D1168409

WITHDRAWN

PARIS

IN AMERICAN LITERATURE

PARIS

IN AMERICAN LITERATURE

by Jean Méral

Translated by Laurette Long

The University of North Carolina Press

Chapel Hill and London

© 1989 The University of North Carolina Press
All rights reserved
Manufactured in the United States of America

The paper in this book meets the guidelines for permanence
and durability of the Committee on Production Guidelines
for Book Longevity of the Council on Library Resources.

93 92 91 90 89   5 4 3 2 1

Library of Congress Cataloging-in-Publication Data

Méral, Jean.
    Paris in American literature.

    Translation of: Paris dans la littérature
    américaine.
    Bibliography: p.
    Includes indexes.
    1. American literature—History and
criticism. 2. American literature—French
influences. 3. Paris (France) in literature. I. Title.
PS159.F5M4713   1989   810'.9'324436   88-33910
ISBN 0-8078-1803-8 (alk. paper)

For Régine and Jean-Laurent

CONTENTS

ACKNOWLEDGMENTS

I would like to express my thanks to Professors Roger Asselineau and Guy-Jean Forgue of the Sorbonne; to M. Lilamand of Editions du CNRS, who granted me the translation rights to the original text, which appeared under that publisher's imprint; to my friends and colleagues Marcienne Rocard and Maurice Lévy at the University of Toulouse–Le Mirail; and, last but not least, to Laurette Long, who translated the French text, and Ron Maner, who edited the manuscript.

PARIS

IN AMERICAN LITERATURE

INTRODUCTION

This book examines the presentation of Paris in American literature from the beginnings of that presentation in the mid-nineteenth century to the present day. Such a task is not in fact as big as it may seem. The book does not set out to draw up a detailed historical census of American expatriate writers, nor does it attempt the still more difficult task of evaluating the possible ways in which the French capital exerted an influence on them. The lives of the writers and what they wrote are two different things, and a systematic analysis of the works themselves reveals that—whatever the impact of Paris on the writers' lives or their ways of thinking—the importance of Paris as a literary theme in American writing is limited. The present study explores, through the texts themselves, the way in which the city of Paris constituted an authentic subject for literary treatment and analyzes the different responses of American writers to the challenge of understanding and describing the capital.

This is the first time the subject has been looked at from such an angle, and the relevant body of critical works is small. In a curious book entitled *The Paris of the Novelists* (1919) Arthur Bartlett Maurice provides a rapid, panoramic survey of novels by writers of all nationalities set wholly or partly in the French capital.[1] In an unpublished doctoral dissertation in history, "Pilgrimage to Paris: The Background of American Expatriation, 1920–1934," Warren Irving Susman conducts an exhaustive investigation into the social and economic factors affecting the great migration of the 1920s. George Wickes, in his book *Americans in Paris, 1903–1939,* tries to evaluate the influence of the capital on writers like Gertrude Stein, John Dos Passos, Ernest Hemingway, and Henry Miller, while in a more recent study, *Published in Paris,* Hugh Ford looks at American and English works published in the capital. The best general study is an article, "City for Expatriates," which appeared in an issue of *Yale French Studies* devoted to Paris in French literature and in which Joseph H. McMahon argues that, except for Henry James in *The Ambassadors,* Paris has never really been a fertile source of inspiration for American writers.

What exactly is meant by the term "American literature" in this study? Paris has inspired a vast range of publications by Americans if we include travelogues, guidebooks, magazine articles and purely autobiographical works. Consequently, I ruled out various books of memoirs containing interminable and irrelevant anecdotes about the Lost Generation but at the same time tried to keep the selection criteria sufficiently elastic to include works like *The Autobiography of Alice B. Toklas, A Moveable Feast,* and Anaïs Nin's *Diary,* all of which are more difficult to categorize. The final corpus examined here turned out to be fewer than two hundred titles, grouping the short stories by collection.

Although the indispensable starting point is the text itself, my approach is not limited to purely formal considerations. An analysis of lexis, metaphor, and structure would not, on its own, yield very much. Starting from the basic postulate that a special significance attaches to the mention of Paris by American writers, I have tried to define this significance and to examine the different ways in which the city of fiction relates to the city of reality. While remaining in constant contact with the texts themselves, I also take account of historical or sociological factors that might throw light on them. How do American writers react to a myth that is not part of their own culture? It is rare that their version of the city acquires a mythical value of its own. What we perceive in their writings is more like the echo of another nation's myth apprehended through a foreign sensibility and a foreign experience. This study is not, therefore, a simple recounting of the myth of Paris; it does not view Paris from the narrow perspective of myth. What, then, of the wider perspective of "the poetry of Paris," which Pierre Citron defines in the following way: "We may roughly define as 'poetic' any text in which the author has not set out to convey the reality of Paris . . . but in which he has sought to express this reality through something else; to give us a new version of it by transforming, distorting, systematizing; often by making it more beautiful, but sometimes by making it more ugly."[2] Even this is too restrictive, for many American writers did indeed "set out to convey the reality of Paris." Of course the very existence of a Parisian "reality" for these writers presupposed a choice and an intention on their part, and that makes anything relating to Paris in their writing significant. Consequently, we shall be looking at a variety of ways in which American writers responded to the city—its prosaic as well as poetic aspects—and at a wide diversity of images that are the literary equivalent of simple daguerreotypes as well as surrealist paintings.

The book is organized chronologically into certain broad divisions. Literary Paris reflects on the whole the changing fortunes of real Paris. The First World War marks a dramatic break in literary history as it does in world history: on one side of this major divide stands the Paris of Henry James; on the other, worlds apart, stands the Paris of the Lost Generation. The chapters are grouped around the important milestones of 1914, 1919, 1930, and 1940, which mark the subject's major phases. At times a book such as this necessarily tends toward being a catalogue, or a descriptive and rather eclectic guidebook. But underlying the recitation of individual authors and titles is a framework intended to provide a more cogent analysis in which the works of each period are critically examined in the light of social, literary, and wider cultural factors.

CHAPTER **I**

FROM THE IMAGINARY
TO THE REAL

The most rich and complex response to Paris in American literature prior to
the First World War is found in the works of Henry James—most notably in
The Ambassadors—and in certain novels and short stories by Edith Wharton. A contemporary writer of lesser stature, Robert W. Chambers, is important because of the sheer volume of what he wrote about the capital in
stories on Parisian manners in the 1880s and in historical novels set against
the backdrop of the Franco-Prussian War and the Commune. But the motif
of Paris was first introduced into American literature well before the publication of *Madame de Mauves* in 1874 and *The American* in 1877, in works by
Edgar Allan Poe, Oliver Wendell Holmes, and Mark Twain.

Edgar Allan Poe introduced the idea of a mysterious Paris, turning for
inspiration to French writers who had already explored this aspect of the
city. Oliver Wendell Holmes, in his poem "La Grisette," described bohemian
Paris. And Mark Twain depicted the city as it was seen through the eyes of
the tourist in *The Innocents Abroad*. These three writers, the first to use
Paris as literary subject matter, explored the subject in a partial and fragmen-
tary way. Others, following in their footsteps, stayed fairly close to the
models set forth by these pioneers and did not appreciably extend their field
of vision. Mysterious Paris continued to thrive in detective novels and works
of fantasy, while bohemian Paris figured in various minor works. Thus, even
as James and Wharton were writing about the capital from a different
perspective, others continued to exploit these two aspects of the subject in an
episodic way right up until the First World War. Although the motifs of
mysterious Paris and bohemian Paris are neither the most significant nor
indeed the most typically American elements of the literature of the second
half of the nineteenth century, they do underline the important fact that it
was through the medium of literature that the theme of Paris passed from
France to America, reminding us of the close links between the literatures of
the two countries.

The tourist's vision of the capital, as presented by Mark Twain, may seem rather superficial, but it does have the merit of embracing the city in its entirety without presuppositions, and, more importantly, it reflects the reactions of the average American face-to-face with the concrete reality of the capital. In fact, the first authentic version of the American in Paris is probably neither the student nor the artist, with their vision colored by romantic fancies, but the tourist, with traces of American soil clinging to his boots.

These aspects of the city that were first highlighted by nineteenth-century writers have tended on the whole to remain marginal to the full development of the Parisian theme in later writings. The title of this chapter, "From the Imaginary to the Real," does not imply that Paris was initially perceived as an idealized city which the authors dreamed about before they actually discover it. It simply seeks to draw attention to the different versions of the city as they emerge one by one from literature. First Paris appears as a mysterious and imaginary city; then myth takes a step toward reality in the portrayal of bohemian life in the capital; and finally the city is shown firmly anchored in the reality of everyday life, observed through the eyes of average Americans conscientiously fulfilling their roles as tourists and pilgrims. This movement from the imaginary to the real will be examined briefly in a number of minor works and looked at in more detail in the works of Henry James and Edith Wharton.

Mysterious Paris

Apart from Washington Irving's fantastic tale "The Adventure of the German Student" (1824), random descriptions of Paris in the *Journals* of the same author, and a rather dull narrative by James Fenimore Cooper called *A Residence in France,* which was published in 1836, the first texts of any importance for this study are three short stories by Edgar Allan Poe. These owe nothing to direct observation, for although the author was a schoolboy in England from 1815 to 1820, he never ventured across the Channel. His case, though unique, is in one respect exemplary. Poe's mysterious Paris is a fantasy city which, oddly enough, resembles the metropolis described by writers who knew the capital well. The city of mystery is a city that has nothing to do with real experience but filters into American literature through successive layers of French literary tradition.

Eugène Sue's *Mystères de Paris,* despite its resounding success in both France and America, appeared after Poe's Parisian stories, and cannot be regarded as the fountainhead of the mysterious city tradition. Burton R. Pollin has pointed out[1] that Poe got most of his information about Paris from translations of *Notre-Dame de Paris* and Louis Léonard de Loménie's *La Galerie Populaire des Contemporains*. Yet even if Sue did not have a direct influence on Poe, he remains nonetheless, along with Balzac and Hugo, one of the principal explorers and creators of the Parisian underworld. He was, in fact, an explorer in the literal sense of the word: he researched his subject in scrupulous detail before recreating in mythical terms the world of the slums, a world that inspired a whole new kind of popular literature after the publication of the *Mystères*. It is an offshoot of this literature that was transported across the Atlantic and flowered on the North American continent.

In America as in France, this flowering occurred in the field of popular literature. Posterity has deemed it fit to allow the mantle of oblivion to fall discreetly over the names of writers such as Archibald Clavering Gunter, Guy Wetmore Carryl, Cleveland Moffett, and Louis Vance (all, however, mentioned in the *Biographical Index* and *Who's Who in America*), who were the principal, though not the only, exponents of mysterious Paris. Archibald Clavering Gunter (1847-1907) was born in Liverpool, and went to the United States when he was six. Raised in California, he moved in 1879 to New York, where he founded the Home Publishing Company with the express aim of publishing his universally rejected manuscript *Mr. Barnes of New York* in 1887. This first novel, which recounts the adventures of a rich and impudent young American traveling through Europe, sold more than a million copies. According to the *Biographical Index,* Gunter, despite his evident stylistic infelicities, was the most widely read American novelist between 1887 and 1894. Louis Vance (1879-1933) remains best known as the author of *The Lone Wolf,* published in 1914. The character of the Lone Wolf, caught between the world of crime and the forces of law and order, subsequently appeared in half a dozen novels as well as films and radio serials. Vance, who managed to hit upon the right blend of crime and romance, giving him his first success, acknowledged having earned more than one million dollars between 1905 and 1921. He died in a fire that he himself accidentally started, but in circumstances that gave rise for a time to rumors that he was murdered. Cleveland Moffett (1863-1926) was an American who died in Paris after living there for over twenty years. A versatile journalist, he achieved a degree of success with his play *Money Talks* in 1906. He was the translator of Paul Bourget, wrote numerous screenplays, and was a militant activist for U.S. intervention in the First World War. He wrote two detective stories about Paris—*Through the Wall,* published in 1909, and *The Seine Mystery,* which notwithstanding its relatively late publication date of 1925 will be discussed in this chapter. Guy Wetmore Carryl (1873–1904), who died at the age of thirty-one, was considered, while a student at Columbia University, to be one of the most promising writers of his generation. He too was a journalist, and he lived in Paris from 1896 to 1902. The city is the setting for his novel *The Transgression of Andrew Vane* (1904) and the stories in *Zut and Other Parisians* (1903). All four of these writers used a setting popularized by Eugène Sue and a detective plot of which Poe was one of the originators.

In connection with the works considered here, it is worth mentioning "The Mystery of Marie Rogêt," a story by Poe that provides an extreme example of the way in which the city of mystery is divorced geographically from the real city. The plot of the story revolves around a heinous crime identical to one actually committed in New York. In his fictional version, Poe suggests possible solutions to the American case, which had not been solved at the time he wrote the story. It soon becomes evident to the reader that although the story is supposed to take place in Paris, the geography of the city resembles that of New York. Poe sticks to the geographical area within which the crime was committed, but transposes it to the French capital, throwing up a smokescreen of imaginary names—the Rue Pavée Saint Andrée, the Rue des Drômes—to mingle with real ones—the Palais Royal, the Barrière du Roule, and the Faubourg Saint-Germain. But the distances given between one place and another,[2] combined with the certainty that the Barrière du Roule is not on the same side of the river as the Rue Pavée Saint Andrée and the Rue des Drômes, make it impossible to reconcile the story's geography with the actual layout of the city. The Rue Pavée Saint Andrée is meant to be Nassau Street, while the Barrière du Roule corresponds to Weehawken, New Jersey. Assuming that the Barrière du Roule of the story is in fact the Rue Barrière du Roule, now renamed Rue de Sablonville, in the seventeenth arrondissement, or the Avenue du Roule in Neuilly, Marie would have to live miles away from the perfumery in the Palais Royal where she worked.

Little by little, the Seine grows until it has reached the same proportions as the Hudson. Large sailing ships go up and down it; little fishing boats ply valiantly between its distant banks;[3] the tangy smell of the ocean fills the air. Paris loses its normal contours to become a long, emaciated city stretched out on both banks of the river, and the reader, confronted with this unfamiliar vision like something in a hall of mirrors, is seized by a sensation of vertigo. Paradoxically, the French names, instead of helping, only add to the feeling of disorientation. What is one to make of the Rue Pavée Saint

Andrée, fluctuating between two genders, or the names of newspapers like *Le Commerciel* and *La Mercure*? The effect is, of course, unintentional, but it is no less important on that account. For Poe's story—although it contains some surprisingly traditional elements in the depiction of the city—draws attention to one of the mysterious city's special properties, namely that we cannot pin it down to the city of everyday reality. The mysteries of Paris belong to no particular district. The city of the aristocracy, of the tourist, or of the student is not comparable to the city of the criminal, whose scale is the scale of imagination. The points of contact that do exist between the city of the surface and the city of the underworld are few and far between. Mark Twain mentions one of them, the Morgue, which he describes as "that horrible receptacle for the dead who die mysteriously and leave the manner of their taking off a dismal secret."4 The Morgue exposes to the light of day the wreckage cast up by nighttime Paris; it is the place of clues, identifications, and reconstructions. In *Through the Wall* the detective Paul Coquenil goes to la Motte-aux-Papelards to examine a corpse, which is presented to him fully dressed and sitting on a chair as if it were alive.5 The Morgue, sinister enough in what it exposes, is made even more sinister by what it suggests: the existence of a Janus-faced city.

Certain parts of the city are particularly conducive to this atmosphere of mystery. First and foremost is the Zone, an outlying district full of the twilight shadows that envelop the city. In Frank Berkeley Smith's story "Thérèse" a young girl is attacked by a cab driver at night at the end of the Rue de Vaugirard and takes refuge from her pursuer in the Zone. She literally and figuratively crosses the barrier separating the normal from the bizarre, and her flight takes on the sacrilegious nature of a descent into hell:

> Thérèse slunk by the hovel in the shadow of a factory wall. As she did so for some moments her heart again seemed to stop beating. There were men inside the cabin: she could hear their oaths and laughter. The remaining hovels in the group lay tucked away in some small truck gardens. These low shanties, patched with stray boards and roofed with odds and ends of the scrap heap, were notorious shelter for a colony of Apaches, part of a vicious band smoked out of their stronghold on the outskirts of Menilmontant, where they had lived the year before in a deserted quarry.6

In *The Lone Wolf* the Zone de Belleville is the home of the secret headquarters of the band of Apaches led by Popinot.7

The warren of narrow streets around Les Halles, described by Louis

Vance, harbors stealthy, occult activities beneath the appearance of a ne-
cropolis: "It's a silent web of side ways and a gloomy one by night that backs
up north of les Halles: old Paris, taciturn and sombre, steeped in its memories of grim romance. But for infrequent, flickering, corner lamps, the street
. . . was as dismal as an alley in some city of the dead. Its houses with their
mansard roofs and boarded windows bent their heads together like mutes at
a wake, black-cloaked and hooded; seldom one showed a light; never one
betrayed by any sound the life that lurked behind its jealous blinds."[8]

But it is above all the Seine, sink of crime and turpitude, with its dark,
slimy waters dividing the city, that forms the main axis of mysterious Paris. It
is on the river's banks, where bands of villains roam, that Marie Rogêt's
body is cast up: "Here are the very nooks where the unwashed most
abound—here are the temples most desecrate. With sickness of the heart the
wanderer will flee back to the polluted Paris as to a less odious because less
incongruous sink of pollution."[9] The river lends its name to the title of
Cleveland Moffett's novel *The Seine Mystery,* which tells the story of a
novelist, Launay, whom someone attempts to drown in a desire for revenge.
The attempt fails, and Launay, by dressing a floating corpse in his own
clothes, is able to begin a new life under a false name. The Seine, which holds
the key to many a dark mystery, thus keeps the secret of this strange rebirth.
In *The Transgression of Andrew Vane* the convoluted plot reaches its dramatic denouement on the banks of the river with a crime and a suicide.
Indeed, the Seine is so indispensable to the landscape of mysterious Paris that
David Belasco, in his melodrama *The Stranglers of Paris* (1881), does not
hesitate to change its course so that its waters lap against the walls of the
Grande Roquette, which in fact are nowhere near the river: in Act 5 of the
play, Sophie Blanchard, whose husband has been condemned to the convict
ship through a miscarriage of justice, vainly tries to drown herself outside
the prison one night.[10] Perhaps the author felt that this new location would
make readers more aware of the imminent departure of the convicts. Or
perhaps he imagined these dark waters, crossed by the boat of the ferryman,
would be convenient for introducing the motif of death.

The architecture of criminal Paris is in one sense far removed from that of
the grand avenues, with their new buildings, but in another sense it is very
close, constituting, as it were, the backs of the elegant facades that are the
more familiar aspect of the city's scenery. "Even if you knew your way about
Paris you had to lose it in order to find it to Troyon's,"[11] Louis Vance writes at
the beginning of *The Lone Wolf.* In order to reach this hidden city, one must
plunge into the parallel world of houses invisible from the street, into a

tangle of alleys and byways. The adventures of Maurice, the amateur detective of Archibald Clavering Gunter's *That Frenchman,* lead him from the narrow streets of the Maubert Quarter to the suburban villas of the Rue des Vignes in Passy.[12] In Cleveland Moffett's "The Mysterious Card Unveiled" the narrator, trying to prevent a murder, enters "a black-mouthed, evillooking alley, so narrow and roughly paved that the carriage could scarcely advance,"[13] somewhere between the Boulevard Saint-Germain and the Seine. "Lone Wolf" Michael Lanyard also dodges into an alley to try to shake off a pack of Parisian gangsters in hot pursuit of him.[14] In "The Murders in the Rue Morgue" Poe describes the street from which the story takes its name as "one of those miserable thoroughfares which intervene between the Rue de Richelieu and the Rue de St. Roch."[15]

The houses, too, are unusual and often sinister. In "The Murders in the Rue Morgue" Dupin and the narrator live in "a time-eaten and grotesque mansion, long deserted through superstitions . . . and tottering to its fall in a retired and desolate portion of the Faubourg St. Germain."[16] The villa Montmorency, where Detective Coquenil lives in *Through the Wall,* seems, with its high walls and single iron gate opening onto the Rue Poussin,[17] like an ancient fortress. Troyon's as well huddles defensively against possible intrusion from the outside world, repelling even the boldest visitor with its twisted and nightmarish architecture: "From the court a staircase, with an air of leading nowhere in particular, climbed lazily to the second storey and thereby justified its modest pretensions; for the two upper floors of Troyon's might have been plotted by a nightmare-ridden architect. . . . Above stairs, a mediaeval maze of corridors long and short, complicated by many unexpected steps and staircases and turns and enigmatic doors, ran every-which-way and as a rule landed one in the wrong room."[18] In *That Frenchman* and *The Lone Wolf* the houses often have two entries and sometimes even a secret passage leading to the street.[19] In *Through the Wall* the arch-criminal Groener escapes from the pursuing Coquenil through Mme Cécile's house in the Rue Tronchet. A house of easy virtue and easy exit, the place is a surrealists' delight, communicating with various streets and arcades which facilitate a quick getaway.[20] Perhaps the most extreme example is the confessional in Notre-Dame that has two exits due to architectural modifications of the cathedral.[21] But the most striking architectural feature of the mysterious city is the catacombs, where both Coquenil and the innocent victim, Alice, take refuge from the diabolical Groener.[22] The best description of the awesome diversity of subterranean Paris can be found in two works of historical fiction by S. Weir Mitchell, "A Little More Burgundy" and *The*

Adventures of François, in which the heroes, common to both works, spend no fewer than six days underground.[23]

Such urban architecture, in addition to being admirably suited to the twists and turns of the detective novel, is symbolic of the Janus-headed city that hides many a dark enigma. The climate, too, is in harmony with the generally sinister atmosphere of the mysterious city, particularly in *The Lone Wolf.* Paris is cold and rainy; the bare silhouettes of trees stand out against a lowering sky; the rain beats down on café tables on deserted terraces; and the Bois de Boulogne suddenly looks remarkably like Siberia. Louis Vance's novel presents us with a lugubrious vision of an anti-Paris, captured in the following passage: "It was bitter cold in the wind sweeping down from the west, and it had grown very dark. Only in the sky above the Bois a long reef of crimson light hung motionless against which leafless trees lifted gnarled, weird silhouettes. While [Michael] watched, the pushing crimson ebbed swiftly and gave way to mauve, to violet, to black."[24] Similar descriptions can be found in most detective novels and also in a novel of manners about the American aristocracy in Paris, *The Inner Shrine,* written by Basil King and published in 1909. In one part of the novel, the rich Mrs. Eveleth, terrified that her son has gone off to fight a duel, anxiously awaits his return, on the balcony of her house on the Quai d'Orsay. In the early hours of the morning, she watches the spectacle of the awakening city:

> On the swift, leaden-colored current of the Seine, spanned here and there by ghostly bridges, mysterious barges plied weirdly through the twilight. Up on the left the Arc de Triomphe began to emerge dimly out of the night, while down on the right the line of the Louvre lay, black and sinister, beneath the towers and spires that faintly detached themselves against the growing saffron of the morning. High above all else, the domes of the Sacred Heart were white with the rays of the unrisen sun, like those of the City which came down from God.[25]

The city is shrouded in a haze of mystery that has something to do with the nature of crime itself but also with the enigma posed by the solving of crimes. "The Mysterious Card" is the only example in which the solid detective work that is the basis of such literature strays into the realm of fantasy. More often than not, the mysterious element is provided by the criminal world itself, but it is also a part of the search for the criminal. In the labyrinth of dark alleyways a minotaur lurks—perhaps the assassin, perhaps the rival gang bent on revenge, perhaps even the police. All of them represent evil, but the oversimplification of many popular novels is absent here. Nothing is clearcut; good and evil are relative, and dependent on circumstances. Paris is a jungle where the forces of law and crime are locked together in a struggle for survival. It is the privileged theater of operations of a police force with a secret branch. The American writers are familiar with the *Mémoires* of Vidocq and the multiple Balzacian incarnations of this famous chief of the Bureau de Sûreté. M. G., the prefect of police in "The Purloined Letter," explains his supreme powers thus: "I have keys, as you know, with which I can open any chamber or cabinet in Paris."[26] In *That Frenchman* the head of the Bureau de Sûreté, M. Claude, who also appears in *The Stranglers of Paris,* complains in 1868 that he is no longer at liberty to arrest whomever he pleases as he was able to do just after the coup d'état.[27] The seemingly disparate milieux of criminals, politicians, and policemen are in fact all bound up together. In *The Lone Wolf* the chief of the Belleville Apaches, Popinot, whose name is borrowed from Balzac, is really a corrupt police-man, while De Morbihan, to all intents and purposes a highly respected French aristocrat, is an international gangster. As for Groener, the assassin hunted by Detective Coquenil, he turns out to be the baron de Heidelmann-Bruck, brother-in-law of the prime minister himself.

In his novel *Baron Montez of Panama and Paris* Archibald Clavering Gunter uses the Panama scandal to expose the collusion that existed between the worlds of business, politics, and international crime. With virtuous in-dignation, the author vents his hostility toward "the foreign adventurers who came to Paris, lured by the millions spent and squandered upon the Canal," among whom "the greediest, the most devouring" were "the Swiss, the Ger-man, the man of all nations."[28] The elegant facade of urbane social rela-tionships masks the fact that the city has been taken over by rogues and villains. Dupin risks his life to get hold of the "purloined letter" in the Poe story of that name; had he not managed to replace it by a fake, he "might never have left the ministerial presence alive."[29] In *Through the Wall* the alleged Groener is set free on government orders, and Coquenil, dismissed and in danger of his life, is left to solve the case single-handedly. The baron is finally unmasked in the middle of the courtroom scene, at the very moment he is sitting alongside the judges, watching the trial of the innocent victim whom he hopes to see condemned in his place. Without this public coup de théâtre, which leads to the baron's suicide, Coquenil would never have succeeded in revealing the truth. The universal corruption of mysterious Paris extends to the press, which is only too ready to sell itself to the highest bidder—with the notable exception of the *New York Herald,* according to Gunter.[30] The network of corruption spreads its long and poisonous tenta-

cles from Paris to other capitals; in *That Frenchman* the amateur detective
Maurice pursues the would-be assassin of the Prince Imperial as far as
Russia.

There are few differences between this American version of criminal Paris
and that found in French literature. It is in fact a potpourri put together from
the works of Eugène Sue, Alexandre Dumas, Honoré de Balzac,[31] Gaston
Leroux, and Maurice Leblanc. *The Seine Mystery* and, more particularly,
That Frenchman and *The Lone Wolf* are part of the detective novel tradition
of which Poe was one of the founding fathers. Dupin preceded Sherlock
Holmes as the archetype of the intellectual detective whose powers of deduction give shape to stories that turn on the solution of a central problem. He is
the remote ancestor of Maurice Leblanc's Arsène Lupin, whose exploits are
full of allusions to his famous predecessor. Maurice, dandy and art lover,
also resembles Dupin, but in addition has something of Sherlock Holmes, his
elder by a few years.[32] In comparison with these two, Coquenil, a bachelor
who divides his affections between his mother and his dog César, is more
like a modern antihero. But Coquenil knows from the beginning that his
success is assured and that he will triumph over his colleague and rival
Gibelin, thanks to his calm and unruffled powers of deduction. Like Arsène
Lupin, he is a master of disguise and can make himself look like whomever
he chooses with the same ease as his arch-enemy Groener. Michael Lanyard,
a foundling like Gaston Leroux's Rouletabille, has a more ambivalent position as far as the law is concerned, due to his special status of "gentleman-
burglar," although he possesses neither the benevolent anarchism nor the
freewheeling panache of Arsène Lupin.[33]

The connections between these American novels and popular French literature are fairly evident. To point out the fundamental affinities that exist
between American Paris and notions of crime and mystery, we must refer to
the myth of the great city, born from the prodigious urban development
caused by the industrial revolution. The birth of the proletariat adds a minor
component to this myth: the mysterious slums which are related to the
medieval "cour des miracles." The slums of both London and Paris had
already found their way into literature in the mid-nineteenth century, not
just in the works of Sue, Hugo, Balzac, and in popular French novels but also
in Paul Féval's *Mystères de Londres* (1848) and in the works of Charles
Dickens. Paris, like other great cities, provides a perfect setting for crime.
The murder of Marie Rogêt is identical to that of Mary Cecilia Rogers,
committed in New York, as if some sort of occult symmetry existed between
the two metropolises. The same symmetry seems to be at work in "The

Mysterious Card," in which the principle of evil reincarnated in the person of Richard Burwell is the same principle that has exerted its nefarious influence on both cities since time immemorial. New York's Water Street finds its counterpart in the narrow streets bordering the Seine and the charnel house of the Picpus cemetery. If Poe chose to set three of his tales in the French capital, it is doubtless because Paris, with its powerful mythology, evoked more than any other city the atmosphere of crime, horror, and fantasy that had earlier been found in Gothic castles.

Poe also felt that Paris had special affinities with crimes of mystery. For him crime represented an enigma, a mystery that could obviously be unraveled since all the mysteries of the universe are capable of being unraveled—simply as a matter of "ratiocination." But while Paris is the city of murder and horror, it is also the city of the intellect, of science, of books, where knowledge has its esoteric side. The circumstances in which the narrator meets Dupin in "The Murders in the Rue Morgue" are revealing in this respect: "Our first meeting was at an obscure library in the Rue Montmartre, where the accident of our both being in search of the same very rare and very remarkable volume, brought us in closer communion." The two friends spend several hours a day reading, and Dupin, though far from rich, is always buying books: "Books, indeed were his sole luxuries, and in Paris these are easily obtained."[34] The capital, city of books, plunged in the strange atmosphere of occult sciences, provides a favorable climate for crime but, to an even greater degree, for deduction. And indeed, though the general picture of the police is not morally edifying,[35] writers do pay tribute to the sleuthlike talents of some of its members as well as to the modern scientific methods employed in the prevention of crime and the pursuit of truth.

In *That Frenchman,* for example, Maurice plunges into the study of the effects of carbonic acid in order to prevent the murder by asphyxiation of the Prince Imperial.[36] *Through the Wall* pays homage to the work of Alphonse Bertillon, whose department of anthropometry was to be found at the prison of La Santé.[37] The reader also follows for forty or so pages Coquenil's interrogation of Groener,[38] during which the detective tries to discover the latter's true identity. As part of his interrogation, Coquenil subjects the prisoner to a carefully crafted word association test. After this, a doctor monitors his unconscious reflexes while he watches a series of images projected by a magic lantern. Gradually, it emerges that the prisoner's guilt is in some way connected with the fire at the Bazar de la Charité. This psychosomatic technique of lie detection, which in 1907 belonged mainly to the realm of fantasy, is firmly entrenched in the Dupin tradition of "ratiocination." The application of the intellect to the solving of mysteries has simply taken a technical turn in a further effort to penetrate the most secret thoughts of the criminal. Thus, ranged against the evil masterminds of mysterious Paris are detectives who bring into play all the powers of human logic in an effort to get at the truth, and who thereby demonstrate the crucial role of science.

Before leaving the subject of mysterious Paris, mention should be made of a specious relationship that the American reader might be inclined to draw between certain inhabitants of the city and the people who represent one particular aspect of his own tradition. One can reasonably ask to what extent the Parisian slums, with their native Indians, represent a European version of James Fenimore Cooper's prairie. Roger Caillois believes that the transition from the adventure novel to the detective novel, which resulted from the metamorphosis that took place in nineteenth-century cities, "comes of the change in scene from Cooper's savannah and forest."[39] Is such a transition evident in the texts just considered? It is a tempting hypothesis, but a superficial one. Cooper's influence on the French adventure novel is indeed indisputable. Balzac, Dumas, and Hugo all drew on his accounts of the American frontier when describing the hidden mysteries of the capital, and Eugène Sue openly acknowledges his debt to the American writer: "Everyone has read the admirable accounts in which Cooper, the Walter Scott of America, described the savage customs of the Indians. . . . We shall try to depict for the reader a number of episodes in the life of a different group of barbarians, who are as much outside civilization as the savage tribes so vividly portrayed by Cooper."[40] Cooper had his imitators, but soon—with the publication of *Le Père Goriot* by Balzac in 1834, as Pierre Citron points out—comparisons between Paris and the vast tracts of the American wilderness were no more than literary clichés. There followed an identification between the natives of the New World and the savages inhabiting the banks of the Seine, an identification that gained even more credence by the presence of real Indians in Paris, or of mythomaniacs who claimed to be Indians.[41] By the time Gunter, Moffett, and Vance appeared on the scene, Mohicanism had become mere verbal coloring, and Indians of all hues had long enjoyed the freedom of the city. The literary tradition that leads from Cooper to these writers, symbolized by the metaphorical survival of such tribes, passes without any doubt through the medium of the French novel. It is amusing to discover, however, in *Through the Wall,* that in 1907 Cooper is still the most widely read author in the prison of La Santé.[42]

The term "Apache" deserves particular attention. It became fashionable after 1902, thanks to the journalist Arthur Dupin, who used it to describe the heroes of the gang war triggered by Amélie Hélie, the famous "Casque d'Or."[43] These characters immediately entered into Parisian folklore and became a permanent feature of both French and American literature. As earlier references to them in this chapter suggest, frequent mention will be made of these Apaches in subsequent American novels. Right up until the Second World War, readers can encounter them, though they may well ask themselves if these characters really exist. While some authors claim to have discovered genuine examples of the species, others also boast of having met Arthur Dupin himself.[44]

It is clear that the connections linking mysterious Paris to the world of the American frontier occur randomly throughout the literature at different levels. With the exception of Poe's stories, the works mentioned heretofore are of minor importance and cannot be said to constitute a branch of literary history in their own right. They follow in the aftermath of French novels, and the previously noted hypothesis about the transition from the adventure novel to the detective novel—in the final analysis—does not hold water.

These Indians are not, however, the only people who, through their transplantation to the French capital, bear witness to the powers of absorption of the Parisian myth. Ranged alongside them are Jews, Hindus, Bedouins, and Bohemians. This last group existed as exotic characters well before the notion of the "vie de bohème" was born. Through them, a sort of geographical drift takes place, as the Bohemia of the atlas moves toward the French capital and is gradually absorbed in it, only to reemerge as a new mythical country.

Bohemian Paris

Bohemian Paris, apart from its depiction in short stories glorifying the Latin Quarter, is part of the global vision of the city that emerges from the great works of literature. Mysterious Paris was created out of literary mementoes and writers' imagination; bohemian Paris supplements these with firsthand experience. It is highly unlikely that large numbers of Americans flocked to Paris in the nineteenth century to embrace a career of crime. If they did, history, and more understandably literary history, has chosen to forget them. But many Americans did come to Paris in order to further their education in the period following the Civil War. Through them, the Latin Quarter became an exportable fact of French civilization which was gradually incorporated into the American universe. An American bohemia grew up alongside the French one, the prototype of that which later flourished in the 1920s and 1930s. While American characters are rare birds in the Paris of mystery, where it requires all sorts of artifice to get them into the plot, their more important role in bohemian Paris corresponds to social and historical fact. Consequently, the introduction of the bohemian motif represents a step forward in American writers' apprehension of Parisian reality. To the heritage of myth, it adds the corrective influence of personal observation. It moves away from the imaginary, toward the real.

This move, however, does not mean that the imaginary aspect disappears altogether. Just as mystery writers drew on works like *Notre-Dame de Paris* and the novels of Eugène Sue as their chief sources of inspiration, those who chose to write about the life of students and artists turned to Henri Murger's *Scènes de la Vie de Bohème* for their archetypes. The international celebrity of Parisian bohemia is borne out by the number of references to it in guides and travelogues. Frank Berkeley Smith published *The Real Latin Quarter* in 1901, and Richard Harding Davis devotes several pages to the Left Bank in his book *About Paris,* written in 1895. According to Irving Stone, whose book *The Passionate Journey* is based on the life of painter John Noble, Smith's book played a crucial role in persuading the young man from Wichita to try his luck in Paris.[45] Thirty years earlier, Mark Twain was also writing about the Latin Quarter, pouring scorn on its romantic myth, particularly as it presented the character of the grisette, and his comments give some indication of the American public's familiarity with the subject: "They are another romantic delusion. They were (if you let the books of travel tell it) always so beautiful—so neat and trim, so graceful—so naive and trusting—so gentle, so winning—so faithful to their shop duties, so irresistible to buyers in their prattling importunity—so devoted to their poverty-stricken students of the Latin Quarter—so lighthearted and happy on their Sunday picnics in the suburbs,—and oh, so charmingly, so delightfully immoral." Twain, observing the situation from the viewpoint of the humorist and busy tourist, deemed reality to be a far cry from this romantic fiction: "They were like nearly all the Frenchwomen I ever saw—homely. They had large hands, large feet, large mouths; they had pug noses as a general thing, and moustaches that not even good breeding could overlook . . . they were not winning, they were not graceful; they ate garlic and onions. And as to their vaunted immorality, how *could* they be immoral? The improprieties of animals are not designated by so stately a word as that."[46]

But this sort of diatribe is the exception rather than the rule. The typical grisette of American literature has more in common with the romantic figure described in the first of these passages by Twain. She inspired Oliver Wendell Holmes's 1863 poem "La Grisette," which is the first example in American literature of a celebration of Paris's bohemian life. The poet introduces the lyrical themes of recollections of youth and of budding love blighted by premature death. But his heroine, Clémence, displays the same independent spirit and lack of conventional morality as Murger's women. As he writes of her, "I knew that thou hadst woes to weep / And sins to be forgiven." Holmes evokes the familiar spectacle of the sick student cared for by a tender young girl—"The trailing of thy long loose hair / Bent o'er my couch of pain"—and sketches in the background the urban landscape he knew as a medical student during the July Monarchy. The Rue de Seine, the Eglise Sainte-Geneviève, the boulevards, the quays, Notre-Dame, Saint-Etienne-du-Mont, and the Panthéon mark the boundaries in which was played out Clémence's short life, which ends in the last verse of the poem at the Père-Lachaise cemetery.⁴⁷

Did this first signpost along the road to bohemia lead to a progressive integration of the motif into a final, global vision of the city? Such a progression is not neatly marked out in chronological order, and the issue is further complicated by the fact that the experiences of the authors who contributed to the presentation of bohemian Paris cover a relatively long time span. At the beginning of the period, we find two writers, Oliver Wendell Holmes (1809–94), who lived in Paris from 1833 to 1835, and S. Weir Mitchell (1829–1914), who came to Paris to pursue his medical studies in the early 1850s and later to become a neurologist of international renown. But the latter did not draw on his memories until 1895, when he wrote "A Little More Burgundy." Both authors' experiences were similar to those of Henri Murger, whose *Scènes de la Vie de Bohème* appeared in 1851. The painter Frank Berkeley Smith came to the capital much later, around 1892, and was still living there in 1912, when his book *The Street of the Two Friends* was published. Guy Wetmore Carryl spent six years in the city, from 1896 to 1902, and the Paris of these two writers was that of the Belle Epoque—the city portrayed in *Peter Whiffle* by Carl Van Vechten (1880–1969), which was published in 1922 but set in the Paris of 1907.⁴⁸

Robert W. Chambers (1865–1933) comes somewhere in the middle. He arrived in Paris in 1886, determined to become a painter, and returned to New York in 1893 to begin a long career as a novelist. His first book, *In the Quarter* (1894), was written in an attempt to rival Murger's. The protagonists of this ambitious and complicated novel are an art student, Rex Gethryn, and a singer, formerly a grisette, Yvonne Descartes. They live out their unhappy and tormented love affair against the background of the Boulangist riots. Chambers also draws on his memories to embellish his narrative of a period with which he was unfamiliar, that of the Franco-Prussian War and the Commune. He thus blends direct experience with historical reconstruction, a technique he employed in several dozen books based on different periods in French and American history. The Latin Quarter described by Chambers in most of his short stories corresponds, like that of *In the Quarter,* to the quarter as it was in the period 1886–93. The story collection entitled *The King in Yellow* includes tales of fantasy such as "The Mask" and "The Court of the Dragon," but there are also picturesque accounts of student life in "The Street of Our Lady of the Fields" and "Rue Barrée." The atmosphere of gaiety typical of the Left Bank later inspired "Ambassador Extraordinary," "Enter the Queen," and "Another Good Man," which appeared in a collection called *The Haunts of Men* in 1895. Other stories in the same volume, "The Street of the Four Winds" and "The Street of the First Shell," are set in 1870 and 1871 and draw their inspiration from the same sources as the four novels Chambers wrote about this period in French history, notably *The Red Republic* and *Ashes of Empire.* Two images of bohemian Paris coexist in Chambers's works, the first drawn from his memories of student life and the second from the imagination of the historian. A link between the two is provided in the character of Braith. In 1870, in "The Street of the First Shell," he appears as a young art student of sixteen; in 1888, in *In the Quarter,* he can still be seen at Bouguereau's studio, where he is regarded as a mentor by his young comrades, to whom he recounts the horrific events of the siege and the Commune. Chambers doubtless wished to pay tribute through this character to the real person responsible for arousing his interest in the "Année Terrible."

S. Weir Mitchell's descriptions of Paris in the opening pages of "A Little More Burgundy," where he himself figures in the plot in the third person, give us a different picture from that provided by the recollections of later writers. Mitchell evokes the old *hôtel particulier* at 47 Rue Saint-André-des-Arts—in reality the Hôtel de Vieuville—as it was in 1853, with its high, domed ceilings, its caryatids and licentious frescoes, and its rooms filled with swarms of impecunious students.[49] To Mitchell's description of this pre-Haussmann Latin Quarter, Chambers adds a multitude of further details about places that have already been suggested in the titles of his stories: the Cour du Dragon, the Rue des Quatre-Vents, and the Rue Notre-Dame-des-Champs. The author personifies the last of these settings in the following description: "It is a pariah among streets—a street without a Quarter. It is generally understood to lie outside the pale of aristocratic Avenue de l'Obser-vatoire. The students of the Montparnasse Quarter consider it swell and will have none of it. The Latin Quarter, from the Luxembourg, its northern frontier, sneers at its respectability and regards with d¹sfavor the correctly-costumed students who haunt it."⁵⁰ Chambers, who was briefly an illustrator for *Life, Truth,* and *Vogue,* builds up a collection of vignettes of the Left Bank, in particular of the Jardin du Luxembourg, which is the focal point for the plot of "The Street of Our Lady of the Fields." "Enter the Queen" is set mainly in the Théâtre Bobino, where two students who play in the orchestra get other people to replace them for an evening. Unfortunately, neither student informs the other, and even more unfortunately, their stand-ins are nonmusicians who are incapable of sounding the crucial fanfare that heralds the queen's entry on stage. The adventures of "Another Good Man" reach their finale one evening in Mid-Lent at the Bal Bullier, whose atmosphere is evoked in the following passage:

The dull red and blue woodwork of the Bullier was hung with the banners of all nations. In the musician gallery, Conor and his orchestra banged away at the "March into Hell" and the tables trembled with the crash of the brass. The floor was crowded to suffocation. Imbecile shrieking clowns in ruffles and powder, went madly bounding about. Turks footed it with Russian peasant girls, gendarmes wearing false noses and enormous moustaches locked arms with "ces messieurs" of the Vilette [*sic*] who wore the charming costume of that quarter includ-ing "favoris" and "rouflaquettes."⁵¹

Chambers wrote several hundred pages about the Left Bank, painting a vivid and detailed picture of the lives of its inhabitants. They live in rented studios perched high under rooftops, like Rex Gethryn, whose lodgings are on the sixth floor of a small hotel, or they are pensionnaires at Mme Ma-rotte's. They go to the Crémerie Murphy, the Restaurant Boulant, or the Restaurant Mignon; they frequent the Café Vachette or the Café du Cercle. Sometimes they take a trip out to the countryside, perhaps as far as La Roche; and occasionally they cross the river to attend the masked balls held at the Opéra.⁵² The author's geography is unfailingly accurate, though his street numbers are false, such as 470 Rue Serpente or 340 Rue Monsieur-le-Prince, where he probably adds a zero to an existing number so as to write freely about a real place.⁵³ Carryl and Smith, writing about the Belle Epoque, do not add much to these descriptions, except to include Mont-martre as a center of bohemian life. In Carryl's "Caffiard" Pierre lives in the heart of the Latin Quarter at 13 Rue Visconti,[54] but the Rue des Deux Amis, which gives its name to a collection of stories by Smith, is "a crooked byway halfway up Montmartre."[55] The hero of "Straight-Rye Jones," in Smith's collection, would seem, however, to indicate a return to the Left Bank when he leaves Montmartre to go and live in a strange building that Smith calls "the Hornets' nest," which is described as follows: "It was round and gray, and had a small door as its single entrance and exit for a swarm of three-score of painters and bohemians and their sweethearts, who found refuge within."[56] Here, Smith is obviously talking about La Ruche, the wine pavilion at the international exposition of 1900, which was pulled down and put up again at 52 Rue de Dantzig and provided studios for, among others, Modigliani, Soutine, Zadkin, and Fernand Léger. La Ruche is also the subject of a lengthy description in *The Passionate Journey*, where it is referred to as "the beehive" and where painter John Noble lives for a time.[57]

These stories by Carryl and Smith leave us with an impression of artificiality that comes from their idealized and sterilized depiction of bohemian life. It is a life in which no one suffers, in which no one is unhappy. Providence smiles benignly on lovers and artists, resolving their problems with magical ease. "Caffiard" provides an example of the sort of anodyne conventionality permeating characters and plot. Pierre, a painter, and Mimi, a seamstress, are forced to abandon their plans to picnic in the countryside because they have no money. Pierre comes to announce the bad tidings to Mimi, who is waiting for him in the Café des Deux Magots. The sad story is overheard by Caffiard, the editor of a humorous newspaper, *La Blague*. Fortunately, his eye happens to light upon some cartoons that Pierre has just drawn, and he offers to buy them on the spot, thus enabling all three of them to partake of a happy lunch together on the banks of the Seine.

Such romantic convention imposes itself, above all, on the way in which these writers portray love. The descriptions of what actually goes on are given in such soft focus that they are no more than simple concessions to the norms of the genre. In *Les Mystères de Paris* Sue invented the character of Rigolette, the grisette who couldn't be got into bed, but he had pointed out the anomaly of this characterization. In American stories, the exception becomes the rule, and even the men are remarkably coy. Grisettes and models are shown as essential components of artists' lives, but their intimacy is restricted to scenes on café terraces and picnics in the suburbs. Love is named, but never described. The authors, by exalting it, put it firmly out of reach. Smith, for example, makes only the vaguest allusions to the realities of the situation in this homage he renders to the women of bohemia, in which he seems, more than anything else, to be struck by their civic virtues: "They were honest, for they never stole. They were brave, for they never demanded. They were discreet, with that inborn sense of discretion and contentment which Anglo-Saxon women are ignorant of. They possessed nothing, yet they gave with an unselfish generosity unknown to the rich. They were proud—not of themselves, but of any good fortune that came to those whom they loved."[58]

Carryl and Smith often sound as though they are writing for children. The idea that moral permissiveness may lead to happiness makes them decidedly uneasy. Conscious of the fact that, for many readers, Paris is the home of sentimental involvements, they avoid including in their accounts of such involvements anything that could upset these readers. The same moral prejudice is found in their dire warnings about the perils of drink. In "Straight-Rye Jones" Smith describes a young man's struggles with this vice. Jones, after managing to resist the temptation of bars and cafés, eventually cures himself and goes back to Montana to marry his childhood sweetheart. Carryl's story "Le Pochard" is a similar example, though its ending is more ambiguous. Grégoire is a writer who regularly gets drunk on absinthe. His roommate, Jean, gives him a clockwork toy of a drunk, who looks remarkably like Grégoire, lifting his glass. At the end of the story Jean wins the Prix de Rome and departs for the Villa Médicis, while Grégoire is left behind, alone with his derisory alter ego, whose clockwork is beginning to wear out.

These authors have set out to revise and improve Henri Murger. In their version of bohemian life, money is scarce but real poverty is absent, and the reader is also spared the sordid hospital death scenes that are frequent in Murger's writings. Where Murger talks openly about the various amorous intrigues of his characters, the Americans evade the issue, contenting themselves with discreet references to the subject. They seem to want to initiate American readers into the facts of bohemian life, which they themselves have experienced, but they resort to gift wrapping in order to make such facts acceptable. Evident in such an approach is a desire to proselytize, but also an effort at justification. Bohemian life is idealized, is shown floating in an atmosphere of sunlit youthfulness and joie de vivre in order to convince the reader of the legitimacy of expatriation. In "The Refugees" Smith tells the story of two American painters who fail to adapt to life in New York after a long stay in Paris. Their studios seem altogether too new and Greenwich Village too boring; the steam heating and the elevator are too noisy. In short, the two of them are so disgusted with the lack of atmosphere that they book passage on a ship and are back in Paris nine days later, thereby confirming

Murger's peremptory assertion that "Bohemia only exists and can only exist in Paris."[59]

The Parisian theme is, then, treated here in a superficial way. Whereas mysterious Paris lay somewhere beneath the streets of the city, bohemian Paris floats somewhere above the rooftops on a rosy cloud of unreality. Such a depiction of a milieu that tradition decreed essentially erotic is a step backward from even Holmes's brief sketch. Clémence at least had a few sins to be forgiven. If Smith and Carryl are compared to Chambers, their shortcomings become even more glaring. Chambers's work feels much closer to that of Murger. It is true that Chambers sometimes adopts an air of superiority toward his French characters which is rather exasperating, but this is a fairly general failing among American writers. He also has a tendency to preach,[60] and some of his student characters (Philip Landes, the hero of *The Red Republic,* for example) are so unbendingly virtuous that the author feels a word of explanation is needed: "Landes had inherited healthy blood, and his idea of pleasure did not include the craving ache of vice, but it did include an undue proportion of childish play. He found perfect satisfaction for some of his needs in galloping through Meudon Woods, in fishing the still pools of the Cailette, in romping over the fragrant meadows of Versailles."[61] This sort of American Saint Anthony, sublimating his physical desires through healthy exercise, is fairly rare, however. There are a few militant puritans, like Fradley in "Another Good Man," but Chambers shows the latter eventually succumbing to the infectious spirit of camaraderie of the Mid-Lent festival and allowing himself to join in the universal revelry. We also find one or two resolutely idealistic innocents, like Hastings in "The Street of Our Lady of the Fields," but most of Chambers's characters belong to a group of merry fellows, friends of Richard Elliot and Foxhall Clifford, who reappear from one work to the next and who seem to spend most of their time drinking, joking, and running after the girls. Even the grisette emerges as a more substantial figure. Yvonne, heroine of *In the Quarter,* has led an eventful life as the mistress of an officer since the age of seventeen. In "The Street of the First Shell" Sylvia admits to Jack Trent that she has had a child before meeting him. But although Chambers's vision is colored by a certain somber harshness and a taste for the fantastic, this does not ultimately result in a more profound analysis of bohemian love than that offered by other writers. Even those of his characters who are touched by a tragic destiny retain something of the flimsiness of the heroes of operetta.[62]

Hastings is an exception. He falls in love with a flighty grisette called Valentine, believing her to be a young lady of society. She, finding herself becoming more involved in the relationship than she had anticipated, keeps putting off the moment when she must finally acquaint her virtuous suitor with the facts. At last, after several meetings in the Luxembourg, they take a trip into the countryside, where Valentine confesses her unworthiness and her genuine love for Hastings. But the latter's happiness is not to be denied. He refuses to be influenced by the judgment of society, and the idyll ends favorably.

Yet this happy story has an antithetical side that is pointed up by the rural surroundings in which the action takes place. The setting is not typically Parisian; the city scenes are confined to the Rue Notre-Dame-des-Champs and the leafy glades of the Luxembourg, while other parts of the story take place in the countryside. The prevailing atmosphere is pastoral. Statues of Apollo, Venus, and Eros look down on the lovers' meetings, and in the last sentence of the story Our Lady of the Fields herself seems to bless the happy outcome. In this prelapsarian paradise, only an innocent like Hastings may be rewarded. The course of true love in ordinary life is by no means so smooth, and couples are frequently shown in discord rather than harmony. Chambers seems to share the sentiments expressed by Braith, who recalls his youthful errors in a speech to Rex Gethryn: "Damn this 'Bohemian love' rot. . . . I've seen all that shabby romance turn into such reality as you wouldn't like to face. I've seen promising lives go out in ruin and disgrace . . . lives that started exactly on the lines that you are finding so mighty pleasant just now."[63]

What is most interesting in Chambers's writing is his full and detailed descriptions of the everyday lives of bohemian artists. *In the Quarter,* "Another Good Man," and "Rue Barrée" all take us through the doors of the Académie Julian, founded in 1860, at 31 Rue du Dragon. Bouguereau, Boulanger, and Lefèvre [64] all teach there, and later John Noble will study there under Jean-Paul Laurens.[65] But Chambers also takes us into Boulanger's private class held on the Right Bank near the Passage Brady. The author evokes the atmosphere of the painter's studio in these terms: "The heat was suffocating. The walls smeared with the refuse of a hundred palettes, fairly sizzled as they gave off a sickly odor of paint and turpentine. Only two poses had been completed, but the tired models stood or sat, glistening with perspiration. The men drew and painted, many of them stripped to the waist. The air was heavy with tobacco smoke, and the respiration of some two hundred students of half as many nationalities."[66] Chambers also describes the picturesque figures who are part of the Académie Julian. There is Jules, the secretary, whose job it is to see that the students pay their subscriptions and who also calls the register, changing the order of the names each time so that everyone gets a chance to have a good position in the classroom. There is also Sara la Rousse, a redheaded model much appreciated by everyone, who is the star of the Mid-Lent ball, and M. Cicéri, a former model who now sells paints and artists' materials. New arrivals are forced to undergo an initiation ceremony. They are "crucified" by the older students in the studio on the Right Bank or sent to the "clou" at Julian's, that is to say, locked in the "dust chest."[67]

There are occasional clashes between American and French students, in which Chambers has the Americans coming off best. They also play jokes on their French comrades by recounting "tall tales" of their distant homeland.[68] Foxhall Clifford, in *In the Quarter,* is particularly fond of this pastime, and another character called Arizona insists on walking the streets of Paris equipped with a six-shooter, pretending to be a cowboy. According to Irving Stone, this was a true account of John Noble's behavior.[69] In 1888 we find the Americans complaining about not being able to exhibit their paintings at the Salon, interpreting their exclusion as a consequence of America's decision to levy import duties on works of art.[70] Chambers, describing artists at work, devotes seven pages to an account of one sitting of a model called Elise for Rex Gethryn.[71] Their collaboration, based entirely on the demands of art, is doubtless idealized, but Chambers says that it is exceptional.

These examples give some idea of the kind of documentation found in texts on bohemian Paris. Occasionally Chambers raises the issues of expatriation, money, and the outcome of a period of study in Paris. Rex Gethryn, discouraged by his lack of success, wonders if honesty and integrity are not handicaps for the aspiring painter. His aunt threatens to cut off his allowance if he does not come up with some sort of concrete achievement, like his compatriot Mousely, who has made a fortune by selling to bereaved Americans identical pictures of a dead child ascending to heaven.[72] In broaching such issues, Chambers seems more modern than either Carryl or Smith.

Bohemian life appears in other works where it is integrated with different aspects of the city, and it does not always meet with unqualified approval. In *About Paris* Richard Harding Davis draws an ironical picture of a typical young American who hangs around artists' studios for a few months before devoting himself to the pursuit of pleasure for as long as the allowance he receives from his parents permits. Similarly, in Harry Leon Wilson's *Ruggles of Red Gap* Cousin Egbert pours scorn on the idea that students come to the capital to find cultural enrichment. Egbert, though he has arrived four months ago, admits, "I can't see that I'm a lick more finished than when I left

Red Gap."[73] In *The Ambassadors* Chad's explanations to Mrs. Newsome about why he has moved to the Left Bank are manifestly untrue: "This was the region—Chad had been quite distinct about it—in which the best French and many other things were to be learned at least cost."[74] But the most blatant example of bad faith can be found in James's "Four Meetings," in the character of Caroline Spencer's cousin. He turns up in Le Havre with a farfetched story which nevertheless takes Caroline in. She hands over all the money she has brought for her trip and goes straight back to the United States.[75] Parisian bohemia also raises the issues of expatriation and patriotism; and in *The Guest of Quesnay* by Booth Tarkington, for example, the narrator, a painter, makes his feelings on the matter quite clear: "I am no 'expatriate.' I know there is a feeling at home against us who remain over here to do our work, but in most instances it is a prejudice which springs from a misunderstanding. I think the quality of patriotism in those of us who 'didn't go home in time' is almost pathetically deep and real."[76]

Virtually the only connection that American bohemia has with the rest of the capital is its link with the American colony living on the Right Bank. Miss Elizabeth, in *The Guest of Quesnay,* sums up the situation as being a relationship between the "right bank" and the "wrong bank."[77] The different worlds represented by the Faubourg Saint-Germain and the Latin Quarter have very little to do with one another. It is true that in *The Ambassadors* the faubourg bestows its blessings on the social success of the great artist Gloriani,[78] but apart from this one example the gap between the two worlds is so wide that the young Mme de Bellegarde, in *The American,* despairs of ever being able to realize her dream of dancing with the students at the Bal Bullier.[79] Relations between bohemia and the colony are restricted to worldly and economic matters. In Edith Wharton's novel *The Reef* they are exemplified in the picturesque lifestyle of the Farlow couple, who live in the Rue de la Chaise on the edge of the Latin Quarter. Mr. Farlow is a painter, while his wife writes articles for New England magazines. The alluring titles of her articles—"Behind the Scenes at the Français," "Peeps into Château Life," "Salons of the Faubourg St. Germain," "University Life"[80]—hint at a content that is largely the fruit of Mrs. Farlow's imagination. In her ridiculous versions of Parisian realities, Mrs. Farlow's notions of aristocratic milieux, such as they are, have all been acquired through the American colony. Thus, Wharton uses the Farlows to draw attention to the material ties binding American artists to their compatriots on the Right Bank.

Finally, the motif of bohemia is interwoven with the major theme of the

American hero's Parisian initiation in the works of Henry James. The character of Chad typifies on one level the young artist who has come to sow his wild oats on the Montagne Sainte-Geneviève. After idling away a few months on the Right Bank, he decides to cast his lot with bohemia and its twin pursuit of artistic and amorous fulfillment. Though he soon loses interest in the former, the latter continues to fascinate him, and he abandons himself to a succession of love affairs from which he derives "a special series of impressions . . . all of Musette and Francine, but Musette and Francine vulgarised by the larger evolution of the type."[81]

His stay on the Left Bank is a rite of passage, though the hero's initiation is not yet complete, and it continues on the Right Bank after he goes to live on the Boulevard Malesherbes. Once he has become the lover of an aristocrat from the Faubourg Saint-Germain, Chad has experienced and assimilated the influences of three different Parisian milieux. Though in one way typically bohemian, Chad also represents something beyond this as he passes from new experience to new experience in a series of initiations. By the time the "ambassadors" arrive, Chad's spiritual development is over, and we watch Strether, in his efforts to imaginatively recreate Chad's experience, embark on a spiritual development of his own. Obsessed by the idea of bohemian life, Strether had, while still in America, mused on what such a life must be like. Once in Paris, he ruminates on these ideas again in the Luxembourg in an effort to understand Chad's behavior. Later, guided by Little Bilham, who leads him symbolically across the river, he crosses the threshold into the intimate atmosphere of this "far-away makeshift life, with its jokes and its gaps, its delicate daubs and its three or four chairs, its overflow of taste and conviction and its lack of most else." He will be bewitched: "These things wove around the occasion a spell to which he unreservedly surrendered."[82]

For Strether, bohemia is symbolic of youth and love, and an essential part of his image of Paris. As he observes life in the Latin Quarter, he begins to doubt the puritan principles on which his existence had previously been based. What he sees arouses in him reflections not so much on the mysteries of art but on the mysteries of womanhood. His younger and less experienced predecessor, Longmore, had been the fascinated observer of the duo of Claudine and the painter in *Madame de Mauves*.[83] In this short novel of 1879, James had, before Chambers, exploited the potential of a trip to the countryside. Longmore returns from this pastoral epiphany dazzled and confused, racked with inner turmoil provoked by "the feeling that women were indeed a measureless mystery, and that it was hard to say whether there was greater beauty in their strength or in their weakness."[84] Strether is ready to accept bohemia for what it is. He assumes that Chad has had several love affairs but makes a revealing mistake by considering Chad's relationship with Marie de Vionnet something completely different, more noble and elevated. Subconsciously rejecting Marie's guilt, he is only too willing to believe Little Bilham's assertion that their attachment is entirely virtuous. Strether's blindness can be partly explained by his feelings for Marie, but there is another factor involved that hinges on a sort of dialectic between the two banks of the Seine. Strether wants to sublimate the grace and freedom of bohemian love into something altogether more disembodied. He believes that love undergoes a transformation by passing from one bank to the other; or rather, the final vestiges of a puritan upbringing cause him to reject the notion that an idyll which has captured his imagination by its beauty might have anything to do with sex. His aesthetic sensibility rejoices in the idea of Chad and Marie's love, and he longs to be able to invest their relationship with some sort of moral value as well, even if with a somewhat negative one.

The bohemian motif is dramatically reintroduced at the end of the novel when Strether surprises the two lovers in the country. Like Longmore, he is forced into the role of unwilling voyeur; and he finally realizes that Chad has a mistress in the same way that he had a mistress when he lived in the Latin Quarter and that this mistress is none other than Mme de Vionnet. The episode is similar to that in *Madame de Mauves*[85] but the effects on the two characters are different. Longmore is forced to ask himself a number of questions, whereas Strether is brought face to face with the answer to questions he had been avoiding. At first Chad and Marie try to pass off their meal at the inn as an innocent escapade, but Strether is not deceived and is at last forced to admit to himself the physical nature of their relationship, a relationship like any other.[86] The sublime idyll that Strether had pictured to himself suddenly collapses like a pricked balloon, leaving him with the realization that there is nothing to distinguish what is going on here from the amours of the average grisette. This country outing completes Strether's Parisian education, begun amid the springtime greenery of the Luxembourg.

With the exception of James, and to a lesser degree Chambers, American authors treat bohemia in a superficial way, without attempting to explore the interior world of the artist and how he is influenced by his surroundings. Few of the characters are writers, and the painters seem to cultivate an artistic know-how demanding neither sacrifice nor suffering. Moreover, bohemia is a transitory state, a way of filling in time between school and a career. Some characters abandon it quickly and return home to become model sons and citizens; others, like Chad, are slow to react to their families' entreaties. The rare artists who become famous and settle in the capital for good are shown being inevitably drawn into the bourgeois milieu of the American colony, like John Campton in Edith Wharton's novel *A Son at the Front*. Literary history cannot be changed, but one may be tempted to speculate regretfully on what might have happened if one of these American Saint Anthonys had had a real encounter with a Parisian grisette. It is a meeting that never takes place, and we are left with characters like Faustine in *The Red Republic:* "She was never vulgar, never tiresome, she never lost a certain dainty politeness, even when she lost her temper. Philip Landes supposed she had various affairs about which he knew nothing, and cared less, but for him she was merely an excellent playmate."[87] American literature of this period simply does not do justice to these pretty young women, of whom Murger wrote, "Now like bees, now like crickets, they worked and sang all week long, praying only for blue skies on Sunday, making love in the common way, from the heart, and sometimes flinging themselves out of windows."[88]

At the same time that bohemia's existence as an authentic social milieu was coming to an end with the outbreak of World War I, its use as a literary theme also disappeared. It next resurfaced, entirely transformed, in the writings of the Lost Generation.

Tourist Paris

Logical rather than chronological considerations have dictated the desirability of leaving a discussion of tourist Paris to the end of this section, for the appearances of mysterious and bohemian Paris do not necessarily antedate that of the tourist version of the city. In this third version, the character of the American who has just arrived on the scene is the linchpin of the plot. His function is clear: he is in Paris to observe, to understand, and even to criticize. Whereas the other two versions of the city relied heavily on literary themes that had found their way across the Atlantic, this version relies on the importation of different kinds of Americans into France. Through them, the authors are able to show us what happens when the accumulation of American experience comes face-to-face with immediate Parisian reality. In concrete terms, tourist Paris corresponds to those areas of their behavior and actions. It is not simply the setting for tourist rites, it also involves the way in which such rites are performed. Its role and its importance relative to other factors vary from one work to the next.

Before looking at works of fiction, it is worth mentioning various travel books, which according to the criteria set out in the introduction should not strictly be included in this study. But such works are important in the nineteenth century insofar as they did much to familiarize readers with the capital. They are also noteworthy because they were the first of their kind and were often written by well-known authors. They give readers some idea of what to expect on their travels and serve as entrée to novels with a foreign setting.

A Residence in France, published by James Fenimore Cooper in 1836, is a chronicle with strong ambassadorial overtones. Conscious of the fact that he is representing his country, Cooper keeps his distance vis-à-vis a city that in his eyes represents a dangerous temptation for his fellow citizens. He visits the court of Louis Philippe, and describes Paris as it was immediately after the troubles of 1832. He also visits Notre-Dame, which can now be seen in all its glory as a result of the demolition of the archbishop's palace, which had previously blocked its view. He admires the Louvre, the Palais Royal, and certain *hôtels particuliers.* The details he gives of the cholera epidemic and the uprisings in Montmartre and Saint-Méry—as well as the comparisons he draws between New York and Paris—have a certain documentary interest, but on the whole the account offers little of value.

Oliver Wendell Holmes's descriptions in *Our Hundred Days in Europe* are more interesting. This book is the story of a four-month trip that the author took with his daughter in 1886, and it is memorable chiefly for the way in which Holmes, seventy-seven at the time, looks at the city where he was once a student. The account of this sentimental pilgrimage is full of benevolent and touching humor. The city, through what has remained and what has changed, recalls the fleetingness of time, and the old man is forced to the melancholy conlusion that "Paris as seen by the morning sun of three or four and twenty and Paris in the twilight of the superfluous decade cannot be expected to look exactly alike."[89]

A thorough and systematic essay written two years later by William Crary Brownell and entitled *French Traits* provides a sharp contrast to Holmes's personal style. The author, one of the most penetrating literary critics of his time, draws an exhaustive comparison between the French and American ways of life. Brownell takes almost all his examples—with the exception of Chapter 8, "The Provincial Spirit"—from what goes on in the capital, illustrating what he says with details that visitors will have seen for themselves. In *About Paris,* which was dedicated to Paul Bourget, Richard Harding Davis gives a memorable image of the city as it was in 1895. This book— part guide, part chronicle (it relates, for instance, the Parisians' emotional reaction to the assassination of Sadi Carnot in Lyons)—is written with considerable brio and contains numerous anecdotes that make it a very enjoyable read. It is by no means as superficial as one might think to judge from the many engravings that accompany the text and contains several perspicacious comments on the American colony. The vogue for this sort of book, which was a mixture of narrative, memoirs, essays, and hints for travelers, was firmly established by the end of the century. Theodore Childs wrote *The Praise of Paris* in 1893, and Frank Berkeley Smith authored three such books between 1901 and 1905: *The Real Latin Quarter* (1901), *How Paris Amuses Itself* (1903), and *Parisians Out of Doors* (1905). Such texts become less interesting as they become more numerous.

The fictional side missing from such works is found to a certain extent in *The Innocents Abroad*, despite its autobiographical elements. Mark Twain tells the story of his 1867 Mediterranean cruise on the *Quaker City*, stopping in various countries, in particular Palestine. The Parisian episode is a self-contained entity. The work is based on letters published two years previously by the *Alta California* of San Francisco, the *New York Herald*, and the *New York Tribune*. Twain's pilgrims were real persons: Dan is Dan Slote; Doctor is Dr. A. R. Jackson, and Charley is Charles A. Langdon, who was to become the author's brother-in-law. Yet characters and narrator soon acquire an autonomous existence, and the reader can easily see in them fictional creations. What makes this travelogue different from the others is Twain's idiosyncratic style, which takes precedence over the book's content and desire to inform. The fictional aspect is, as it were, provided by the humor.

But it is not simply through the fact of belonging to the ambiguous genre of the humorous narrative that *The Innocents Abroad* stands apart. Rather, it is due to the fact that Mark Twain was the first writer to appreciate to what extent the American tourist was a potential source of laughter. In some respects, the American tourist is simply a modern variation on Montesquieu's Persians, Rica and Usbek, or even the Voltairean Huron, who one hundred years earlier had looked on the prospect of Paris with the eyes of a naif.[90] The character of the tourist, the foreigner lost in the middle of a city whose customs and language he barely understands, is a creation proper to the quintessentially original and eccentric nature of the humorist. Twain's innocents provide us with the first example of what happens when preconceived ideas and concrete reality meet head-on. Like all tourists, the narrator and his companions are full of notions about Paris that they have absorbed from their reading, and they feel that they know the city without ever having set foot in it. As the narrator observes, "It surprises me sometimes to think how much we do know, and how intelligent we are."[91] But the images they have conceived do not always correspond to reality.

Though he debunks bohemia, Twain seems to accept the existence of an occult Paris. In the Morgue he sees "patrician vestments, hacked and stabbed and stained with red,"[92] and he notices in the Faubourg Saint-Antoine those sordid details that give the area its unmistakable character:

> Little, narrow streets; dirty children blockading them; greasy, slovenly women capturing and spanking them; filthy dens on first floors, with rag stores in them (the heaviest business in the Faubourg is the chiffonier's); other filthy dens where whole suits of second and third-hand clothing are sold at prices that would ruin any proprietor who did not steal his stock; still other filthy dens where they sold groceries—sold them by the half-pennyworth—five dollars would buy the man out, goodwill and all. Up these little crooked streets they will murder a man for seven dollars and dump the body in the Seine. And up some other of these streets—most of them, I should say—live Lorettes.[93]

The narrator is keen to see Paris as it really is, with its good side and its bad. The easy flow of the narrative permits him to juxtapose a visit to Versailles, which he thoroughly enjoys in spite of his antiroyalist sentiments, with a visit to the slums, to poke fun at Parisian wigmakers one minute and Parisian billiard tables the next. He knows how to seize upon the tiny details that the tourist is totally unprepared for, such as coming across the stars and stripes hanging outside the Bal d'Asnières, whose manager is a New Yorker.[94]

But Twain is concerned above all to point out the ridiculous side of accepted tourist rites and rituals and to draw attention to the way in which the naiveté of these visitors is shamelessly taken advantage of. What is the point of rushing off to see some horrible bloodstained robe that Archbishop Affre happened to be wearing when he was killed on a barricade in 1848 or the traces left by a bullet that missed Czar Alexander II and hit a tree in the Bois de Boulogne? How can one help but be surprised that in shops where English is supposedly spoken the employee who possesses this linguistic ability is invariably absent and that in bars boasting a wide range of American drinks it is impossible to get anything like a decent cocktail? Why are the guides constantly racked by hunger and thirst, and why do they drag their clients into all sorts of bizarre shops on the slightest pretext? The reason, according to Twain, is because these same guides "deceive and defraud every American who sets foot in Paris for the first time and sees its

sights alone or in company with others as little experienced as himself."⁹⁵
The redoubtable guide Billfinger, whose prototype remains anonymous,
embodies the suspect and commercial nature of everything he shows to the
tourists. Through the lens of the author's humor, we see a Paris completely at
odds with the one shown us in the previously discussed works of fiction.
Mark Twain, arriving in the capital via Marseilles, unlike the rest of his
compatriots, gives the impression of creeping up on the city by surprise,
from the rear; and by observing it from this new angle, he illuminates certain
shabby and tarnished features of the legend. He takes detours that give him a
different view of things.

The Innocents Abroad is not unique. It stands at the beginning of a literary
tradition that exploits the amusing side of the trials and tribulations of tourists. Its range of comedy is wide, going from the endearingly comic to the
plain ridiculous. We will have to wait until 1915 before finding the same theme
treated in burlesque manner in the first four chapters of Wilson's *Ruggles of
Red Gap.* The narrator, Ruggles, a butler, is put up as the stakes in a poker
game in Paris by his English masters and is won by American tourists.
Through this central character, Wilson is able to make fun of the English,
Americans, and Parisians all at once. The influence of *The Innocents Abroad*
can still be seen, much later, in a burlesque epic by Donald Ogden Stewart,
Mr. and Mrs. Haddock in Paris; a novel by Homer Croy, *They Had to See
Paris;* an entertaining book by Lyon Mearson, *The French They Are a Funny
Race;* and comic scenes in the detective novels of Elliot Paul.

There are few comic episodes related to tourist Paris in the novels of the
late nineteenth century. In *The American,* however, Christopher Newman,
that Christopher Columbus in reverse, who arriving in Paris is convinced
that "Europe was made for him, and not he for Europe,"⁹⁶ has much in
common with Mark Twain's pilgrims. We may recall his naive admiration of
Noémie Nioche's terrible painting, for which he unflinchingly pays the
exorbitant figure she scribbles on a page of his guidebook. Newman, like a
modern Quixote, tries to help the lady earn enough money for her trousseau
by commissioning her to do some copies of the Louvre's great works of art.
Noémie, who makes up for her lack of artistic talent by a considerable flair
as a coquette, has other ideas about how to get on in the world. In "A Bundle
of Letters" James brings out the naiveté of his heroine, Miranda Hope, who
is totally unaware that the pension where she is staying is run on crudely
commercial lines. She defines it as "a kind of boarding-house, combined
with a kind of school; only it's not like an American boarding-house, or like
an American school either. There are four or five people here that have come

to learn the language,—not to take lessons, but to have an opportunity for conversation."[97] Strether offers little potential for comedy, but Sarah Pocock, and to a greater degree Waymarsh, are both amusingly depicted as the sort of American who remains totally impervious to the capital's charm. Speaking of Waymarsh, Miss Barrace wonders, "I show him Paris—show him everything, and he never turns a hair. He's like the Indian chief one reads about, who, when he comes to Washington to see the Great Father, stands wrapped in his blanket and gives no sign."[98] In a way, such characters are the descendants of Mark Twain's innocents.

The various novels relating to tourist Paris occupy widely differing positions in literary history. Alongside works by Henry James and Edith Wharton stand others by Dorothy Canfield, Booth Tarkington, and some minor authors already mentioned. The more fully a novelist explores the general theme of the city, the less important the aspect relating to tourist Paris becomes. In trying to describe this aspect and define its role in different works, a sort of hierarchy emerges. Those novels integrating tourist Paris with a more general study of social milieux stand out at the top of the hierarchy, and a more detailed discussion of them will be reserved for the following chapter.

If we turn to a map of the city, tourist Paris can be defined as consisting primarily of areas on the Right Bank. The tourist has just as many problems as the student penetrating the closed world of the Faubourg Saint-Germain, and its doors do not swing magically open if he waves a Baedeker at them. To be received in the faubourg means the visitor has taken the first step on the road to being accepted in society—or, alternatively, that he has fallen into a well-laid trap or is to be put to some sort of difficult test. Whenever an American man wishes to become a member of Parisian society through motives of ambition or love, he will usually find the object of his desires somewhere in the faubourg: Mme de Cintré, Mme de Vionnet, or Mme de Malrive.[99] There, too, he will find his adversaries: the Bellegardes or Mme de Treymes. In the eyes of the tourist, the Faubourg Saint-Germain is like a distant, shimmering mirage, veiled in mystery.

The places on the Right Bank most frequently described are the newly built boulevards and the city's most famous monuments: the Louvre, Notre-Dame, and the Arc de Triomphe. After 1889 the Eiffel Tower, which is on the Left Bank, is likewise among the most described monuments. But mention is also made of various streets, hotels, and shops that enable the reader to follow the characters' comings and goings. In fact it would be possible to produce from these novels a guidebook to Paris, listing hotels, restaurants, cafés, and theaters, some of which have disappeared but most of which can still be found today. The authors, with the possible exception of Edith Wharton, rarely invent places. Wharton's characters stay at the aptly named "Nouveau Luxe,"[100] which may have been based on one particular Parisian institution but which combines the characteristics of all the big hotels catering to an international clientele. The Nouveau Luxe provides an excellent vantage point from which to study American behavior and could be any one of the capital's palatial hotels—the Ritz, the Meurice, or the Bristol. At times, Henry James is coyly reluctant to name places he describes in minute detail, such as the mysterious restaurant on the bank of the Seine where Strether and Mme de Vionnet sample a tomato omelette accompanied by a Chablis the color of straw. The geographical clues provided by the author narrow the possibilities down to either Lapérouse or the Tour d'Argent, but given the fact that the diners are able to look out on the river, dotted with boats, it is probably the latter, whose dining rooms are upstairs.[101]

It would be tiresome to list all the places mentioned. To give a few examples, we know that Christopher Newman stayed at the Grand Hôtel before taking an apartment overlooking the Boulevard Haussmann. Strether chooses a more modest hotel near the Rue de la Paix, while the Pococks live in a palatial hotel on the Rue de Rivoli, like John Durham in *Madame de Treymes.* Chad's apartment is on the Boulevard Malesherbes; Maria Gostrey's little entresol is near the Champs-Elysées, in what James refers to as the Marboeuf [*sic*] district. Newland Archer, in *The Age of Innocence,* stays at the Bristol on the Place Vendôme. In Edith Wharton's story "The Last Asset" Mrs. Newell is living at the Ritz, and the hero of *Mr. Barnes of New York* has rooms at the Meurice, as does Mrs. Headway in James's short novel *The Siege of London.* In the same book, Lady Demesne is at the Hôtel du Rhin, while the Dosson family, in *The Reverberator,* is staying at the Hôtel de l'Univers et de Cheltenham in the Rue de la Paix.

Cafés, theaters, and restaurants mark out the tourists' leisure circuit. The cafés on the boulevards have pride of place: the Café de la Paix, where Ansolini displays an advertisement drawn on his shaven pate in *The Beautiful Lady,*[102] the Café Anglais, the Grand Café, the Riche, the Café de Paris, the Café de Madrid, the Café Le Peletier.[103] The restaurants most frequently mentioned are Laurent, Durand, Paillard, Bignon, Brébant, the Pavillon d'Armenonville, and the Pavillon Henry IV in Saint-Germain.[104] Maxim's is the setting for a short story by Frank Berkeley Smith, "Natka," about the downfall of a Russian baroness who ruins herself for her American lover.

A wide range of theaters is mentioned, from the Opéra down to the cafés chantants of the Champs-Elysées and the cabarets of Montmartre, including the Théâtre Français, the Gymnase, the Variétés, and the Capucines. In *The Ambassadors* James puts the various establishments into different categories. The Français and the Gymnase are acceptable, and Chad may take Mamie Pocock there. Others are more vulgar, like the Variétés, whose program looks particularly interesting to Jim Pocock, and the circus, where Waymarsh takes Sarah.[105] The Opéra provides the setting for the scene in which Morton Carlton pursues the princess Aline[106] and for the incident witnessed by Christopher Newman that will lead to the death of Valentin de Bellegarde.[107] Chad and Strether meet again in the Français,[108] as do Littlemore and Nancy Beck in *The Siege of London*.[109] Undine Spragg, in *The Custom of the Country*, prefers the "little theatres," probably those of the boulevards, while Miranda Hope puts the Palais-Royal at the head of her list, since her guidebook gives it two stars.[110] In *The Age of Innocence* May Archer, who is on her honeymoon in Paris, adores the cafés chantants. The cabarets Le Ciel and L'Enfer are the setting of Carryl's short story "A Latter-Day Lucifer" in *Zut and Other Parisians*. Maxime Perrot, who is an "angel" (that is, a waiter) in Le Ciel is fired after trying to swindle a group of Americans. Seeking revenge, he takes the place of a "demon" in L'Enfer and, slipping into Le Ciel through a side entrance, spreads confusion throughout the establishment.

Tourist Paris also provides a series of vignettes that trace the changes in the city landscape and offer an interesting retrospective for the modern reader. Occasionally, historical events and minor local happenings are mentioned. In 1893 Archibald Clavering Gunter denounces the perils of Parisian traffic, and in 1908 Booth Tarkington comments on the quantity of blue smoke emitted by motor cars.[111] James remarks on the whiteness of the new building facades,[112] and Tarkington gives details of the balloon rides that may be taken from the Porte Maillot.[113] This bric-a-brac of souvenirs shows that the authors know the city intimately, and the use of such details drawn from their own experiences is primarily aimed at building up an atmosphere of verisimilitude that will engage the reader's interest. Still, the tourist Paris of fiction, though solidly embedded in that of reality, undergoes a subtle metamorphosis.

This metamorphosis first takes the form of an embellishment. It is true that tourist Paris is confined to the elegant neighborhoods, so the atmosphere of luxury that pervades it, like the atmosphere of luxury that surrounds these neighborhoods, is real. But often a desire to idealize the tableau of the city is evident. For Strether, Paris is a "huge, irridescent object, a jewel brilliant and hard."[114] For Miranda Hope, it is "truly elegant" and "very superior" to New York.[115] John Durham thinks it has a "look of having been boldly and deliberately planned as a background for the enjoyment of life."[116] When the climate is mentioned, the time of year is inevitably spring or summer. Strether arrives one fine day in March and leaves in August. Miranda Hope finds the climate "remarkably cheerful and sunny."[117] In Dorothy Canfield's novel *The Bent Twig* art-critic Felix Morrison, watching the sun set behind the Arc de Triomphe, exclaims: "Oh, Paris! Paris! . . . Paris in April! There's only one thing better, and that we have before us— Paris in May!" A little later, Canfield gives a lengthy description of the passage from May to June. "The days were like golden horns of plenty, spilling out sunshine, wandering perfumed airs, and the heart-quickening aroma of the new season. The nights were cool and starry. Every one in Paris spent as much as possible of every hour out of doors. The pale-blue sky flecked with creamy clouds seemed the dome, and the city the many-colored pavement of some vast building, so grandly spacious that the sauntering, leisurely crowds thronging the thoroughfares seemed no crowds at all, but only denoted a delightful sociability."[118] In short, the tourist lives in an artificial year, from which winter is excluded and which is aptly referred to by a word denoting its limited duration, "season."

The shock caused by the spectacle of luxury and beauty turns into dizzy excitement in the overwhelming atmosphere of carnival that fills the city. It is not by chance that the places most frequently mentioned are cafés, restaurants, and theaters. These temples of pleasure impart their festive atmosphere to the city as a whole, and the visitor cannot long remain insensible to this pervasive mood of joyful intoxication and good-natured folly. Writes Tarkington, "Since King Charles the Mad, in Paris no one has been completely free from lunacy while spring-time is happening. There is something in the sun and the banks of the Seine. The Parisians are born intoxicated and remain so; it is not fair play to require them to be like other human people. . . . The strangest of all this is that it is not only the Parisians who are the insane ones in Paris; the visitors are none of them in behaviour as elsewhere. You have only to go there to become as lunatic as the rest."[119] The "gaieté parisienne" is inherent in the city the tourist discovers. Its outward signs are everywhere visible, and when it is expressed through laughter, the tourist falls victim to the contagion and is caught up in the general hilarity.

Yet words like "drunkenness" and "madness" take on a special meaning. The way these Americans let their hair down is harmless in the extreme. For Strether, it means starting to smoke;[120] for Waymarsh, an evening alone with

Sarah Pocock.[121] The Americans in *Ruggles of Red Gap* drink in the company of several jolly coachmen at the Rendez-Vous des Cochers Fidèles before setting out in search of further thrills riding the wooden horses of a merry-go-round.[122] These are innocent pleasures. None of these authors—though they all agree that Paris is "the temple of Pleasure"[123]—ventures a few steps further to explore more occult ceremonies. No tourist goes so far as to prolong his revels by participating in the rites practiced by the goddesses of venal and transitory love. Until World War I, festive Paris is a daytime phenomenon, and the absence of any real noctambulist excludes all contact with the Paris of mystery.

Faced with the good-natured harmlessness of such pursuits, one might justifiably conclude that they are not a true reflection of reality. Without doubt, respect for convention led many writers to impart a rosy tint to this aspect of Paris. The tourist, like Cinderella, retires from the scene on the stroke of midnight, avoiding those dark and disturbing elements of nighttime Paris that will be revealed for the first time in the novels of the First World War. The celebration of the city fulfills, above all, one of the novel's basic functions, that of making the reader dream.

The precise role and relative importance of tourist Paris can be determined by an examination of the way it appears in different works. These fall into two categories: books in which the exploration of Paris is restricted to its purely touristic aspects and those in which the theme is more fully developed, where an examination of tourist Paris is used primarily to lead into a more profound exploration. In both categories, the importance of the motif in relation to the plot and characters varies considerably. It may be entirely extraneous to the plot or may be incorporated in it with varying degrees of success. For instance, in *The Beautiful Lady* and *The Guest of Quesnay* Tarkington uses Paris as the setting for one or two scenes, and then the city fades into oblivion as the characters move elsewhere. Both novels begin in Paris, on the boulevards, after which one moves to Italy and the other to Normandy. For the narrator of *The Guest of Quesnay,* the magic of Paris is sufficiently potent to seduce him away from the Bay of Naples: "But even on Capri, people sometimes hear the call of Paris and wish to be in that unending movement: to hear the multitudinous rumble, to watch the procession from a café terrace and to dine at Foyot's. So there came at last a fine day when I, knowing that the horse-chestnuts were in bloom along the Champs Elysées . . . was off for the banks of the Seine."[124] The reader may be excused for thinking that this sudden return indicates a permanent location for the plot, but the city merely revives the narrator's flagging inspiration, and off he goes to Normandy to paint pictures. The first thirty pages set in Paris have no obvious link with the rest of the book, though the long, opening description of the boulevards is an anthology piece.

In other novels of this type Paris constitutes the basis for a separate episode. An example of this occurs in Book II of *Mr. Barnes of New York,* where the hero's adventures in Paris are recounted in a section entitled "An Episode of the Paris Salon." The hero arrives in Paris after various adventures in Corsica to continue his escapades at an art exhibition before dashing off to engage in further exploits in Monte Carlo. In *The Princess Aline* by Richard Harding Davis a painter, Morton Carlton, falls in love with the princess of the title and follows her from London to Paris and then to Constantinople and Athens. In spite of various setbacks to his suit, he nonetheless relaxes sufficiently while in Paris to recall the pleasant memory of his student days: "The trees hung heavy with leaves over his head, a fountain played and overflowed at his elbow, and the lamps of the fiacres passing and repassing on the Avenue of the Champs Elysées shone like giant fire-flies through the foliage."[125] In such novels, Paris is a decorative addition guaranteed to go down well with the public. Its depiction is limited to a series of lithographs scattered throughout the narrative, and it is the superficial exploitation of what Pierre Citron calls "the exterior charm of Paris."

A different situation occurs in the novels of Henry James, Edith Wharton, and Dorothy Canfield and in *The Transgression of Andrew Vane.* Carryl's uneven and generally ill-focused work runs the gamut from fantasy to study of manners; but mixed with the incredible plot are pertinent observations on the behavior of Americans in Paris. For Carryl, James, Wharton, and Canfield do not simply limit tourist Paris to its rather clichéd charm but work it in with a fuller exploration of the city and the way it is linked with the destiny of certain characters. These include Christopher Newman; Chad and Strether; John Durham and Fanny de Malrive in *Madame de Treymes;* Longmore in *Madame de Mauves;* Undine Spragg in *The Custom of the Country;* Sylvia Marshall in *The Bent Twig;* and Andrew Vane. Yet it is justifiable to single out tourist Paris in these books. These characters are initially introduced as tourists but respond to the city's challenge by establishing a whole network of relationships with it. Tourist Paris consists also of a psychological stage in the development of certain characters ready to embark on their Parisian adventure. This stage may be described as one of heightened receptivity in which the characters, having shed their cultural habits, stand open and vulnerable to the city's influence. This state of receptiveness can be opposed to the reaction of the humorist faced with some new and surprising custom. Whereas the humorist instinctively takes a protective step backward, the receptive character takes a step forward. Tourist Paris explains why; it fleshes out a city that has also a spirit and a soul.

Tourist Paris exists within clearly defined limits and is transitory and often false. The tourist moves in a closed universe. The only Parisians he meets are guides, concierges, coachmen, waiters, and his personal servants, often from the provinces. He thus lives in the center of a Paris from which most Parisians are excluded, as though his arrival has frightened them away. This is the lesson that Mark Twain points out to his compatriots. But it is also the conclusion reached by the receptive hero, who is now determined to go beyond his condition as a tourist.

The metaphor of the theater fittingly describes the American visitor's isolation. Paris, a city of theaters, is itself a marvelous spectacle, but a spectacle of illusion and artifice that the visitor observes without taking part in. The texts themselves often show him in the role of spectator, sitting on some café terrace watching the passing crowds: "The multitudes seem to go as actors passing to their cues," observes Tarkington, adding: "Your place at one of the little tables upon the side-walk is that of a wayside spectator."[126] It is now up to the tourist to decide if he will leave his seat in the audience and take his place with the actors in the theater of the city.

CHAPTER 2

PARISIAN MILIEUX BEFORE 1914

American Perspectives

The American hero who goes beyond his condition as a tourist enhances and refines his experience in two ways. First, he acquires a new social culture through the circles in which he begins to move, and secondly he undergoes a process of initiation that brings about subtle changes. In the works that form the basis of the next two chapters, the characters are given a wider field of action leading to a more comprehensive and global view of the city. Fifteen or so novels and short stories are involved, whose literary merit varies widely but which together provide a detailed and coherent picture of contemporary Parisian society.

As soon as one attempts to determine how these American heroes see the capital, a problem arises. Their perception is complicated by the question of authorial distance and by the wide range of characters expressing their opinions of Paris. Simply to make two groups, the praisers and the detractors, is not very helpful, since fools may praise and wise men criticize. The main difficulty lies in unscrambling the author's real message, blurred and distorted by the cacophony of his characters' voices, the complaints of his disgruntled tourists, the raptures of his delighted aesthetes, the ripostes of his exasperated patriots, and the nostalgic reminiscences of his epicureans. The characters' behavior, their social and political significance, are open to different interpretations. The briefest exchange of opinion raises the question of whether or not what the characters are saying is also what the author thinks. And, of course, it would be entirely possible, through selective juxtaposition of specially chosen passages, to put forward contradictory images of the city in any one work.

American Paris can be considered as consisting of more or less the same places that make up tourist Paris. Although members of the American colony occasionally move out to the suburbs, like the Carnbys in *The Transgression of Andrew Vane,* the vast majority are to be found firmly entrenched in the rich and elegant neighborhoods of the Right Bank. Mme de Mauves constitutes a notable exception, living out in Saint-Germain-en-Laye, from whose heights—the symbol of her apparent moral elevation—she contemplates the distant city below. But as the characters are generally received into Parisian society, American Paris begins to encroach on the sacred enclave of the Faubourg Saint-Germain. The protagonists' deeper experience of the city does not give them a broader view of it. Rather, it adds richness and tone to the depiction of the urban setting, without extending the range of vision. While the city of the tourist consists above all of streets, that of the initiate consists of houses. The new, rich apartments of the Carnbys, the Tristrams, or Mrs. Marshall-Smith in *The Bent Twig,* reflect the owners' neutral lifestyles, caught between an urge to display their wealth and a desire to imitate French taste. The decor is usually modern, and the walls are hung with avant-garde (that is, impressionist) paintings. Their experience is different from that of their compatriots in Rome, who have taken over many of the city's decaying palazzi. Americans in Paris do not supplant the Parisian aristocracy, which is so deeply rooted in the faubourg that this physical setting engages with their lives almost as if it were a living natural habitat. The high walls surrounding its *hôtels* are the concrete symbols of an easily recognizable caste whose way of life remains a constant source of interest and astonishment to the Americans. James drew two completely different portraits of such a milieu. In *The American* it is seen through the eyes of an outsider, Newman, whereas in *The Ambassadors* it is depicted from the inside as an open, airy environment bathed in an atmosphere of artistic refinement. But although the Bellegardes in their sinister dwellings seem caricatures when compared with characters in other works of this period, their fundamental traits recur, less marked but still recognizable, in novels by Edith Wharton.

Cut off from the street by their paved "court of honor," these *hôtels* usually present a solid, time-blackened facade to the outer world. To penetrate them is like an act of transgression, or sacrilege. Stepping inside the Bellegardes' residence, Newman feels "as if he had plunged into some medium as deep as the ocean, and as if he must exert himself to keep from sinking."[1] In *Madame de Treymes* John Durham is ill at ease visiting the Hôtel de Malrive outside the season. "The thought of what he must represent to the almost human consciousness which such old houses seem to possess, made him feel like a barbarian desecrating the silence of a temple of the earlier faith."[2] These somber vaulted dwellings, uncomfortable and inhospitable, seem to gird themselves against light and joy, the present, and life itself. Even in the gardens, where nature asserts its rights, the observer feels as if he is at the bottom of a well, and the reader, looking up at these high walls, has the impression he is slowly sinking. Yet the very function of these ancient walls is to withstand the passing of centuries and remain the incorruptible guardians of old prejudices and strange, outmoded customs.

The contrast between these dwellings, sunk in a sort of hollow, and the old family châteaux, set in high, hilly country, is symbolic of the decline of the aristocracy deplored by Valentin de Bellegarde on his deathbed. The French nobility serves as little purpose as its derisory provincial fortresses. It continues to live out its unproductive existence entombed in dark Parisian mausoleums. The impression of this decline is particularly strong in *The American*. The Christian name of the last of the Bellegardes, Urbain, not only suggests the deceptive refinement of his manners, but also reminds us of this passage from feudal glory to sterile encystment in a city caste. The interiors of these ancient dwellings in the Faubourg Saint-Germain give us an image of the families who live there. The Bellegardes' house, built in 1627, is a vast, dark edifice, cold and so old-fashioned that Valentin wants to show it to Newman as a joke, just to see his reactions. In *Madame de Treymes* John Durham's sister Kate shudders at the thought of how freezing it must be in the Hôtel de Malrive in winter. The austere drawing rooms have an air of theatrical artificiality, as if specifically planned to serve as the correct backdrop for family tableaux. The thick walls and the austere, forbidding interiors all convey the impression of existing expressly to protect the way of life of a tightly knit clan. The prominence given to such residences is an indication of the centrality of the aristocracy in the literature of this period.

The meeting between Americans and Parisians, impossible in the context of tourist Paris, can now take place, but within strictly defined limits. It may be defined as the meeting between different aristocracies. Almost all the American protagonists are millionaires. Strether, who in many respects represents an inversion of the myth of the American, is nonetheless a wealthy intellectual. The men in these novels manage from afar fortunes that they have acquired through hard work, inheritance, or plain good luck. Newman's empire was built shortly after the Civil War; Chad's wealth derives from the family company, which manufactures a household object the author declines to name; Mr. Dosson's riches result from his business acumen; Littlemore, a somewhat indolent pioneer, has the good fortune to inherit a silver mine that has fallen into disuse but later turns out to be extremely profitable. Most of the time, the American women enjoy a similar amount of financial independence, resulting from an opportune marriage, a lucrative divorce, or a timely widowhood.[3]

Once in Paris, the protagonists meet up with their rich compatriots in the American colony, and both newcomers and residents alike share the same impatience to cultivate Parisian nobility. They consider its members to be their approximate counterparts and frequently succeed in becoming members themselves through marriage. Consequently, the narrative frame encompasses a social setting that is relatively restricted and homogeneous, and from which members of the urban proletariat are conspicuously absent. The literature of the period is quite unconcerned with anything outside the way of life of the wealthy; and this outlook can be explained by reference to the authors' social origins. Henry James and Dorothy Canfield were both members of the middle, or upper middle class, whereas Edith Wharton was definitely patrician. Their main concern is to depict the experience of Americans in Paris rather than to depict Paris itself, and, as they all worked from life, their studies were unable to go beyond the social boundaries that limited their personal observations.

The images of Paris in these authors' works show the close relationship of the Parisian theme to what James called "the American-European legend," that is to say the literary account of the American adventure in Europe. Discounting *The Marble Faun,* published in 1860, Paris can be seen to lie at the origin of what chronologically are the first instances of international intrigues in American writing, in *Madame de Mauves* and *The American,* published in 1874 and 1877 respectively. However remarkable this chronological priority may be, the fact remains that subsequently the "Parisian" novel was to become but one aspect of the "European" novel. This closeness of the Parisian to the European theme constitutes an ever-present problem for this study, particularly for the period preceding the First World War and particularly for the writings of Henry James. The American-European legend has already been critically examined by other writers, notably Marie-Reine Garnier in *Henry James et la France* and Christof Wegelin in *The Image of Europe in Henry James.* Here, the intent is not simply to apply the observations and conclusions of these critics to the more restricted subject of Paris. Nor is it to try to evaluate the relative importance of the Parisian microcosm in the genesis of the European myth in its totality or to try to weigh the Parisian experience against the experience of other great metropolises. The main concern is to establish what was fresh and original in American writers' responses to Paris and to define the peculiar harmonies and dissonances set up between city and protagonists.

From the evidence of the texts themselves, Paris emerges during this period as the most important, if not the only, place on the imaginary map of

France. The Côte d'Azur, later rechristened the Riviera, does not begin to play a literary role until the 1920s. The northeastern provinces have not yet become notorious as scenes of battle. The provinces in general conjure up ideas of châteaux, spas, and the odd seaside resort. For perfectly valid reasons, no other city serves to adjust or alter the image that the capital gives of the whole of France. But if Paris's primacy within France itself is unquestionable, its importance in Europe is far more difficult to evaluate, especially, for example, when comparing it with London. A superficial examination would suggest that the two cities provide more or less the same literary potential as exemplars of their nations, whereas Rome suffers through sharing with other cities such as Florence and Venice its role as representative of Italian civilization. But beyond these impressions, it is impossible to be more specific without proceeding to an examination of London, Rome, Florence, Venice, and other European cities, similar to the one undertaken for Paris.

There are, however, European elements that are part of the Parisian scene. The cosmopolitan nature of American Paris is borne out by several factors. First we are struck by the characters' geographical mobility. In some novels, such as *The Custom of the Country* and *The Bent Twig,* which are, strictly speaking, more international than Parisian, Paris is firmly situated in a European context by the characters' numerous trips. But even in works set more specifically in the capital—*Madame de Mauves, The American, The Ambassadors,* "Mrs. Temperly," and "The Last Asset"—the protagonists constantly come and go, making one aware of the presence of neighboring countries. Longmore is forever talking about his plans to visit Brussels in order to see the works of the Flemish painters; Newman travels throughout Europe and, like John Durham, goes to London, where Noémie is busy pursuing her career as a successful courtesan. Valentin de Bellegarde dies in Switzerland as the result of a duel. Chad comes back from the south of France to meet Strether, and later the second group of "ambassadors" will disperse to neighboring countries. In Paris itself, several characters are neither French nor American: the famous artist Gloriani is Italian, as is Mme Dandelard, a lady who gradually slips toward the brink of the demimonde in *The American,* and Roviano, who is part of the international set of *The Custom of the Country.* Stanislas Kapp, the successful adversary of Valentin de Bellegarde, is Alsatian and therefore, at the time, German, like Baronness Adelschein, who is Undine Spragg's friend, and Herman Heidenmauer, one of the heroes of "Collaboration."

The presence of England is even more strongly felt. The travelers, who often arrive and leave via Liverpool, meet lots of English people in Paris:

Lord Deepmere, Mrs. Bread, and the anonymous cousin of Mme de Cintré in *The American;* Lord Demesne in *The Siege of London;* and Schenkeldorff, Mrs. Newell's protector, in "The Last Asset." The French and British aristocracies are related by blood. Mme de Cintré is half English. Diane Eveleth, whose maiden name is de la Ferronaise, is half Irish. Numerous links are forged between America and France with or without the help of the American colony. Mrs. Tristram, Maria Gostrey, and Euphemia Cleve, who later becomes the baronne de Mauves, are all educated at French convents. In *The Transgression of Andrew Vane* Margery Palffy has an American mother and a father who is from Bordeaux. In *The Reverberator* Gaston Probert's position in the aristocracy is quite remarkable.

> Born in Paris, he had been brought up altogether on French lines, in a family which French society had irrecoverably absorbed. His father, a Carolinian and a Catholic, was a Gallomaniac of the old American type. His three sisters had married Frenchmen, and one of them lived in Brittany and the others much of the time in Touraine. His only brother had fallen, during the terrible year, in defence of their adoptive country. Yet Gaston, though he had an old legitimist marquis for his godfather, was not legally one of its children; his mother had, on her death-bed, extorted from him the promise that he would not take service in its armies. . . . The young man therefore, between two stools, had no clear sitting-place: he wanted to be as American as he could and yet not less French than he was.[4]

This extreme example illustrates how the transition between America and Paris takes place gradually, thereby cushioning both the characters and the American readers from too much culture shock. The presence of such milieux that bridge the gap between the two nations is comforting and reassures readers as to the importance of their own country. Furthermore, it allows comparisons to be drawn between Americans who are Europeanized and those who are not.

Along with the fundamental opposition between recent arrivals and old, established members of the colony, the authors under consideration here enjoy comparing the Americans with the British, who get pretty short shrift. It is rare to find an English character treated sympathetically. Mrs. Bread, in *The American,* is perhaps an exception, though she is occasionally narrow-minded.[5] Lord Deepmere personifies the boorishness of the English aristocracy. When he is discovered with Noémie, he attempts to hide his confusion "with the inferior grace of a male and a Briton."[6] He prefigures the equally lumpish character of Lord Demesne, Mrs. Headway's victim in *The Siege of*

London, whose stupidity is remarked upon several times by the author. Valentin de Bellegarde's English cousins fill him with a sarcastic irritation that seems to have the author's approval: "Imagine a woman who wears a green crape bonnet in December and has straps sticking out of the ankles of her interminable boots! My mother begged I would do something to oblige them. I have undertaken to play *valet de place* this afternoon. They were to have met me here at two o'clock, and I have been waiting for them twenty minutes. Why doesn't she arrive? She has at least a pair of feet to carry her. I don't know whether to be furious at their playing me false, or delighted to have escaped them."[7] In describing Raymond de Chelles, Edith Wharton slips in a biting authorial comment about the English nobility: "If Raymond de Chelles had been English he would have been a mere fox-hunting animal, with appetites but without tastes; but in his lighter Gallic clay the wholesome territorial savour, the inherited passion for sport and agriculture were blent with an openness to finer sensations, a sense of the come and go of ideas."[8] Nettie Wincher, after becoming the marquise de Trézac, remarks to Undine that the Parisians make conversation more easily than do the English and that "here people don't go on looking at each other for ever as they do in London."[9] The only good thing about the English would seem to be their accent, "the distinctively British accent which, on his arrival in Europe, had struck Newman as an altogether foreign tongue, but which, in women, he had come to like extremely."[10]

Lampoons of this kind can also be found in the books discussed in Chapter 1. As far as Frank Berkeley Smith's narrator in "The Enthusiast" is concerned, his friend Briston carries the idea of the phlegmatic Englishman to excess. "Briston is a stone,"[11] he declares. The character of Ruggles provides a hilarious example of a kind of arrogant and obtuse Anglocentrism. For him, Paris has meaning only in relation to London, and this lends a distinctive flavor to his description of the city: "We now crossed their Thames over what would have been Westminster Bridge, I fancy, and were presently bowling through some sort of Battersea part of the city."[12] Finally, the English, with their characteristic appearance, stand out clearly amid the crowds of people on the boulevards, as Tarkington observes when he characterizes them as "ruddy English, thinking of nothing, pallid English, with upper teeth bared and eyes hungrily searching for sign-boards of tearooms."[13]

This critical tendency on the part of authors who are not known to be especially Anglophobe is all the more surprising insofar as there is no mitigating praise. The persistence of national prejudices and the memory of historical squabbles are not enough to explain it. It would appear to be specifically the English in Paris, rather than the English in general, who arouse such animosity in the American writers. Doubtless this is part of a subconscious attempt to divert attention from their own embarrassment and difficulties by focusing on the ridiculousness of their Anglo-Saxon cousins. Perhaps too, in their attempts to analyze the complex reactions provoked by the capital, they see the English attitude as over-simplistic. The ambivalent status of the British, who are at one and the same time Europeans and Anglo-Saxons, is well suited to the role of initiator. But in reality they never play such a role, and it is apparently their lack of intelligence in their response to Paris that makes them the primary butt of American criticism.

In the majority of these American books, English is the language of communication for the characters. The texts themselves—with the remarkable exception of "Les Metteurs en Scène," which Edith Wharton wrote in French—are, of course, written in English. But realism and credibility, to say nothing of elementary common sense, dictate that the characters must either have an interpreter or speak the same language. The novelists are faced with the options of making the Parisians speak English, having the Americans speak French, or stressing the characters' mutual difficulty in understanding each other. When a character gets into difficulties expressing himself, it is, oddly enough, a Parisian groping for the right English expression more often than an American struggling with the local language. For example, M. Nioche, in *The American*, who used to be an accountant in England, has developed a peculiar jargon all his own. "The language spoken by M. Nioche was a singular compound, which I shrink from the attempt to reproduce in its integrity. He had apparently once possessed a certain knowledge of English, and his accent was oddly tinged with the cockneyism of the British metropolis. But his learning had grown rusty with disuse, and his vocabulary was defective and capricious. He had repaired it with large patches of French, with words anglicised by a process of his own, and with native idioms literally translated."[14]

Dorothy Canfield's characters are intellectuals who generally speak French. This is also the case of John Durham, in *Madame de Treymes,* whose accent is so perfect that he could easily pass for a Parisian. But, on the whole, the novelists tend to push to the extreme the first of the previously noted options. Consider, for example, the striking proficiency in English of Mme de Cintré, Mme de Vionnet, Diane de la Ferronaise, Margery Palffy, and the Proberts, all of whom are virtually bilingual. In addition, Mme de Brive in "Mrs. Temperly," all the Bellegardes, M. de Mauves, and Raymond de Chelles, speak fluent English. The French reader may find it easy to believe that the international set of *The Custom of the Country* is more or less polyglot; but the linguistic gifts so generously bestowed on Parisians are a little harder to swallow, and it is somewhat disconcerting to find an aristocratic society that is so resolutely turned toward the Anglo-Saxon world.

But there is more to come. As a sort of compensatory process, the writers try to create a certain linguistic local color. They endeavor to render palpable the presence of French as part of the surroundings. The most elementary way of doing this is by sprinkling the texts with French words, a technique frequently employed by James in *The American* and *The Ambassadors*. Each of these novels contains a hundred or so insertions of this kind. They crop up during conversations or as part of the narrative itself and are thus attributable to both characters and author. In addition, a large number of words and expressions are transposed from French to English. For example, like Frank Berkeley Smith and Guy Wetmore Carryl, Henry James bows to the custom of using the word "breakfast" to translate the French word "déjeuner," meaning "lunch." Despite the fact that he is bilingual, Valentin de Bellegarde uses a literal translation of a French expression when he says to Newman "and only yesterday I was yawning so as to dislocate my jaw."[15] It is above all in *The American* that we find a large number of transpositions of this kind. Various characters use them, as well as the narrator himself. Sometimes they appear without explanation, while at other times they are accompanied by a sort of warning, such as "as they say here," "according to the French phrase," or "as we say." Mrs. Tristram, talking about Mme de Cintré says, "She belongs to the very top of the basket, as they say here."[16]

So far we have seen examples involving the narrator or English-speaking characters; but when the protagonists speak French, the authors apply themselves single-mindedly to reconstituting, in English, a literal, word-for-word translation. Consequently, a character in "Natka" expresses himself by saying, "I demand a thousand pardons, Monsieur, but you will be very amiable to give me a little fire."[17] In "Zut" we find expressions such as "name of a name, hast thou no heart," "your affairs march to a marvel," and "I counsel you to take care."[18] This sort of procedure is occasionally amusing and can be used for comic effect. George Du Maurier uses it freely in *Peter Ibbetson,* where it is part of a little game that Peter and his friend Mimsey like to play. Generally speaking, however, it seems regrettable that such a rudimentary technique should have become incorporated into the rules of the genre right up to the present day. Do the authors, by going in for such linguistic overkill, wish to remind readers that the Parisians speak French? Do they simply wish to have a little innocent amusement and to divert bilingual readers to the exclusion of others? In reality, what emerges is a complete travesty based on false premises, which leads to situations in which, to convey the notion of *tutoiement,* the characters end up talking like Quakers. This sort of heavy-handed picturesqueness, which could be applied to any foreign language, often gives the impression of being an unfair caricature. Though the author may not wish to deride, the reader may well be tempted to do so.

The fact that the Parisians speak a language other than English appears on the face of it to be a purely concrete phenomenon. The difficulties that arise in passing from one language to the other, in attempting to use foreign words to express one's thoughts and feelings, are rarely brought out. Henry James does it occasionally. He notes, for example, that when Mme de Vionnet is surprised in the company of Chad in the countryside, she begins to speak French. To Strether's eyes, she seems suddenly vulnerable and on the defensive, hiding behind the protective barrier of her native tongue. But such examples are few and far between. On the whole, by granting some of their creatures linguistic gifts so that others may understand them, the novelist-creators dodge the problem. They have not really tried to come to grips with the communication problems that their American characters are faced with. And yet the contact with a foreign language could be one way of penetrating more fully into a new social milieu and, ultimately, a part of the characters' own self-discovery. But it is rarely suggested that the visitor's itinerary should include an exploration of the language. The poetry of the words themselves, and the gap between word and thing, escape him. While in Paris, he keeps to his own language, clinging to it as if it were a lifebuoy in order not to lose his sense of identity. He is neither immigrant, not expatriate, but, as the title of James's novel indicates, a veritable ambassador. He carries on his shoulders the entire weight of the American condition.

In his essay *Le Roman Américain 1865-1917: Mythes de la Frontière et de la Ville* Bernard Poli demonstrates how the decline of the frontier explains American writers' interest first in their own great cities and then in those of Europe. For him, the heroes of *The American* and *The Ambassadors* come to Paris seeking a new spiritual frontier that does not exist in America. Poli quite rightly insists on the archetypal quality of Newman, who continues the saga of *The Virginian*—even though Wister wrote this later—in American mythology. "Whereas the story of the Virginian ends when he becomes a prosperous businessman and marries into an old New England family, that of the American begins when, having established himself as a powerful financier and member of the New York Stock Exchange, he decides to break through yet another barrier and to go to Europe to look for what he is unable to find in the United States: artistic culture, and the most perfect wife imaginable."[19] Looked at from this angle, Paris represents one of the final goals in the march toward the East and urban civilization. The French capital provides a new opportunity to fulfill the American dream. Here the fictional characters discover a way of life that, by its differences and similarities to their own, gives rise to questions about the bases of American society and its aspirations to progress. These questions arise primarily from the characters' measuring themselves against different milieux within Parisian society.

Social Groups

The American Colony

The American colony, in which the principal protagonists never become completely integrated, is a hybrid group that, like the English, has often failed to comprehend the city fully. The important part it plays in the literature of the period, which bears no relation to its real historical role, derives from the fact that it constitutes an intermediary body whose function is to introduce the newcomer. So, for example, it is Mrs. Tristram who presents Newman to Mme de Cintré, and Mrs. Draper who arranges a meeting between Longmore and Mme de Mauves. Andrew Vane is welcomed by the Carnbys on his arrival, and, in *Madame de Treymes,* the Boykins permit John Durham to play the role of ambassador to Fanny de Malrive's in-laws on several occasions. The colony's superiority to the new arrivals derives principally from its relatively long acquaintance with the capital. The Boykins and the Carnbys pride themselves on having been in Paris for twenty-five years, and the Tristrams for six, though the reasons for their expatriation are not very clear. Jeremy Carnby is able to explain his presence by the fact that he manages the European end of a large insurance company from his office on the Place de l'Opéra. Mr. Tristram's presence is harder to account for, and the life he leads does little to enlighten the reader on this point. His ambitions are prosaic: "to hold out at poker, at his club . . . to shake hands all round, to ply his rosy gullet with truffles and champagne, and create uncomfortable eddies and obstructions among the constituent atoms of the American colony."[20] As for Mrs. Tristram, the author observes less severely that she consents to live in Paris "because it is only in Paris that one could find things to exactly suit one's complexion. Besides, out of Paris it was always more or less a trouble to get ten-button gloves."[21] But the awkward position in Parisian society of this ill-suited couple is by no means universal among their set, for not all members of the colony are alike.

At a social level higher than that of impecunious couples like the Farlows or unambitious members of the bourgeoisie like the Tristrams are active people like the Carnbys, society types like the Boykins, and creatures of ridicule like the Palffys, Mrs. Lister, and Mrs. Shallum.[22] And at the very top of the social pyramid comes the dyed-in-the-wool aristocracy of novels such as *The Custom of the Country* and *The Bent Twig*. These aristocrats, who are also members of New York high society, are a world apart. Their movements follow the rhythm of the seasons, and Paris is a favorite stopping place on their rounds of pleasure. For the heroes of the novels being considered here, the colony embodies the dangers of expatriation rather than its temptations, and it is often in reaction to its habits that they acquire a better understanding of Paris. Although James mentions the colony in *The American,* he introduces it into *The Ambassadors* only to point out that Chad rarely frequents it.[23] Maria Gostrey, Miss Barrace, and Little Bilham are far too independent-spirited to be members, and Gaston Probert scarcely knows that the colony exists. It is only seen as glorious by characters like the naive Delia Dosson, who dreams that one day her sister Francie will become a member. "She believed the members of this society to constitute a little kingdom of the blest; and she used to drive through the Avenue Gabriel, the Rue de Marignan and the wide vistas which radiate from the Arch of Triumph and are always changing their names, on purpose to send up wistful glances to the windows (she had learned that all this was the happy quarter) of the enviable but unapproachable colonists."[24]

At the opposite extreme from this idealized picture, the colony is shown as teetering indecisively halfway between Paris and America. Its relationship to the latter is marked by the ambiguity common to all expatriate groups; as Mrs. Carnby observes, "I'm extremely doubtful as to the exact location of 'God's country,' and even if you were to prove to my satisfaction that it lies between Seattle and Tampa, I'm not sure I would want to live there. America's a kind of conservatory on my estate. I don't care to sit in it continually, but, at the same time, I don't like to have other people throwing stones through the roof."[25] Against this measured opinion, which seems to represent the sincere feelings of the author, may be set the fantasies of the Boykins, who, "in the isolation of their exile . . . had created about them a kind of phantom America, where the national prejudices continued to flourish unchecked by the national progressiveness."[26] Newman is irked by Mr. Tristram's attitude toward the United States. "He irritated our friend by the tone of his allusions to his native country, and Newman was at a loss to understand why the United States were not good enough for Mr. Tristram."[27] The colony's chronic national identity crisis creates a gulf between its members and new arrivals and is further exacerbated by the uncomfortable position the colony occupies in Paris. Its members' acceptance into the Faubourg Saint-Germain often occurs at the expense of a blow to their self-esteem. Sometimes they cut ridiculous figures, as does Mr. Tristram, who mistakes one of the Bellegardes' servants for a duke.[28] Sometimes the Parisians exploit the Americans' snobbery. The Boykins are invited to Mme d'Armillac's charity sale on the implicit understanding that they will spend a lot of money. A sort of underground warfare erupts between the two groups from time to time, and the Boykins, who are participants in it, remind John Durham of "persons peacefully following the course of a horrible war by pricking red pins in a map."[29]

Finally, for the protagonists in these novels, the colony represents neither a model nor an ideal. Some protagonists criticize the fact that the colonists fawn on the nobility, servilely copying its manners. In *The Bent Twig* Austin Page, watching the Americans who frequent the salon of Mrs. Marshall-Smith, exclaims, "Don't they do it with true American fervor. . . . It would take a microscope to tell the difference between them and a well-rehearsed society scene on the stage of the Français! That's their model, of course."[30] The colony lives wrapped up in its own narrow and sterile world. Cazeby, the diplomat in Carryl's "The Next Corner," describes its members as spending most of their time wondering "how the Choses can afford to do what they do, and why the Machins cannot afford to do what they leave undone."[31] For Mrs. Carnby, who is not averse to the odd culinary metaphor, the colony is "as much like America as a cold veal cutlet with its gravy coagulated . . . is like the same thing fresh off the grill."[32] The authors are generally severe, but their views are echoed in nonfictional accounts by other authors, such as William Crary Brownell and Richard Harding Davis. The latter, in *About Paris,* says of the American colony,

> They are continually on the defensive; they apologize to the American visitor and to the native Frenchman; they have declined their birthright and are voluntary exiles from their homes. The only way by which they can justify their action is either to belittle what they have given up, or to emphasize the benefits which they have received in exchange, and these benefits are hardly perceptible. They remain what they are, and no matter how long it may have been since they ceased to be Americans, they do not become Frenchmen. They are a race all to themselves; they are the American Colony.[33]

The Aristocracy

If the literary fate of the American colony is, so to speak, the consequence of internal politics, the same cannot be said of the way in which the aristocracy is described, which throws into relief one particular aspect of the relationship between the French and Americans. The previously noted descriptions of residences in the Faubourg Saint-Germain give a clear indication of how the authors see the people who live there. The faubourg arouses contradictory reactions ranging from annoyance and moral condemnation to surprise and admiration. It provokes attitudes of patriotism—or, on the contrary, criticism—of America.

Although the nobility does not appear in *The Transgression of Andrew Vane*, its role in the novels of James and Wharton, and also in *The Inner Shrine* by Basil King, is so great that it completely eclipses that of all other social classes. What the authors show us of the aristocracy is usually presented as being the fruits of experience of a hero both perspicacious and vigilant. But if we look behind this hero to the figure of the author, we see that the way the aristocracy is judged varies according to the author's own experiences. In *The American*, for example, we perceive James's resentment at finding that the doors of the salons were not flung open to receive him. The novel is also a reply to a play by Alexandre Dumas fils, *L'Etrangère*, which James saw in Paris and disliked. *The Ambassadors*, on the other hand, was written at a time when James was widely received in the faubourg. The rancors, disappointments, waves of gratitude—the whole private war that James waged with the capital—passed into his writing at some time or another. The same is true of Edith Wharton, though she arrived— both in Paris and on the literary scene—at a later date. Perhaps the fact that she was part of the New York aristocracy also gave her a certain advantage over James. In any case, her observations are more satirical, but more serene, than James's and convey the impression that she was better acquainted with the sort of characters she describes. Basil King focuses above all on moral problems, and the discussions he engages in seem particularly suited to his training for the ministry.

In *The American* James restores to the nobility the role of traitor that it once shared with monks in American Gothic novels like *Julia and the Illuminated Baron* by Sarah Wood (1800). In this respect, *The American* makes the transition from Gothic novel to international novel. The Hôtel de Bellegarde and the convent of the Rue d'Enfer provide Gothic elements reminding us of a period a hundred years earlier. Despite the distance that separates James from "our friend" or "our hero," he seems to be in agreement with his character's prosecution of the nobility. Newman, the straightforward arche-type of the Western hero, with his vast territories and majestic schemes, reacts to Paris like a pioneer spurred on by the historical epic of America. He is unable to accept the uselessness and arrogance of this wholly self-con-tained milieu whose elaborate and complicated traditions are enacted in a vacuum sealed off from all social responsibility, if not all moral obligation. James supplies his hero with the average American reader's prejudices against all hereditary aristocracies.

The French aristocracy, in contrast to the British, is not involved in govern-ment. The Bellegardes do not recognize the Bonapartes, and the baron de Douves, Gaston Probert's brother-in-law, is a convinced Legitimist. One looks in vain for a character such as Lord Warburton, the gentleman with progressive ideas, who appears in *The Portrait of a Lady*. But the authen-ticity of the French aristocracy is beyond question, and the doubts that hover around some Italian and Polish titles never cast the least shadow on their French counterparts. The aristocracy in Paris is a highly organized, elitist milieu with its own internal hierarchy, whose summit is occupied by the figure of the Duchess.[34]

This special caste, whose every tradition goes against the grain of demo-cratic sentiment, remembers only too well the role it played in the American Revolution. Newman, listening to Mme de la Rochefidèle talking about the good Dr. Franklin, finds this moral debt hard to take. James does not spare his hero this embarrassing encounter, which establishes him as a descendant of Benjamin Franklin, and also emphasizes how far Lafayette's ideals are re-moved from those of contemporary aristocratic society. This reference to the American Revolution also draws attention to affinities between the nobility and the Hamiltonian ideal. Leaving aside its inexcusable economic and politi-cal uselessness, the nobility can be seen as a milieu that succeeded in organiz-ing around itself a harmonious urban way of life. Doubtless the Federalists, whom Jefferson accused of wanting to establish an aristocracy based on birth, ultimately preferred to take English society as their model; yet intermittent bursts of admiration for the Parisian nobility reveal a repressed elitism that is often typical of American democrats. Aristocratic appreciation of the refine-ments of life in the haut monde corresponds to middle-class, businesslike appreciation of quality—the quality of a man or a product—which can be seen in the persistent American quest for the biggest and the best. As the nobility represents the best that French society has to offer, the American visitor automatically turns in their direction. There he may find, as Chris-topher Newman bluntly says, "the best article in the market."[35]

James's attitudes, whether of praise or of condemnation, are always extreme. The poisonous atmosphere surrounding the Bellegardes should not mislead us, but conversely the idealized picture of an aristocracy open to the arts and liberated from the restraints of a strict social code that we find in *The Ambassadors,* is also atypical. *The American* deals with archetypes, and *The Ambassadors* with personalities. Strether and Mme de Vionnet each tries in his own way to resolve the problem of adapting to a different personal and social situation. In contrast, Urbain de Bellegarde, Christopher Newman, and the extremely negative Mme de Cintré are old-fashioned national types, or fairy-tale characters. Everything in *The American* that was reminiscent of the sort of puritan society depicted in Hawthorne's novels disappears in *The Ambassadors.* The narrow-mindedness, the blinkered attitudes, are there to be found in characters like the Pococks, who voice the criticisms once expressed by Newman—but which now have a different meaning.

What are the fundamental characteristics of the nobility? They attach great importance to the family and to the code of honor, but, at the same time, they display a lack of moral seriousness, most often manifested in adultery. American writers are primarily concerned with the relationship between the individual and the group. On the one hand, they deplore the restrictions imposed on the characters by their aristocratic milieu, but, on the other hand, they criticize the overt or devious ways through which members of the clan are permitted to escape from its laws. They champion individual liberty and morality. This is illustrated at a basic level in Bronson Howard's play *One of Our Girls,* whose very title betrays national pride. Through the character of Kate Shipley, an eighteen-year-old American who comes to Paris to visit her cousins, the author launches a biting attack on the noble family of the Fonblanques. These aristocrats embody to an astonishing degree everything that the contemporary public could possibly despise. The end result now seems rather farcical, and one wonders that such extreme caricature should have appealed so strongly to New York theatergoers of 1885. Howard's comments about the system of dependencies among the members of the family lose their savor in the context of his unmitigated scorn. Mrs. Tristram gives a more restrained version of how the system of family authority operates, in explaining why Mme de Cintré is not free to do as she wishes: "In France you must never say Nay to your mother, whatever she requires of you. She may be the most abominable old woman in the world, and make your life a purgatory; but after all she is *ma mère,* and you have no right to judge her. You have simply to obey. . . . Her brother is the *chef de la famille,* as they say; he is the head of the clan. With those people the family is everything; you must act, not for your own pleasure, but for the advantage of the family."[36] In *The American* family politics may even lead, by a dialectic of reversal, to the murder of the all-powerful father. The clan reacts against any member who weakens it from within or against any foreign element— such as Newman—that may threaten it from without. But the family cell is also part of a far larger ensemble, which Fanny de Malrive describes to John Durham in these terms: "There is nothing in your experience—in any American experience—to correspond with that far-reaching family organization, which is itself a part of the larger system, and which encloses a young man of my son's position in a network of accepted prejudices and opinions. Everything is prepared in advance—his political and religious convictions—his judgements of people, his sense of honour, his ideas of women, his whole view of life."[37] Thus the aristocracy manages, if not to quell any desire for independence manifested by its members, at least to present a unified front in terms of appearance and behavior. John Durham becomes aware of this as he observes a group of aristocrats in Mme de Malrive's salon. "All these amiably chatting visitors, who mostly bore the stamp of personal insignificance on their mildly sloping or aristocratically beaked faces, hung together in a visible closeness of tradition, dress, attitude and manner, as different as possible from the loose aggregation of a roomful of his own countrymen."[38]

American writers also call into question the social and moral legitimacy of the code of honor. For the French reader their arguments inevitably recall the conflict between bourgeois and aristocratic morality common in French literature in the seventeenth century. Things are by no means so clear for the American public, which explains why James and, even more so, Basil King, take pains to show how the system works. Honor, they remind us, has lost all personal and moral significance and has become the mere practice of a sterile social code. Newman is an impotent and shocked spectator of this process that will result in Valentin's death, and he protests vehemently. Struck by the disproportionate relationship between cause and consequences, he challenges the passive acceptance of such rituals. "Because your great-grandfather was an ass, is that any reason why you should be?"[39] he asks Valentin. Like James, Basil King stresses the fact that, in the end, honor is the stick used by other members of the caste to take the measure of a person. In *The Inner Shrine* he develops the notion of social morality over against personal morality as the notion on which the opposition between Parisians and New Yorkers hinges. Although American, George Eveleth has become part of the French nobility through marriage and is therefore obliged to fight a duel with Bienville, who has claimed to be his wife's lover. The duel takes place, and no one is injured; but George, knowing he is on the verge of bankruptcy, takes advantage of the occasion to commit suicide. His action remains undiscovered, and, as a result, the honor of the dead man and the honor of the survivor are both satisfied. That of Diane Eveleth, however, is compromised. Although she in fact has nothing with which to reproach herself, she has, like Daisy Miller, allowed appearances to give the opposite impression. It takes her a long time to redeem her reputation and clear herself of shame in the eyes of the man she loves. Bienville, whose behavior is socially justifiable, is nonetheless struck by remorse and publicly confesses, while in New York, that he has slandered Diane. He is convinced that this confession will make him a social outcast and prevent him from marrying Marion Grimston. She, however, reminds him that honor in New York and honor in Paris are two different things: "We regard these things differently here from the way in which you do in France. It may be true, as you say, that in losing your honor you've lost all—in French eyes; but we don't feel like that. We never look on any one as beyond redemption. We should consider that a man who has been brave enough to do what you've done to-day has gone far to establish his moral regeneration."[40]

Dueling is shown in American texts as an exotic custom totally foreign to the Anglo-Saxon way of life. Mrs. Eveleth, for example, considers it as "brutal senselessness."[41] But duels, like debts, are the attributes of a French gentleman. In the closing lines of A Hazard of New Fortunes, William Dean Howells defines Christine Dryfoos's future husband as "a nobleman full of present debts and duels in the past."[42] A rapid survey of American literature show that duels, though infrequent, do occur. In Charlotte Temple (1791) Montraville, the seducer, fights with Belcour near Charlotte's tomb. In The Virginian the hero measures up to the villainous Trampas. But, by and large, such duels are rare, and during the period under consideration they more often than not have some sort of connection with Europe and Paris. In addition to the duels fought by Valentin de Bellegarde and George Eveleth, other examples can be found in Howard's plays. In The Banker's Daughter the comte de Carojac insults Howard Routledge in the foyer of the American embassy and kills him in the sword fight that ensues, before he is himself defeated by John Strebelow. In One of Our Girls the comte de Crébillon fights two duels, one with Henri Saint-Hilaire and the other with Captain Gregory. In a short story by Frank Berkeley Smith, "The Arrangement of Monsieur de Courcelles," the American attitude toward such affairs of honor is conveyed through the character of Jack Hollister. M. de Courcelles has a taste for fashionable duels, which he enjoys arranging, if not actually provoking. He manages to push two gentlemen into calling each other out over a trivial matter. But he fails to reckon with the righteous indignation of Jack, who intervenes in the situation and, demanding that M. de Courcelles put up his fists in classic Anglo-Saxon fashion, gives him a good public thrashing. The spell of the ritual is broken by this act of sacrilege and the duel cannot take place.

Women are often the cause of duels, which therefore serve as an intermediate step between the cult of honor and the practice of gallantry. The aristocracy must follow the rule of a fashionable game that Bienville describes as follows: "The people among whom [Diane] and I were born—in France—in Paris—engage in this game as a sort of sport, and we call it—love. It isn't love in any of the senses in which you understand it here. We give it a meaning of our own. It's a game that requires the combination of many kinds of skill, and, if it doesn't call for a conspicuous display of virtues, it lays the greater emphasis on its own few, stringent rules."[43] This is in fact a simplified version of the situation, for this kind of amusement may run the entire gamut from politeness to passion. Its practice is favored by the idleness and egotism of high society. And yet the character of Don Juan, whose genetic stamp would seem to be an essential part of the aristocratic makeup, appears nowhere in these writings. The seducers are disappointingly dull, and the coquettes lacking in any trace of artful perfidy. The authors have instinctively made their protagonists bourgeois. Their aim is to reveal the existence of adultery rather than to portray love or passion.

The subject of adultery enters the American novel in works like *Madame de Mauves* and others written at about the same time. Leslie Fiedler ironically points out just how scrupulously the theme had earlier been avoided: "One remembers William Dean Howells, realistic American novelist, who in forty novels did not treat adultery once."[44] In *Madame de Mauves* James does not simply introduce the character of the unfaithful husband—last in line of a family famous for the chronic and hereditary adulterousness of its males—but presents a husband who actually goes so far as to push his own wife into committing adultery with Longmore. As Mme de Mauves's maiden name, Euphemia Cleve, suggests, the spirit of Mme de Lafayette hovers over the composition of this *Princesse de Clèves* in reverse. Adultery is ubiquitous in the capital. Mme de Treymes is the mistress of the prince d'Armillac; the princesse Estradina, in *The Custom of the Country,* has regular clandestine rendezvous; Mme de Vionnet has had another lover before becoming Chad's mistress; and, finally, Mme de Mauves's anonymous friend, suffering from two simultaneous jealousies, is more upset by the betrayal of her lover than by that of her husband.[45]

The novels bring out one of the reasons why such irregular situations are common, namely the refusal of the Catholic church to recognize divorces in spite of the fact that they became legal under the Third Republic. As Maria Gostrey says, "Ces gens-là don't divorce you know, any more than they emigrate or abjure—they think it is impious and vulgar."[46] *Madame de Treymes* is basically the story of a divorce that never takes place, just as *The American* is the story of a marriage that never occurs. The Malrive clan has no intention of allowing Fanny Frisbee to escape without implementing the law that gives custody of a child to its French father if the mother is American and remarries. Mme de Treymes draws the following moral from such a law: "We abhor divorce—we go against our religion in consenting to it—and nothing short of recovering the boy could possibly justify us."[47] What bothers the writers more than the passive acceptance of edicts pronounced in Rome is the time-honored Parisian custom of intelligent, if unprincipled, adaptation to social norms. For example, Mme de Treymes deliberately deceives John Durham by letting him believe that Fanny will get her divorce. She lies in order to get enough money out of him to cover her lover's gambling debts. Such a lie, in itself sordid, must be regarded in the context of the constant struggle of this lady to comply with the obligations of her rank and the dictates of her heart. If it is true that noblesse oblige, it is also true that it often involves its members in sorry compromises. Some liaisons are acceptable in the eyes of society, while others are not, and thresholds of tolerance may vary from one minute to the next. Mme de Trézac's advice to Undine is easier to give than to follow: "Between ourselves . . . a woman with tact, who's not in a position to remarry will find society extremely indulgent . . . provided, of course, she keeps up appearances."[48] To do what one wants while also doing what one ought demands constant vigilance, and it seems harder to survive in Parisian high society than in the New York of *The House of Mirth*.

The reforming zeal of the Americans cannot comprehend this useless waste of energy. To be constantly working around rules that are respected in appearance and broken in reality seems like a particularly futile way of doing things. Surely it would be easier simply to change the rules! But tradition prevails, and the constant saga of this derisory form of courtly love continues. What with the half-divorces implicit in separation, and the half-truths such as those that constantly beset Strether, aristocratic love seems doomed to eternal half-measures. It also relies sometimes on the help of a sort of halfway house in society, whose very name calls attention to its implicit compromise, the demimonde.

The Demimonde

The demimonde, which is, as it were, the seamy side of the aristocracy, is rendered disproportionately important by this proximity to the nobility. Its name, which entered into current usage in 1855 with the younger Dumas's play *Le Demi-Monde,* conjures up both the *aventurière* with a dubious past and the authentic courtesan. But where the former tries to conceal her way of life, the latter openly flaunts it. It is an almost exclusively female milieu, characterized by the ambiguity of its position in society and the chronic laxity of its morals. Its presence in American novels is not limited to the description of the one or two cocottes indispensable to any portrait of Paris at the time but includes characters who are relatively central to the plot.

The demimonde is rather international. It is amusing to observe Archibald Clavering Gunter, in *Mr. Barnes of New York,* firmly planting the American flag in this small and sensitive area of French territory. Bowing to the patriotic imperatives of the popular novel, he informs us that "la belle Blackwood," whose portrait adorns the walls of the Salon de Paris, is none other than Sally Spots, come all the way from a small village in Ohio to forge a romantic career in the French capital. In "The Last Asset" Mrs. Newell represents another version of the American presence in this particular milieu. The demimonde may also be said, in a wider sense, to include the bands of *aventurières* who gravitate toward American millionaires. These aristocrats of money use such subalterns to conceal their various transgressions and irregular conduct. They set up around themselves a demimonde on an international scale, which consists of schemers and opportunists. Baroness Adelschein is on the fringe of this corrupt milieu that moves, with the seasons, from Paris to the spas, and from the spas to the Mediterranean resorts. Intrigues abound: the princesse Estradina uses Undine as a cover for one of her amorous liaisons, as Bertha Dorset uses Lily Bart in *The House of Mirth* and as Mrs. Vanderlyn will later, in an identical situation, use Suzy Branch in *Glimpses of the Moon.* Lily Bart, wrongly accused of being Mr. Dorset's mistress, and Undine, pushed toward an affair with Raymond de Chelles, both risk their reputations. Undine's divorce and the scandal attendant upon her escapade with Peter Van Degen could easily have terminated with the heroine falling to the same level as these unscrupulous hangers-on: "Roviano, Madame Adelschein, and a few of the freer spirits of her old St.

Moritz band, reappearing in Paris with the close of the watering-place season, had quickly discovered her and shown a keen interest in her liberation.
It appeared in some mysterious way to make her more available for their
purpose."⁴⁹

James is particularly fascinated by the idea of the woman who gradually
slides into the world of the demimonde, and the subject is taken up twice in
The American. Mme Dandelard's case is treated almost clinically, with Newman and Valentin coolly weighing the lady's chances of remaining honest in
Paris. An Italian abandoned by her French husband, Mme Dandelard seems
to have no alternative but to become a member of the demimonde, given that
she is poor, beautiful, and stupid. Newman, who sees it as his natural duty to
gallop to the rescue of imperiled virtue, finds his generous impulses severely
checked after visiting the potential victim. He never explains why he abandons the idea of saving her, but we presume that he found her altogether too
willing to suffer her fate. Valentin refuses to seduce her. Rather than picking
this ripe fruit, he prefers to watch it fall of its own weight. As he explains to
Newman: "To see this little woman's drama play itself out, now, is for me, an
intellectual pleasure."⁵⁰ While Mme Dandelard is, to a certain extent, the
victim of social forces, Noémie Nioche, carefully planning her entry into the
demimonde, knows exactly what she is doing. Despite her open advances to
Newman, she fails to seduce him and turns instead to Valentin. When he
asks if one of her paintings is for sale, she replies ingenuously, "Everything I
have is for sale."⁵¹ For her the passage into the world of romantic intrigue is
not a fall but, on the contrary, a sort of social elevation that she wishes to
enjoy to the utmost. After the rivalry between Valentin and Stanislas Kapp,
and the ensuing duel, Noémie's Parisian success is assured, yet it is on the
other side of the Channel that she really attains the summit of her career, by
becoming the mistress of Lord Deepmere.

The two preceding examples are entirely in keeping with what happens in
French literature, where entry into the demimonde is either a question of
ambition or necessity. But is it possible to move in the opposite direction? Is
it possible to recover one's respectability? The answer given by the French
theater is a clear no. James is struck to see how in *L'Aventurière* by Emile
Augier (1848) and *Le Demi-Monde* society often gets rid of these intruders
by all sorts of underhanded tricks of which the audience is supposed to
approve. Though the context is a little different, *The Siege of London*—in
which over half the action takes place in Paris—is interesting in this respect.
According to Philip Rahv,

The idea of *The Siege of London* came to James one evening in the autumn of 1877, after witnessing a performance at the Théâtre Français of *Le Demi-Monde,* a play by the younger Dumas. The problem of the play was whether under certain circumstances a gentleman would be justified in "telling on" a lady whom he had once loved though never respected. Typically enough, James found the moral insensibility of the French playwright to be nothing less than "prodigious," and he was sufficiently provoked to think of attempting to pose the same problem through the medium of characters of his own nationality.[52]

James decided to plead the case for the demimonde against the clannish reactions of the aristocracy. His hero, George Littlemore, is interested in such moral issues: "He had seen *Le Demi-Monde* a few nights before, and had been told that *L'Aventurière* would show him a particular treatment of the same subject—the justice to be meted out to unscrupulous women who attempt to thrust themselves into honorable families. It seemed to him that in both of these cases the ladies had deserved their fate, but he wished it might have been brought about by a little less lying on the part of the representatives of honor."[53] Suddenly the problem debated on stage becomes real when Littlemore encounters at the theater one of these "unscrupulous women" from the American West in the company of an English lord. Unlike Olivier de Jalin and Don Fabrice in the French plays, Littlemore declines to reveal the past of Nancy Beck, alias Mrs. Headway, thus causing no obstacle to her marriage to Lord Demesne. His only concession is to admit to the lord's mother—but only after it is too late—that Mrs. Headway is indeed "not respectable." Without being particularly sympathetic to his heroine, James nonetheless wished to give her her chance. He acknowledges her enterprising spirit and pioneering tenacity, and one could say that Mrs. Headway provides a link between the "nouveau monde" and the demimonde.

Such a comparison should not, however, obscure the fact that the demimonde in the strictest sense of the term constitutes a unique milieu. M. Lejaune of the Académie Française, in "The Point of View," observes on a visit to New York that the city offers no American equivalent to it. In Paris, the cocotte is one of the city's institutions, a reassuring figure, financed and kept in good working order by the aristocracy. The demimonde replaces the nocturnal, bawdy Paris censored by literary convention. It is an erotic substitute that does not offend the contemporary reader.

Guy Wetmore Carryl describes the system in detail in "The Tuition of Dodo Chapuis." Two courtesans, Thaïs de Trémonceau and Gabrielle de

Poirier, are rivals for the favors of a naive young man from the provinces. Carryl writes about the sumptuous lifestyle of the two women, one of whom is kept by a Brazilian millionaire, the other by a Russian millionaire. Both frequent the Café de Paris, the Pavillon d'Armenonville, the Auteuil race course, the Palais de Glace, the Folies-Marigny, and the Elysée-Palace-Hôtel. Gabrielle writes the odd serial for *Le Journal* and occasional short stories for *Le Gil Blas Illustré*. Thaïs sings from time to time at the Folies-Bergère. Gabrielle lives in a luxury apartment on the Avenue Kléber, and Thaïs lives in a private townhouse in the Rue de la Faisanderie. Each has her own carriage and pair in which she drives up and down the Allée des Acacias three times an afternoon during the season. In *The Transgression of Andrew Vane* Carryl completes this piece of detailed reportage by a more intimate portrait of the character of Mirabelle—whose last name is also Trémonceau. Mirabelle, who is the accomplice of the master blackmailer Radwalader, is supposed to compromise Andrew, who is planning to get married, and thus render him susceptible to blackmail. Instead, she falls in love with him and ends up coming to his defense, a development that allows Carryl to exploit the theme of the big-hearted courtesan.

The demimonde surrounds the Parisian aristocracy and the American colony with a halo of eroticism. The aristocrats make and break the reputations of the cocottes, and one of the duties of the colony seems to be to find out their names and know their caprices. At any rate, this is the way that Mr. Tristram understands it, admitting that one of his dreams is "to know the names of all the cocottes."[54] The polymorphous milieu of the demimonde forms a sort of interstitial tissue linking these two other social groups. And in this role of mediator, it can be beneficial, as when it allows the aristocrats to escape from the rigidity of social conventions; but, at the same time, this subordinate milieu may also represent a danger. Mirabelle can, if she wishes, prevent Andrew Vane's marriage, while Valentin pays with his life for his brief infatuation with Noémie.

CHAPTER 3

LIFE IN PARIS BEFORE 1914

The Parisian Adventure: Lessons and Morals

Parisian society often seems to American eyes to be a sort of twilight zone, a milieu that violates all their terms of reference, shakes up their latent romantic images, and unsettles their moral principles. Caught between their dreams and concrete reality, between the admiration of the tourist and the need for moral clarification, the Americans are disoriented. On discovering this notorious example of old urban civilization, they suddenly realize that life is not as beautifully simple as they thought. The colony is only half American; the aristocracy arouses feelings of admiration and contempt; the demimonde represents a phenomenon they have trouble coming to terms with. The characters are often ill at ease, and their feelings reflect the embarrassment of their creators, who project onto them reactions and judgments that they themselves are unwilling either to assume or to avoid.

This ambiguity is particularly noticeable in passages where the dichotomy between American virtue and Parisian vice is stated in no uncertain terms. Mme de Mauves says to Longmore: "My marriage introduced me to people and things which seemed to me at first very strange and then very horrible, and then, to tell the truth, very contemptible."[1] In the same vein, Margery Palffy gives Andrew Vane her views on Paris: "I could not attempt to make you understand how I loathe Paris, and how homesick for America I am. Here—I can't express it, but the shallowness and the insincerity and the—immorality of these people gets into one's blood. It's all pretence, sham, and heartless, cynical impurity."[2] In *Madame de Treymes* the only time that Fanny de Malrive feels secure is when she is with her compatriots. She contrasts the Parisian atmosphere with "that clear American air where there are no obscurities, no mysteries."[3] But are such reassuring oversimplifications actually representative of what the authors think? In the case of Robert W. Chambers, they quite likely are, to judge from the vehemence of his homily against the American colony at the Bal de l'Opéra:

And you over there—you of the 'American Colony', who are tossed like shuttlecocks in the social whirl . . . why should you come? American women, brought up to think clean thoughts and see with innocent eyes, to exact a respectful homage from men and enjoy a personal dignity and independence unknown to women anywhere else,—why do you want to come here? Do you know that the foundations of that liberty which makes you envied in the old world are laid in the respect and confidence of men? Undermine that . . . and fix at that moment on your free limbs the same chains which corrupt society has forged for the women of Europe.[4]

It seems likely too, that, in *The American,* James shares something of Newman's contempt for the nobility. James nursed some animosity toward Paris at the time he wrote *The American,* and expressing his opinion through Newman was perhaps a way to assuage his feelings of guilt about being an expatriate. But how much weight does he attach to the censure of Mme de Mauves? Toward the end of the book, he turns her into an excessive character, whose inhuman treatment of her husband leads him to commit suicide. Similarly, the bitterness of Fanny de Malrive seems surprising if we set *Madame de Treymes* alongside Wharton's New York novels such as *The House of Mirth,* in which the clarity of the American air is singularly modified.

What emerges as important in these works is the progressive revelation that urban civilization rests on a fundamental imbalance between the moral and the social. The writers become increasingly aware that Parisian society is built like an arch, where the very fact that each stone has a tendency to fall guarantees the structure's enduring solidity. The social edifice is able to maintain itself thanks to the interaction of elements that, taken on their own, are destabilizing factors. The complex equilibrium of the old metropolis is an implicit challenge to the sententious gravity of the puritan ethic. William Crary Brownell warns his readers against a form of moral prejudice that in his view warps the judgment of his compatriots: "What would be vice among us remains in France social irregularity induced by sentiment. The distinction is, I think, the most important of all that can be observed in any judgement of France by Americans."[5] It would be wrong to say that the American novelists misconstrue things completely. In fact, they often denounce the disarray into which Paris throws such puritan morality, and there is, for instance, a far greater spirit of tolerance and understanding in *The Ambassadors* than there was in *Madame de Mauves.* Yet even James and

Wharton seem on occasion to take refuge in moral aggressiveness as a means of resisting a reality that they see as threatening.

By his ironic injunction "Go East, Young Woman!" in the title of one chapter of *Le Roman Américain,* Bernard Poli draws attention to the fact that women, by the late nineteenth century, had become more significant than men in this return to the East. The wife and mother who followed the covered wagons along the trails to the West found her role changed to that of guide in this cultural volte-face. It is she who will henceforth embody the worldly and aesthetic aspirations of the new urban society, and it is not surprising that she should decide to cross the Atlantic in order to discover new role models. But there is another interesting protagonist: the young woman born into this new urban milieu, who has just reached a marriageable age at the moment when her mother is preparing to set off on a reconnaissance mission to Europe. Her presence explains why the relationship between Paris and America is most frequently symbolized by the marriage of an American woman to a French aristocrat.

Historical reality concords perfectly in this regard with James and Wharton's distinct preference for female characters. The literary type of the young American woman abroad corresponds to a well-authenticated historical figure, and it is natural that such a character should tempt the novelist. Yet her extraordinary development in the works of Henry James suggests that there may have been other reasons for her attractiveness as a protagonist. James's biography makes it clear that he knew little of American businessmen. Furthermore, the impression made by his cousin, Minnie Temple, may also explain his partiality for heroines. Even the mysterious wound he suffered in Newport, interpreted by some critics as accidental castration, could in psychoanalytical terms justify the novelist's preference for female characters. As in James's works, in Edith Wharton's novels and stories the heroes are generally easily forgettable characters, and in her books about Paris it is the heroines who are all-important and provide the pivotal focus for the plot. Here, too, some explanation seems to lie in the author's own experience, for Wharton's biography reveals that, with the exception of Morton Fullerton, the men in her life—notably her husband, confined to a mental hospital from 1910 onwards, and Walter Berry, who greeted her affection with some indifference—were all in one way or another a disappointment to her. Michael Millgate sees this as one explanation for the feebleness of her heroes compared with the masculine vigor of her heroines.[6]

The numerical supremacy of such female characters is self-evident.

Though Newman and Strether are male, and though the latter's importance in the exploration of Paris is crucial, we may set against these two, in addition to Mme de Mauves, the heroines of James's short stories; the main female protagonists of Edith Wharton like Undine Spragg, Mme de Malrive, and Mrs. Newell; and Sylvia Marshall, the central character of *The Bent Twig*. A survey of marriages reveals that in almost every case a young American woman marries a man from Paris. George Eveleth is one of the few exceptions to this rule. In order to discover the motives that lie behind such marriages, one must look at the romantic idealism to which the young American woman is so susceptible, as evinced, for example, in the story of Mme de Mauves. The young heroine, carried away, like Emma Bovary, by an overactive imagination, has since childhood dreamed of marrying a gentleman whose noble birth will be, to her, a guarantee of his virtue. Like Flaubert's heroine, she is betrayed by the books she reads, in which the old Legitimist nobility is described in idyllic terms. She is far less attracted by the idea of living in Paris than by the idea of breathing the rarefied atmosphere of this superior aristocratic world. Her love, born among the green mountains of the Auvergne, suffers its first moments of disillusionment on the banks of the Seine. For Euphemia, the dazzle of the family coat of arms far outshines the dazzle of the Faubourg Saint-Germain, and her dream is to live as far away from the capital as possible. Her husband, however, will only agree to live as far outside the center as Saint-Germain-en-Laye, whose provincial name is also a constant reminder of the capital and whose situation places Euphemia somewhere in between the reality she wishes to flee and the distant province where the memory of her lost illusions still lingers.

For the heroines who come after Mme de Mauves, the myth of the aristocracy is inseparable from the myth of Paris. For them, the modern Prince Charming with his chivalric attributes is the urbane, refined gentleman of society, leading a life of exquisite elegance in the patrician circles of the capital. For the Americans, French nobility and the Parisian aristocracy are more or less the same thing. The prestige of the Faubourg Saint-Germain owes much to the fact that the French aristocracy, unlike the British, is a surviving relic of a bygone era. The contrast between American and European civilization is more marked in Paris than in London; and although Rome and other Italian cities offer a greater degree of aristocratic exoticism, they are unable to match the formidable battalions of nobles ranked in close formation on the Left Bank of the Seine. The Parisian nobleman devotes his energies to cultivating worldly pleasures, and he is as much responsible for the art of gracious living as is the noblewoman, perhaps even more so. A complementarity is thus set up between the position of the nobleman in Parisian society and that of the woman in the new urban culture of the United States, where women aspire to ideals of distinction and elegance while their husbands and fathers engage in the efficient pursuit of turning the concrete world to profitable ends. American women, free from all material worries, understandably find similarities between their existence and that of Parisian gentlemen. The aims of both would seem to be identical and their association, therefore, a logical consequence.

This is where the misunderstanding arises. Just as Euphemia Cleve finally realizes that breeding is not synonymous with virtue, characters like Fanny de Malrive discover that, behind the apparent refinement of Parisian nobility, lies a lack of moral seriousness that is incompatible with the puritan conscience. A victim of her own romanticism, Fanny, like Newman and Isabel Archer, takes her place among the ranks of deceived innocents. Her story is a double failure, as she is forced to remain a prisoner of the milieu she rejects, after having so much aspired to be a part of it. Yet failure is not universal. If, for Bernard Poli, the story of Americans in Paris is not one of success, we should note that he limits himself exclusively to the cases of Newman and Strether. In the perspective of his study, which retraces the history of the American hero at the end of the nineteenth century, both characters provide good illustrations of the passage from the cult of success to failure. For the first time in his life, Newman comes up against an insurmountable difficulty, the pride of the Bellegardes, while Strether rejects the work- and achievement-oriented ethic that is the guiding principle of life in Woollett. But Newman, however well he fits in with the myth, offends against historical reality. The Bellegardes' rejection is fairly unconvincing, and James himself admitted in the preface to the New York edition that things would have taken a different course in real life. As for Strether, the questionable defeat he experiences in Paris must be set against its accompanying initiation.

It would be particularly unjust to place all Franco-American marriages under the sign of disillusioned romantic ideals. It is true that American innocence is deceived in *Madame de Mauves, The American,* and *Madame de Treymes,* but elsewhere the heroine's career does not inevitably trace the downward curve of a love story with an unhappy ending. And the very term "love story" is of questionable applicability, since quite a few of these stories have little to do with sentiment. The romantic idealism that appears as a motivating force in the early works of the period yields gradually to social ambition or even simple cupidity in the later ones. The genre changes in the direction of comedy of manners and even the picaresque novel—already pointed out in relation to the demimonde—an example of which may be found in the adventures of Ella Poore in *The Tattooed Countess* by Carl Van Vechten. The working out of financial arrangements, which was not really the issue in *The American,* gradually assumes more and more importance in the marriages depicted by American writers. Restoring the family's coat of arms to its former prosperity and glory is certainly a factor behind the marriage alliances formed in both *The American* and *Madame de Mauves.* But in the former the Bellegardes' pride takes precedence over all other matters, and in the latter M. de Mauves cannot simply be reduced to a fortune hunter: he is eventually driven to suicide through feelings for his wife.

Marriage, particularly in the short stories, now begins to look like what Mrs. Tristram calls "a compromise."[7] It ceases to be the logical end to an idyll and becomes instead the clinching of a deal. Romance is turned into an industry with marriage as the end product. Wharton's short story "Les Metteurs en Scène," in the collection of the same name, provides an ironic illustration of this. Two characters, Blanche Lambart, an American, and Jean Le Fanois, a Frenchman, go into partnership to arrange aristocratic matches for the young heiresses of the New World. One of these heiresses, Catherine Smithers, refuses the young man who is presented to her and persuades Le Fanois that he himself should marry her. But she dies of pneumonia shortly before the wedding, leaving Blanche a legacy of one million dollars on condition that she marry Le Fanois. Unfortunately, however, Catherine's mother has already made arrangements to marry the young Frenchman. This caricature of the role of money in marriage, combined with the development of a character like Mrs. Smither, paved the way for Edouard Bourdet's comedy *Le Sexe Faible* (1929), in which the American women lay their dollars on the table to bid for whatever Frenchman strikes their fancy.

"Les Metteurs en Scène" ridicules the artificial and conventional nature of marriage. Certain rules must be observed. For example, it is simply not respectable to have parents who are divorced, and Mrs. Newell, in "The Last Asset," prefers to be a kept woman rather than divorce and remarry. But convention also demands the presence of a father, and thus Mr. Newell, after a lot of hard bargaining, finally agrees to a walk-on role at his daughter's wedding. If the characters should happen to fall in love, as do young Hermione Newell and Louis du Trayas, this is only a happy coincidence that serves as a romantic counterpoint to the sordid transactions preceding their union. The central character in this story is the unscrupulous mother, whose name puts her in the clan of Newmans and Newsomes, but above all signifies that she "knew well" what she was doing. Mrs. Newell plans the strategic moves in her Parisian campaign with meticulous thoroughness. She refuses to get a divorce and insists that her daughter should convert to Catholicism. Her campaign ends successfully, but it involves a gamble, which, had it failed, would have resulted in the naive Hermione's fall into the ranks of the demimondaines. The omniscient narrator adds this comment to the description of the wedding: "The fact that the girl took her good fortune naturally and did not regard herself as suddenly snatched from the jaws of death, added poignancy to the situation."[8]

Ambition as a driving force is above all exemplified in the character of the mother or the mature woman who has made up her mind to get the very best out of the circumstances. There appears in these works a type of female character whose long journey from the Far West and speedy rise in society have only whetted her appetite for adventure. Mrs. Headway, whose aspirations to get to the top of the social ladder are indicated by her name, is one example of the type. Another example, Mrs. Temperly, in the story that bears her name, is an abusive mother who has left California for Paris with the firm intention of marrying off her three daughters, Dora, Effie, and Tishy. Unlike Mrs. Headway, Mrs. Temperly is thoroughly respectable, but her amiable exterior hides an implacable will. Helped by the marquise de Brives, she manages in the space of five years to have the whole of Paris at her feet and thus expects for her daughters "not only every advantage and every grandeur, but every virtue under heaven, and every guarantee."[9] Her ambition pushes her in the same direction as Euphemia Cleve. Yet Dora is set on marrying a penniless American painter, Raymond Bestwick, a match that her mother will not hear of, at least not until her sisters have made their long-awaited grand marriages. And so Dora, the rebel, puts herself at the service of her sisters, somewhat like Cinderella. Effie's success is more or less assured, but Tishy is totally lacking in charm; and the story ends on a note of disillusionment: "Tishy is decidedly a dwarf, and Raymond's probation is not yet over."[10]

Paris may prove corrupting for those who choose it as a promising theater for their ambitions. As her name suggests, Mrs. Temperly is a woman of vigorous temperament, but it is the force of the Parisian myth, crystallizing what Raymond Bestwick calls her "Napoleonic designs," that finally drives her coldly to sacrifice her daughters' desires to her own ends. *The Inner Shrine* plays on this same theme. Mrs. Eveleth has given up everything to ensure the social success of her son, a sacrifice which will result in his ruin and suicide. Here personal ambition is linked with national pride, as Mrs. Eveleth admits to her daughter-in-law, "I was pleased with his success in the little world of Paris just as I had been flattered by my own. When he fell in love with you I urged him to marry you, not because of anything in yourself, but because you were Mademoiselle de la Ferronaise, the last of an illustrious family. . . . I encouraged him when he built this house. I wanted to impress you; I wanted you to see that the American could give you a more splendid home than any European you were likely to marry, however exalted his rank."[11]

The integration of characters into Parisian society implies, over and above a certain number of spiritual affinities, considerations of a financial and economic order. It is the result of an exchange. The money earned in America permits the purchase, in Paris, of noble titles and attributes indispensable to the social standing of rich Americans. It is an understood fact that dowries are extremely important. The wealth of the American heiresses facilitates their marriage with Frenchmen, just as, conversely, the poverty of well-born Frenchwomen makes a mésalliance acceptable. Newman's fortune is sufficient to make the Bellegardes give some initial consideration to his offer. As for Diane de la Ferronaise, she had only "a poverty of a *dot* which had been the chief reason why her noble kinsfolk had consented to her marriage with an American."[12] In "The Point of View" Mrs. Church knows only too well that she will never be able to marry her daughter off without a dowry; and M. de Mauves's penniless sister encourages Longmore's courtship. The prestige of the dollar also plays a role in the metamorphosis of Nettie Wincher, Undine Spragg, Fanny Frisbee, and even the romantic Euphemia Cleve, who become respectively the marquise de Trézac, the comtesse (and later marquise) de Chelles, the marquise de Malrive, and the baronne de Mauves.

In Chapter 38 of *The Custom of the Country* Wharton gives a humorous exposé of the fashionable art of "fumer ses terres" (literally "fertilizing one's land"). Hubert, younger brother of Raymond de Chelles is up to his ears in debt when he is provided with an opportunity to resolve his financial problems in the shape of a young heiress fresh from Nevada, whom he meets at a skating rink. Raymond promises to pay his brother's debts on the understanding that Hubert will pay him back when he inherits from his father-in-law. But the transaction becomes extremely complicated due to the fact that Raymond has rented to the father-in-law in question a magnificent apartment in the family town house for a period of twelve years, on condition that he pay for the installation of electricity and central heating throughout the building. Cultural complementarity is not the central issue in this story, which turns on the struggle to save the old family residence and in which the Franco-American alliance is translated into a farce about plumbing. What does it matter if the birthplace of the heiress does not yet figure on any map and that her father is not so much a general as a "General Manager"?[13] The deal is concluded to the satisfaction of both parties, though Miss Looty Arlington, whose first name suggests looting and booty, seems to be the absolute winner in this strange compromise.

The jingle of dollars does not always produce a husband, nor titles of nobility lead inevitably to romantic infatuation. The confrontation between American ambition and romanticism, on the one hand, and Parisian cupidity and pride, on the other, gives rise to a whole series of situations which form a picture of a new kind of marriage of convenience. Whereas the Americans, in the name of individual liberty, denounce the arranged marriages common among the nobility, they are in fact creating new conditions for these marriages. The snobbery that is a motivating factor in such arranged marriages is intended for a specific audience. Everything that happens in Paris is closely followed in America. Paris, again, is a theater, and while the spectators across the Atlantic may be remote, they are extremely attentive. Paris sets the seal of social approval on the change in status of arrivistes such as the Dryfooses in *A Hazard of New Fortunes:* "News has come from Paris of the engagement of Christine Dryfoos. There the Dryfooses met with the success denied them in New York; many American plutocrats must await their apotheosis in Europe, where society has them, as it were, in a translation."[14] Americans regard a stay in Paris as proof of increased social status that will impress their compatriots. It is a way of skipping various stages in the conquest of the East. Paris acts as an arbiter of taste and also as a court of appeals where sentences passed on the other side of the Atlantic are reconsidered. In *The Siege of London* Mrs. Headway wishes to avenge her poor reception in New York by a success in Paris. As she says to Waterville, "If once I'm all right over here, I can snap my fingers at New York! You'll see the faces those women will make!"[15] Paris plays a role in the petty warfare waged in American salons and permits the settling of old scores at long distance. Here the character of the journalist enters the story. One of his many functions consists precisely in reporting the European destinies of the expatriates. In many works, he is the telegraph wire stretched across the Atlantic. He links the two continents, and, as the name of the newspaper *The Reverberator*—in the short novel of that title—indicates, is the sounding board for the events he witnesses.

The Americans' experiences in Paris affect both the myths and the reality of their own urban society and the way these evolve. We have observed how Parisians exploit the American colony and deceive innocents, but it should not be forgotten that the American in Paris can be a predator as well as a victim. The theme of deceived innocence is only one side of the picture. Set against the victims of the Parisian social order are innocents who return from their adventure in the capital with the same starry-eyed, romantic notions they had when they left the United States. Like Miranda Hope, whose ecstatic effusions have already been mentioned, Louis Leverett, the decadent Parnassian aesthete of "A Bundle of Letters" and "The Point of View," returns to Boston with all his clichéd images of the capital fully intact. From Boston he writes to a friend still in Paris:

> I am a stranger here, and I find it hard to believe that I ever was a native. It is very hard, very cold, very vacant. I think of your warm, rich Paris; I think of the Boulevard St. Michel on the mild spring evenings. I see the little corner by the window (of the Café de la Jeunesse) where I used to sit; the doors are open, the soft, deep breath of the great city comes in. It is brilliant, yet there is a kind of tone, of body, in the brightness; the mighty murmur of the ripest civilization in the world comes in; the dear old *peuple de Paris,* the most interesting people in the world pass by.[16]

Louis sees Paris solely through the filter of his literary souvenirs, his admiration for Théophile Gautier and the Francophile Swinburne. His real encounter with the city opens up not the slightest breach in the united front of his enthusiasm. In contrast, Marcellus Cockerel, in "The Point of View," who describes himself as "a roaring Yankee," finds only subjects for criticism and complaint: "You must know that, among the places I dislike, Paris carries the palm. I am bored to death there; it's the home of every humbug. The life is full of false comfort which is worse than discomfort, and the small, fat, irritable people give me the shivers."[17] Between these two extremes, the majority of the characters can be grouped along with what James, in the preface to *The Reverberator,* calls "passionless pilgrims." The supreme irony of *The Ambassadors,* and Strether's final discovery, is the fact that Chad himself is one of these pilgrims. It seems that in Chad, as in most American characters, the romantic and the consumer wage an eternal conflict.

Paris, the mythical goal, the place where literary illusions crumble, the miniature melting-pot for transatlantic patricians, is also the place to buy a new wardrobe for the ladies, to finish the education of both children and parents, to marry off daughters, and to taste a whole range of pleasures forbidden in the United States. For the "passionless pilgrims," Paris relates to their own country mostly insofar as it serves to produce a flattering echo of their expatriation. Apart from that, it is no more than a consumer object, a toy to be played with and then discarded.

Apart from the criticism of morals and the comparisons drawn between individuals and customs, there would seem to be little, if any, questioning of social structures, or any kind of sustained social critiques by American novelists writing about Paris. Whenever the Americans, fired by the spirit of democracy, begin to criticize the French aristocracy, their censure is often based on misconceptions about its relation to the prevailing political system. *The American,* set in the period of the Second Empire, describes a Legitimist family that has nothing to do with the current regime, and in other novels, France is a republic like the United States. As far as the economic system is concerned, the complex workings of the capital are ignored, and money is mentioned only in relation to marriage arrangements or the characters' social success. These novelists are not concerned with the same problems that preoccupied their contemporaries writing on the subject of America, like Theodore Dreiser or Upton Sinclair, or indeed those that preoccupied French writers of the same period, like Emile Zola. There is no trace of naturalism in their works and not the slightest reference to the industrial revolution and the condition of the working class.

One notable exception in this regard is found in *The Bent Twig.* Austin Page is a young millionaire mineowner from Colorado, whose fortune lies heavily on his conscience. He sees only too clearly what Parisian luxury implies in terms of human suffering and exploitation. While Sylvia Marshall and art critic Felix Morrison indulge in rapturous comparisons of Paris, Athens, and Corinth, Page sees in the spectacle of the capital the outer show of ill-gotten and squandered wealth. The grandiose vision of the Place de la Concorde is overshadowed for him by a much more somber vision. "It makes me think of a half-naked, sweating man, far underground in black night, striking at a rock with a pick,"[18] he says to his friends. His long walk through the city marks a turning point for the young man. Immediately afterward, he leaves for America, where he donates his entire fortune to the state of Colorado. This awakening of his political consciousness takes place against the sumptuous background of the French capital. Austin Page's reaction is the first sign of a troubled radicalism inspired by Paris, foreshadowing the questions and self-doubts of Dos Passos's characters in novels of the First World War.

The Characters' Initiation

The initiation of the characters is not simply a passage from innocence to experience and does not necessarily lead to a complete and wholehearted acceptance of a way of life that is reputedly superior to their own. As the Americans are not necessarily innocents, it may be better to describe what they learn in Paris as a new way of looking at life rather than an entirely new way of living. Not only their experience but also their consciousness is enriched by their contact with the capital. Their education may be at times completely negative, resulting in a total rejection of Parisian values. This is the case for Fanny de Malrive, who, asked if she is "still so good an American" after fifteen years in the capital, answers fervently, "Oh, a better and better one every day."[19] The keenest aficionados of the Parisian way of life are not necessarily real initiates, and extreme devotees such as Mr. Tristram or Louis Leverett come across as ridiculous characters on the whole. Marie-Reine Garnier, in her book entitled *Henry James et la France,* and Charles Cestre, in his article "La France dans l'Oeuvre de Henry James," argue that "l'art de vivre" and "la joie de vivre" may be taken as values against which the protagonists' progress, like that of their creator, can be measured. Their acceptance of these new values is a sign of intelligence and wisdom. They have seen the light and duly become converts. "The wisdom of these new characters," says Garnier, writing about *The Ambassadors,* "was a tribute to the glory and hospitality of our capital." And she goes on to say, "It did not reserve its favors exclusively for its own children, but, on the contrary, impartially bestowed its good sense on all those who approached the city in a spirit of learning rather than of conquest."[20] Such dogmatism, tinged with patriotic pride, is perhaps a little out of place. Christof Wegelin has a few ironic comments to make about Cestre's interpretation of the role of the Proberts, in *The Reverberator,* who are taken as being the author's spokesmen simply because they identify totally with the capital.[21] To speak of the characters' initiation does not mean deciding who is right and who is wrong, nor does it imply the passing of a subjective judgment on two lifestyles. It means looking at the way in which hero and city meet, a meeting in which the city transcends its physical and social reality and becomes a veritable protagonist.

The first influence that the city exerts on the characters can be observed in specific changes that take place in their outer appearance. A sort of mimicry takes place, which, if it is deliberately cultivated, may seem ridiculous. The protagonists become more refined; their sense of elegance is heightened;

and, both physically and psychologically, they acquire a greater flexibility. When John Durham again meets Fanny Frisbee, now Mme de Malrive, he is astonished at how much she has changed: "She was the same, but so mysteriously changed! And it was the mystery, the sense of unprobed depth of initiations, which drew him to her as her freshness had never drawn him." He tries to analyze her transformation and defines its causes: "Yes, it was the finish, the modelling, which Madame de Malrive's experience had given her that set her apart from the fresh uncomplicated personalities of which she had once been simply the most charming type. The influences that had lowered her voice, regulated her gestures, toned her down to harmony with the warm dim background of a long social past—these influences had lent to her natural fineness of perception a command of expression adapted to complex conditions."[22]

Similarly, Chad's transformation, as perceived by Strether, plays an important part in Chapters 7 and 8 of *The Ambassadors*. It is made more dramatic by the doubly theatrical appearance of the young man in the Comédie Française box and the long meditation that it provokes in Strether. This apparent change of identity is not simply a question of age. Chad is virtually unrecognizable, and Strether is forced to take account of this new factor that upsets the delicate balance of his mission. "Chad had been made over. That was all; whatever it was, it was everything. Strether had never seen the thing done before; it was perhaps a specialty of Paris." During their conversation at the café, Strether reflects on the metamorphosis of his young friend:

> It had cleared his eyes and settled his colour and polished his fine square teeth—the main ornament of his face; and at the same time that it had given him a form and a surface, almost a design, it had toned his voice, established his accent, encouraged his smile to more play and his other motions to less. He had formerly, with a great deal of action, expressed very little; and he now expressed whatever was necessary with almost none at all. It was as if, in short, he had really, copious perhaps, but shapeless, been put into a firm mould and turned successfully out.[23]

This harmonious blending of character and city may only be skin deep and does not automatically imply an acquiescence in the city's values. Mme de Malrive cannot help being transformed by a society she despises—and of which she is a prisoner. In Chad's case, he has managed to acquire an air of superficial refinement while basically remaining rather vulgar and morally weak, and it is this outer polish that deceives Strether. Such changes, maybe even as simple as a change of accent, clearly show the implacable persuasiveness of the city. John Durham soon becomes aware of this: "It gave him a sense of the tremendous strength of the organization into which Fanny de Malrive had been absorbed, that in spite of her horror, her moral revolt, she had not reacted against its external form."[24]

Paris imposes itself on those who live there. The city not only works subtle changes on the characters' attitudes and behavior, it also claims them physically, appropriating their bodies and playing on them as it wishes. Is not the very air of the city, as Strether discovered, "infectious"?[25] The tourists' state of entranced wonder is followed by an education of the senses. The characters are plunged into a whirl of sensations, filled with a multitude of colors, smells, and sounds. The incessant vibration of the capital produces an answering vibration in the Americans. Even those who are most reticent, like Waymarsh and Sarah Pocock, are not entirely impervious to this riot of feelings. The rather unreceptive Mr. Dosson, in *The Reverberator,* for example, spends hours in the courtyard of his hotel, drinking in the Parisian atmosphere. "The April air was mild; the cry of women selling violets came from the street and mingling with the rich hum of Paris, seemed to bring with it faintly the odour of the flowers."[26] Undine Spragg becomes aware of the fundamental harmony that exists between the city and her innermost being: "As she looked at the thronged street, on which the summer light lay like a blush of pleasure, she felt herself naturally akin to the bright and careless freedom of the scene. . . . Her senses luxuriated in all its material details."[27] Strether, a sensitive and acute observer, analyzes for his own pleasure the charm of a Parisian evening: "It was the evening hour, but daylight was long now and Paris more than ever penetrating. The scent of flowers was in the streets; he had the whiff of violets perpetually in his nose; and he had attached himself to sounds and suggestions, vibrations of the air, human and dramatic, he imagined, as they were not in other places, that came out for him more and more as the mild afternoon deepened."[28]

These reactions, whether they are skin deep or more profoundly penetrating, are continued on a psychological level. It is possible that the characters' sensory relationship with the city, like their emotional one, may be a relationship of conflict. Generally speaking, however, it appears that the pulsations of Parisian life push the characters in the direction of their natural inclinations. Strether, for example, wondering whether to send Mme de Vionnet a *pneumatique* informing her of his arrival, is influenced by the special atmosphere of the post office. "If he at last did deposit his missive it was perhaps because the pressure of the place had an effect." James chooses the metaphor of the post office to convey the idea of the correspondences connecting the innumerable and different parts of the city's great body. Strether, we are told, "was carrying on a correspondence, across that great city, quite in the key of the Postes et Télégraphes in general, and it was fairly as if the acceptance of that fact had come from something in his state that sorted with the occupation of his neighbours."[29]

Pathetic fallacy is common in these works, and the protagonist's dilemma is objectified in the city's physical movements. The crowd, the weather, the air of the streets are the different harmonies accompanying the characters' interior recitatives. Summer rain, a sinister, chilly rain, is falling during Sylvia Marshall's long walk through the city in *The Bent Twig*. Having learned that Austin Page has given away his fortune, the young woman now finds herself faced with a difficult choice. In the scene where Strether visits Mme de Vionnet for the last time, a storm rumbles in the distance. The characters, moving about the city, recognize landmarks expressing in concrete form their moods and feelings. Sylvia, in quest of her true identity, comes face-to-face with the artistic representation of her struggle in front of the Panthéon. "In the rainy twilight the fierce tension of the Rodin 'Thinker' in front of the Pantheon loomed huge and tragic. She gave it a glance of startled sympathy. She had never understood the statue before. Now she was the prey to those same ravaging throes. Above her on his pedestal, the great, bronze, naked, tortured man ground his teeth as he glared out from under the inexorable limitations of his ape-like forehead, and strove wildly against the barriers of his flesh."[30] In *The Siege of London* Houdon's statue of Voltaire, in the foyer of the Comédie Française, adds a contrasting touch of skepticism to the conversations that go on at its feet. Like an extra character, it seems tacitly to encourage Littlemore to enjoy himself watching the comedy of manners that is being enacted around him. In such ways, a physical and psychological exchange is set up between the city and the characters. Paris, acting as the agent of an ambiguous determinism, molds and seasons their development.

But the capital's most obvious role—and one that is doubtless the least interesting for French, especially Parisian, readers—is to instruct the visitor. It is unnecessary to launch into a lengthy review of the capital's historical and cultural riches. But those riches should be called to mind in order to understand why, for Americans, no matter how long they stay in Paris, it will always be a city of museums and historical landmarks. Under the naive gaze of Christopher Newman, Paris is the place where one is able to find the most beautiful things in the world—hence his desire to obtain copies of the Louvre's greatest masterpieces. For John Durham, Ralph Marvell, Louis

Leverett, Sylvia Marshall, Felix Morrison, and, above all, Strether, Paris triggers a whole series of correspondences between present and past, between one form of artistic expression and another. Sylvia Marshall, looking at the Champs-Elysées, cries, "Isn't it the key to Rubens—bloom, radiance, life expansive!" and Felix Morrison agrees, adding, "And Chabrier should set it to music."[31] The Americans are fascinated by the way in which the past, a past that seems remote in comparison with their own brief national history, is constantly rendered so dramatically present. The Middle Ages, the reign of Louis XIII, and the First Empire are daily brought back to life before their very eyes as they visit Notre-Dame, the Hôtel de Bellegarde, and Mme de Vionnet's apartment. In *The Ambassadors* the multiple allusions to this historic and cultural heritage are perfectly integrated with the texture of the novel. The reader's difficulty in grasping them all is in keeping with the book's complexity. But in other works we find the characters sometimes making erudite comparisons that are less successful. *The Bent Twig* is particularly redolent of such pedanticism, which probably explains the later appearance of a scholarly edition of the work, with annotations and suggested research topics.

But what is the city's influence on the psychology of artists? In what way is Paris a special and favored place for artistic creation? The answer is not evident. The spectator and art lover finds his sensibilities and visual acuity sharpened and enhanced. But what of the creative artist? Dorothy Canfield attempts a reply to the question through the metaphor of the city as a horn of plenty. Paris is an eternal spring of creative energy at which the artist may drink. Henry James, in *The Ambassadors,* sees things differently. If we are to take the original vocation of Chad, or at least Little Bilham, seriously, then Paris has had a detrimental effect on his artistic development. Here, for the first time, we encounter the idea that Paris may, paradoxically, produce in the American artist a sort of sterility. To the observer or thinker Paris offers such a rich field of investigation that the artist may, like Strether, be content simply to play the role of voyeur, to watch from a distance, from a balcony or the river's edge, content to try and understand what he sees rather than express it in a creative act. Little Bilham came to Paris intending to be a painter, but, as the narrator notes, "His productive power faltered in proportion as his knowledge grew." What remains from this failure is "his beautiful intelligence and his confirmed habit of Paris."[32] The sheer plenitude and riches of the Parisian harmonies may actually hamper artists' creativity and, by educating them, render them impotent. This idea will be taken up repeatedly by the expatriates of the 1920s. In the years preceding 1914, the artist is perceived from the outside and is never a fully engaged protagonist. The novelists never draw on their own experience as literary subject matter. They do not attempt to define the influence that Paris had on them personally. Most of the artists in the books are painters; and if their art is a particular way of looking at things, they are in this respect symbolic of all American characters, including tourists and journalists, whose primary function is to observe. The capital provokes a sensory awakening—it cultivates, teaches, sharpens the characters' aesthetic perception—but it is not clear that it encourages creation.

The city's greatest contribution, however, lies in the opportunity it affords men for a real sentimental education, a deeper knowledge of women, and a new conception of love. Andrew Vane's romantic initiation takes place in exceedingly banal circumstances. Known at Harvard as "Galahad Vane," the hero finally loses a virginity worthy of his namesake in the arms of Mirabelle Trémonceau. Convention dictated that the scene should take place between the ending of one chapter and the opening of the next, but it is nonetheless, historically speaking, the first literary instance of the real seduction of an American in Paris. The heroes' apprenticeship, however, involves more than a sexual awakening, and a gradual discovery of women takes place in different and subtle ways. Thanks to the good offices of Mirabelle, Carryl's hero discovers undreamed of complexities in the female character.

> Lately he had been conscious of noticing things about Mirabelle which had never been part of his analysis of another woman. . . . Now, for the first time, he was conscious that a woman is never wholly silent—that a whisper of lace or a lisp of silk speaks the movement that is unapparent to the eye. Already he had found that her frown can be mirth-provoking, and her smile of a sadness beyond description. Already he was become weatherwise in his understanding of the ripples of expression blown by the shifting winds of inner thought across her eyes.[33]

Similarly, John Durham perceives in Mme de Treymes an extra dimension that American women lack: charm. As William Crary Brownell writes, in French, "le charme prime la beauté,"[34] and this further gift has been granted to Mme de Malrive's sister-in-law. "She was a beauty, if, beauty, instead of being restricted to the cast of the face, is a pervasive attribute informing the hands, the voice, the gestures, the very fall of a flounce and the tilt of a feather. In this impalpable *aura* of grace Madame de Treymes' dark meagre presence unmistakably moved, like a thin flame in a wider quiver of light."[35]

Strether goes much deeper into the heart of things. All through *The Ambas-*

sadors, he struggles to understand the true nature of Mme de Vionnet and to situate her in relation to other women he has known. Surprise follows surprise, and he finally discovers that behind the mysterious figure of the lady of society stands the figure of a grisette abandoned by her lover. Thus there is no break between the comfortable myths of bohemian life and the real life of an aristocrat of the Faubourg Saint-Germain. This discovery by the intellectual from Woollett of what Leslie Fiedler calls "the genital aspect of the case,"[36] is crucial for our understanding of the American vision of Paris before the First World War. This simple revelation, made infinitely dramatic by the book's logical progression leading up to it, extends beyond *The Ambassadors* to illuminate other works. The meeting on the river bank inaugurates the first fully rounded vision of woman as an essentially protean creature. As Miss Barrace remarks, Mme de Vionnet's personality has many different facets: "'She is various. She's fifty women'—'Ah, but only one'—Strether kept it clear—'at a time'—'Perhaps. But in fifty times.'"[37] U. C. Knoepflmacher notes that Mme de Vionnet is simultaneously "queen" and "quean."[38] It is unclear whether Strether, deep down, ever manages to reconcile these two conflicting aspects. Does he leave Paris because his illusions have been shattered or because his initiation is complete? Interpretations may differ, but the essential thing is the discovery itself. Strether is suddenly confronted with the revelation that all the evidence had been leading up to: Mme de Vionnet is Chad's mistress. Strether's worldview cannot accommodate this fact. Like Mme de Treymes and even Mirabelle Trémonceau, with her lesser virtue, Mme de Vionnet exemplifies a new kind of woman. Leslie Fiedler's distinction between "fair maiden" and "dark lady" no longer holds true, as he himself points out.[39] The Parisian quest that Christopher Newman, the "new man," embarked on in *The American* finally ends with the meeting with a "new woman," a category to which Mme de Cintré definitely did not belong.

And so the mysterious double figure of the Parisienne, in which bacchante and angel are merged, perfumes the air of the city with the subtle musk of the bedchamber. For Strether, Mme de Vionnet is both Cleopatra and Venus, and the city itself, which encourages the characters to indulge in the delights of sensual pleasure, basks in an aura of paganism, or even animality. It is a tropical swamp, a jungle, a Babylon, a seraglio, an oriental bazaar.[40] Longmore considers M. de Mauves to be a real pagan. Strether wonders whether Chad is "a pagan," or if on the contrary he has become "a gentleman," and if the mysterious character who keeps him in Paris is "a brute" or "a woman."[41] The span of these metaphors situates the capital outside of time. Like the sea to which James often compares it, the city survives the ebb and flow of time while remaining eternally feminine. To borrow the cut-and-dried conclusion of a popular French song, "Paris is a woman"—a fact borne out by the grammatical structures of the language used to describe it. Pierre Citron has shown that in French mythology the capital has been given, successively and simultaneously, both genders; but when it is personified in American literature, Paris is always feminine. She is an accomplice for Undine Spragg, an adversary for Fanny de Malrive, and a rival for Margery Palffy. And Andrew Vane admits to Margery: "I know I'm not wrong—something's come between us, and that something is just what I've said—Paris! Isn't it?"[42] In Carryl's story "Papa Labesse" Paris is a courtesan. Marcelle, sick and exhausted, coming back to the Butte Montmartre to end her miserable existence as a prostitute, identifies with the city: "I have come back to the Butte, Papa Labesse—come back to die. For now there is no-one to receive me save Paris. She will take me, thou knowest, she who has made me like herself."[43]

The gradual development of this new concept of womanhood cannot by itself account for all the different aspects of Paris and, in particular, its social structure. But it does provide a new axis around which may be grouped the thematic constellations of hedonism, the elegant patterning of social relationships, and the aristocracy's connections with the demimonde. Paris acquires through this female figure a unity that is in marked contrast with the diversity Henry Adams saw in contemporary society and that can remain a fertile source of spiritual energy. The best symbol of this cult of femininity, which began with the worship of Aphrodite and continued in the Middle Ages with the worship of the Virgin, is the Cathedral of Notre-Dame. Far from representing the secular might of the Catholic church, it becomes instead a refuge, a museum, a haven of calm, in which floats an atmosphere of spirituality tinged with paganism. Newman goes there to meditate before giving up the idea of vengeance on the Bellegardes; Sylvia Marshall, during a visit to the cathedral, thinks she hears the voice of the man she loves echoing around the vaults; and Strether, a regular visitor, one day discovers within the cathedral a modern version of the ancient goddess of love, whose Christian name recalls the Virgin, as he gazes at the face of Mme de Vionnet in prayer. It is the mystery of love's suffering that pushes all these troubled souls toward this sanctuary.

James's answer to American moral aggressiveness lies in the affirmation of a new kind of woman. *The Ambassadors* makes this connection clear: the dreams of bohemia have found their way into real life, and the characters learn that moral beauty may exist outside the narrow world of puritanism. It may be found in the elegant and refined world of society and may, indeed, be what finally explains and justifies that world.

CHAPTER 4

PARIS IN CRISIS: HISTORICAL AND GEOGRAPHICAL ASPECTS

The Turning Point of Two Centuries

The First World War marks a turning point in American literature. That much is agreed upon, though the exact date assigned to the turning point varies from one historian to another, some choosing the year 1910 as the end of an era, and others 1912, 1914, or even 1917. As Martin S. Day explains the turning point in the preface to the first volume of his *History of American Literature,* "There are several reasons why the terminating date of this treatment is 1910. Many of the major writers of the nineteenth century continued to write into the early years of the twentieth," and "an old literary spirit was dying and a new one being born a few years before the First World War."[1] The war was not the sole factor shaping this radical transformation, whose origins are to be found much earlier, but it did in a dramatic and brutal way bring new literary inspiration to a whole generation of young writers, face-to-face with such an overwhelmingly novel and tragic experience that it inevitably passed into their writing.

This general change in American literature also affected the Parisian theme and its development. Among authors already mentioned, Edith Wharton and Dorothy Canfield chose wartime Paris as the setting for several novels. Toward the end of his life, Henry James was interested in the conflict as a journalist and also as a controversialist who was convinced that American intervention was a political and moral necessity. In "England at War," "The American Motor Ambulance Corps in France," and other essays published under the title *Within the Rim,* his primary aim is to keep the American public informed about the war. Richard Harding Davis, who died in 1916, the same year as James, also left accounts of Paris during the early days of the war, notably in *With the Allies* and the short story "Somewhere in France," in which the adventures of the German spy Marie Gessler end in the prison of Saint-Lazare.

New writers of a younger generation also describe the capital—first and foremost John Dos Passos but also more minor literary figures such as Elliot

Paul and Owen Johnson. Gertrude Stein, evoking wartime Paris in *The Autobiography of Alice B. Toklas,* also belongs to this new generation of writers despite her relative age—she was forty in 1914. William Faulkner gives a brief description of the city in *A Fable,* published in 1954, thus drawing our attention to the way in which the war exerted an influence on the imagination of American writers for a considerable period of time. *The Marne,* by Edith Wharton, and *Home Fires in France,* by Dorothy Canfield, both appeared in 1918. Canfield subsequently published *The Day of Glory* in 1919 and *The Deepening Stream* in 1930, two years before Wharton returned to the theme of the war with *A Son at the Front,* in 1932. Dos Passos drew on his wartime experiences in *One Man's Initiation: 1917,* published in 1921, *Three Soldiers* (1921), and *1919* (1932) as well as a lesser-known work published in 1954, *Chosen Country.* The unifying factor behind all of the works discussed in this section is not, however, when they were written, but rather the fact that they all deal with the same subject, wartime Paris.

In literature at least, the period of the war did not end on 11 November 1918. Wartime Paris, from American writers' point of view, was a phenomenon extending well beyond the armistice. Through necessity or inclination, American servicemen linger on in the capital instead of going directly home. During the winter of 1918–19, their ranks are swollen by successive waves of civil servants, advisers, and diplomats who arrive to negotiate the peace. The city is shown as being less rapidly transformed by peace than it was, four years earlier, by mobilization. The Parisian episodes of *Three Soldiers* all take place after the armistice. In spite of its title, *1919,* like *Chosen Country,* covers the last two years of the fighting. As for the beginning of the period, it is covered in *The Marne* and *A Son at the Front,* both of which describe a wartime city of August 1914, and *The Deepening Stream,* which opens in early 1915. In the perspective afforded by these works, the war lasts from mobilization until the middle of 1919.

Several books begin with, or refer back to, the period before the war. *The Wasted Generation,* by Owen Johnson, starts around 1914, though the life of the capital in preceding years is occasionally recalled in flashbacks. In *The Green Bay Tree,* published in 1925, Louis Bromfield tells the story of Lily Shane from 1900 to 1920. Although the descriptions of prewar Paris are purely imaginary, the author uses his experience as an ambulance driver to provide material for the period of the war itself. In the trilogy *U.S.A., The 42nd Parallel* contains passages about prewar Paris in relation to the character of J. Ward Moorehouse, who plays an important part in *1919.* . Two novels stand apart from the rest, *Chosen Country,* and *The Deepening*

Stream. Although the most important episodes in both books take place after the outbreak of hostilities, they contain full and detailed descriptions of Paris as it was well before 1914. A succession of different and changing images is thus built up as their plots develop. In *Chosen Country*, a largely autobiographical work, the hero, Jay Pignatelli, spends much of his childhood moving about, and he visits Paris several times before eventually ending up there as an ambulance driver in 1917. As luck would have it, he is billeted in the same hotel where his family used to stay when he was a child. His reminiscences of the past, scattered widely throughout the novel, allow the reader to see the war in the context of a longer period.

The Deepening Stream is particularly interesting for our study. Matey Gilbert, the heroine, is the youngest daughter of an American academic who has maintained a long-lasting, close relationship with one of his former classmates at the Sorbonne, Paul Vinet, who has become a teacher in a Parisian lycée. Matey's life is divided between Paris and America. Her first experience of Paris comes when she is thirteen, during a sabbatical year of her father's. In 1901 she returns once more, this time to pursue her studies at the Sorbonne, while living at the Vinet apartment in the Rue de Fleurus. In 1908, at age twenty-four, she marries a distant cousin, Adrian Fort, who has spent time in Paris studying painting at the Studio Colarossi—referred to as "Minarossi" in the book—and their honeymoon brings them to the capital once again. The book's significance would be amply justified by the number of pages devoted to Paris up to this point in the story, but the Forts' involvement with the capital is not over. It is at the precise moment when they seem to be firmly settled in Rustdorf, in Rip Van Winkle country, that war breaks out in Europe, and Adrian, after some hesitation (for he is a Quaker), gives up his job in a bank and enlists in an ambulance corps. The Forts finally arrive in Paris again in 1915 and go to live with Mme Vinet, who is now a widow.

For the following 125 pages of the book, the war is described from a point of view that is simultaneously American and French. Canfield, through her close acquaintance with both American and French academic milieux, provides a comparative study in which the lifestyle of French middle-class intellectuals is portrayed in minute detail. The Vinets, though not rich, have an "at home" day, a maid, a person who waxes the floors, and even, surprisingly, a private tutor for their four children. By the time the war breaks out, the reader is intimately acquainted with the family and feels more keenly the significance of the changes that such a catastrophe inevitably brings. The maid is forced to return to her native Brittany, the floor-waxer and tutor are called up, and one after the other, the two Vinet sons are killed in action. To a greater degree than *Chosen Country, The Deepening Stream* is a book of transition, not simply because Parisian life is described over a period of more than twenty-three years at a major turning point in history but also because for the first time in American literature the French middle class is depicted.

Samuel Merwin's novel *The Honey Bee*, like *The Deepening Stream,* marks a break with tradition. The heroine, Hilda Wilson, is a fashion buyer for a New York firm whose work has brought her regularly to Paris for the past eight years. The city plays a crucial role in her sudden discovery in 1914 of the sterility of her existence and in her decision at the age of thirty-two to give up everything and abandon herself to a totally new way of life in which she lives from day to day, like the honey bee of the title, which occasionally ceases its activity and feeds upon the reserves of the hive. Through a chance encounter with two young fellow Americans, a dancer and a boxer, Hilda is introduced into the world of the music hall and the boxing ring. Hilda, who is neither a tourist nor a student, discovers a hitherto unknown Paris that causes her to rethink, and finally to reject, her past life. This five-hundred-page novel, sometimes didactic, sometimes discursive, follows the progressive changes in the main character against the background of political crisis. Through her contact with the city, Hilda is made aware of the drawbacks of puritanism and the fundamental injustice of the female condition, yet, somewhat in the manner of Strether, she returns to New York in November 1914, armed with a new maturity. Merwin's novel, published to critical acclaim in 1915, was in advance of contemporary writings on the Parisian theme in that it revealed the existence of a new, bohemian working class, which would be subsequently described by the British novelist Jean Rhys in the 1930s. In addition, *The Honey Bee* is strikingly modern in the sort of issues it raises, and this, too, stamps it as a work of transition bringing down the curtain on the Belle Epoque and highlighting the significance of the year 1914.

All the authors mentioned so far lived in the capital for varying periods of time between 1914 and 1918. Edith Wharton hardly set foot outside Paris during the whole of the fighting. Her work with the Red Cross and organizations such as The Accueil Franco-Américain—set up to provide aid for the children of Ypres—American Hostels, and Children of Flanders earned her the Legion of Honor in 1916. Dorothy Canfield and her husband also worked for various charities for the wounded and the orphaned, and they became closely acquainted with the daily life of the capital during the three years they lived there. From 1916 onward, Gertrude Stein owned her own ambulance, which Alice B. Toklas drove under the auspices of the American

Fund for French Wounded. John Dos Passos enlisted with the Norton-Harjes group in 1917, returned to the United States in 1918, and came back again as an ordinary soldier in early November—experiences he shared with the majority of his characters. Elliot Paul served with the American army, while William Faulkner joined the Canadian air force.

The image of Paris evoked by all of these writers grows directly out of their own experiences. It is colored by the memories of men and women who voluntarily elected to share the city's historical destiny at a particularly difficult time. Their concern for realism and the accumulation of the small details of daily life, which are an essential part of their representation of the city, mark a definite break with the way the image of Paris was presented in the first decade of the twentieth century. But it would be wrong to describe such literary developments as resulting entirely from the war's catalyzing effect. In fact, even before the war, the breach between the real world and its literary representation had already begun to open. The war, by throwing in new and unknown quantities, exacerbated the situation and ultimately split apart cracks dating from an earlier period.

The conclusions presented in the last chapter were based largely on an analysis of *The Ambassadors*. James, by placing woman at the center of an elegant, aristocratic, and art-loving society, fused his limited perception of a milieu that was historically doomed with an idealized vision of a perfect society. Paris is America in reverse. James apparently started from an analysis of American society in order to throw into relief those aspects of contemporary Paris that stood in dramatic contrast. Thus against the American search for material possessions he set the Parisian quest for spiritual values; against the restrictions of puritanism, the tolerance of hedonism; against the vulgar cult of success, a philosophical acceptance of failure. The end result is that Paris symbolizes, despite the wealth of concrete detail with which it is described, a sort of abstract way of life, the culminating point and logical outcome of a dialectic between the two civilizations. The city is viewed from above, refracted through the prism of a personality profoundly affected by the conflict between the Old World and the New. James weaves together the different strands of the Parisian theme with consummate art, but the city whose glorious past he evokes seems fixed inexorably in the present, with the most conservative social group imaginable at its center. Despite *The Ambassadors*'s recurrent time symbolism, despite the contrast between Woollett's time measured by the ticking of the clocks and the time of the capital measured by lived experience, the urban setting finally comes across as having the same immutability as most utopian kingdoms.

The contrast between the two cultures is aesthetically flawless. The juxtaposition of the flow of human destiny with the changeless nature of the city puts the reader in mind of Faust, whose presence hovers over the book. Nonetheless, this picture of Paris in the last years of the nineteenth century seemed as early as 1903 to belong to a bygone era. The reader discovers its wrinkles, little by little, as he discovers those of Mme de Vionnet. James captures the city like a butterfly on a pin, allowing one to contemplate the richness and brilliance of its color but also its eternal fixity. From the fertile soil of an old theme, James produced an authentic, blossoming poetry of the city; but it is a poetry that, by its special nature, forbids all further development.

This particular archaism is perhaps less pronounced in the works of Edith Wharton. The author of *The Custom of the Country* seems more preoccupied by changes in American social habits than by the habits of Parisian society. The rise of the nouveau riche is seen as an exclusively American phenomenon. The Parisian aristocracy remains, for her, the same as ever and is portrayed in her books as a veritable protagonist of heroic proportions. While the American aristocracy exhibits visible signs of change, the French aristocracy seems destined to last for eternity. The Nouveau Luxe restaurant, a meeting place for the French and American elite, provides a setting that highlights this emerging contrast. Wharton exaggerates the monolithic and unchanging aspect of the French nobility in order to throw into relief the individual revolts it engenders, but also to underscore the contrast between Paris and New York. Fanny de Malrive and Lily Bart face two very different kinds of adversary. But Wharton's Paris, like that of James, shows what is fundamentally an eleventh-hour society, which will not long outlive the century that gave it birth. Booth Tarkington, too, presents in *The Beautiful Lady* a picture of Paris that is basically nostalgic. By fulfilling the expectations of the American public with an image of Paris corresponding to that which already exists in their collective consciousness, he offers a version of the city that is outdated and turned toward the past.

Consequently, even as early as *The Ambassadors,* the Parisian theme seems to have arrived at an impasse, partly because James seemed to have produced the definite version and partly because literature had not kept pace with history. The Paris of pre–World War I novels, in its outer appearance and social institutions, seems almost the same as it was, historically, throughout the Second Empire, and even in relatively late works faint echoes of Offenbach can still be heard in this city of the Belle Epoque. There is no doubt that the ground was already prepared for some sort of change when history took the dramatic turn whose impetus propelled literary Paris into the twentieth century. The new role that circumstances imposed on the capital, giving it a unique status among European cities, radically affected the Parisian motif and closed the gap between literature and reality. No other city—not London, bombarded by Zeppelins; not Berlin or Vienna, both of which disappeared in hostile territory; not Rome or other Italian cities, whose logistical importance was only minor—was able to rival in prestige the great city behind the lines that, on two occasions, found itself perilously close to the action.

While some works can be seen as transitional between the two periods, the contrast between the literary Paris of the Belle Epoque and that of the war is extreme. It can be clearly illustrated by comparing two works by the same author, *Madame de Treymes* and *The Marne,* for example, or *The Bent Twig* and *The Deepening Stream.* The gulf that separates them is enormous. It is as though Gloriani's garden were suddenly subjected to a bombing attack by the Gothas or Mme de Vionnet were discovered bandaging the wounded in Neuilly. With the outbreak of war, an old order is swept away. The carriages of *Ruggles of Red Gap,* the Rendez-vous des Cochers Fidèles, the whole of horsedrawn Paris, vanishes, lost in the approaching cloud of smoke from the taxis of the Marne.

For the first time in this study, we are confronted with works in which Paris is shown as having a historical dimension. It may seem surprising that the capital's national destiny has not so far been evoked. One reason is that the major literary works on which this study is based were all written during the relatively calm period of the Third Republic, which, from its origins until 1914, afforded few historically dramatic events for the American public. But there are some works—historical novels and short stories—written before 1914 that take as their subject matter the more turbulent periods of the city's history, notably the 1789 revolution and the Commune. In their vast crowd scenes and dramatic action sequences, these works foreshadow the literature of the First World War.

Revolutionary Paris in Historical Fiction

No American writer, it would appear, was on hand to witness the dramatic events of some of the city's great historical crises: the revolution of 1789, the uprisings of 1830 and 1848, the siege of 1870, and the Commune. Certainly no one drew directly upon his recollections of such periods in fictional works accessible to the researcher. All that can be found are occasional references to the Franco-Prussian War and the strong anti-German sentiment of the generation who grew up in the aftermath of the defeat of

Sedan. In *The Reverberator* Gaston Probert's brother is killed in the 1870 war, as are the husband, father, and brother of Mme de Brindes in "Collaboration." This short story by James depicts, through the characters of Mme de Brindes and her daughter Paule, a kind of vengeful and extreme form of patriotism that was to resurface during the First World War. But the central issue in the story is the incompatibility of the sexes, which James portrays as being stronger even than that between Frenchman and German. Paule de Brindes is a Lysistrata in reverse who breaks off her relationship with the poet Félix Vandemer because of his collaboration (the term has a premonitory ring) with the German musician Herman Heidenmauer in the composition of an opera. In the end, Félix leaves Paule in Paris and goes away with Herman.

The lack of firsthand reports obliges one to look for illustrations of the most eventful moments of the city's past in historical novels and dramas. The twenty volumes of *America's Lost Plays* provide meager pickings. Though a few plays are set in Paris, at least in part (*Rose Michel* by Steele MacKaye, *Thirty Years or the Gambler's Fate* by William Dunlap, *The Two Sons-in-Law* by Howard Payne), the city's role in them is extremely limited. The same can be said of *Roads of Destiny*, an early work by O. Henry, which takes place during an imaginary ancien régime. Archibald Clavering Gunter capitalizes on the scandalous reputation of the French Regency in his two long novels featuring the financier John Law, *A Princess of Paris* and *The King's Stockbroker*.

The French Revolution had already been treated in *Modern Chivalry*, Hugh Henry Brackenridge's huge picaresque novel. In the second part of this work, published in 1815, Teague O'Reagan goes to Paris, where he meets various French revolutionaries. Henry James's short story "Gabrielle de Bergerac," which appeared in 1869 in the *Atlantic Monthly*, has the same revolutionary background. Gabrielle, after marrying her younger brother's tutor, dies on the scaffold along with her husband and various Girondists. S. Weir Mitchell describes an episode in the Reign of Terror in his story "A Little More Burgundy," in which he introduces the character of François the thief. The same episode and character reappear in a lengthy book *The Adventures of François, Foundling, Thief, Juggler and Fencing Master during the French Revolution*. François, the picaro whose progress is summed up in the book's title, is interested in the human side of great historical events and thus presents the dramatic moments of the Revolution from the viewpoint of the man in the street. Owen Johnson's novel *In the Name of Liberty* (1905), set in the same period, recalls *A Tale of Two Cities*, published in 1859.

According to the *Cumulative Book Review Digest* of 1905, Johnson's book was a great success, at least as far as the critics were concerned. It tells the story of a young man, Barabant, from the provinces, who arrives in the capital and immediately embraces the Girondist cause. He is arrested during the Terror but is saved from the guillotine by Nicole, a young flower seller whom he has married in prison. Nicole imitates the heroic gesture of Sidney Carton and takes her husband's place on the tumbril.

Robert W. Chambers wrote four novels and several short stories about the events of 1870–71. *Lorraine,* set on the eastern front, and *The Maids of Paradise,* about the Army of the Loire, only marginally involve the capital. However, *Ashes of Empire* deals with events that took place in Paris between 4 September 1870 and March 1871, and *The Red Republic* closely follows the progress of the Commune. In the first of these two books, two American war correspondents, Cecil Bourke and Jim Harewood, fall in love with twins, Yolette and Hildé Chalais, and protect them during the siege from looters and from spies who are interested in the strategic position of their house close to the fortifications. In *The Red Republic* numerous adventures are strung together by means of a slender plot. During the early days of the uprising, an American, Philip Landes, becomes the protector of Jeanne de Brassac, whose father was the victim of a heinous crime. Philip braves death a hundred times; he is wounded on several occasions, arrested, and at one dramatic moment in the story faces summary execution—but, needless to say, the gun does not go off. At the end of the book, the Commune is finished and destroyed, Philip recovers the Brassac diamonds, and, of course, he gets the girl.

Together, S. Weir Mitchell, Owen Johnson, and Robert W. Chambers devote some sixteen hundred pages to the subject of Paris. Though they describe many different aspects of the capital, the reader will find no surprises in their literary representation. It depicts an animated city that serves as the backdrop to a series of well-known historical events. Description and narration alternate with predictable regularity. Occasionally, one is reminded of the city of *Les Mystères de Paris,* as when Mitchell's young François, having run away from a choir school on the Ile Saint-Louis, ends up wandering through strange alleys and narrow streets:

> Quite at a loss, he wandered once more through the slums of the Cité, and soon lost himself in the network of narrow streets to the north of the cathedral, hearing as he went, strange slang, which his name-sake François Villon would have better understood than he. The filth of the roadways and that of the tongues were here comparable. . . . Far away

he paused breathless in a dark lane which seemed unpeopled, and where the houses leaned over like palsied old scoundrels who whisper to one another of ancient crime. Even to a boy the place was of a sudden terrible. There was murder in the air.[2]

In the Name of Liberty, like *The Adventures of François,* focuses mainly on the revolutionary Paris of the Right Bank, situated around the Place de la Révolution, the Tuileries, the Palais Royal and the Place de Grève. Chambers's novels are set in different parts of the city. In the preface to *Ashes of Empire* the author says that he has changed various place-names—a fort, a "porte," and two streets. But there is evidence to suggest that the main episodes take place near the Porte de Saint-Cloud, while other scenes occur at the Hôtel de Ville and in the Belleville Quarter. In *The Red Republic* Philip Landes, scouring the city in search of Jeanne de Brassac, covers every inch of the capital.

It is hard to say just how much historical research has gone into these books. In Archibald Clavering Gunter's account of the Regency, one has the impression that it is not very much. Similarly, Owen Johnson sets his romantic plot against a revolutionary background that is fairly sketchy. For the nonspecialist, *The Adventures of François* provides more evidence that the author possessed some knowledge of the history he was writing about. Mitchell, who was a neurologist, gained the same reputation for rigorousness and probity in his fictional works that he enjoyed in his scientific publications. Martin S. Day notes, for instance, that seven years of research went into *Hugh Wynne: Free Quaker.*[3] As far as sources are concerned, the most up-to-date information about the Revolution and the Commune at the end of the nineteenth century must have been Hippolyte Taine's multivolume *Origines de la France Contemporaine,* which appeared from 1876 to 1896. Chambers, dealing with a more recent period, was able to draw on the recollections of eyewitnesses as well as the plentiful literature on the Franco-Prussian War and the Commune that began to appear from 1871 onward. In the preface to *Ashes of Empire* he acknowledges as sources a certain "commandant Rousset"[4] and an "officier de marine"—in French in the text—who in all likelihood provided him with the necessary technical details about movements of gunboats and what sort of artillery was used. In *The Red Republic* he sketches the historical background by using a technique similar to that of Dos Passos's "Newsreels," though more rudimentary.

Reality is blended with fiction in a variety of ways in these books. Thanks to their creators, the heroes always manage to be in the right place at the right time. François not only sees Marie Antoinette on her way to the guillotine but is also lucky enough to spot the painter Jacques-Louis David at work on his famous sketches nearby. Barabant witnesses the bloody events of 10 August and 9 Thermidor. In *Ashes of Empire* Harewood participates in the sortie at Le Bourget, and Bourke sees the assaults on the Hôtel de Ville on 31 October 1870. Philip Landes is particularly favored by destiny and manages to be present at practically every event of importance in connection with the Commune: the fighting of 18 March, the arrest of General Lecomte and General Thomas, the fusillade of 22 March. He is even in the middle of a conversation with Archbishop Darboy when the latter is arrested; later, at the prison of Grande Roquette, he sees Darboy leaving for the firing squad. From time to time, minor historical figures move to the foreground, actually playing a part in the plot of a book. Amar and Grégoire, who were members of the Convention, and Flourens, one of the leaders of the Commune, become in *The Adventures of François* and *The Red Republic* respectively, authentic fictional characters.[5]

The heroes are able to get close to historical celebrities with providential ease. François plays the clown before the actor Talma and reads Robespierre's palm. Philip Landes chats with General Dombrowski, and his friend Alain de Carette visits the Louvre to talk to Thiers and MacMahon. In *Ashes of Empire* Bourke informs General Trochu of the presence of German spies. On 4 September 1870, Yolette and Hildé give up their cab to a lady in a hurry who turns out to be none other than the escaping Empress Eugénie. Upton Sinclair will later push this technique of fortuitous juxtaposition to its limits in the Lanny Budd novels, but perhaps the most extreme example among works considered here occurs in another scene from *Ashes of Empire*. In it Hildé strokes a carrier pigeon that has landed on her windowsill; then, when the bird has flown away, the narrator reveals to us that it bears a message for the governor of Paris, announcing the destruction of the Army of the East.

In order to make past events more real to readers whose knowledge of history is only superficial, the novelists attempt to forge a link between those events and the present. Sometimes this is done by linking the past that is narrated with the present narration. So it is the nephew of Gabrielle de Bergerac himself who relates the latter's life story to the narrator. Similarly, in "A Little More Burgundy" old M. Des Illes, in 1853, gives S. Weir Mitchell a preliminary account of the adventures of François, which he, too, was involved in as a child; but the biggest surprise for the reader in this story comes when he learns that the butler who has just served the drinks is none other than François himself, now almost a hundred years old. The authors also try to weave in bits of their own national history with that of France. Hence the husband of Gabrielle de Bergerac fought alongside the American insurgents, as did the son-in-law of M. de Ste Luce in *The Adventures of François*. Through real and fictional characters, Chambers plays up the importance of Americans in the crisis of 1870–71. First, German-Americans are shown in an unfavorable light. In "The Street of the First Shell" the German-American banker whom George West asks for help seems unusually well fed at a time when the siege is at its height. In the same story the student Hartman is convicted of treason and executed. In *Ashes of Empire* Speyer and Stauffer, correspondents for American newspapers written in German, turn out to be spies who are digging a tunnel beneath the fortifications from the house of the Chalais sisters. In a similar vein, Buckhurst, a New York gangster wanted by the police, begins a new life of crime with the francs-tireurs of Belleville.

Other Americans are shown in a more favorable light and make positive contributions to the resistance by setting up organizations such as the American Ambulance and Public Assistance. George West raises funds for this group, while Jack Trent enlists in the army, taking part in a counteroffensive. Ambassador Washbourne, who intervenes on behalf of Archbishop Darboy and whose residence is sacked during the events of Bloody Week, is often referred to in the texts. He settles Franco-American problems and is the first diplomat to give official recognition to the Third Republic, a gesture that earns him and his country instant acclaim in the capital. In *The Red Republic* the revolutionary students Sarre, Rigault, and Tribert reproach him with having censored the newspapers that he received during the siege, but according to Philip Landes he is "the only foreign representative in Paris who stuck to his post."[6]

The primary aim of these novelists is, quite clearly, to write adventure stories set against the background of a city in upheaval. This is indicated in their subtitles, where Chambers talks of "romance" and Mitchell of "adventures," as well as in the plots themselves, which bear witness to the authors' penchant for unpredictable and exciting situations. In some respects, the way in which they recreate this city of adventure belonging to a bygone era recalls the birth of the Paris of *Les Mystères*. In the latter, there was a transposition in space down toward the underworld of the city. The city of adventure moves back through time to periods that were particularly rich in dramatic moments and tense situations that were well suited to the working out of individual human destinies. However, the authors of historical adventure stories do not wish to transport their readers to imaginary realms that are totally foreign to their experiences. The fact that they make an obvious attempt to relate what they are describing to the experiences of their public, indicates, perhaps, that they were more concerned with didacticism than escapism. Their aim is not only to inform the reader of historical facts previously unknown to him but also to point up the lesson of all this history so different from his own. This lesson is essentially one of political conservatism.

The events narrated in *In the Name of Liberty*, whose title derives from Mme Roland's well-known declaration "Liberty! So many crimes are committed in thy name!" are such that this same title acquires a ring of bitter skepticism. Its epilogue, in particular, underlines the futility, the ultimate pointlessness, of the Revolution. Dossonville, returning from exile, discovers a Paris during the Empire in which there remains not the slightest trace of the spirit of 1789. Like Owen Johnson, S. Weir Mitchell has little sympathy for the Jacobins. Chapter 10 of *The Adventures of François* is called "How Pierre Became a Jacobin and How a Nation Became Insane." For him, the painter David is completely heartless and Robespierre a monster. Amar and Grégoire are constantly depicted in an unfavorable light. The Girondists have a better reputation. Barabant is a member of the faction, as is the husband of Gabrielle de Bergerac. The way in which Mitchell describes Marie Antoinette on her way to the scaffold is aimed primarily at enlisting the reader's sympathy for the ancien régime. It is true that the aristocrats are not always shown as being without fault, but even though they may be frivolous, they still know how to behave elegantly and courageously when they are in prison. And is it not true that they are the real friends of the common people, since it is they who offer François, the expert thief, the opportunity to reform? The latter sides with them without hesitation, explaining his behavior by the following profession of faith: "I am an aristocrat. I am at the top of my profession. I like naturally the folks who are on top."[7]

Chambers, in *The Red Republic*, is at pains to point out the faults of the Versailles government. Thiers is shown as ridiculous and cruel. The popular refrain "C'est Adolphe Thiers qu'on me nomme / Sacré nom d'un petit bonhomme" punctuates the bloody consequences of his decisions. Philip Landes, forced at one point to fight alongside the Communards, witnesses various atrocities perpetrated by the Versaillais. Nonetheless, the members of the Commune are shown as being much worse than the country's lawful representatives. They are nothing but a bunch of ill-disciplined drunks and cowards who cannot even agree among themselves. Weser kills Tribert; Sarre wants to force Philip to get rid of Rigault; Archie Walton, although he is a colonel in the Garde Nationale, dies at Grande Roquette, where he is imprisoned with soldiers of the government. But Chambers, in his profound aversion to chaos and anarchy, mixes bandits and revolutionaries indiscriminately. In his eyes, Flourens, Sapia, and Blanqui are assassins, and real looters such as Mon Oncle, Bibi-la-Goutte, and The Mouse are hardly distinguishable from the soldiers of the Garde Nationale. The Comité Central is "an obscure band of cutthroats who sat like buzzards watching the agonized city, until their moment should arrive to fatten on its ruins."[8] Chambers brutally attacks Leon Gambetta, and is even more scathing about Ernest Renan: "See him as he eats! His chin is fat, his belly fatter, his fat white fingers are spread out on either knee, the nails offensively untrimmed. He preaches universal brotherhood; he is on good terms with humanity. Incidentally he talks much, and familiarly about our Savior—and eats, eats, eats."[9]

In what way do these books prepare us for the literature of World War I? To begin with, there are certain superficial similarities. In all of these works, we see individual destinies being shaped by great historical events. But the way in which the facts are presented differs between the books of the First World War and earlier books. In these earlier novels, the heroes' adventures are summarily embroidered onto the historical narrative with little concern for verisimilitude. In the novels about World War I, the memories of the dramatic moments the authors have lived through inspire them with a greater respect for historical fact. In particular, the city no longer serves simply as a foil for the successive exploits of the hero. Its destiny and the destiny of the protagonist are more skillfully fused together, and the amalgam between real and imaginary characters also disappears. Moreover, the city of the war is less consistently described. Its presence in the novels is not built up through an accumulation of patiently researched detail but reduced to the concentrated residue of an intense experience. It is the creation of an eyewitness rather than that of a scholar. It is biographical rather than bibliographical.

Yet, these historical novels do contribute one or two important elements to the Parisian tableau. First, they show the capital in a state of complete upheaval, ruled by violence and death, an image in stark contrast to the visitors' impression of a city whose perfect harmony seems eternal. This new vision is incorporated into the general myth of Paris through a series of latent images. Typical of many descriptions of the city in chaos is Chambers's account of how it looked during Bloody Week:

Heavy explosions shook the city to its foundations; the splendid rue Royale was blazing, and the Ministry of Finance, its noble facade dripping with petroleum, caught fire and sent a roaring pillar of flame into the sky. Ruffians from Belleville and the Faubourgs dashed pails of petroleum over museums and palaces, or pumped it out of fire-engines, directing streams of kerosene from the great fire hose over wall, roof and spire. The Tuileries vomited flames from every window, the Louvre, the Palais Royale [*sic*], the Conseil d'Etat, the Palace of the Legion of Honor, all were burning.[10]

Although the circumstances are different, some descriptions of the Prussian bombing in 1871 or of the arrival of refugees in *Ashes of Empire* foreshadow scenes in novels of the First World War. Certain segments of Chambers's novels bear an uncanny resemblance to passages by Canfield or Wharton. Faced with the threat of German hegemony, for example, Chambers reacts exactly as Wharton later does in *The Marne*, when he has Cecil Bourke observe that "France, with all her faults has done more for human progress, human liberty—for everything that makes life worthwhile—than all the other European nations put together."[11]

But these similarities are more coincidental than essential. Examining different periods in the city's history, however, the authors also highlight what is essential—the unstable and changing nature of the city. Here the tragic and the absurd rub shoulders. It is as if the city dons a series of masks, changing its appearance from one minute to the next and from one neighborhood to another. When Philip Landes comes down from Montmartre on the evening of 18 March, he finds the boulevards packed with a joyful crowd completely indifferent to the events of the day: "That part of the city was perfectly tranquil. People sat smoking in front of all the cafés, precisely as if they knew nothing about the bloody tragedy of the rue des Rosiers. In front of Tortoni's, gay groups of ladies and gentlemen sipped their cordials, and street fakirs thronged the sidewalks and pressed their wares as usual. All the theatres were open and blazing with gas, vehicles crowded along the Boulevard des Italiens, and the terraces of the Café de la Paix."[12] Similar contrasts occur in wartime Paris, divided as it was between its role as a city of strategic importance and a city for the recreation of soldiers. For S. Weir Mitchell, Paris is quick to forget the past, without heart or memory. It is also frightening, for, in opposition to the elegant metropolis, aristocratic and refined, there exists an unpredictable city, plebeian, brutal, and barbarous, inciting its inhabitants to revolution and murder. It is just such a city that Strether is aware of while storm clouds gather on the horizon: "From beyond the window, and as from a great distance . . . came, as if excited and exciting, the vague voice of Paris. . . . On the eve of the great recorded dates, the days and nights of revolution, the sounds had come in, the omens, the beginnings broken out. They were the smell of revolution, the smell of the public temper—or perhaps simply the smell of blood."[13]

American writers are also struck by what they see as the Parisians' attitude of frivolous irresponsibility toward fundamentally tragic situations. Thus Mitchell depicts the prisoners of the Convention calmly playing cards while waiting to be executed. And Chambers describes how, in the early hours of the siege of 1870–71, an animated crowd begins to form, like expectant theatergoers, to see the Prussians take up their positions. While soldiers of the Commune are busy building barricades on the Place Saint-Sulpice, Philip Landes overhears a conversation in which a group of students and grisettes makes fun of a bandy-legged officer. "'His legs are Renaissance architecture—ladies, François Premier,' said a student . . . 'Not Renaissance,— Moorish!' put in another student. 'Look at him now as he stands—the rear view—a perfect Moorish arch! Those legs, ladies! admire this fragment from the Alhambra, imported by the government at enormous expense for the instruction of the Paris public!'"[14] This refusal to take things seriously, with its accompanying element of black humor, amazes the novelists. Yet in registering their surprise at this apparent paradox between the spirit of revolution and the spirit of festival, they unwittingly put their finger on one of the key factors in the peculiarly Parisian atmosphere—the urge toward transgression that two such apparently different impulses exemplify. The special gaiety that was first observed by the tourist seems, then, to have the same origin as the city's revolutionary atavism.

What effect does all this virile brutality have on the feminine nature of the capital? Pierre Citron notices a change in the attitude of French poets at the moment of the 1830 revolution. Paris, traditionally perceived as feminine, suddenly becomes masculine.[15] Does the same thing happen in American literature? The answer, on the grounds of such limited evidence as the texts provide, is tentative. If we see the city as being personified in various fictional characters, we must set beside the figure of François, who owes much to Gavroche in *Les Misérables,* the far more heroic figures of Nicole and Faustine. The former sacrifices her life for that of Barabant, and the latter, who is in love with Philip Landes, cold-bloodedly gives herself to Tribert for the revolutionary ideal and is later killed on a barricade while pleading for the life of Archbishop Darboy. Both these women, the flower seller and the grisette, are much more appropriate symbols of the city than Barabant, who is a provincial or, of course, Philip, who is an American.

Yet the mythical character of the city does acquire new attributes through its association with blood and violence. Its physiognomy is modified. Simultaneously victim and executioner, blood-stained and bloodthirsty, the woman-city provokes images of holocaust, rape, and parturition. In this collage of images, the *tricoteuses* of *In the Name of Liberty*, who knit while they await the beheadings, or the sinister Quatre-Pattes of *The Adventures of François* recall the Fates of antiquity, while the *pétroleuses,* throwing kerosene bombs during the Commune, may be seen as minor incarnations of the Furies. Even at the height of the insurrection, the city seems to preserve its femininity, though it is a femininity in which the perfumes of the boudoir have been overlaid with the dark smell of blood. In a text about the 1870 war by William Faulkner, Paris is depicted as a humiliated but eternally victorious woman. This image, close to the one that appears in the historical novels we have been considering, may be seen as an epigraph to the literary representation of the Paris of the First World War:

> [She was] never more dreamed after and adored than now, while in abasement. Never more was she, not France's Paris but the world's, the defilement being not only a part of the adored immortality and the immaculateness and therefore necessary to them, but since it was the sort of splendid abasement of which only Paris was capable, being capable of it made her the world's Paris: conquered—or rather, not conquered . . . the desired, the civilised world's inviolate and forever unchaste, virgin barren and insatiable; the mistress who renews her barren virginity in the very act of each barren recordless promiscuity, Eve and Lilith both to every man in his youth so fortunate and blessed as to be permitted within her omnivorous insatiable orbit.[16]

The Chronicle of Wartime Paris

Wartime Paris has distinctive geographical and historical features. Historically, the inhabitants live out their collective adventure in the context of a larger and much more universal drama. The portrait of the city stands out against a background of dates and events of worldwide significance, captured at a moment of change imposed by circumstances. But although the city's own local and personal chronicle is largely subordinate to the development of the war, the latter, for all its repercussions on the life of the capital, is nonetheless something that is taking place elsewhere. The few dozen miles that separate Paris from the front are sufficient to afford a sense of perspective and relative calm that permit the city to act as a sort of moral conscience.

What emerges, in effect, is a secondhand chronicle, in which the city is shown as a great unanimous being, a collective soul, whose reactions to the distant fighting are felt more strongly than its reactions to incidents in which it is immediately involved. Whereas many Americans saw the Parisians as cynical and indifferent, Troy Belknap, the young hero of *The Marne,* "was not shocked by the seeming indifference of Paris: he thought the gay theatres, the crowded shops, the restaurants groaning with abundance, were all healthy signs of the nation's irrepressible vitality. But he understood that America's young zeal might well be chilled by the first contact with this careless exuberance."[17] The city vibrates in spontaneous sympathy to reports of events such as the sinking of the Lusitania or rumors of atrocities or impending mutiny. Its destiny is so closely bound up with the fighting that even during the bombings, the Parisians are mainly concerned about what is happening at the front. "It was so obvious that the strained look on every face was not caused by the random fall of a few shells, but by the perpetual vision of that swaying and receding line on which all men's thoughts were fixed."[18] Edith Wharton's style is well suited to this sort of personification. For instance, after the announcement of the counteroffensive of April 1918, "Paris, irrepressibly, burst at once into abounding life. It was as if she were ashamed of having doubted, as if she wanted, by a livelier renewal of activities, to proclaim her unshakable faith in her defenders. In the perpetual sunshine of the most golden of springs she basked and decked herself, and mirrored her recovered beauty in the Seine."[19] Conversely, when the Chemin des Dames is retaken by the Germans on 25 May, "the air of Paris, that day, was heavy with doom. There was no mistaking its taste on the lips. It was the air of the Marne that [Troy] was breathing."[20] Through the use of personification and pathetic fallacy, the authors are able to give indirect commentaries on the military situation.

But reality soon imposes itself on the city in a more visible way. The collapse of the front line at Soissons in 1918 is made manifest in the capital by the sudden arrival of young girls in white dresses evacuated in the middle of their first communion ceremony and accompanied by the presiding bishop. Similarly, the first battle of the Marne, in August 1914, pushes the first ragged wave of refugees into Paris. "Every day the once empty vistas were filled with trains of farm-wagons, drawn by slow country horses, and heaped with furniture and household utensils; and beside the carts walked lines of haggard people, old men and women with vacant faces, mothers hugging babies, and children limping after them with heavy bundles. The fugitives of the Marne were pouring into Paris."[21] Gertrude Stein, who was still in London at the time, was told about the atmosphere of these first days of war by Parisians. Taxis, she learned, were no longer allowed out of the city center, and her friend Alfy Maurer described to her how he saw France's gold pass right under his nose: "I was sitting there and then I noticed lots of horses pulling lots of big trucks going slowly by and there were soldiers with them and on the boxes was written Banque de France. That was the gold going away just like that."[22]

The early days of the war gave rise to fewer descriptions than the later ones, doubtless because there were no American writers in the capital at the time, apart from Edith Wharton and possibly Samuel Merwin (the vividness and precision of certain scenes in *The Honey Bee* suggest that Merwin witnessed them at first hand). Richard Harding Davis was already at the front, and Gertrude Stein did not get back to Paris until 15 October. The final days of the Belle Epoque were observed by Wharton, who found herself in a situation similar to that of her hero, John Campton, in *A Son at the Front*. "In the hotel, in the hall, on the stairs, he was waylaid by flustered compatriots . . . who appealed to him for the very information he was trying to obtain for himself: how one could get money, how one could get hold of the concierge, how one could send cables, if there was any restaurant where the waiters had not all been mobilised, if he had any 'pull' at the Embassy, or any of the steamship offices, or any of the banks."[23] According to her biography, Wharton had just got back from a trip to Spain, after which she planned to go directly to Stocks, her home in England, when she suddenly found herself marooned in Paris with no money and no servants, forced to camp out in a deserted apartment, while on the other side of the Channel her entire household impatiently awaited the arrival of essential funds. It is astonishing that the novelist, who had lived in the Rue de Varenne for five years, and had spent some time in Berlin the previous year, seems not to have had the slightest idea that war was imminent. If we are to believe Gertrude Stein, Wharton's case is typical: "Americans living in Europe before the war never really believed there was going to be a war."[24] Edith Wharton indirectly criticizes her own lack of foresight by making her American characters in the same predicament utter incredible recriminations: "Why couldn't Germany let our government know? After all, Germany has no grievance against America. . . . And we've really spent enough money in Europe for some consideration to be shown us."[25]

Wharton records the different stages in the city's metamorphosis. *A Son at the Front* begins on 30 July 1914. The Avenue Marigny looks the same as ever: "In the golden decline of day, the usual throng of idlers sat under the horse-chestnuts of the Champs-Elysées, children scampered between turf and flowers, and the perpetual stream of motors rolled up the central avenue to the restaurants beyond the gates."[26] Two days later, however, with mobilization, the boulevards are transformed by the dense crowd pressing into the streets. "Hardly any vehicles were in sight: the motor omnibuses were already carrying troops to the stations . . . and only a few taxis and horsecabs, packed to the driver's box with young men in spick and span uniforms, broke through the mass of pedestrians which filled the whole width of the Boulevard. This mass moved slowly and vaguely, swaying this way and that, as though it awaited a portent from the heavens. In the flare of electric lamps and glittering theatre-fronts the innumerable faces stood out vividly, grave, intent, slightly bewildered."[27] But Paris settles down to wartime conditions. Children no longer play on the Champs-Elysées, and the city reminds Gertrude Stein of the way it was in her childhood. "It is strange, Paris is so different but so familiar. . . . I see what it is, there is nobody here but the french (there were no soldiers or allied there yet) you can see the little children in their black aprons, you can see the streets, it is just like my memory of Paris when I was three years old. The pavements smell like they used (horses had come back into use) the smell of french streets and french public gardens that I remember so well."[28]

Edith Wharton does not write about the end of the war in *The Marne* or *A Son at the Front,* but Dorothy Canfield, in "The Day of Glory," narrates in detail the events of 11 November 1918, in particular the demonstrations in front of the Strasbourg statue on the Place de la Concorde.

> As far as the eye could reach, the vast public square was black with the crowd, and brilliant with waving flags. A band up on the terrace of the Tuileries, stationed between the captured German airplanes, flashed in the air the yellow sheen of their innumerable brass instruments, evidently playing with all their souls, but not a sound of their music reached our ears, so deafening was the burst of shouting and singing as the crowd saw its goal. . . . We shook out our flags high over our heads, as we passed, we cast our flowers up on the pedestal. . . . At the base of the statue a group of white-haired Alsatians stood. . . . Theirs was the honor to arrange the flowers which, tossed too hastily by the eager bearers, fell to the ground.[29]

In *1919* the armistice surprises Dick Savage in Tours, but Eveline Hutchins, Eleanor Stoddard, and J. W. Moorehouse are all caught up in the general rejoicing of the capital. Recounting the various tribulations of Eveline, lost in the middle of a delirious crowd, Dos Passos tries to give his reader some idea of what it was like to be in Paris at that time:

The next moment, she was marching arm in arm with a little French sailor in a group of people mostly in Polish uniform who were following a Greek flag and singing *la Brabançonne.* A minute later she realized she'd lost the car and her friends and was scared. She couldn't recognize the streets even, in this new Paris full of arclights and flags and bands and drunken people. She found herself dancing with the little sailor in the asphalt square in front of a church with two towers, then with a French colonial officer in a red cloak, then with a Polish legionnaire who spoke a little English and had lived in Newark, New Jersey, and then suddenly some young French soldiers were dancing in a ring around her holding hands.[30]

The most interesting scenes in American accounts of Paris between the beginning and the end of the war are those that describe the various air raids on the capital. In *1919* and *Chosen Country* Dos Passos gives several such descriptions. As the Zeppelins, Gothas, and Fokkers only attacked on clear nights, moonlight is often an ingredient in these strange and unreal scenes painted by Dos Passos. Eveline Hutchins and Raoul Lemonnier watch a bombing raid from the heights of Montmartre as if they were theatergoers. "They stood on the porch of the Sacré Coeur and saw the Zeppelins come over. Paris stretched out cold and dead as if all the tiers of roofs and domes were carved out of snow and the shrapnel sparkled frostily overhead and searchlights were antennae of great insects moving through the milky darkness. At intervals came red snorting flares of the incendiary bombs. Just once they caught sight of two tiny silver cigars overhead. They looked higher than the moon."[31] The same scene recurs, in almost identical circumstances, in *Chosen Country,* where it is witnessed by Jay Pignatelli and Reggie Coleman. Dos Passos deliberately divests such incidents of their essentially dramatic elements. When Eveline is caught in a Fokker raid, for example, the biggest risk she runs comes from a drunken French colonel keen to take advantage of the situation. In a similar scene, Dick Savage also tries to accost a strange woman. In "Camera Eye 35" Dos Passos quotes the song about Big Bertha, "'Suis dans l'axe, 'suis dans l'axe, 'suis dans l'axe du gros canon!" and describes how a shell falling into the Seine produces a miraculous catch of fish for the Parisians.

In *The Deepening Stream* the tone is different. Canfield narrates in detail the events of 21 March 1918, the first day Big Bertha was fired. Everyone is mystified by this apparent series of daytime bombings, during which no planes can be heard. The notion that Paris is actually within range of a piece of enemy artillery is unthinkable. Perhaps the Germans are experimenting with a new toxic weapon? Canfield describes the basement of a lycée where a group of gradeschool children assemble with their mothers. The headmistress appeals to their courage and patriotism, and gets them to enact a scene from Molière. Matey Fort notes in particular that she forbids them to pray.

Other passages relate episodes which, though minor, are nonetheless indicative of the American presence. At the beginning of the war, John Campton, in *A Son at the Front,* watches as the American recruits for the Foreign Legion march past. Troy Belknap does the same in *The Marne:* "Then one day, in the sunny desert of the Place de la Concorde, he came on a more cheering sight. A motley band of civilians, young, middle-aged and even gray-headed, were shambling along together, badged and beribbonned, in the direction of the Invalides; and above them floated the American flag. Troy flew after it, and caught up with the last marchers. 'Where are we going? . . . Foreign Legion' an olive-faced 'dago' answered joyously in broken American. 'All 'nited States citizens . . . Come and join, sonnie.'"[32] Three years later, in *The Deepening Stream,* the Forts watch the arrival of the first regular American units who will participate in the Independence Day parade. The scene takes place on the morning of 3 July 1917, near a freight yard. After their initial shock at the sinister appearance of these soldiers, the crowd gives them an enthusiastic greeting. The Forts, however, with their ingrained Quaker and academic background, feel no common bond of sympathy with these totally alien-looking compatriots. "Here were lean, lanky, stony-faced men all of an age apparently, and certainly all of one predatory breed, with bulging jaw muscles, hard reckless eyes, and leathery skins burned to a uniform sallow brown by the sun of the Mexican border. . . . And now they were marching by the crowd on the side-walk—*left*! right! *left*!—swinging their long legs from loose hips, their hard small eyes impassive and expressionless in the leathery faces with the high cheek-bones."[33] The following day, 4 July 1917, John Campton watches the great military procession from the terrace of the Tuileries.

In the period immediately following the armistice, certain events stand out. First is the return of the prisoners at the Gare du Nord, the subject of a long description in *The Deepening Stream.* Among the wounded, Matey Fort comes across the husband of one the Vinet girls, who has been missing for four years. But the most newsworthy event is the arrival of President Wilson. In the biographical chapter of *1919* devoted to "Meester Vilson," Dos Passos describes the president's visit with a few deft, ironic strokes: "At the station in Paris he stepped from the train on to a wide carpet that led him, between rows of potted palms, silk hats, legions of honor, decorated busts of uniforms, frockcoats, rosettes, boutonnières, to a Rolls-Royce."[34] In *The Deepening Stream* Wilson's arrival is witnessed by Matey Fort, who, mingling with the crowd, bitterly observes the growing excitement of the Parisians: "When the guns boomed out a distant warning of the arrival of the train at the station the crowd surged forward in a rush that made Matey tremble. A woman near her shocked her by saying hysterically, 'It's on our knees we should be!' Every one made way so that the children could see. An escort of bicycle police flashed by. Down the street a sound of frantic cheering broke out. There was no military music, no roll of drums, only a car rolling quietly along the pavement."[35] The general strike of 1 May 1919 is described in *Three Soldiers* and *1919*. In the former the scene is closely observed by deserters, stuck in their hideouts, watching developments in the secret hope that a revolution will make it possible for them to come out of hiding. In the latter "Camera Eye 40" gives a series of impressionistic sketches of the day's events, the serious tone of which contrasts with the mood of Eveline Hutchins, Don Stevens, and Paul Johnson, who follow the progress of the strike much as if it were some popular fête. Finally, the last collective adventure of the war is provided by the victory parade of 14 July 1919, briefly depicted by Gertrude Stein in *The Autobiography of Alice B. Toklas:* "We saw it all, we saw first the few wounded from the Invalides, in their wheeling chairs wheeling themselves. . . . All the nations marched differently, some slowly, some quickly, the french carry their flag the best of all, Pershing and his officers carrying the flag behind him were perhaps the most perfectly spaced."[36]

The New Geography

Although the map of Paris was not suddenly transformed as if by magic, producing a whole new list of names and places, and although many traditional features associated with particular neighborhoods remained the same, the face of the city shows definite signs of change during the First World War. Its life is organized around new patterns, focusing on areas which have a direct relevance to what is happening in the war. The first thing that strikes us is the capital's new geographical relationship to the rest of the country. Many of the traditional routes leading to Paris are too dangerous to use or are simply cut off altogether. Paris can only be reached from the south, usually from Bordeaux. The soldiers of *One Man's Initiation*, Dick Savage in *1919*, Jay Pignatelli in *Chosen Country*, David Littledale in *The Wasted Generation*, and the Fort family in *The Deepening Stream* all arrive by this new route. In the reader's imagination, the familiar shape of the French hexagon seems to have undergone a distortion, pushing Paris farther north toward the vague, uncertain boundaries of a war-torn country. And this imaginary topography corresponds to what was happening in strategic terms: Paris suddenly becomes the crossroads of war and peace, the intersecting point for those returning from the war and those leaving for it. Soldiers stream endlessly in and out of the city. Paris is the hub of a turning universe in which railway stations suddenly acquire a dramatic significance. The Americans arrive and depart at the Gare d'Orsay or the Gare d'Orléans (now Austerlitz). The Gare de Lyon links the capital with the Italian front and the eastern theaters of operations. Above all, the Gare du Nord and the Gare de l'Est stand out on the Parisian landscape as the two prime symbols of the war, bringing its disquieting reality into the heart of the city. One day, Matey Fort goes to the Gare du Nord to meet her husband, who is returning from the front. In the turmoil and chaos of the teeming station she misses him, and she stands for a long time observing the by-now-familiar scenes of arrival and leave-taking. Dorothy Canfield evokes the same atmosphere in "A Little Kansas Leaven": "No one who has not seen the Gare de l'Est night after night can ever imagine the sum of stifled human sorrow which filled it thickly, like a dreadful incense of pain going up before some cruel god. . . . The great court outside, the noisy echoing waiting-room, the inner platform which was the uttermost limit for those accompanying the soldiers returning to hell,—they were not only filled with living hearts broken on the wheel, but they were also thronged with ghosts."37

Hospitals and relief centers also spring into prominence. As might be expected, the most frequently mentioned is the American Hospital at Neuilly. Richard Harding Davis sings its praises in *With the Allies* and explains how the organizers of the hospital also created an autonomous ambulance service operating out of the new building of the Lycée Pasteur. Before receiving his repatriation orders, Dick Savage works in an annex of the American Hospital on the Avenue du Bois-de-Boulogne. In *A Son at the Front* the painter René Davril dies in an establishment near the Palais Royal where Mrs. Talkett works. George Campton undergoes treatment in a reeducation center near the Bois de Boulogne and in a hospital in the Rue de Rivoli, which would appear to be housed in the Hôtel Continental. The big charitable organizations that throw an umbrella of salvation over the city are not always given precise locations. Dorothy Canfield, for example, through motives of discretion, or perhaps to underline the fact of their omnipresence, gives no definite address for the numerous offices in which Matey Fort battles against inexcusable bureaucratic absurdities of various American organizations. The administrative headquarters of the Red Cross, where Eleanor Stoddard and Eveline Hutchins work, is in the rue de Rivoli. In "A Little Kansas Leaven" and *The Deepening Stream* Canfield describes what was known as a "vestiaire"—a sort of independent help center and ladies workroom, which was set up through private initiative but received supplies from larger organizations. Ellen Boardman helps Mrs. Putnam, a New England aristocrat, to keep the books for the vestiaire she has opened in the Rue Pharaon, whose general appearance is somewhat disorienting:

> At the rue Pharaon, number 27, Ellen was motioned across a stony gray courtyard littered with wooden packing-cases into an immense, draughty, dark room, that looked as though it might have been originally the coach and harness-room of a big stable. This also was strewed and heaped with packing-cases in indescribable confusion, some opened and disgorging innumerable garments of all colors and materials, others still tightly nailed up. . . . In one corner on a bench, sat a row of wretchedly poor women and white-faced, silent children, the latter shod more miserably than the poorest negro child in Marshallton.[38]

Mme Vinet and Matey Fort work in another vestiaire in the Rue Pascal. In *The Marne* Mme Lebuc, the former governess of Troy Belknap, works for a refugee organization where the young man finds the mother of M. Gantier, his tutor who was killed in action. John Campton is one of the founders of "The Friends of French Art," an association set up to help the families of artists who have been drafted, which has its headquarters in a famous restaurant at the Palais Royal, which can only have been le Grand Véfour. A picturesque confusion reigns throughout:

> Behind the plate-glass windows young women with rolled-up sleeves and straw in their hair were delving in packing cases, while, divided from them by an improvised partition, another group were busy piling on the cloak-room shelves garments such as had never before dishonoured them. Campton stood fascinated by the sight of the things these young women were sorting: pink silk combinations, sporting ulsters . . . and fringed and bugled garments that suggested obsolete names like "dolman" and "mantle." . . . Was it possible that "The Friends of French Art" proposed to clothe the families of fallen artists in these prehistoric properties?[39]

The coming of peace divests such places of most of their importance. After 11 November, the main focus of military Paris shifts to the Hôtel

Crillon, which henceforth becomes the symbol par excellence of American diplomacy. For Dos Passos "the hub of this Paris was the hotel de Crillon on the place de la Concorde, its artery the rue Royale where arriving dignitaries . . . were constantly parading escorted by the garde républicaine in their plumed helmets."⁴⁰ Inside the hotel, the corridors "were lively as an anthill with scuttling khaki uniforms, marine yeomen, messenger boys, civilians; a gust of typewriter clicking came out from every open door. At every landing groups of civilian experts stood talking in low voices, exchanging glances with passersby, scribbling notes on scratchpads. Miss Stoddard grabbed Dick's arm with her sharp white fingers. 'Listen . . . it's like a dynamo.'"⁴¹ Dick Savage comes here to try to get his repatriation orders revoked. Jay Pignatelli, in similar circumstances, bumps into an old friend, Mortlake, as he is visiting the hotel. In *Three Soldiers* Aubrey, the journalist, turns up regularly in the middle of the night in hopes of gleaning confidential tidbits from the tipsy diplomats on their way to bed. Matey Fort is invited to dinner there by her brother, who is a member of the American delegation. Moorehouse has his headquarters in the hotel, and it is there that he gives his last press conference before returning to the United States. Lily Shane, in *The Green Bay Tree,* comes across the Governor there, her former lover and the father of her son Jean. The Crillon is the place where everyone meets and where all important decisions are made. John Andrews, venturing into the lobby on one occasion, is put off by the atmosphere. "It had the smell he remembered having smelt in the lobbies of New York hotels,—a smell of cigar smoke and furniture polish. On one side a door led to a big diningroom. . . . There was a sound of jingling spurs and jingling dishes from the restaurant, and near where Andrews stood . . . sprawled in a leather chair a fat man with a black felt hat over his eyes and a large watch chain dangling limply over his bulbous paunch. He cleared his throat occasionally with a rasping noise and spat loudly into the spittoon beside him."⁴² Despite the fact that President Wilson stayed at the Hôtel de Murat, the Crillon is without doubt the dominant symbol of 1919.

The war also gives other areas of the city new meaning. For Dos Passos, the Rue Sainte-Anne brings to mind the brutality of the Military Police, who had their headquarters there, and the Rue Saint-Honoré, with its office of the School Detachment, recalls those soldiers with permission to continue their studies in Paris. For Don Stevens in *1919,* the Rue du Croissant is the tragic reminder of Jean Jaurès's vain efforts to avert the war, while the Square du Vert Galant reminds Scott Bronson, in *Chosen Country,* of Henri IV's great scheme for the unification of Europe at the beginning of the seventeenth century. Jay Pignatelli thinks the name of the Rue de la Paix should now be changed, and John Andrews finds the architecture of the Place des Victoires particularly incongruous in the circumstances. "He came to an oval with a statue of a pompous personage on a ramping horse. 'Place des Victoires,' he read the name, which gave him a faint tinge of amusement. He looked quizzically at the heroic features of the sun king and walked off laughing. 'I suppose they did it better in those days, the grand manner,' he muttered. And his delight redoubled in rubbing shoulders with people whose effigies would never appear astride ramping-eared horses in squares to commemorate victories."[43]

But perhaps the most significant change relates to festive Paris. The war has a direct bearing on this aspect of the city, giving it a distinctive character, which, curiously, is little affected by the coming of peace. The diplomats who arrive after the armistice regard the city as having the same cathartic function that it had had as a city behind the lines. In the broken time scale of *1919*, for example, it is often impossible to tell whether certain festivities take place during the war or after it. The essence of Parisian festivity, residing in the art of juxtaposing the serious and the frivolous, has a certain autonomy that allows it to remain impervious to outside events. But, in other respects, the festive city is transformed after 1914. It becomes associated with different places and establishments, and changes from a daytime to a night-time phenomenon. Tourist Paris, however, with its more conventional, daytime aspects, does not disappear altogether. In the middle of the war, Pignatelli gives his friend Scott Bronson a detailed tour of the city center. John Andrews visits Malmaison with Jeanne and wanders through the countryside near Herblay and Chartres with Geneviève Rod. Moorehouse and his entourage go to Chantilly on a picnic. The special situation of American soldiers and civilians—their relative affluence, their culture, or at least their curiosity—enables them to keep in touch with what remains of the tourist infrastructure. The traditional jewels in the city's crown are often mentioned: the Café de la Paix, the Ritz, Maxim's, and the Opéra.[44] There are now many new hotels, some of which are being used as billets. Above all there are lots of restaurants: exclusive places like the Tour d'Argent, Larue, Voisin, and Noel Peters, but also the Poccardi, the Weber, the Médicis, and the Madrid, or even the Rat qui Danse, the Taverne Nicolas Flamel, or Rumpelmeyer's tearoom.[45] Apart from the Opéra, where General Goureau attends a performance of *Castor et Pollux,* various theaters are mentioned. Among these are the Opéra Comique, featuring *Louise* and *Pelléas et Mélisande;* the Odéon; the Olympia, where Herman gets thrown out in a scene in

Three Soldiers; and the Théâtre Caumartin, where Staunton Wills, in *1919*, sees an actress he particularly likes.[46] In an unnamed theater Martin Howe hears the public break into a spontaneous rendering of "La Madelon" in *One Man's Initiation*. In another theater there is yet another performance of *Cyrano de Bergerac*, which Heineman claims to have seen "twice sober and seven other times."[47] John Andrews, a former student at the Schola Cantorum, often goes to the Salle Gaveau, the Concerts Colonne, and the Concerts Lamoureux.

The numbers of cafés mentioned is surprisingly small. Apart from the Café de la Paix, the establishment that is described at greatest length is the little café where John Andrews works on his musical scores. Jay Pignatelli and Scott Bronson make a pilgrimage to the Café de Paris to drink a toast to the memory of Flaubert and Turgenev, John Andrews is a regular at the Rohan, and the Napolitain is mentioned in *1919*. By and large, however, the war seems to have deprived Parisian cafés of the special privileges they once enjoyed in the eyes of the Americans. One reason for their declining popularity can be found in their rapidly dwindling terraces, hard hit by the chronic shortage of waiters and the wartime lighting restrictions. It is as if the spirit of Parisian gaiety, directly affected by the spectacle of the city huddled around its dim blue lights, has moved indoors and set up quarters in dark, enclosed places. In any case, the Parisian atmosphere is now exemplified not so much in the large open cafés spilling out onto the pavements but in the discreet intimacy of places like Harry's Bar. Harry's, with its walnut panelling and inviting gloom, heralds the arrival of the cabaret, private and anonymous, as the new center of the Paris of pleasure. With the exception of the Noctambules, all these cabarets are to be found somewhere on the hillside of Montmartre. Jay Pignatelli visits a gypsy cabaret there, and Daughter, after leaving the Folies Bergère, spends an eventful night at the Hermitage with George Barrow. Moorehouse invites Eleanor and Eveline to go dancing at the Abbaye, whose interior is entirely decorated with Allied flags. John Andrews and his friends visit the Lapin Agile, made fashionable among Moorehouse's coterie by Edgar Robbins, rechristening it Freddy's, a corruption of the name of Frédé, the singer. "Robbins' favorite hangout was Freddy's up back of Montmartre. They'd sit there all evening in the small smokycrowded rooms while Freddy, who had a big white beard like Walt Whitman, would play on the guitar and sing. . . . People at the tables would get up and recite long poems about La Grand'route, La Misère, L'Assassinat or sing old French songs like *Les Filles de Nantes*. If it went over everybody present would clap hands in unison. They called that giving a bon [*sic*]."[48]

Montmartre is the true heart of the festive city, the inevitable last stopping place for the nightwalkers before they split up and scatter into the shadows below. As Henslow says in *Three Soldiers,* "The Butte is the boss on the middle of the shield. It's the axle of the wheel. That's why it's so quiet, like the centre of a cyclone or a vast whirling rotary circus parade."[49] This description underscores the violent forces sweeping through the city, a relentless whirling motion in which the characters are caught up willy-nilly. The protagonists rush from one place to the next; Moorehouse and his little group start the evening at the Poccardi, move on to the Opéra, continue their rounds at the Café de la Paix and the Abbaye, and finally end up at the Lapin Agile. Daughter has cocktails at the Ritz and dinner at the Hermitage before moving on to Maxim's; from Maxim's she goes to a hooligan's ball, from the ball to Les Halles for an onion soup, and, as dawn breaks, from Les Halles to an airplane ride that will end in death. This acceleration in time, like a sped-up replay of a film, contributes to the disjointed, disoriented nature of nighttime Paris.

Montmartre is also the gateway to the closed and secret world of prostitution, a world hinted at since the beginnings of the Parisian theme in American literature, but never directly discussed, which finally enters American fiction forthrightly through the novels of Dos Passos. Prostitution is omnipresent. It is most notable in Montmartre, but we see it elsewhere: on the Place Saint-Michel, on the boulevards, around the Gare Saint-Lazare, in front of the unknown church near a metro station where Jay Pignatelli meets a prostitute called Jeanne. When night falls and the cafés lower their metal grilles, the *filles de joie* take possession of the city. Dick Savage discovers their existence on his first night in the capital. "There was almost no traffic but the boulevards were full of strollers in the blue June dusk. As it got darker women leaned out towards them from behind all the trees, girls' hands clutched their arms, here and there a dirty word in English burst like a thrown egg above the nasal singsong of French."[50] The same surprise, described in almost identical terms, awaits Martin Howe and Tom Randolph in *One Man's Initiation:* "Everywhere girls of the streets, giggling alluringly in hoarse, dissipated tones, clutching the arms of drunken soldiers, tilting themselves temptingly in men's way as they walk along."[51]

Touts are on the lookout for soldiers wanting a good time; Jay and his friends, for instance, are solicited by "an individual with patent leather hair and eyes in deep creases above high flushed cheeks, dressed in a sort of Balkan uniform."[52] The pimp and the prostitute lead the reader over the threshold of the "maisons closes." After meeting Suzette, Minette, and Annette, in a shelter, Dick Savage and his friends are taken to "a closely shuttered house where they were ushered into a big room with livercolored wallpaper that had green roses on it. An old man in a green baize apron brought up champagne and the girls began to sit on knees and ruffle up hair. Summers got the prettiest girl and hauled her right into the alcove where the bed was with a big mirror above the whole length of it."53 Later Dick meets up with some Australians and goes off to a different place. "They tried to get a show put on, but the madam said the girls were busy and the Australians were too drunk to pay attention and started to wreck the place."54 To the girls who work in such establishments, Reggie Coleman, in *Chosen Country,* prefers the ordinary street walker, with her enticing aura of mystery and adventure, inviting the passerby to step from the world of normality into the other world behind the shuttered facades of small hotels. It is to one of these that Jay takes Jeanne; and Dick, too, accompanied by one of these ladies of the night, goes into "a little hotel on the back street behind his own."55

The Paris of sexual pleasure is only one step away from the city that offers more conventional pleasures of good living. But to reach it demands from the prospective voyager a special effort, a casting-off into the unknown. This is what Jay feels, naively regarding the spectacle of all the women offering themselves to his gaze as he walks along the boulevards. "He was remembering a picture he'd seen that morning at the Louvre. The pavement of the grands boulevards were quays, like the quays of Casanova's Venice, where in the dim spring light in the scent of lily of the valley you embarked for the island of carnal love: *Embarcation [sic] pour Cythère.*"56 This departure, symbolizing the character's amorous initiation, also corresponds to a new departure in the literary representation of the city. Dos Passos introduces a Paris in which the bedroom of the "hôtel de passe" is a key image. After the theater, the restaurant, the café, and the cabaret, diverse characters in American war novels now move on to this room. Lost in a disintegrating urban universe, separate and anonymous, it provides a shelter for loves that have no past and no future. "L'homme sans nom et la femme sans nom, vont faire l'amour a l'hotel [sic] du néant," Dick Savage tells his companion for the night. But the room within this "hôtel du néant" exists. It is a real part of the city's landscape, hitherto unmentioned, masked by more conventional monuments. Dos Passos acknowledges its existence and gives it its rightful place on the map of the city. A new aspect of the capital is finally revealed to the reader as the door swings open: "There was a big bed, a bidet and a lot of heavy claret-colored hangings."57

CHAPTER 5

ACTORS AND SPECTATORS
IN THE PARIS OF WORLD WAR I

Costume Characters

The period of the First World War brought the emergence of new types of characters whose functions were related directly to the capital's new and urgent needs. Literature had, up to this point, presented an image of Parisian society constructed around easily identifiable groups, but this structure begins to disintegrate, as evinced in the novels of writers like Edith Wharton, during the war. In the cataclysmic upheaval of the war, characters are shaken up and jostled into new positions, creating new relationships and social patterns. Each character is now seen literally or figuratively in some kind of uniform.

Within this realignment, traces of the old order may still be found through various characters who have managed to adapt, to accomplish some sort of transition that enables them to survive the shake-up. Several characters of this sort appear in Wharton's novels. The nobility is represented by Mme de Tranlay and her daughter in *A Son at the Front,* who, like the duchesse de Murols, attended Madge Talkett's salon. Mme de Dolmetsch belongs to the sisterhood of *aventurières.* Fortin-Lescluze is a member of the upper classes, a professor of medicine. *A Son at the Front* recalls the American colony of prewar days, with characters like John Campton, who is a painter; Brant, a banker; the Talketts; Adele Anthony; and Boylston, a student. Julia Ambrose, who divorces Campton to marry Brant, has received an upbringing—split between a Parisian convent and a Venetian palace—similar to that of certain Jamesian heroines. *The Marne,* too, offers a portrait of a milieu we are familiar with from earlier novels—rich, cultured, and international. The central character, Troy Belknap, is the son of a family of Europeanized millionaires, who comes to France each year with his mother to rejoin his governess and continue his studies in French culture with his tutor, M. Gantier. Troy, a model hero, whose decision to enlist in the army befits his noble image, is a somewhat irritating character, strongly reminiscent of the comtesse de Ségur's heroes. Similarly, the mawkishly idealized Francophile milieu, still effortlessly bilingual, seems to come from an earlier age. Dos Passos's hero Jay Pignatelli also has links with the past, thanks to a childhood in some respects comparable to Troy's; but Jay, unlike Troy, perceives the wartime capital in a way that is totally free of any emotional associations with the earlier part of his life. The relics of the past that can be found in the literature of this period are scattered randomly and achieve some sort of coherence only in passages whose function is either introductory or retrospective.

The characters in these novels come from a far wider range of social backgrounds than before. The Vinets in *The Deepening Stream,* Geneviève Rod in *Three Soldiers,* Honorine Bruhl in *Chosen Country,* and Raoul Lemonnier and Maurice Millet in *1919* are all members of the educated middle class. The Davrils, to whom John Campton offers assistance, are working-class people, like the Gantiers, or the family of the soldier that Ellen Boardman meets at the Gare de l'Est in "A Little Kansas Leaven." Olga, the mistress of Dick Savage's brother comes from a milieu bordering on the underworld. The war has effectively destroyed barriers of birth, wealth, and education, allowing people from different backgrounds to mix freely. Wharton occasionally deplores the results of such interaction, which—describing the random assortment of guests at the Talketts' salon—she dubs "war promiscuities."[1] Through the medium of war charities and similar institutions, people are now able to form relationships outside their own social groups. A striking example of changing social mores occurs when George Campton's batman is invited to the Brants'. The war also transforms the relationship between Mme Vinet and her maid. John Campton shares the joys and sorrows of his concierge so intimately that he asks her to pose for him.

The Americans are affected by a further change. Before the war, only those with adequate financial means could enjoy the luxury of a trip to Europe. This does not mean that all American visitors to Paris were millionaires. Eveline Hutchins, Matey Fort, and J. W. Moorehouse, for example, none of whom are from particularly wealthy backgrounds, have all visited the capital before. But Eveline is the daughter of a clergyman, Matey the daughter of an academic, and Moorehouse a social climber who "married money." The war changes this state of affairs, and the new tourists are in uniform, traveling at the army's expense or financed by some kind of charity. They can be regarded as "Grand Tour upstarts" insofar as the war has granted them the privilege of a trip to Paris, often involving an extended stay in luxurious conditions. To some degree, Eleanor, Daughter, and Dick Savage all belong to this category. Ellen Boardman, a typist from Marshallton, Kansas, is an exception. A member of the working class, she is transformed into a figure of patronage when she draws out all her savings and comes to Paris at her own expense to volunteer her services. Once her small nest egg has vanished, she simply goes home like Cinderella after the ball. Her idealism transports her beyond the boundaries of her class, giving her a role that would not normally have befallen her. The same is true of Matey Fort, who uses her aunt's legacy to run help centers. She is temporarily assigned the role of philanthropist, a role for which her background has not prepared her and whose more social and worldly side she rejects completely.

Rich and poor, Eastern intellectuals and Midwestern rustics, are all thrown together in the capital in a proximity that does not fail to produce friction. The members of the American colony who have survived the beginning of the war and chosen to remain are none too pleased by these successive waves of nurses and ambulance men who, resplendent in their new uniforms, plant their organizations in the city like flags in a newly conquered territory. Wharton's irritation is evident, describing the "wasp-waisted youths in sham uniforms who haunted the reawaking hotels and restaurants in the frequent intervals between their ambulance trips to safe distances from the front."² The new arrivals, in their turn, develop their own system of social snobbery based on how long people had been in the capital and how many times they had been to the front. All of them, without exception, turn resentfully on those Americans who come to make peace after the fighting is over and who act as if they were the ones responsible for winning the war. A quotation from *The Autobiography of Alice B. Toklas* summarizes the general attitude toward these late arrivals: "Gertrude Stein described one of the young men of the peace commission who was holding forth as one who knew all about war, he had been here ever since the peace."³ Class reactions to the Americans brought to Paris by the war are also evident, as may be seen in the remarks of a distinguished American lady reacting to the vulgarization of volunteer work: "I disapprove wholly of those foolish American volunteers . . . ignorant, awkward, provincial boors, for the most part, knowing nothing of all the exquisite old traditions of France, who thrust themselves forward. They make America a laughing-stock."⁴

The Americans, along with all the other characters, fall into their allotted place in the great scheme of national strategy, where no behavior is innocent and where the mere fact of being in Paris carries within it its own justification. Like pawns on the city's chessboard, they are each given a second identity through the roles they play and the costumes they wear. The war draws a divide that cannot be crossed in the city's international milieux. On one side are those who are French; on the other, those who are not. This produces one or two surprises: Mme de Dolmetsch's lover, Ladislas Isidor, who everyone presumed to be a foreigner, is suddenly called up. George Campton, though American, did his national service in France, and therefore he, too, is mobilized. Wharton exploits this unusual situation in order to underscore the disadvantages of dual nationality, as she did in *Madame de Treymes* in regard to French divorce laws. George's parents are Americans, but he, like his father, was born in Paris; consequently, on his return from Harvard, he is considered French, whereas his father, who has lived in Paris all his life, is technically considered a neutral until 1917. The tangible proof of belonging to the country consists, for the men, of the document that John Campton examines as his son is sleeping in a room at the Crillon, a "thumbed and dirty red book the size of a large pocket diary . . . it was the livret militaire that every French citizen under forty-eight carries about with him."[5] Again, Wharton focuses attention on the identity crisis suffered by the American colony and on the ambiguity of its position. Relegated to the limbo of neutrality until 1917, Americans in Paris are unhappy with their role as foreigners. The questions that John Campton asks himself are typical of those asked by all the expatriates of Edith Wharton's set. "But *was* he a foreigner, Campton asked himself? And what was the criterion of citizenship if he, who owed to France everything that made life worth while, could regard himself as owing her nothing, now that for the first time he might have something to give her."[6]

Just as the war highlights the hitherto ill-defined contours of nationalities, it draws a line between the sexes, pigeonholing individuals in a simplistic and categorical way. Its basic and elementary rigor allows us to review the newly emergent Parisian types and to proceed to a roll call of the different characters. The soldiers are, by far, the most numerous. First, there are the French, visible everywhere in their uniforms whose basic color was changed in 1916 from madder red to sky blue. But there are the Allies, too, Englishmen, Australians, New Zealanders, Poles, and also Serbs, whose uniforms resemble those of the Americans after 1917. For the most part, they are in Paris on leave, strolling up and down the main boulevards, christened "Cosmopolis" by John Andrews, in contrast to the quieter Left Bank, which is slightly off the beaten track. Equally familiar are the uniforms of the American ambulance men serving with the various organizations that spring up and sometimes disappear: the Norton-Harjes group and the divisions of the Red Cross, to which Dick Savage belongs one after the other; the Quaker organizations where Adrian Fort works; the companies attached to the French army, like the one Henslow works for, or the Near East Relief and the Italian

Red Cross. Two new types stand out in Dos Passos's works: first of all, the "Y man," the representative of the YMCA, the fumbling earnest spokesman of official policy, whose uniform is adorned with a crucifix, and second, the "Red Cross major," a burlesque soldier petrified at the sound of the shelling, who makes sure he conducts his war from the relative safety of his office in the Crillon, or in the Rue de Rivoli. It is thus that Moorehouse makes his entry on the Parisian scene, anxiously scanning the sky when there is a full moon, terrified at the thought of an air raid. After the armistice, members of the School Detachment, like Jay Pignatelli, Paul Johnson, and John Andrews, hang about the benches of the Sorbonne, an incongruous sight in their worn uniforms.

Although other characters are in civilian clothing, the reasons for their presence in the capital are quite clear. There are journalists like Jerry Burnham and Don Stevens who appear in *1919,* Aubrey in *Three Soldiers,* and Hibbert Hopewell and Carl Humphries in *Chosen Country;* bureaucrats and civilian experts like Robbins and Rasmussen; and diplomats like Francis Gilbert. And, waiting on the sidelines, are those who are too old to fight, the impotent Gérontes of the bloody farce. As John Campton says to his friend Dastrey, "Men our age are the chorus of the tragedy, Dastrey; we can't help ourselves. As soon as I open my lips to blame or praise I see myself in white petticoats, with a long beard held on by an elastic, goading on the combatants in a cracked voice from a safe corner of the ramparts. On the whole I'd sooner be spinning among the women."[7] The women, too, are noncombatants; but they have their allotted part in this new distribution of roles. Streetwalkers, posted at intervals along the route of soldiers on leave, seem little more than cardboard cutouts. Other women appear simply as victims, as do Mme Gantier and, to a certain extent, Mme Vinet, but the great majority of women devote themselves to the traditional task of ministering to the sick and wounded. With a few exceptions, these women all appear dressed as nurses.

The nurse's uniform is a part of wartime reality, and the Americans, more than the French, seem to get a great deal of pleasure out of wearing it. Troy Belknap is amused to see them on the Atlantic crossing, "cocked-hatted, badged, and gaitered—though most of them apparently, were going to sit in offices of Paris war-charities, and Troy had never noticed that Frenchwomen had donned khaki for that purpose."[8] Madge Talkett, reporting to the hospital for duty, creates a new image for herself which takes John Campton by surprise: "A Red Cross nurse advanced: not the majestic figure of the Crimean legend, but the new version evolved in the Rue de la Paix: short skirts, long ankles, pearls, and curls."[9] George's mother undergoes a similar transformation: "She had made herself a nurse's face; not a theatrical imitation of it like Mme de Dolmetsch's, not yet the face of a nurse on a warposter, like Mrs. Talkett's. Her lovely hair smoothed away under her strict coif, her chin devoutly framed in linen, Mrs. Brant looked serious, tender, and efficient. Was it possible that she had found her vocation?"[10] A hierarchy is established among the women, starting with subalterns like Ellen Boardman, moving up to people with a certain amount of influence like Matey Fort, and finishing, at the top, with powerful entrepreneurial figures like Mme de Tranlay, Mrs. Whitlock, and Mrs. Belknap. The latter's largesse, while suffering from the pneumonia that kept her in the capital in 1914, confirms her right to privilege. "Meanwhile, having quite recovered, she rose from her cushions, donned a nurse's garb, poured tea once or twice at a fashionable hospital and on the strength of this effort, obtained permission to carry supplies (in her own motor) to the devastated regions."[11]

Finally, half hidden in the wings, away from the footlights, are other, furtive characters, with different roles. First and foremost in this new version of *Les Mystères de Paris,* is the spy, to whom it is difficult to ascribe a particular costume. Who exactly is he? The innocent-looking waiter in the corner café? The mysterious person who tried to rob and kill the dispatch rider that John Andrews meets at Malmaison? He blends into the shadows of the wall on which Eveline Hutchins reads the warning "Méfiez-vous les oreilles enemies [*sic*] vous écoutent."[12] He is the object of the attempts by French journalists in 1917 to deliberately exaggerate the importance of American aid. In *The Autobiography of Alice B. Toklas* Gertrude Stein seems to think that spy-mania is not an imaginary illness. It is her opinion that Udel, the art collector, was working for the German secret service, along with the sculptor Honnebeck, who in 1914 photographed all the cities in the north of France from the top of church belfries, claiming that the views he obtained reminded him of Delaunay's paintings. But the invisible spy is not the only one who challenges the system or secretly plots its downfall. There are also deserters, soldiers gone AWOL, who, in *Three Soldiers,* hide out at the "Chink's" in the Rue des Petits Jardins, and, in *Chosen Country,* members of the "Club des Communards," where socialists gather in a part of the Buttes-Chaumont carefully avoided by the police. The bargeman who rescues John Andrews is a confirmed anarchist. Guided by the author in "Camera Eye 41," the subjective eye of the camera surprises a group of anarchists having a picnic on the banks of the Seine, their mood providing an ironic counterpart to the prevailing spirit of patriotic militancy in the city.

This chorus line of characters gives an initial image of Parisian wartime society. The sheer numbers of the protagonists, particularly in 1919, tend to diminish their individual significance, and their ceaseless, manic activity gives them the air of automatons who can be reduced to immobility at the throw of a switch. But this emphasis on the importance of wearing a uniform has other implications. For men and women involved in a collective adventure that surpasses their understanding, their costume also serves as a disguise. Their roles presuppose the hidden tensions common to all actors. Inside each uniform is an individual; inside each individual, a personal conflict mirrors the vast historical conflict in which he or she is an actor.

Morale and Morals

In the literature of the First World War, under the combined effect of a new moral permissiveness and the direct or indirect presence of danger and death, the individual's behavior and system of values are considerably modified. Furthermore, the breakdown of traditional social relationships leaves a vacuum that will be filled by a new type of social interaction more suited to the circumstances. Its keynotes are make-believe and improvisation. Finally, political morality enters Parisian life for the first time, affecting the characters in different ways depending on the dictates of their individual consciences. All decisions, collective or individual, will henceforth be influenced by the problematic relationship between morale and morals, by the delicate balancing act of keeping up one's spirits and not succumbing to the pressure of events while at the same time keeping up standards and preserving some sort of ethical system.

The individual characters see the fact of wearing a uniform in different ways. For some, it is an embarrassment or even a form of mutilation. Jay Pignatelli and Dick Savage are punished for their pacifist beliefs, and John Andrews, who wanted to be a musician, ends up unloading sacks of cement in a disciplinary battalion in Passy. Figuratively, in the case of Andrews, and literally, in the case of Davril in *A Son at the Front,* a uniform leads to the death of the artist. The failure of these Americans to adapt to a situation of their own choosing calls into question the nature of their initial decision. In the American collective consciousness, however, wearing a uniform has other, quite different, implications. First, it offers a kind of protective coloring for unsophisticated characters like Dan Fuselli in *Three Soldiers* or Martin Howe in *One Man's Initiation.* Secondly, it has sexual connotations that are in keeping with those of Paris. It defines the individual simplistically, reducing him or her to an identity consisting of two elements, national and sexual. The soldier, conforming to military norms that do not accord with civilian morality, is now able to give free rein to his instincts and to live out his fantasies. At the same time, losing his identity, he becomes a sort of mass-produced sex object of a basic and interchangeable kind. When Jeanne says to Pignatelli that she is not a prostitute because she only goes with soldiers,[13] she is doubtless identifying all her different partners with one single image in her imagination, *the* soldier. In its emphasis on increased sexual availability, the uniform acts as an antidote to traditional puritanism. Paris, city of debauchery par excellence, is beyond the soldier's wildest dreams. "I'd heard that Paris was immoral, but nothing like this,"[14] says one of the characters of *One Man's Initiation.* This aspect of the capital comes to be seen as a veritable "battle of Paris," in which the characters all take part, and in which some are comparatively innocent victims, as is Fuselli, who ends up getting syphilis. As the song quoted by Dos Passos says: "Oh that battle of Paree / It's making a bum out of me / Toujours la femme et combien."[15]

What is new about the situation is that the women are now a part of it. Female sexual liberation is well under way. Canfield, in *The Deepening Stream,* gives an ironic description of a young volunteer from Iowa, dazzled at the mere thought of Maxim's and determined to live life to the full while she is in France.[16] This young woman, bent on gathering rosebuds while she may—like Eleanor, Daughter, and Eveline in *1919* or even Madge Talkett in *A Son at the Front*—testifies by means of her "fast" lifestyle to the progress of the feminist movement. The emancipation of these women reaches its apotheosis through the experience of a city that introduces them to the pleasures of carnal love.

The city's climate of eroticism is no doubt heightened by the proximity of death, which brings the characters face-to-face with their own obsessions and fears. Wharton mocks those who, with the outbreak of hostilities, are unable to conceal their "war funk." "On the whole the women behaved best: the idiotic Mme de Dolmetsch had actually grown beautiful through fear for her lover. . . . The men had made a less creditable showing—especially the big banker and promoter, Jorgenstein, whose round red face had withered like a pricked balloon."[17] The characters seek the necessary moral strength to face up to the permanent threat of danger and bereavement in whatever way they can. Mme Vinet finds comfort in Beethoven, while her daughter Mimi rejects her secular upbringing and turns to religion. George Campton's mother seeks refuge in the irrational and pays frequent visits to Madame Olida, the clairvoyant. In *1919* Maurice Millet explains to Eleanor and Eveline the mystic faith that burns inside him. "He stayed till late in the evening telling them about miraculous conversions of unbelievers, extreme unction on the firing line, a vision of young Christ he'd seen walking among the wounded in the dressingstation during a gasattack. Après la guerre he was going into a monastery. Trappist perhaps."[18] The two girls are sufficiently impressed to go and light candles in Notre Dame.

With the exception of Owen Johnson, Edith Wharton is the only writer to draw attention to the war's role as a force for moral regeneration and heroism. Hitherto dissolute characters like Fortin-Lescluze in *A Son at the Front* or Maurice de Saint-Omer in *The Wasted Generation* undergo a metamorphosis, becoming responsible and courageous officers. Troy Belknap, still clad in his ambulance corps uniform, seizes the rifle of a dead soldier and joins in the fighting. Benny Upsher in *A Son at the Front* and Alan Littledale in *The Wasted Generation* enlist in the British army by pretending to be Canadians. George Campton volunteers for the front a second time after having been seriously wounded. Edith Wharton stresses the moral solitude of such combatants on their return to the capital. John Campton, unlike his ex-wife, tries to understand their son's behavior. When Madge Talkett offers to become his mistress, George's reaction is symbolic of his refusal of all compromise. As he explains to his father, he wants her for his wife, not his mistress, and he knows she will never divorce her husband. An affair, which might be justified under the circumstances, is for him unthinkable. In his undeviating quest for absolutes and his rejection of all half measures, George offers an ideal combination of morale and morals. But his is an extreme case, and in the world of ordinary mortals the social comedy plays on.

In spite of events in Europe, the salons of Paris continue to flourish, their members continue to meet and converse, with each one striving to outshine the others. Americans who failed to escape from the capital in August 1914 can be heard proclaiming—*after* the victory of the Marne—that they stayed of their own free will. Mrs. Belknap is one of these. Yet during the worst moments of the offensive, the main concern of such characters is not the safety of France but the safety of the family jewels. In *A Son at the Front* Harvey Mayhew, in the Hague for a few days for the peace conference, makes the most of having been taken prisoner by the Germans. Declaring loudly upon his departure, "I shouldn't, in any case, allow anything so opposed to my convictions as war to interfere with my carrying out my mandate,"[19] he subsequently returns bristling with warlike intentions and becomes famous for his "Bureau des Atrocités" at the Hôtel du Nouveau Luxe. Both Wharton and Canfield are bitter in their condemnation of the

frivolous irresponsibility and selfishness of those American nurses who orga-
nize a comfortable existence for themselves remote from the realities of war,
rather like tourists, and for whom a trip to the front is an escapade, a well-
earned reward. A contrast is drawn between characters like Matey Fort,
working quietly behind the scenes since 1915, and stars of the charity show,
like the recently arrived Mrs. Whitlock, who instantly occupies center stage
thanks to her money and contacts. Canfield writes witheringly about the
fashionable and aristocratic side of French and American war charities. In
"A Honeymoon . . . Vive l'Amérique," published in the collection *Home
Fires in France,* she describes the imaginary character of the duchesse de
Sazarat-Bégonine.

> The very fact that I know the Duchesse de Sazarat-Bégonine is a startling
> proof of the extent to which, in the pursuit of her war-relief work, she
> has wandered from her original circle! It shows, as nothing else could,
> what a thorough sport she was in the pursuit of her new game, stopping
> at nothing, not even at promiscuous mingling with the obscure. She was,
> if you will allow me the expression, the as des as of the fashionable war-
> relief world in Paris. As in the case of Guynemer, when she mounted her
> aerial steed in pursuit of big cash donations to her *oeuvre,* all the lesser
> lights abandoned hope for theirs.[20]

After the armistice, Mrs. Whitlock says to Matey Fort, who has never been
to the front, "Why, you poor child! . . . We must get a permit for you at
once—it'll be easy to manage some mission or other for you. Though of
course now . . . I forgot about the armistice—there's really nothing to
see."[21] The social comedy also has its baser side. Both John Campton and
Mme de Dolmetsch resort to a certain amount of string-pulling in order to
protect, respectively, their son and lover.

Around the beginning of 1916, to judge from the texts, in particular *A Son
at the Front,* Paris begins to rally and to adapt itself to a war that seems likely
to continue for some time. On pretexts that are more or less specious, the
capital begins to live and to enjoy itself again. Gertrude Stein, returning
from Majorca, is struck by the difference after a year's absence: "We came
back to an entirely different Paris. It was no longer gloomy, it was no longer
empty."[22] Edith Wharton explains the change as follows: "The war still
raged; wild hopes had given way to dogged resignation; each day added to
the sum of public anguish and private woes. But the strain had been too
long, the tragedy too awful. The idle and the useless had reached their
emotional limit, and once more they dressed and painted, smiled, gossiped,

flirted as though the long agony were over."[23] The author traces all the minute indications of the change. Although Mrs. Brant does not resume her bridge sessions, she does start to have her nails done again. The presence of the marquise de Tranlay at the Talketts' salon bestows on it the moral sanction of a Parisian nobility that knows how to bury its sons and marry off its daughters with heroic realism. It meant "that mothers had to take their daughters wherever there was a chance of meeting young men, and that such chances were found only in the few 'foreign' houses where, discreetly, almost clandestinely, entertainment had been resumed. You had to take them there . . . because they had to be married (the sooner the better in these wild times, with all the barriers down), and because the young men were growing so tragically few, and the competition was so fierce."[24]

Not everyone has the aristocratic frankness of the marquise, and the Americans are forced to keep up their spirits with slogans such as "forget the war" and "business as usual," the latter generally attributed to Winston Churchill. As Harvey Mayhew says, everyone now has a "duty to rest," and the catch phrase of the Talketts at one period is "be subversive." This apparently seditious attitude is a sort of game in which other, more severe, injunctions to "carry on" or "do your bit" can be temporarily forgotten. The resumption of social life that Wharton describes perhaps accounted to some degree for the widespread feeling of malaise that took hold of the troops in 1917. The social set, whether playing at being at war or playing at forgetting it, is constantly playing at something. John Campton is struck by the theatrical aspect of Mrs. Talkett's salon. Concerts are held there, as they are at Mrs. Brant's, for the benefit of The Friends of French Art. One day, Campton arrives at his ex-wife's house in the middle of a rehearsal. "At the far end of the great gilded room, on a platform backed by velvet draperies, stood Mr. Mayhew, a perfect pearl in his tie and a perfect crease in his trousers. Beside him was a stage-property tripod surmounted by a classical perfume burner; and on it Mme de Dolmetsch, swathed in black, leaned in an attitude of affliction. Beneath the platform a bushy-headed pianist struck an occasional chord from Chopin's 'Dead March.'"[25]

Campton sees these givers of galas as no more than pathetic actors; for him, "this playing at Bohemia seemed a nursery-game."[26] He tries to capture the galas' social atmosphere, their feeling of dreamlike unreality, by painting Madge Talkett in her salon. In this city, reminiscent of "a bankrupt theatre,"[27] these puppet characters seem even more illusory when viewed against the tragic events that are being enacted in the background. Some of the actors, however, manage to keep a firm enough hold on reality to exploit the situation for their own ends. Mme de Dolmetsch maneuvres Harvey Mayhew into electing her treasurer of The Friends of French Art with the express intention of embezzling some of the group's funds. Boylston opens John Campton's eyes to the fact that "lots of people are beginning to speculate in war charities—oh, in all sorts of ways."[28] This kind of salon gangsterism, the extreme end of fashionable intrigues, is to a certain extent the reflection of what is going on at the national level. Although the novelists' principal concern is not to show how great supranational interests influence the course of national politics, both Canfield and Wharton draw attention to the powerful eddies that swirl just below the surface of the city's influential and well-connected circles. And Dos Passos is more explicit: many of his characters clearly reflect his Marxist-inspired analysis of the situation.

The primary index of American capitalism is, paradoxically, the American Red Cross. Matey Fort, forgetful of the gigantic scale on which her country does things, is astonished at the huge quantities of supplies that suddenly inundate her little vestiaire. In the space of a few days, American war relief organizations invade the city, rapidly taking over enormous buildings which they fill with "typewriters, steam radiators, roll-top desks, telephones, and self-possessed ladies in khaki uniforms, ready to bind up the wounds of war on a large scale."[29] Adrian Fort gives vent to his skepticism at the sight of such ceaseless activity by quoting the phrase of William James: "The minute anything gets big, it gets wrong."[30] And in fact the Red Cross turns out to be an inhuman administrative machine, churning out decisions that are sometimes in direct opposition to its humanitarian aims. A center for convalescent children that Matey Fort has set up in Hendaye is threatened with closure in the middle of the winter simply because of a problem of interdepartmental reorganization. It is saved only by the intervention of Mrs. Whitlock, who, though she has no idea of what is going on, has sufficient influence to pull the necessary strings. The Red Cross has its own publicity department, whose chief, in *1919,* is J. W. Moorehouse, former head of public relations for Standard Oil. Eleanor and Eveline's job consists of disseminating a rather scandalous sort of propaganda whose sole aim is to raise funds. The two of them spend their time "pasting pictures of ruined French farms and orphaned children and starving warbabies into scrapbooks to be sent home for use in Red Cross drives."[31] Similarly, Harvey Mayhew is spectacularly successful at diverting American donations toward Paris as a result of his powerful rhetoric on the subject of war atrocities. The political morals to be drawn from these examples are that money is all-important and that the end justifies the means.

Further evidence of capitalism at work can be seen in characters like Jorgenstein in *A Son at the Front*. He represents the stereotype—not untinged with anti-Semitism—of the arms dealer, disappearing and appearing mysteriously, letting it be known that he has the ear of various ministers. Under normal circumstances, the doors of the American colony would have been closed to such a person, but the influence of the financier increases in proportion to his wealth, and eventually John Campton resigns himself to being in his company. As a reward for his services, Jorgenstein is knighted by the king of England in 1916. John Campton and Matey Fort, both speaking for their creators, are horrified to discover that the war may be a source of profit—and not simply for people like servants, whose wages, alas, are constantly going up. Campton curses "this hideous world that was dancing and flirting and money-making on the great mounds of dead."³² Matey learns that Mrs. Whitlock has vastly increased her fortune by speculating in steel, and Moorehouse, who rushes straight to the Bourse at the announcement of the armistice, also appears to be a well-informed player of the stock exchange. Jerry Burnham, expressing the views of Dos Passos, comes straight to the point. For him the war will never end because it is "too damn profitable, do you get me? Back home they're coining money, the British are coining money; even the French, look at Bordeaux and Toulouse and Marseilles coining money and the goddam politicians, all of 'em got bank accounts in Amsterdam and Barcelona."³³

A polarization occurs between idealism, patriotism, and goodwill on the one hand, and amorality, greed, and selfishness on the other. The numerous intrigues that take place during the peace treaty negotiations make it brutally clear, now that things are over, that the war was not just about territorial liberation and the preservation of basic human freedoms. The appropriation of the world's raw materials by American and British companies is described in *The Deepening Stream* and *1919*. Robbins outlines for Dick Savage his view of how world politics depends on oil. "It used to be King Coal, but now it's Emperor Petroleum and Miss Manganese, queen consort of steel. That's all in the pink republic of Georgia. . . . That's what this damned idealist Wilson can't understand, while they're setting him up to big feeds at Buckingham Palace the jolly old British army is occupying Mosul, the Karun River, Persia . . . now the latrine news has it that they're in Baku . . . the future oil metropolis of the world."³⁴

The character of President Wilson, an actor on the Parisian stage for the space of a few months, incurs diverse criticism. Through Matey, who acts as a brake to Mme Vinet's enthusiasm, Dorothy Canfield voices her doubts as to the President's politics and indeed his personality. Wilson reminds Matey of her father, the impulsive and idealistic university professor, and when he passes by, she sees "a long bony college professor's face, with the pleased smile on the thin lips."[35] In Matey's eyes, Wilson is the dupe of his own advisers. When she is invited to dinner at the Crillon, she is brought face-to-face with the reality of political hypocrisy and duplicity. The tactics of the American delegation, as one diplomat puts it, are to "let the old Man talk. He loves to. And what harm does it do? Makes a nice occupation for him. When it comes right down to what is going to be *done* he won't have a look-in. He can't! The big world's no college campus."[36] Matey is so sickened by what she hears that she collapses on a bench outside the hotel, physically and morally drained. But the most severe criticism of Wilson comes from Dos Passos, who, in his representation of him as a character exemplifying the corruption of moral idealism, hypocrisy and lies, treats him more severely than any other historical figure in the *U.S.A.* trilogy.

Different Modes of Perception

Both Wharton and Canfield offer an image of wartime Paris that is at odds with the one they give of the prewar city. Each of them, however, has a basic ideology that affects their vision of the capital. Both are ardent Francophiles. For an academic like Canfield, Paris was the symbol of culture and refinement of manners, and for Wharton this second aspect of the city was particularly attractive. Both writers, in literature as well as life, did not hesitate to leap to the defense of their chosen country. This attitude is most noticeable in a kind of propaganda underlying their descriptions of the city. France must be helped in her struggle; civilization, threatened by the German barbarians, must be saved. This conveniently simple way of seeing things was completely serious, and it was shared by Richard Harding Davis, and even Henry James, about whom Olivia Coolidge said, "It is extraordinary to think of Henry James, that kindly, sedentary, civilized, aging man, talking of being seated on the stomach of William of Hohenzollern, squeezing out reparations."[37] The emotionalism of this viewpoint comes through clearly in the writing. It would be interesting to know at precisely what moment certain sections of *Home Fires in France, The Day of Glory,* and *The Marne* were written. Generally speaking, all three books were written before the armistice and perhaps before America's entry into the war. Canfield and Wharton seem to be pushing the idea of American intervention, even though, given the delay in publication, they appear to do so too late. We have already seen the important place accorded in these works to Americans who volunteered for active service. As the Franco-American of "A Little Kansas Leaven" says, "I couldn't give the old country the go-by when trouble came."[38] Wharton and Canfield share this sentiment and wish to convey the feeling to their American public. As has been pointed out on numerous occasions, this damages the aesthetic equilibrium of their novels; and critics, who have completely forgotten *Home Fires in France* and *The Day of Glory*, give short shrift to *The Marne* and *A Son at the Front*. The patriotic senti-ment toward France as an adopted homeland expressed in these novels is astonishingly aggressive. It takes the form of ardent professions of faith that are often maudlin and embarrassing. For the adolescent Troy, France is a beloved person he longs to defend: "France, his France, attacked, invaded, outraged—and he, a poor helpless American boy, who adored her, and could do nothing for her—not even cry, as a girl might."[39] For Troy's friend, Sophy Wicks, France is a guide: "France, which she hardly knew, had merely guessed at through the golden blur of six weeks' midsummer trip, France had drawn her with an irresistible pressure; and the moment she had felt herself free she had come: 'Whither thou goest I will go . . . thy people shall be my people. . . .' Yes, France was the Naomi-country that had but to beckon, and their children rose and came."[40] In *A Son at the Front* the author, who intervenes in the narrative, defines her adopted country as "an idea: that was what France, ever since she had existed, had always been in the story of civilization; a luminous point about which striving visions and purposes could rally. . . . To thinkers, artists, to all creators, she had always been a second country. If France went, western civilization went with her."[41]

Although Wharton and Canfield share the same pro-French militancy, two of their later works, *A Son at the Front* (1923) and *The Deepening Stream* (1930), show that in other respects their opinions diverge considerably. Can-field's tone changes between *Home Fires in France* and *The Deepening Stream*. The war is now seen in a longer perspective, as playing a formative role in the education of the heroine. Paris is shown as awakening her dor-mant sensuality, giving rise to an amusing scene where Matey flings herself passionately into the arms of her husband in the Square du Carrousel. Her sexual liberation is underlined by the presence of Lafayette, looking down approvingly from his pedestal! But her experience of the war in Paris also affects Matey's moral education, confirming her choice of fundamental val-ues and finally convincing her, through what she sees after the armistice, that the world has gone mad. Canfield's former militancy, expressed here only through the pathetic character of Mme Vinet, has been replaced by a feeling of disgust and repugnance. Yet Canfield cannot entirely forget the spirit in which she wrote *The Day of Glory,* and she allows Matey a brief moment of enthusiasm: "For one whole day, the eleventh of November, she put her doubts aside."[42] This fleeting and distant acknowledgment looks back to lines written in a very different tone and spirit.

In all probability, Canfield's disillusionment dates from the early 1920s, although in *The Deepening Stream* she attributes a sense of disillusionment to her heroine as early as 1918. Matey's collapse is brought about by the Paris of the armistice, the exasperating presence of her brother Francis, and, above all, Mrs. Whitlock, whose coquettishness in the past almost destroyed the marriage of Matey's parents. The Forts find it impossible to stay in the capital, where everything is a bitter reminder of their betrayed ideals. Paris saved from destruction does not portend the rebirth of civilization. The cosmopolitan capital in which American diplomats call the tune is, on the contrary, the symbol of human failure, and even of original sin. The Forts make their escape as fast as possible and, in fleeing, are saved. But their country, the "home" to which they return, is not really America; it is Rustdorf, an imaginary village in the Hudson Valley, whose Dutch name means "village of rest." Rustdorf and Paris are at the opposite ends of a parabola. In the former, one may find peace of mind through Quaker nonviolence, meditation, and deep human relationships, whereas Paris is henceforth given over to lies, greed, and physical and moral violence. The French capital is not simply the mirror of a nation; it reflects a moment in the history of the entire world. The debate has moved to a different level from that of opposition between countries or between the Old World and the New. It now involves the acceptance or rejection of the world itself and leads to a religious crisis.

Wharton's attitude is more difficult to pin down. The same ideology that lay behind *The Marne* can still be found in *A Son at the Front.* Wharton continues to be a firm supporter of the French right wing and its traditionally nationalistic policies. Her characters echo the same simplistic and reassuring version of reality as the generals, platitudes that will be turned to derision in the mouth of J. W. Moorehouse in *1919,* which sometimes reads like an unintentional satire of Wharton. Wharton's self-willed brainwashing, which colors and distorts her perception of the city, is doubtless the result of the personal crisis she was going through at the time. Her final ties with the United States were severed in 1913, the year of her divorce. The same year saw the publication of *The Custom of the Country,* the last book she wrote about the American aristocracy before the war. When she tried to resume the same theme later on, in 1922, with *The Glimpses of the Moon,* the attempt demonstrated the difficulty she had treating a contemporary subject. Between 1913 and 1922, she published two studies on France, *Fighting France from Dunkerque to Belfort* (1915) and *French Ways and Their Meaning* (1919), and two retrospective novels, *Summer* (1917) and *The Age of Innocence* (1920). Four works on France, written over a period of eight years, underline the importance for Wharton of the country in which she had chosen to live. But this new direction in her writing, with its accompanying desire to return to the past, is, as Marilyn Jones Lyde points out, a sign of the author's growing confusion as she lost her traditional sources of inspiration.[43] Wharton had previously got the raw material for her social critiques from her observation of an aristocratic society that was virtually wiped out by the war, and the novelist now stood disarmed before an incomprehensible present.

A study of wartime Paris seemed to offer a fresh avenue of exploration, but Wharton created her own version of contemporary reality that, although historically accurate, was fundamentally a hollow fiction based on a past that was finished and dead. At the same time that she was busy rejecting America for France in her personal life, she was struggling to create the literary illusion that the two countries were still intimately linked in an idealized relationship exemplified by characters from practically extinct milieux. Her background and upbringing—she was the youngest child of a tradition-bound family in the New York of the Civil War period—made her feel more at home with the old, Paris-centered France of Paul Bourget and the comtesse de Fitz-James, as R. W. B. Lewis has shown in his biography. What might have been a new source of inspiration for her is compromised from the outset by the narrowness of her vision. In her books about the war, she does portray characters from a wider range of social backgrounds, and her social analyses are often perceptive. Paradoxically, though, it is the puppets of the salons who, ultimately, have more substance than the main protagonists, who appear as mere silhouettes projected on the screen of the city by the author's interior shadow theater. John Campton, who resembles Walter Berry, has a certain credibility as the novelist's alter ego, sharing her disappointment and disillusionment, but heroes like Troy Belknap and George Campton strike us as pure fantasy figures, the sons she never had, the bearers of too obvious a message, the symbols of a mythical America whose destiny is indissolubly linked with that of France. Troy takes his French tutor's place in the battle, but isn't it the ghost of this same tutor who brings the wounded hero back to safety in the closing section of *The Marne*? George dies in Paris on 6 April 1917, the day the United States declares war, as though his sacrifice is both the sign and the condition of ultimate victory, and as if he is reincarnated in the American soldiers who began to arrive in France. Yet these two protagonists are empty of all substance. According to Marilyn Jones Lyde, if Wharton "could perceive in the young men going off to war only idealized and insubstantial George Camptons and Troy Belknaps, youths who were contemporaries of Dos Passos, Fitzgerald, Faulkner, and Hemingway, then her failure to understand the disillusion and bitterness which mushroomed after the armistice was . . . a hopeless struggle for comprehension which may be compared without extravagance to a valiant, last-ditch battle against overwhelming odds."[44]

Wharton's brand of optimism masks an unconscious yearning for the past. She scornfully rejects the new America—an attitude she would maintain in later works—and in *The Marne* she mercilessly satirizes the limited ideas of plebeian volunteers like Hinda Warlick. Her desire to turn the clock back is particularly noticeable in the opening pages of *The Marne,* when John Campton inexplicably takes his son to stay at the Crillon. This is not simply so that he can show George the magnificent spectacle of the Place de la Concorde. Wharton had other motives: writing the book after the signing of the peace treaty, she wished to restore to the hotel its authentic historical role as a great palace and to teach her readers of 1923 a little lesson. The real Crillon, she seems to be saying is the one I have always known, not the one the whole world discovered in 1918. If Wharton manages to escape the profound disillusionment of Canfield, it is perhaps because her version of wartime Paris is the product of a process of autosuggestion. Her attitude has something propitiatory about it, as if by ignoring or concealing the signs of change in the city, she will actually succeed in wishing them away. It is interesting to note that the plot of *A Son at the Front* stops short in 1917. One of the reasons for the book's curtailment might simply be that it suited the author to remain silent about what happened later. What followed the peace had no place in her reassuring schema. Even a description of what happened after 1917 would have soured her bland moral fable and made it impossible for her to continue the narrative further while still keeping reality at arm's length. The flaws of Wharton's portrayal of wartime Paris offer an indirect testimony to the spiritual crisis that accompanied her decline as a writer.

For Dos Passos, the year 1917 brings the revelation of war, and his characters, who are all to some extent biographical, respond to the bewildering spectacle of the capital in a totally different way from the heroes of Wharton and Canfield. As the full title of his first novel, *One Man's Initiation, 1917,* indicates, this year marks a turning point. In "Camera Eye 28," "the first year of the century" is as much 1917 as 1919. "Tomorrow I hoped would be the first day of the first month of the first year."[45] In fact, the two years are complementary. The first provides a brutal discovery of war, arousing hope for a better future. The second brings the progressive confirmation of a feeling of disillusionment at which the author has already hinted. The Paris that Wharton turned her eyes from lies exposed to the gaze of this young man of twenty-one at an acutely critical moment in history, marked by the widespread malaise of the troops, America's decision to enter the war, and the Russian Revolution. Everything Wharton refused to see makes a strong and vivid impression on Dos Passos, resulting in a vision of Paris that is full of freshness and originality, unfettered by long and close association with France in the past. For Dos Passos, it is simply a country that reawakens certain childhood memories, and the characters through whom he speaks are for the most part unfamiliar with Europe. Paris is kept at a distance, and Tom Randolph, John Andrews, Dick Savage, and Jay Pignatelli, like their real-life contemporaries, retain, in Malcolm Cowley's words, "their curious attitude of non participation, of being friendly visitors who, though they might be killed at any moment, still had no share in what was taking place."[46] They are voyeurs, sometimes watching from above, as we have seen, the spectacle of Paris bombarded by enemy planes.

Yet this fresh and modern version of the city, its cobwebs swept away, is not a faithful mirror of reality. Dos Passos selects those aspects of the capital that allow him to express his personal ideology. In *Three Soldiers* Paris is identified with the impersonal system against which John Andrews vainly struggles, as exemplified by the American army and its military police and the French bourgeoisie worried about law and order. The city, uniformed and repressive, has something of the same feel as the Manhattan that Dos Passos was to describe some years later, and this is totally at odds with the traditional image of the capital. In *1919* Paris provides the opportunity for a more ambitious critique. Dos Passos projects onto the period between 1917 and 1919 questions and doubts that came to a head in the Depression. A communist sympathizer, he tried to bring out in his writing the fundamental opposition between the world of capitalism and the world of revolution, hence the importance he assigns to the date of 1 May 1919. In selecting episodes and characters primarily for their political significance, he does the exact opposite of Wharton. Instead of creating a vision of a present arising like a phoenix from the ashes of the past, he turns the spotlight of the 1929 economic crisis onto a recent period of history. The Paris of *1919* is subjected to the searching, partisan scrutiny of the author. Is it not true, as Robbins says, that "Paris is the hub of the world . . . unless it's Moscow"?[47]

Yet this vision of Paris highlights the behavior of certain Americans who exemplify their country's slide toward squalid postwar profiteering. Social success and recognition are now the rewards for the most undeserving of the "Grand Tour upstarts," the ones with the least integrity, like Eleanor Stoddard and J. W. Moorehouse. False values replace real ones in accordance with Gresham's law, and the Americans lose the moral superiority they had once enjoyed. Many are shown as disoriented and devitalized. Moorehouse, Eleanor, Eveline, and even Dick Savage bear the mark of frustration and sterility. As the name of the latter suggests, they are savages who set up camp for a short time within the confines of the city. They bring with them their neuroses and their sense of failure, trying unsuccessfully to adapt to a society that still retains a human dimension. Freed from the ancestral shackles of puritanism, they are nonetheless incapable of fully participating in the city's pleasures. Eleanor is more or less sexless; Dick, whom Don Stevens calls "a goddam fairy,"[48] is possibly a homosexual, and all of Moorehouse's vitality seems to be centered in his larynx. In their company, love is an eternal impossibility, and death a constant possibility. Henry Savage's mistress, Olga, receives a thousand francs for consenting to an abortion. Daughter, who is expecting Dick's child, provokes the accident that ends in her death. The "cadaverous looking individual in a frock coat"[49] who follows Eveline on the Champs Elysées symbolizes the gulf looming at the feet of all these characters, whose failure, for Dos Passos, reflects the failure of capitalism. The city's significance is now associated with liberty and revolution, and, in "Camera Eye 39," with ideas of spring, reawakening, and the possibility of artistic creation. Its meaning, relative to the one it had in *Three Soldiers,* has apparently changed.

Dos Passos's image of Paris owes much to a historical coincidence. Of the vast number of characters who poured into the capital during this period, many already had the status of fictional heroes. These were the American students whom the war brought to Europe. As Malcolm Cowley said, "The ambulance corps and the French military transport were college-extension courses for a generation of writers."[50] Neither Wharton nor Canfield seemed to realize the significance of this new influx of visitors, living out on a vast scale the individual experiences of heroes in earlier novels. Reality overtook fiction, and many of the young Americans landing in France were real-life descendants of Jamesian heroes. Dos Passos was able to express his own

thoughts and feelings through these characters without too much fictionalization. The same classical education and culture colors their discovery of the city,
and their aloofness, their lack of involvement, is also part and parcel of their
intellectualism. They construct an elaborate game of allusions and correspondences in which Paris becomes a self-referential construction, where the
mirror of history and the mirror of the present create an endless series of ever-
receding images. This temporal perspective is particularly noticeable in *Three
Soldiers* and *Chosen Country*. John Andrews imaginatively relives the Paris of
the eighteenth century, that of Manon, of Diderot and Voltaire—a time that,
like 1919, seemed to be essentially a period of waiting, a Paris "full of pompous
ennui of the past and insane hope of the future."[51] Jay Pignatelli identifies with
Poggius, a humanist of the late Middle Ages, who visited Paris during the
Hundred Years' War. He reads Gibbon, as well as Henry and Brooks Adams,
and attends courses on Amer-Indian tribes at the Sorbonne. By playing on his
characters' culture, Dos Passos situates a contemporary chronicle in a historical and philosophical perspective.

He also reworks the theme of bohemia. John Andrews becomes the lover
of a seamstress called Jeanne, and, in *Chosen Country,* Jay Pignatelli has a
mistress of the same name. Both girls are travesties of the traditional grisette.
The first Jeanne has been forced to leave her home in Laon and come to Paris
to earn her living. When John invites her to his room, she replies simply, "I
suppose one must pay for one's dinner."[52] The second Jeanne has become a
prostitute in order to support her mother. In both cases there is no possibility
of romantic love, and Dos Passos has deliberately chosen to disfigure this
archetypal couple in order to make it quite clear that times have changed.
The student now wears a uniform, and the grisette is merely the victim of
economic circumstances. About Paris, given over to soldiers and whores,
Scott Bronson explains: "War and bad times is when they flower. In good
times they lie dormant in society like a worm in a cocoon. The hot sun of
war brings them out. . . . The soldier and the whore destroy. The soldier
destroys life. The whore destroys love; they have deep affinity for one
another."[53] Much more than Wharton or Canfield, Dos Passos creates an
atmosphere of melancholy and ennui. In *Three Soldiers* and *Chosen Country*
a sad, rainy city reflects the human degradation seen by the author. The final
images of Paris in *1919* show that "the pinnacles and buttresses of Notre
Dame looked crumbly as cigarash in the late afternoon sunshine."[54] Paris,
associated elsewhere with the first morning of a new century, seems here to
suggest not only the decline of civilization but the end of the world itself.

These contradictory images of Paris are not due to differences in the books themselves. Although the underlying ideology of *Chosen Country* is diametrically opposed to that of *Three Soldiers,* the Parisian episodes are in fact very similar. The conflicting versions of the capital arise, within each book, directly from the author's novelistic technique. Dos Passos breaks the regular sequence of narration, description, and dialogue, and the descriptive fragments are often meant to reveal the particular state of mind of the character/spectator. Because the characters' modes of perception are different, the overall vision of the city is composed of multiple, varying elements. Besides, in *1919,* four "Camera Eye" sections are about Paris (Numbers 35, 39, 40, and 41). These texts are difficult to interpret, in particular Number 39 with its use of collage, calligrams, and automatic writing.

Most of what is innovative in Dos Passos's representation of Paris is already present in *Three Soldiers,* published in 1921, which had an influence on the writers of the 1920s. What is new is that Dos Passos prefers Paris to the Parisians. He passes over the different Franco-American groups without comment. His field of observation is the street with its colorful characters, its sounds and smells. His range of vision goes well beyond the elegant neighborhoods, and, for him, Paris is also the damp and steamy bistros where bargemen drink their absinthe, the public baths floating on the Seine, or what John Andrews discovers at four in the morning in Montmartre: "Paris way a slate-grey and dove-color lay spread out like a Turkish carpet. . . . Here and there blue smoke and brown spiralled up to lose itself in the faint canopy of brown fog hung high above the houses."[55] Paris is also the incredible existence of the painter De Clocheville: "They say he never goes out. Stays here and paints, and when friends come in, he feeds them and charges them double."[56] Dos Passos explores Parisian time and space in search of a new poetry. He discovers a modern city, a city of the common people, in which the eye of the observer is constantly surprised, and which bears no resemblance to the one that Wharton and Canfield describe from the inside. For Dos Passos, Paris is envisaged as a lump of raw material viewed from without.

CHAPTER 6

THE GREAT MIGRATION: PARISIAN ASPECTS

The Reconstruction of Paris

The Paris of the 1920s makes a relatively rapid entry into literature, with roughly two-thirds of the relevant works being written during the decade itself. There is no very clear break with the preceding period. Some writers disappear from the scene. Dorothy Canfield returns to America, like her heroine Matey Fort, while Dos Passos drops out of Montparnasse life to pursue his travels elsewhere. Others, like Edith Wharton, Elliot Paul, Gertrude Stein, and e. e. cummings manage a sort of transition. New writers arrive in the capital, and some, like Ernest Hemingway and F. Scott Fitzgerald, could well have witnessed the events that took place at the end of the war had their military orders been different. Others, who arrive after the peace, to discover Paris or renew a previous acquaintance, include Sherwood Anderson, Sinclair Lewis, William Carlos Williams, Elmer Rice, Donald Ogden Stewart, Thomas Wolfe, and Glenway Wescott.

A number of works by minor literary figures also throw light on the way Paris was perceived by American writers during this period. Maurice Samuel's novel *The Outsider,* the melodramatic account of a love affair between a Parisian working girl and an American ex-soldier, paints a gloomy picture of the immediate postwar period. *They Had to See Paris* is a lighthearted book by Homer Croy that was made into a hit movie in 1926. *The French They Are a Funny Race,* by Lyon Mearson, is supposedly the diary of Edgar Bowman, a Chicago bank clerk and amateur inventor, who had come to Paris in search of some "background." In reality, the work is also a sort of keepsake book for the author's friends, written in a good-humored style halfway between literary pastiche and student spoof. *The Professors Like Vodka,* by Harold Loeb, is a novel about Russian émigré circles in Paris that introduces the fanatically anti-Semitic character of Cleopatra. The plot is based on a real-life incident that Loeb recounts in his book of memoirs, *The Way It Was. The Selbys,* by Julian Green's sister, Ann, is an ironic account of American businessmen and bankers in Paris thinly disguised as an innocuous romance. William Van Wyck's book in verse, *On the Terrasse,* is a sort of apologia for Montparnasse. In *The Innocents of Paris* C. E. Andrews strings together stories based on the wanderings of the narrator-guide through the capital. He also inspired with this book an "all-talking" film starring Maurice Chevalier. Finally, three works involve the Parisian theme to a lesser degree but still deserve notice: *American Beauty, The French Wife,* and *The Eater of Darkness.* The first, a novel by Arthur Meeker, focuses on the international set of Paris and Dinard, and contains characters clearly copied from Jamesian models. The "American beauty" of the title is Angela Vane, whose search for a husband, largely at the instigation of an ambitious mother, encounters many obstacles. In *The French Wife* Dorothy Graham offers a variation on the theme of international marriages with the story of Denise de Lambesc, an American widow who prefers to marry one of her compatriots and return to America rather than embark on a second marriage with a French aristocrat. *The Eater of Darkness,* by Robert M. Coates, which is considered to be the first American surrealist novel, begins and ends in the Latin Quarter.

It would be reasonable to assume from the preceding list, and more particularly from the prestige attached to some of the names on it, that the 1920s would produce a vast number of works relevant to our study. The titles that spring immediately to mind—*The Sun Also Rises, Tender Is the Night,* or "Babylon Revisited"— seem to be but the tip of a great literary iceberg. Yet, as Joseph H. McMahon points out, one of the most common misconceptions about American literature is to imagine that Paris is a major theme for the writers of the Lost Generation.[1] This misconception can be explained first by the assumption that because so many writers came to Paris, they must therefore have written about their surroundings, and second by the fact that innumerable pages have been published about the lives of these writers in literary memoirs.

Artists like George Antheil, George Biddle, and Jacob Epstein, or well-known social figures such as Margaret Anderson, Mabel Dodge Luhan and Peggy Guggenheim, have all left memoirs of the period. Poets like John Gould Fletcher, Harriet Monroe, and Hilda Doolittle have published autobiographies containing accounts of the capital. Gorham Munson remembers his life in Paris in a 1932 article in the *Sewanee Review* entitled "The Fledgling Years," while Caresse Crosby describes her cosmopolitan existence in the capital in *The Passionate Years* (1953). Poet Claude McKay, an important figure of the Harlem Renaissance, writes about his various visits to Paris in *A Long Way from Home* (1937). And Burton Rascoe, journalist and literary critic, continues his autobiography—begun with *Before I Forget* (1937)—in *We Were Interrupted* (1947), in which he talks about the 1920s and, in Chapter 7, gives his impressions of Paris after 1924.

The relative importance of the capital in such works varies considerably. In some it is simply the backdrop to certain episodes. In others it is the chief center of interest. Janet Flanner, who wrote for the *New York Times* under the byline "Genêt" and was a well-known figure in American Paris, devotes the major part of *An American in Paris* (1940) to an account of the capital during the 1920s. In *Shakespeare and Company* (1956) Sylvia Beach tells the story of her life as the owner of the famous bookshop of the same name, and her role as confidante to the writers of the Lost Generation. Samuel Putnam recalls the Roaring Twenties in *Paris Was Our Mistress* (1947), and the Canadian Morley Callaghan throws light on the relationship between Hemingway and Fitzgerald in 1929 in *That Summer in Paris* (1963). Finally, in *Paris, France*, published after the outbreak of World War II, in 1940, Gertrude Stein describes everything that France and its capital represented for her for a period of forty years.

These works can be ignored on the grounds that they are nonfictional. Some yield interesting information and provide details of dates or locations that are a helpful "way in" to the literature proper, but many are nothing more than a series of loosely connected and tedious anecdotes in which the descriptions of people and things Parisian are sometimes wildly inaccurate.[2] Strictly speaking, *A Moveable Feast* ought to be classed with these works, but one can argue that it contains limpid vignettes of Montparnasse that complement those in *The Snows of Kilimanjaro*. Indeed, Hemingway himself wrote in the preface, "If the reader prefers, this book may be regarded as fiction. But there is always the chance that such a book of fiction may throw some light on what has been written as fact."[3] The same idea is echoed by Frederick Kohner, author of *Kiki of Montparnasse* but better known for his novel *Gidget*. A roman à clef rather than a biography or autobiography, *Kiki of Montparnasse* is a spicy narrative based on the author's affair with the famous model.

In all, thirty or so works constitute the basis of this chapter. To those already mentioned, we may add the following authors and titles. Thomas Wolfe's novel *Of Time and the River* (1936) contains a 140-page section about the hero's stay in Paris in 1924–25. The same hero, rechristened George Webber, returns to Paris four years later in *The Web and the Rock* (1939). In *Dark Laughter* (1925), parodied by Hemingway in *The Torrents of Spring* (1926), Sherwood Anderson looks back at the period following the end of the war. Elmer Rice's play *The Left Bank* (1931), set in an apartment on the Boulevard Montparnasse, focuses on the problems of expatriation. Donald Ogden Stewart gives a comic account of the tribulations of American tourists in *Mr. and Mrs. Haddock Abroad* (1924) and *Mr. and Mrs. Haddock in Paris* (1926), a theme that was taken up by e. e. cummings in the play *Him* (1932). In *The Glimpses of the Moon* (1922) and, more noticeably, *The Gods Arrive* (1932), Edith Wharton attempts to depict a city and a milieu with which she has fewer and fewer connections. Glenway Wescott's "The Whistling Swan" (1928) exposes the seamier side of expatriate finance. And two books in which the capital figures prominently are *A Voyage to Pagany* (1928), in which William Carlos Williams examines the relationship between the artist and Europe, and *Dodsworth* (1929), by Sinclair Lewis, whose hero is particularly relevant to our study.

Though this selection may seem dauntingly large, the number of pages actually involved is relatively small. The major problem in dealing with this period is not one of size but rather of how to separate the literature itself from the myths that subsequently grew up around its creators. Two main sources of interference lie between the reader and the text. The first is the amount of hoopla surrounding the entire decade; the second is the importance of the new intellectual and literary values that emerged from the period and that successive generations of writers and critics have brought to our attention. Our main difficulty, then, is to disentangle the Parisian theme from these surrounding elements, which are closely bound up with it.

The return to normal life brings a return to familiar types. The student, the tourist, the millionaire, the aesthete, and the man in the street all recover their former importance. Montparnasse, a secondary myth grafted onto the myth of Paris, reintroduces the motif of bohemia. Historians have frequently pointed out the affinities between the 1920s and the period that followed the American Civil War. For the Parisian theme, the 1920s are also a period of reconstruction. The return to civilian life is described in *1919* and *Three Soldiers,* as we have seen, as well as in three other novels: *Dark Laughter, The Outsider,* and Elliot Paul's *The Amazon.* The waves of uniformed characters recede, leaving a city that, though superficially battered, is fundamentally unchanged. Various signs point to this return to "business as usual." The racecourses have opened again, and in *The Amazon* ex-soldier John McCann wins a small fortune thanks to a tip from the shoeshine boy at the American Express office. Once demobilized, some Americans go home, whereas others choose to stay on in a city where the exchange rate is becoming more favorable daily. In *Dark Laughter* Fred Grey treats himself to a year off in the capital before returning to Old Harbor, Indiana, to sort out family problems. Like Mortimer Long in *The Outsider,* John McCann has no fixed ideas about how long he will stay in Paris, but he ends up marrying a Frenchwoman and thus staying forever. The American deserters can now safely come out into the open, finding work driving taxis or doing odd jobs. *The Outsider* paints a dramatic picture of those who wait too long before going home, and who, after the initial euphoria has worn off, end up as criminals, drug addicts, or down-and-outs.

Yet the memory of the war persists, and traces of it can be found throughout the entire decade. The Church of Saint-Gervais, for example, which was bombed on 29 March 1918, now figures on the tourist circuit. Hotel employees are quick to capitalize on stories of their military exploits. Battles are commemorated in ceremonies held at the Arc de Triomphe. In *Tender Is the Night* a group of Gold Star Mothers stand out starkly amid the habitual clientele of the Hôtel Roi George (in reality, the Georges V). But they are not the only ones who make a pilgrimage to the battlegrounds and war cemeteries. These spots are visited in the same novel by Dick Diver and his friends, as well as by Pike Peters and his family in *They Had to See Paris* and the Sterns in *The French They Are a Funny Race.* But the war has, above all, left a mark on those who were actually a part of it: Jake Barnes, with his symbolic wound, Brett Ashley, Abe North, and the Elinor of *Of Time and the River,* literary cousin to Eleanor in *1919.* The sinister character whom Dick Diver meets near the Passy Studio, and who has been compared to the beggar in *Madame Bovary,* is a symbol of fate but also of the war, in which he served as a member of the Eighty-fourth Division. Remnants of the war litter the texts: black armbands, red ribbons, multicolored decorations, artificial limbs, and the iron masks of the "gueules cassées," (soldiers wounded in the face). Franco-American relations will be affected for some time by the problem of the Allied war debt. The events of 1914–18 are writ large in ruins and monuments, in people's memories, and even in their unconscious reflexes. The instinctive reaction of the passersby when a bomb is thrown at a Ukrainian general causes the narrator of *Kiki of Montparnasse* to observe that the Parisians "had acquired great skill in this dropping-down manoeuvre during the last weeks of World War One."[4]

Anti-German sentiment is surprisingly quick to disappear. Alberta Snyder, the "Amazon" of Elliot Paul's novel, is depicted as gradually becoming aware of the unhealthy aspect of her blind patriotism. As lieutenant of a signals regiment, she succeeds in leading her female recruits into battle by passing them off as men. Motivated by intense hatred of the Germans and a persistent fear of rape, she orders her soldiers to take poison rather than allow themselves to fall into the hands of the enemy alive. But Alberta does not have sufficient time to put her plan into action when she herself is captured, and she ends up falling in love with her captor, a German pilot. After the armistice, the conscience-stricken heroine stays in Paris, where the narrator, an American journalist, determines to reunite the lovers. Hermann, the erstwhile enemy, arrives in the capital: "He was in France for the first time in ten years, and he too had loved Paris. He saw upon the faces of the men and women who moved along the sidewalks the same marks of suffering, resignation, abandon or gaiety which he had seen in Berlin or in London. He was like a ghost among them. Once a famous French aviator passed, and Hermann started involuntarily from his chair."[5] The novel ends on a note of reconciliation. It also pokes fun at the then-fashionable preoccupation with Freudian themes, for the handsome Hermann arrives in the capital just in time to snatch his still-pure heroine from the clutches of a lesbian rival.

For John McCann, in the same novel, the war is a sort of second birth trauma, an event of such overwhelming significance that the armistice becomes for him the first day of a new calendar. Yet, at the same time, it also marks the end of things, the stopping of the clock. McCann is quite simply unable to imagine his fellow soldiers growing any older once they are back home. The same paradox is described in *The Outsider*. Mortimer Long sees his demobilization order as a "rebirth certificate," but he views his arrival in Paris as a quest for what his friend Cray calls "the right not to be," a rejection of all responsibility and a search for solitude and anonymity. Mortimer sees in the Seine "the river of forgetfulness," bathing the city of the "unremembered"; and when he climbs to the top of Montmartre, he does so not in order to launch a challenge to Paris, like Rastignac in the Père-Lachaise Cemetery, but to mark his renunciation of the world itself.[6] The end of the war is for him an end to growth and indeed a regression. He withdraws into himself, gradually assuming the fetal position, which is also that of the soldier huddled in shell-battered trenches. Paris represents in Freudian terms a sort of surrogate womb to which the hero longs to return.

In *Dark Laughter* Anderson continues these explorations of Freudian themes with his narration of an event that took place in Paris just after the end of the war, the Bal des Quat'z Arts of 1919. The orgiastic celebrations that traditionally accompany such an event do not here express a feeling of joy at the new peace but rather a rejection of everything. The ball is an artificial hell whose aim is to shock the civilized world, to punish it for making such a war possible. It marks an end to deception, a destruction of old values, and hails the arrival of a Dada-inspired revolution and of a decade whose twin symbols are profanity and black humor. It expresses the artist's hatred of the bourgeoisie, the soldier's hatred of the noncombatant patriot, and man's hatred of woman. The latter is a modern Bathsheba, betraying man as Bathsheba betrayed Uriah. She must now be punished and degraded in this sombre bacchanalia. This episode introduces the idea that Paris offers an opportunity for debauchery and nocturnal revelry leading to a state of emotional violence that is the psychological equivalent of the physical violence of war.

Moving from this transitional period to the twenties themselves, the first thing we notice is an unprecedented closeness between American Paris and the Paris of reality. Though the former is still relatively narrow and enclosed, the fact that many Americans have been involved in the war, combined with the large increase in their numbers during the period—a socioeconomic phenomenon examined by Warren Irving Susman in *Pilgrimage to Paris: The Background of American Expatriation*—leads to an increased familiarity with the capital. Never before has Paris been so marked by the American presence, as Henri Valentino observes in his humorous novel *Les Américains à Paris au temps joyeux de la prospérité,* in which the author takes a look at both the usual and unusual aspects of this peaceful invasion. The authors, and the characters who represent them, seem to have got rid of many of the prejudices and biases that had affected their writing before the war. They are now much more at ease with the city, and whereas we see Claude Wheeler in Willa Cather's *One of Ours,* admitting, while trying to decide whether or not to enlist, that he is less frightened by German bullets than by French etiquette, he later revises his opinion, observing that "one's manners wouldn't matter in the Marne tonight, the night of the eighth of September 1914."[7] This somewhat naive reflection is nonetheless significant in helping to explain why, after the war, the Americans, particularly those who had been engaged in active combat, were no longer obsessed by a feeling of inferiority.

The result of all this is a clarification of emotional ties and a reevaluation of the Parisian myth. Authors and characters alike shed their preconceptions and try to see things as they really are. As Ernest Earnest writes: "Hemingway's generation of Americans was the first to approach Europe without the blinders of Puritanism."[8] It is true that the new permissiveness makes it possible for certain aspects of Parisian life to be treated with more flexibility and assurance, allowing the discovery of the capital to take place in an atmosphere free from moral constraint. Jake Barnes, for example, rebukes Robert Cohn for, among other things, his tendency to look for reasons to dislike Paris in H. L. Mencken and other critics. One of the first consequences of this is the disappearance of the socioeconomic groups described in previous chapters. The demimonde makes its exit from literature, as it does from real life; the American colony sees its special identity threatened not only by the encroaching French but also by the diluting effect of all the expatriates flooding into the city. In *They Had to See Paris* two characters symbolize successive generations of Americans in Paris: Miss Mason, who has lived in Paris for over forty years, stands for those of the period just before *The Ambassadors,* while Mrs. Aspinwall—strongly reminiscent of Edith Wharton—represents those from the beginning of the century and the war years. Miss Mason continues to drive around the city in her private carriage, while the lifestyle of Mrs. Aspinwall, holder of the Légion d'Honneur, faithfully mirrors that of the aristocracy of the 1900s. Both these characters, as may be expected, deplore the arrival of so many of their compatriots, whom they regard as shameless upstarts.

The nobility suffers most. Only a few lightweight characters like Fran Dodsworth or Mrs. Peters are shown as being still susceptible to the glamor of noble titles. In *They Had to See Paris* the nobility is exposed as degenerate, and in *Dodsworth* the "noble" Mme de Penable is really an adventuress. Previous American attitudes toward this milieu are now the subjects of parody and ridicule. Mrs. Peters, in *They Had to See Paris,* following a time-honored maternal tradition, wants to marry off her daughter Opal to a French aristocrat. She singles out the well-preserved marquis de Brissac as a suitable candidate, but her designs are thwarted by her husband, who, judging the prospective bridegroom's request for a dowry to be exorbitant and taking a closer look at the gentleman in question, calls off what is clearly a very bad deal. Homer Croy pokes fun at duels, and, in *Of Time and the River,* the custom of dueling is revived by a con artist in order to make blackmail victims of unwary tourists. The most amusing piece of satire occurs in *They Had to See Paris.* Mrs. Peters organizes a grand soirée in her château at Mont d'Or, but, lacking the appropriate guests, she forces her husband to *rent,* from a specialist agency, a number of penniless aristocrats who dutifully agree to turn up at the right time for the right price.

Croy's novel provides a complete transition between the end of the nineteenth century and the decade of the 1920s. Whereas Peters is representative of the postwar era, his wife turns constantly toward an outmoded past. In popular novelist tradition, Croy offers his readers numerous digressions into

Parisian history. The facts that he gives, with a fine disregard for brevity, constitute a veritable compendium of James and Wharton. The reader is subjected to lengthy explanations about the nobility, arranged marriages, the role of women, and even verdicts of the French divorce courts in cases where the wife is American. The demimondaine Claudine de Tréville, who makes frequent appearances in the plot, appears as the last example of this dying species. As the reader turns the pages, he discovers a veritable retrospective of American Paris, which may explain the book's special appeal.

The Right Bank

The Different Faces of Paris

The tourist and the artist, and the different banks of the river to which they largely belong, constitute the most interesting aspects of Paris in the 1920s. So far the term "expatriate" has been used to include all those Americans who took part in the great migration of the 1920s. Their number includes many secondary types, which complicates the question of drawing a clear distinction between tourist and artist, or tourist and resident. How are we to define journalists, when some of them, like Jake Barnes, are fully integrated into Montparnasse life, while others, like Krum, with whom Jake shares a taxi from the Quai d'Orsay, have never so much as set foot in the Dingo or the Select? The two extremes are easily identifiable, consisting, on the one hand, of people like the Haddocks, who "do" Paris in four days, and, on the other, of the more or less permanent residents of Montparnasse, or the sixteenth arrondissement on the Right Bank. But between them lies an intricate network of categories crisscrossed by the latitudes and longitudes of snobbery and constituting a hierarchy that Sinclair Lewis defines as follows: at the top come the residents who have aristocratic relatives, next the residents who don't; after those come "Americans who have spent a year in Paris— those who have spent three months—two weeks—three days—half a day— just arrived." Implicit in this pecking order is a descending scale of condescension: "The American who has spent three days is as derisive toward the half-a-day tripper as the American resident with the smart French relatives is toward the poor devil who has lived in Paris for years but who is there mainly for business."[9] The Americans themselves use the term "tourist" derogatorily. In *Kiki of Montparnasse* the term denotes those who arrive at the Dôme, the Rotonde, and the Select after seven o'clock. Fran Dodsworth occasionally tries to hide the fact that she belongs to this category. "One day she was brazen enough to be discovered with the tourists' badge, the Baedecker, unconcealed: the next she wouldn't sit with [Dodsworth] at a side-walk café."[10] In *The Left Bank* long-time resident John Selby dubs those of his compatriots who annoyingly turn up on his doorstep without warning as "casuals from Calais."[11]

Along with such a sophisticated system of segregation go different conceptions of just what constitutes the "real" Paris and a similar ranking of the capital's neighborhoods. John Selby explains to Waldo Lynde, the casual from Calais who has just arrived, that "the Paris that is Paris"[12] is indubitably to be found on the Left Bank. In an essay he wrote for *Vanity Fair,* entitled "Conflicting Aspects of Paris," e. e. cummings makes a distinction between "Paree" and "Paname." Paree, given up to the Americans, consists of comfortable hotels, the Rue de Rivoli (where speaking French amounts to blasphemy), Montmartre, and the Boulevard Montparnasse. Conversely, Paname is composed of all the bistros that serve white Bordeaux, the Porte Saint-Denis, the Théâtre du Châtelet, the Cirque d'Hiver, and the Jardin du Luxembourg. As far as the rest of the city is concerned, Paree and Paname overlap, but, adds cummings, Paname is inhabited by WOLS, "worshippers of life," whereas Paree is inhabited by WOBS, "worshippers of the bathtub." The latter live in the city, whereas the city lives in the former.[13]

Cummings focuses attention on a constant expatriate preoccupation, the quest for the real Paris, the Paris where, to be precise, other Americans do not go, or at least not yet. But those who are particularly eager to find Paname are precisely those who will cause it to degenerate into Paree, and once they have left, it will reassume its original identity. The way in which the first phase of this operation works can be seen in *The Sun Also Rises,* with Mme Lecomte's restaurant. Once upon a time, this was a nice quiet spot, but, as Jake Barnes explains, "some one had put it in the American Women's Club list as a quaint restaurant on the Paris quais as yet untouched by Americans, so we had to wait forty-five minutes for a table."[14] Lyon Mearson gives a comic account of the final phase. True to form, Edgar Bowman is constantly on the lookout for a spot where only Parisians go. After many disappointments, he finally discovers a restaurant as yet unknown to his compatriots: the American Quick Lunch in the Rue Fontaine. Sinclair Lewis defines, satirically, the limits of American Paris. There are four separate towns in the capital. The Americans are familiar with the first three: that of the tourist, that of the student, and that of the cosmopolitan. However, they are totally ignorant of the fourth, which is "a Paris inhabited by no one save three million Frenchmen."[15]

The oft-invoked distinction between Hemingway's Paris and Fitzgerald's

Paris is not simply a question of Left Bank versus Right Bank. While it may be true that Fitzgerald's Paris was largely restricted to the Right Bank, Hemingway's city, on the other hand, is much more widespread, rich and fused with his most intimate experiences. It is not limited to Montparnasse and the Latin Quarter. As Hemingway gained fame and fortune, he moved from one bank to the other, and his knowledge of the capital was considerable. Stadiums, velodromes, boxing rings, racecourses, all of these, scattered throughout the city, were destinations of the author's constant to-and-fro between Left Bank and Right Bank. In one pointed anecdote related by the narrator of A Moveable Feast, which takes its place alongside the other perfidies—doubly posthumous—launched against Fitzgerald, he quotes Georges, a former bellboy at the Ritz who has become a barman, as saying that he has not the slightest recollection of this M. Fitzgerald whose name is on everyone's lips. Thus Hemingway establishes his supremacy over a territory ordinarily attributed to his friend and rival.

The division between the Paris of the tourist and that of the artist is justified on two counts. The first concerns the sheer number of pages written about Montparnasse, firmly establishing it as a new center of artistic life, providing the focus for several works. The second has to do with the emergence of a particular type of male American tourist with a clearly defined psychological profile deriving from the Babbitt archetype in American literature and involving a perception of the city totally alien to that of the artist.

Babbitt in Babylon

Sinclair Lewis's hero has not been slipped into this study under false pretenses. He is a bona fide character in William Van Wyck's On the Terrasse. The protagonist of this poem, stretched to the dimensions of a small book by means of various typographical artifices, introduces himself thus: "Yep, I am George Babbitt, I'm the guy / That Sinclair Lewis put into his book."[16] He confides to an artist by the name of Scott the various reflections inspired by the Café du Dôme and by Montparnasse in general. There are references to Babbitt in other works as well, but he is mainly interesting because so many American tourists of this period are like him in one way or another: Sam Dodsworth and his friend Tub Pearson, Pike Peters, Will Haddock, and, in a more comic mode, Edgar Bowman; also Waldo Lynde, in The Left Bank, and even Charlie Wales in "Babylon Revisited." The primary traits of the Babbitt archetype—the single-minded pursuit of success, fundamentally nationalist and racist attitudes, contempt for the artist and indifference to the world of the spirit—can all be found in the characters listed above, albeit to greatly differing degrees. Dodsworth clearly commands his creator's respect, whereas Tub Pearson just as clearly does not, and consequently the development of each character is different. These men embody the idea of American affluence. Pike Peters has worked his way up from horse doctor to garage proprietor to oil magnate. Tub Pearson is a banker. Sam Dodsworth has just sold his automobile factory and now finds himself in the same position as Christopher Newman fifty years previously. Like James's hero, these men are from the West. Dodsworth and Pearson come, like Babbitt, from Zenith, in the imaginary state of Winnemac, representing Wisconsin, Minnesota, and Michigan. Will Haddock is from Legion, Ohio; Pike Peters from Clearwater, Oklahoma; and Edgar Bowman from Chicago. They do not arrive in France reluctant to place a defiling foot upon the revered soil; on the contrary, they can be provokingly assertive, as in the episode where Tub Pearson tries a bit of heavy-handed humor on the waiter of the Restaurant Voisin. The motive for their being in Paris is not a thirst for culture or a desire to see what they have read about in books. They are in the capital because of their wives, who feel obliged to bow to the dictates of fashion that make a visit to Paris absolutely de rigueur, hence the title of Croy's book. The ambiguity of their motives is succinctly revealed by Donald Ogden Stewart: "'I came to Paris,' said Mr. Haddock, 'to view the priceless monuments of the Old World, to bathe in the age-old splendor of a great civilization, to broaden myself,' he concluded, with a gesture, 'by contact with another race, another—but I'll not say better—form of life.' 'Hurray!' cried the other two. 'And so you came to the Ritz bar!'"[17]

The figure of Babbitt in Babylon offers ample potential for comedy, both through his role of visitor and through his essential Americanness. To the ridiculousness of the tourist in general is added the further ridiculousness of Lewis's hero in particular. Though at first glance Babbitt resembles the rustics of earlier literature, easy game for the locals, this image is misleading, since the locals themselves come in for a fair amount of ridicule. The essential comedy of Babbitt and his ilk lies in their failure to conform to norms that are American rather than French. The reader finds Haddock amusing because he zooms around at twice the speed of the average tourist, while Pike Peters is funny because his attitudes and behavior bear the stamp of the Far West. Both of them would be equally funny visiting New England. To the contrast between Europe and America is added the opposition between East and West, and also between town and country. The comic potential of such a situation was apparent to others in addition to novelists. The press, too, was quick to jump on the bandwagon. As Marie-Reine Garnier reminds us, the *Chicago Tribune* ran a series about the adventures of the Potter family in France, beginning with an installment that appeared on 19 August 1923.[18]

Scenes from Tourist Life

The tourist's first contact with the capital is a shock. In comparison with a city like London, Paris has a much faster rhythm. Dodsworth, journeying through the plains of Picardy, is reminded of the familiar landscape of Illinois and Iowa, but this impression vanishes at the Gare du Nord, where everything dissolves into a disordered whirl. This is a common experience for all the new arrivals and results from a combination of factors—the seething chaos of the platforms, the aggressiveness of the porters, the daredevil driving of the cabdrivers, and the terrifying speed of the traffic, which is rendered doubly nerve-racking by the incessant blaring of horns.[19] For Dev Evans in *A Voyage to Pagany*, "This rock [Paris] sets us spinning as dry land does feet after a ship."[20] After the taxi ride comes the hotel, where the reservations are sometimes casually overlooked, and where the unsuspecting traveler is taken aback as he enters his bathroom and comes face-to-face with a foreign appliance variously described as having the shape of a figure eight or a violin. Will Haddock, surrounded by signs announcing "Dernier Confort," is uncomfortably reminded of the administration of extreme unction. The elevators, conforming to the strict etymological definition of their function, only take passengers who are going up, and they are so slow that Mr. Haddock wonders if they come equipped with a buffet car.

Out in the street again, the visitors pronounce the reputation of Parisian women for beauty and elegance to be overrated, but they are even more disappointed by French men, whom Pike Peters finds effeminate and who arouse in the bosom of Will Haddock an inexplicable urge to "sock" them in the face. Then there are the open-air urinals, the brazenness of lovers embracing openly in the street, and the calm assurance with which a mother is observed "hold[ing] her baby out in a sitting position over the gutter,"[21] all symptoms of the French people's good-humored acceptance of the basic facts of life, to which the Americans react favorably on the whole. Dev Evans, strolling along the banks of the Seine, marvels at the way in which the fishermen, equipped with such gigantic rods, manage to catch such tiny fish. Sometimes, as with Elmer Moffatt in *The Custom of the Country*, the tourist reacts to things in a typically businesslike way. Pike Peters thinks the freight cars are too small and is flabbergasted by the inconvenience of the two-wheeled carts pulled by men or dogs. However, the author does admit that his character is unfamiliar with the finer details of a city tax that may well justify their use. The toll system that forces motorists to stop and declare how much gas they have got in their tanks seems to him to be totally unsuited to modern life and transport. Elsewhere we find Americans complaining about the Parisian telephones, which often do not work and which are usually to be found in some dark, evil-smelling basement.

Like their forefathers in *The Innocents Abroad*, modern tourists often find that their role involves a great deal that is irksome. There is simply no question of embarking on the long tourist circuits that take them from the Louvre to Notre-Dame and then to the Eiffel Tower and Versailles. The same litany of complaints recurs. Mr. Humperschlagel, in *The Web and the Rock*, claims that the Parisians "cheat you right and left—if you don't keep your eyes open, they'll steal the gold out of your teeth."[22] At restaurants, tourists are forced to order too much and, as a consequence, see their bill grow out of all proportion. This happens to Pike Peters in "the Restaurant of the Russian Comedians." Dev Evans experiences another form of cheating when the waiter whisks his half-finished steak from under his nose, perhaps in order to resell it on the side. Act 3, scene 3, of *Him* gives a clear illustration of how the typical tourist trap works. As soon as the unfortunate victim is sighted, the orchestra strikes up a tune, the waiters spring to life, and the maître d'hôtel practically stands on his head to get the client to order the most expensive item on the menu. But perhaps the Americans deserve some of the treatment they get from the staff of the Père Tranquille, as they make not the slightest attempt to differentiate between the various French banknotes, often failing to notice how many zeros there are on each one. Donald Ogden Stewart gives an account of a tour of the city directed by a guide and a bus driver who rival each other in their ignorance of the capital. Guides are, however, on the whole, secondary in importance to the staff of luxury hotels and restaurants. Pike Peters is afraid of the servants, who make him feel nervous and in whose presence he dreads betraying his humble origins. Sam Dodsworth is occasionally irritated by the overattentiveness of the staff of the Grand Universel, who make him feel as if he is in an old folks' home. In spite of this, he and his wife get on well with Mathieu, the waiter, whose authentic English is limited to purely culinary matters.

Mathieu may well be an entirely fictional character, but a comparison of different texts from the 1920s makes it clear that many of his counterparts in American literature are based on real characters. This is certainly the case for Jean and André, in *A Moveable Feast*, obliged by the management to shave off their mustaches for the opening of the new American bar at the Closerie des Lilas. The barman of the Crillon, George [*sic*], whom Bill Gorton and Jake Barnes knew and who was considered by Will Haddock to be "the best bartender in Paris,"[23] was also a real character. Lyon Mearson recalls another André, who worked at the Café de la Paix; and, among the staff of the Ritz, Hemingway remembers Frank [*sic*] and Georges. In *Tender Is the Night* Fitzgerald introduces the figure of Claude and, more notably, that of Paul, who refuses to let Peterson into the hotel because he is black. The author tells us in almost identical terms, in both *Tender Is the Night* and "Babylon Revisited," how Paul used to turn up for work in a car with special bodywork, which he left discreetly parked on the Boulevard des Capucines.

These are tutelary figures of Paree, a place about which the tourists have mixed feelings but which is essential to their well-being. On the one hand, they lament the progressive Americanization of the capital, with its burgeoning ads for Wrigley's chewing gum and its cash registers stamped "Made in USA," but, on the other hand, they are terrified of feeling completely like aliens. According to Sinclair Lewis, Americans in Paris are basically preoccupied with two things: the exchange rate and their feeling of homesickness. Pike Peters is so anxious not to forget Oklahoma that he always wears two watches, one of which tells him what time it is in Clearwater. Furthermore, he installs a radio in his château at Mont d'Or that is powerful enough to receive transatlantic broadcasts. One of his most pleasant memories of Paris is of the occasion on which he identified a fellow Elk in the Café de la Paix and was able to have a conversation with him, after first exchanging the appropriate secret signs. The most commonly heard lament among tourists is "Paris is not Paris. The Americans have spoiled it,"[24] yet these same American tourists are constantly on the lookout for things that remind them of home. They want to find their local newspapers, as well as the big national dailies. The most extreme even expect to find American cooking: the high spot of Mr. Humperschlagel's visit is when he discovers a restaurant serving bacon and eggs and real apple pie. Most tourists do not go this far, but they do expect to be able to lay their hands on their favorite brands of bicarbonate of soda and toothpaste, the razor blades they use, packs of Lucky Strikes, and B.V.D.'s, while constantly marveling at the fact that the capital is changing under their influence.

But shopping is a ritual, just as it was in previous times. Dev Evans, picking up a few things at the Bon Marché, criticizes the complicated way the store is organized and suspects that he has been cheated by the assistant, whereas Dick Diver finds that the relatively modest sums he spends at his

English shirtmaker's bring him a considerable bargain, in light of the quality of the service he receives. This difference in atmosphere and attitude underlines the contrast between the department stores and luxury boutiques. While Mrs. Haddock may buy presents for her friends back in Ohio at the Galeries Lafayette, the tourists, in general, do their shopping only at the most reputable establishments, whose vocation is to serve rich foreigners. Pike Peters remarks that Paris is "a woman's city,"[25] observing how everything is marvelously organized so that women can spend their money in the most pleasant way imaginable. In *Him,* two American women are talking about the dress that one of them has bought at Poiret's for which she remembers having paid with "three of those very big notes, you know, the brown ones."[26] Fitzgerald, writing about shopping in Paris, manages to give the ritual a significance that is poetic as well as economic. In *Tender Is the Night,* Nicole Diver and Rosemary Hoyt frequent the elegant hairdressers, dress designers, and boutiques of the Rue de Rivoli. But while Rosemary, the movie star, represents "new money" with all its attendant showiness, Nicole, heiress to the Warren dynasty, stands for established American capitalism. As the author says, behind her are the workers of an entire continent, all busy paying their tithe. While Rosemary lacks assurance and boldness, Nicole calmly goes about her shopping, a two-page list in her hand, bent on acquiring a large collection of chiefly useless objects: "colored beads, folding beach cushions, artificial flowers, honey, a guest bed, bags, scarfs . . . a dozen bathing suits, a rubber alligator, a travelling chess set of gold and ivory."[27] The two women are the symbols par excellence of the splendor of riches, closely linked to Fitzgerald's passion for beauty. Ravishing and rich, Nicole and Rosemary are in perfect harmony with Parisian luxury. "It was fun spending money in the sunlight of the foreign city, with healthy bodies under them that sent streams of color up to their faces; with arms and hands, legs and ankles that they stretched out confidently, reaching or stepping with the confidence of women lovely to men."[28] Whether the money is new or old, the figure of the beautiful American woman elegantly squandering her dollars on countless luxuries stands alongside the figure of Babbitt, adding an aesthetic and sensual dimension to the confrontation of American wealth with the Parisian scene. Babbitt and Nicole are the two faces of the dollar, which is the symbol of tourist Paris and the main thing separating it from the Paris of the artist.

Montparnasse and Revelry

The Habitat

In the 1920s the boundaries of bohemia were pushed outward with the addition of Montparnasse to the familiar territory of the Latin Quarter. The war had a melting-pot effect on the capital's artistic milieu, making it more cosmopolitan, and establishing the Boulevard Montparnasse as the axis of artistic life and the symbol of everything having to do with American writers in the Paris of the twenties. The most frequently described places by far are the boulevard cafés, which sometimes provide the setting for scenes lasting several pages. At the Select, Dodsworth is approached by a young American called Elsa. She deliberately flirts with him, getting him to buy champagne for all her friends, and then surreptitiously vanishes. In the same café, Nande Azeredo, touched by Dodsworth's evident discouragement, attempts to cheer him up and thus initiates their affair. Many of the Parisian episodes of *The Sun Also Rises* revolve around the Select. It is here that Brett and Jake are introduced to Count Mippipopolous and that Harvey Stone torments Robert Cohn. It is here that Jake acts as arbitrator in the quarrel between Cohn and his mistress. The entire action of *On the Terrasse* takes place at the Dôme. In *A Voyage to Pagany* the same café is the favorite meeting place of the artists who welcome Dev Evans to Paris. The Dôme also appears briefly in *Dodsworth, The Sun Also Rises,* "Mr. and Mrs. Elliot," and *Of Time and the River.*[29] Hemingway meets Pascin and his two female models there in *A Moveable Feast* and describes the regulars of the Dôme as being "people who have worked," while the clientele of the Rotonde are people who give in to "vice and the collective instinct."[30] The Rotonde is also mentioned in *Of Time and the River* and "Mr. and Mrs. Elliot."[31] Jake Barnes speaks of its "sad tables," and he strongly suspects some sort of arrangements between taxi drivers and the owner: "No matter what café in Montparnasse you ask a taxi-driver to bring you to from the right bank of the river, they always take you to the Rotonde."[32] The rivalry between the Dôme and the Rotonde is the subject of a lengthy description in *The French They Are a Funny Race.*

On her return from San Sebastian, Brett Ashley goes to the Closerie des Lilas with Jake Barnes and Bill Gorton. In *A Moveable Feast* it is noted as being the café nearest to Hemingway's apartment at 113 Rue Notre-Dame-des-Champs and as being a quiet place, frequented by people who have been awarded the Palmes Académiques or have been injured in the war. It provides the background for Hemingway's malicious portrait of Ford Madox

Ford and the amusing scene where he advises an aspiring writer, Hal, to give up literature and try his hand at literary criticism instead. It is there that he and Fitzgerald meet for the second time and decide to go to Lyon together. In *A Moveable Feast* Hemingway says that he first met Fitzgerald at the Dingo, in 1925. This café in the Rue Delambre is further mentioned in *A Voyage to Pagany* and *The Sun Also Rises*. Still other cafés and restaurants gradually emerge as part of the expatriate scene as well: the Nègre de Toulouse, which Hemingway sometimes called Lavigne, after its owner, and where he soon became a regular with his own serviette; the Avenue; the Jockey; the Trianon; Michaud, where James Joyce used to eat; Chez Henriette; the Café Damoy; and the Café de Versailles. Although quite a long way from the Boulevard Montparnasse, the Brasserie Lipp is also part of the scene in *A Moveable Feast:* the author refers to a meal he had there accompanied by a liter of beer called a "distingué."[33]

Midway between the well-known cafés and restaurants and the anonymous private rooms are the small furnished lodgings where some Americans live. The stage directions for *The Left Bank* state that the play takes place in a hotel on the Boulevard Montparnasse. In *Of Time and the River* Eugene Gant lives in the Hôtel des Beaux-Arts, where Oscar Wilde died. Dev Evans is at the Hôtel Beausoir, and it appears that Mike Campbell and Brett Ashley mistakenly take a room in a brothel in the Rue Delambre. The contrast between such lodgings and those on the Right Bank is striking, even if we leave aside the worst of the former, like the miserable hotel in which Verlaine died and in which Hemingway rented a room to work. They exhale an air of sadness and poverty, of shabby outmodedness, that British novelist Jean Rhys captures perfectly in *Good Morning, Midnight* and *After Leaving Mr. Mackenzie.*

Near the banks of the Seine is the café on the Place Saint-Michel in which Hemingway wrote for some time. Elliot Paul, in *The Amazon,* introduces American readers to the Rue de la Huchette, a street that was to have far more importance in his later works. In the chapter of *A Moveable Feast* called "People of the Seine," Hemingway sketches the quays from the Halle aux Vins to the Quai Voltaire. (This is where Rose Frank lives in *Dark Laughter.*) Near the Tour d'Argent a bookseller displays the English books left behind by visitors in the rooms above the famous restaurant, and it is here along the banks of the river that the Latin Quarter meets the world of the bouquinistes, whose chaotic jumble both fascinates and appalls Eugene Gant. The activity of anglers fishing in the Seine for gudgeon, which, as we have seen, inspired derision in a character like Dev Evans, is strongly defended by Hemingway as "serious and productive."[34] His interest in their activity, which is centered on the islands in the Seine, seems to annex the islands to the Left Bank. Mme Lecomte's restaurant, too, is somehow made to seem part of Montparnasse by the fact that Jake Barnes and Bill Gorton return from it on foot, a more or less unheard of exploit, in *The Sun Also Rises*.

But by far the most memorable images of the Left Bank are Hemingway's descriptions of the Place de la Contrescarpe and its surroundings in *The Sun Also Rises*, "The Snows of Kilimanjaro," and *A Moveable Feast*. The fact that certain impressions of Paris recur often in Hemingway's writing, as they did in that of Dos Passos, indicates how strongly they affected the writer— and for Hemingway, these recurring impressions come, most often, from the area of the Place de la Contrescarpe. The Braddocks' dance club, mentioned by Ford Madox Ford as a character in *A Moveable Feast*, is held in a "bal musette" at 74 Rue Cardinal-Lemoine, the house where Hemingway lived for a time. Jake Barnes rapidly sketches his impressions of the neighborhood as night is falling, a description which is taken up again in more detail in "The Snows of Kilimanjaro" and *A Moveable Feast*. The local inhabitants, dubbed variously by Hemingway as "sportifs" and "drunkards," are the direct descendants of the 1871 Communards. Their narrow world is marked out by the wine cooperative, the horsemeat butcher, the dairy, the terminal of the S bus, and, finally, the Café des Amateurs, "a sad evilly run café where the drunkards of the quarter crowded together," which Hemingway steered clear of "because of the smell of dirty bodies and the sour smell of drunkenness."[35] The dying Harry, in "The Snows of Kilimanjaro," remembers its "sprawling trees, the old white plastered houses painted brown below, the long green of the autobus in that round square . . . the sudden drop down the hill of the rue Cardinal-Lemoine to the river, and the other way, the narrow crowded world of the rue Mouffetard." And this is followed by the remark, doubtless a reflection of Hemingway's own feelings, that "there never was another part of Paris that he loved like that."[36]

The Inhabitants

When it comes to talking about the inhabitants of the artist's Paris, the many character portraits in *A Moveable Feast* pose a problem. It is true that Ezra Pound, Ford Madox Ford, Sylvia Beach, James Joyce, and Wyndham Lewis were all part of American Montparnasse. So, to a lesser degree, were Pascin, Evan Shipman, Ralph Cheever Dunning, and Ernest Walsh. But what about Gertrude Stein, a monolithic figure who stood on her own, or Fitzgerald, whose taste for luxury inclined him more toward the Right Bank? The characters in *A Moveable Feast* are not especially representative of Montparnasse. Often Hemingway chooses to include them in order to justify some of his own actions or simply to settle old scores. However, they do deserve mention, just as other real characters found in various novels of the period do. William Carlos Williams alludes in *A Voyage to Pagany* to Van Cleve, Harland, Walsh, Salter, Léger, George Andrews, and Mary Lloyd. And his hero Dev Evans, on his way to Sylvia Beach's place at 12 Rue de l'Odéon to pick up his mail, notices the two models Kiki and Zaza sitting outside the Dôme.[37] In "The Snows of Kilimanjaro" the author briefly voices his suspicions regarding a "Romanian who said his name was Tristan Tzara, who always wore a monocle and had a headache."[38] In *The French They Are a Funny Race,* Lyon Mearson manages to drop the names of a good twenty or so close friends. In the descriptions of the various cafés in *Kiki of Montparnasse,* Kohner lists the most well known customers, who include, apart from the Americans, Braque, Marcoussis, Derain, Utrillo, Matisse, Picasso, Tzara, and Ilya Ehrenbourg. The most colorful character is Gitche Manitou, a Cherokee chief who read Plato in French and was studying at the Sorbonne. He was an attraction at the Dôme, and, according to the author, his return to the United States coincided with the start of Kiki's drinking.

As for imaginary characters, there is not much point in weighing out the respective parts played by real-life models in the final makeup of fictional heroes. For *The Sun Also Rises,* this has already been done by Harold Loeb in *The Way It Was.* Brett Ashley is modeled on Lady Duff Twysden. Harvey Stone owes a great deal to Harold Stearn. Bill Gorton is probably Donald Ogden Stewart. Robert Cohn is a mixture of Harold Loeb and Robert McAlmon. Braddocks, who liked to arrange dancing evenings reminds us of Ford Madox Ford. In works of fiction, one of the author's concerns is to create characters representative of their milieu. An examination of the inhabitants of Montparnasse reveals, among other things, the relative importance of writers and a marked change in sexual attitudes. It also reveals the existence of what Sinclair Lewis calls "hobohemia," a collection of peripheral figures like Nande Azeredo, who was "half Portuguese, half Russian and altogether French . . . had been married three times and once shot a Siberian wolf."[39] Claiming to be a sculptor, Nande makes a living by producing wax mannequins for shop windows. There are still a number of painters around, like the Greek Zizi in *The Sun Also Rises,* Joe Walker and Tom Burnside in *Dark Laughter,* or the miniaturist Gillespie and the illustrator Jack Keipp, both of whom are Elsa's accomplices in the café scene in *Dodsworth*. Fred Grey in *Dark Laughter* and Ross Peters in *They Had to See Paris* both come to Paris to learn to paint, like so many before them. Lorry Spear is a theater designer in *The Gods Arrive;* Bess Evans, in *A Voyage to Pagany,* is a music student. Rose Frank, in *Dark Laughter,* is a journalist, like Jake Barnes, although the latter seems to have more serious literary ambitions. The increase in the number of characters who are writers, and the fact that they are often major protagonists, is particularly striking in comparison with the place accorded to writers in the literature from before the war. The hero of *A Voyage to Pagany* is a poet. Many of Jake Barnes's acquaintances are novelists—not just Robert Cohn but also Bill Gorton, Robert Prentiss, and Frances Clyne, whose work is published in various magazines. Elsa, in *Dodsworth,* also wants to write novels; and, with the character of Vance Weston, Edith Wharton chooses a novelist as protagonist and through him is able to express her views on Parisian bohemia in *The Gods Arrive.*

But the most remarkable thing about Montparnasse is its atmosphere of moral permissiveness and the relative freedom with which writers discuss such matters. There are prostitutes, whose appearance seems perfectly natural on both banks of the Seine. On the Right Bank we see them at the Père Tranquille, in *Him;* Pike Peters notices them as he walks through the streets; and Edith Wharton introduces at least one in *Glimpses of the Moon*. On the Left Bank the narrator of *Kiki of Montparnasse* admits to being wary of venturing into the Rue d'Odessa, an unhealthy place in more than one respect. Kohner also gives a lengthy description of the lavish opening celebrations of the Sphinx, run by Mme Carnevali, which underscores the importance of this establishment in neighborhood life. However, as Dodsworth remarks, "There are few professional prostitutes to be found at the Dôme or the Select, no matter how competent were some of the amateurs."⁴⁰

Also, starting from the explanations Gertrude Stein obligingly gives to the young Hemingway in *A Moveable Feast,* the reader may also begin to explore homosexual Montparnasse. As Esther Walker says to Aline Aldridge in *Dark Laughter,* shortly after attempting to seduce her: "Over here you've got to look out for both women and men."⁴¹ Starwick, in *Of Time and the River,* and Dev Evans are homosexuals. Starwick has a long-lasting affair with Alec, a Frenchman he meets in a bar. Dev Evans wants to rediscover in Paris the kind of relationship he had in New York with his friend Jack Murphy. In *On the Terrasse* Babbitt is naively astonished by what he sees at the Dôme:

Fairies and Lesbians, these words are new
To George F. Babbitt and the Babbitt Gang.
Look at that thing that calls itself a man,
Making fool eyes at that boy over there
Painted and frizzed . . . [42]

Hal, the would-be literary critic, is told by Hemingway to go and join his fellows at the Petite-Chaumière and later earns himself an obscene remark that confirms what had been suggested by the opening part of the conversation.[43] In "Mr. and Mrs. Elliot" the poet gives up his place in the medieval marriage bed to his wife's girlfriend summoned from Boston. Hemingway claims in *A Moveable Feast* that Zelda Fitzgerald aroused her husband's jealousy not only through her relationships with other men but also with women. The scene in *The Sun Also Rises* in which the prostitute Georgette dances with a group of homosexuals, one after the other, watched by Brett and Jake, exemplifies the ambivalence and confusion of sexual relationships in Montparnasse as a whole.

Drug-taking is described in graphic detail in *The Outsider,* particularly in the scene where Ezra Rich smokes opium. Babbitt several times remarks on the habit in *On the Terrasse,* and other references can be found in "The Whistling Swan." In *A Moveable Feast* Hemingway describes his mission of mercy to deliver opium to Ralph Cheever Dunning when the latter was going through withdrawal symptoms.

Reading on, a clear picture begins to emerge of the various characters, even down to the sort of clothes they wear. Ross Peters, for example, goes in for an exaggerated version of anything he considers to be French and fashionable. Wyndham Lewis usually wore a wide-brimmed black hat, and, according to Hemingway in *A Moveable Feast,* looked like an actor in *La Bohème.* Who could forget, after reading *The Sun Also Rises,* that Brett once did not wear stockings, and after reading *A Voyage to Pagany,* that Delise took hers off in public, claiming to dance better with bare legs? Extravagance, whether it applies to clothes, conversation, or spending money, is an essential part of artistic behavior. Yet, observing the Brownian movement that operates in this breeding ground of artists, one is struck by its artificial nature. The different characters collide, attract, and repel each other like particles in a test tube. Groups form and dissolve on café terraces; rivals confront each other; lovers quarrel. Can these restless, manic characters really be artists? It is sometimes difficult to see what relationship can exist between the city that gave birth to bohemia, and this modern travesty.

Real Parisians are as scarce on the Left Bank as they are on the Right. The reader comes across the odd concierge, like Mme Duzinell in *The Sun Also Rises;* various waiters; dropouts, like the tramps in the Place de la Contrescarpe; a prostitute or two, like Georgette; and even the occasional goatherd. The artist population is almost exclusively Anglo-Saxon. Montparnasse has become the American annex, a bohemia thrown open to the public, with rules for its misrule. Its nooks and corners, its discreet intimacy, its poetic attics sheltering lovers, have almost entirely disappeared. One or two traces of the old atmosphere can still be found here and there. *The Eater of Darkness,* for example, opens with a picturesque evocation of narrow streets and a studio of the Latin Quarter. Starwick's apartment is described in a few lines in *Of Time and the River,* and in *Dodsworth* Sinclair Lewis gives a more detailed picture of Nande Azeredo's lair: "It was an insane little flat: three rooms, just under the roof, looking on a paved courtyard which smelled of slops and worse, and was all day clamorous with quarrelling, children playing, delivery of charcoal, and the banging of garbage cans." Dodsworth is met by an unfamiliar chaos as he enters: "Her dishes were cracked, her cups were chipped; the plaster walls were rain-streaked. . . . Her clothes were in heaps and there was no concealment of sanitary appliances. And everywhere were instruments for the making of noise: a phonograph which by preference she turned on at three in the morning, rattles and horns left over from the last carnival, a very cheap radio—fortunately out of order—and seven canaries."[44] In *A Moveable Feast* Hemingway recalls his apartment in the Rue Cardinal-Lemoine "that had no water and no inside toilet facilities except an antiseptic container, not uncomfortable to anyone who was used to a Michigan outhouse." In spite of those drawbacks, he adds, "with a fine view and a good mattress and springs for a comfortable bed on the floor and pictures we liked on the walls, it was a cheerful gay flat."[45]

Hemingway, in fact, is the only writer of this period who manages to convey an atmosphere of bohemian life as it first appeared in literature, with its contrast between an urban environment steeped in sadness and disillusion and a local population radiating ardor and enthusiasm. He succeeds in capturing all the melancholy of the damp and foggy winter, overshadowed by the memory of Verlaine's death, a melancholy that, for Hubert Redd in "The Whistling Swan," also brings back memories of Gérard de Nerval. The heights of the Contrescarpe as described by Hemingway in "The Snows of Kilimanjaro" and *A Moveable Feast,* conjure up this bohemian atmosphere. The author draws the eye to the mournful picturesqueness of the old houses, with their water closets on each landing, and the regular visits of the sanitary wagons, whose colors of yellow and saffron recall the paintings of Braque. Although Hemingway never went hungry to the same degree as Jean Rhys—who describes five days without food in her short story "Hunger"—he was sometimes unable to afford a meal, and he speaks of hunger as being "healthy," adding, "The pictures do look better when you're hungry."[46]

It seems likely that the sharpness of the images in *A Moveable Feast,* their clear, hard definition, owes something to the memory of this hunger. It does not stem solely from the fasts imposed by a poverty that was, after all, relative. It derives also from an appetite for loving and living, for reading and writing, and it takes the form of a passion whose elements of restraint and liberation were consciously cultivated by the young Hemingway. Although expressed in far more sober terms, Hemingway's feeling here is akin to the romantic frenzy that fed the lyric flights of Henri Murger. On the cover of the Bantam edition of *A Moveable Feast,* an anonymous critic claims that the book is "savagely written, full of love and bitterness." The same thing could equally well have been said of the writing of Murger, whose cruelty is sometimes overlooked. More than a hundred years after the publication of *Scènes de la Vie de Bohème,* Hemingway vividly brings back the poverty and squalor, the idealism and despairing passion, of the original. What he wrote about the Contrescarpe in *A Moveable Feast* is doubly poignant in that it is associated with the death of the novelist Harry in "The Snows of Kilimanjaro" and with the thought of suicide that was a constant obsession with Hemingway at the time.

With the exceptions just mentioned, Montparnasse is viewed from without, a fact that is in keeping with its essentially public nature. The literary presentation of artistic Paris, while undoubtedly having more substance than that of tourist Paris, is nonetheless superficial and limited mainly to Americans. It offers a view of contemporary Parisian manners that is narrow and restrictive, and thus of limited historical value. It is with some justification that e. e. cummings situates the Boulevard Montparnasse in the kingdom of Paree. There, in fact, tourists and artists mingle to such an extent that Montparnasse, in one sense a distinct ghetto or game preserve, also stands for the paradoxical synthesis of the two banks of the Seine under the common banner "America." Still more, however, the two banks of the Seine are united through the sacred rite of carnival, of festival, which, as it did in 1919, careens through the city like a whirlwind, sweeping away old boundaries and establishing its own kingdom of misrule.

Revelry

In *The Sun Also Rises* the episodes set in Paris concentrate more or less exclusively on Jake's adventures from the end of the afternoon to the following dawn on three different occasions. The hero's normal daytime occupations—his job, for example—are hardly mentioned, apart from his visit to the Quai d'Orsay. The idea of festivity is struck by the title of *A Moveable Feast* and also by the title given to the edition of *The Sun Also Rises* published in England, *Fiesta*. Paris and Pamplona are linked in the book, but whereas many of the Spanish festivities take place during the day, festivity, in Paris, is always associated with the night. There are two kinds of festivity: the first is private in nature and restricted to one particular place and group of people,47 and the second—more common—is public and involves some kind of journey through the city. Jake Barnes, Dev Evans, Dick Diver, Pike Peters, Sam Dodsworth, Eugene Gant, and George Webber all engage in their own personal nocturnal explorations of the capital. For Jake, it is a sort of routine. Pike Peters and Dodsworth allow their itinerary to be determined by chance and improvisation. Dick Diver, on the other hand, plans his "quick Odyssey over Paris"48 down to the last detail, the star feature being the shah of Iran's car, which he has somehow managed to get hold of for the occasion. For all these wanderers, what Thomas Wolfe calls the "kaleidoscopic circuit of the night"49 eventually leads them to the cafés near Les Halles or the Gare Montparnasse as dawn breaks over the city. *Of Time and the River,* like *The Sun Also Rises,* contains three different nighttime episodes in which Eugene Gant explores Paris, twice with Starwick and once with Ann. In Sinclair Lewis's novel, Dodsworth's memorable night out with Tub and Matey Pearson lasts for six pages, and revels of a similar nature and length can be found in *A Voyage to Pagany, They Had to See Paris,* and *The Professors Like Vodka.*

Some of the high spots of Paris by night had already been described in novels about the First World War. Others are now mentioned for the first time. Eugene Gant and his friends visit the Moulin Rouge, the Tabarin, Le Coq et l'Ane, the Bolée, and the Rat Mort, where Starwick is challenged to a duel. In "Babylon Revisited" Charlie Wales makes a return visit to the Casino de Paris and Bricktop's, and he mentions the closing down of the Caveau des Poètes. Will Haddock goes to Luigi's and the Ciro. Sinclair Lewis gives a detailed description of the Caverne Russe des Quarante Vents, where Tub Pearson plays the middle-aged seducer.50 The Zelli is mentioned in *The Sun Also Rises, Mr. and Mrs. Haddock in Paris,* and "Babylon Revisited." According to Jake Barnes, "Inside Zelli's it was crowded, smoky, and noisy. The music hit you as you went in."[51] In *The Web and the Rock* Thomas Wolfe gives a colorful account of the luxurious brothel visited by George Webber. One night, Eugene Gant and Starwick venture so far into the slums around the Boulevard Sébastopol and Les Halles that two policemen discreetly follow them in order to make sure they come to no harm.

Homer Croy, like Mark Twain, takes a dim view of the local industry of nighttime distractions and sums up as follows his heroes' night out in Montmartre: "They rushed from one stuffy, bizarre restaurant to another. . . . They ate among coffins and tombs, they ascended into heaven, and they went down into the expensive depth of hell, and all in the name of Pleasure." Le Lapin Agile made a particularly bad impression on the author, as may be seen from his description of the entertainer there, Frédé: "An old man with a tangle of grey hair and a long white beard, wearing a red suit and peasant's boots and looking like Santa Claus, appeared with a guitar." Croy goes on to give details of the performance: "He made a speech which was supposed to be witty, eyed the girls, and sang some sort of a love song. . . . On and on he sang, now and then stopping to crack a feeble, suggestive joke and wiping his mouth with the back of his hand. A fat woman, evidently connected with the establishment, came out and he engaged her in what was supposed to be a humorous word combat, passing compliments on her decayed charms, while the waiters came again with their dirty mops and requests for drinks."[52]

The mood of these revels varies. The atmosphere of *Mr. and Mrs. Haddock in Paris* is one of lighthearted gaiety in which the characters experience a sense of liberation and release. Life is suddenly full of boundless possibilities, and, as Will Haddock remarks to Mrs. Abercrombie, with whom he is sharing a cab, "This Paris is a funny place. . . . Here I am, for example, driving around in a strange carriage with a strange lady in evening clothes at seven thirty in the morning; and yet it all seems perfectly natural and perfectly right."[53] The same spirit inspires Bill Gorton's wisecracks about wanting to stuff every animal he sees and Fitzgerald's fondness for practical jokes, which is shared by many of his characters. Dick Diver and company manage to convince the staff of the Ritz that General Pershing wishes to be served caviar and champagne in the lobby in the middle of the night. Later they construct a labyrinth out of various pieces of furniture, which they christen a "waiter's trap." In "Babylon Revisited" Charlie Wales reminisces about the time he stole a tricycle in the middle of the night in order to ride around the Arc de Triomphe and about having tried to make a phone call to the president of the republic. This lightheartedness is in keeping with the city's own mood during celebrations on 14 July, which can be heard offstage in Act 2 of *The Left Bank,* and those on New Year's Eve, which accompany Eugene Gant's reunion with Starwick. A further note of amusing eroticism is added by e. e. cummings in *Him,* where the two American tourists, "The Fairly Young Lady" and "The Older Lady," desirous of sampling their own version of the local specialties in the form of two drunken men, ask the waiter to bring them two "ombs," one "stewed" and the other "boiled."[54]

It is in a more sombre mood that Sinclair Lewis describes Dodsworth, bored and depressed by his marital problems, looking for solace in the city's bars. Likewise, there is no gaiety in the description of Starwick's increasing debauchery or Abe North's involvement in various escapades that will indirectly result in murder. Such dissipation is reflected in the writers' perception of the city. Thomas Wolfe is conscious of the evil spell cast by the nighttime city, radiating a magic that is black rather than white. He uses the words "magic" and "magical" several times in connection with the capital in *Of Time and the River.* The city is a mysterious and enchanted labyrinth, a poisonous flower that lures the visitors with its fatal beauty. The nocturnal fantasy orchestrated by Dick Diver is set against an urban backdrop with the unreality of a theater set. Episode dissolves into episode, and baroque characters flit across the footlights and disappear into the wings: the Indian chief George T. Horseprotection, the manufacturer of artificial voice boxes for dolls, the fairy-tale Scandinavian prince. As presented by Fitzgerald, the episode has a texture and feel without equivalent in Hemingway's writing. In *The Sun Also Rises* night is merely an absence of daylight. In *Tender Is the Night* it is palpable; it has its own peculiar consistency. While the opposition implied by the sun and the night of the titles is doubtless fortuitous, Fitzgerald's choice of title does indicate his strong affinity for nighttime scenes. The motive behind Dick's arranged outing is to impress Rosemary and to outshine the party in the Rue Monsieur and the lavish distractions of Hollywood. Rosemary, dazzled by her feelings for Dick, fails to see the sham, the artificiality, of the spectacle that unfolds for her. The bizarre mix of characters, the flickering incoherence of scene and time, the childish jokes, and the pitiful and worrying presence of Abe North—all of these are lost on her. The shady, slightly illegal air of many of Fitzgerald's characters is noticeable here, where the reader has the strong impression that he has fallen in with a bunch of moonshiners.

This brings us to the final and perhaps most crucial aspect of Parisian revelry: drunkenness. By this we do not mean the metaphorical intoxication of Booth Tarkington but the literal drunkenness to which many of the protagonists succumb at one moment or another. Starwick has the longest drinking bout, lasting for a full ten pages in *Of Time and the River.* A quick total of the various drinks imbibed by the heroes of *The Sun Also Rises* permits us to gauge the importance of alcohol in the lives of the expatriates: in the eighty-four pages on Paris in the Scribner edition, there are seventy-five references to alcoholic drinks. Getting drunk affects characters in different ways and reveals different aspects of their personalities. Dodsworth gets drunk because he feels depressed. Bill Haley, in *The Professors Like Vodka,* experiences hallucinatory symptoms and thinks he sees the dean's wife sitting at a table in the Dingo. Mortimer Long, in *The Outsider,* experiences a sort of mystic elevation, whereas Starwick's drunkenness is the symbol of his conviction that he is a failure. For Tub Pearson, drinking is an attempt to escape from his Babbitt-like condition, and for Dev Evans, it is a source of pleasure and even of poetic inspiration. William Carlos Williams, describing his hero's intoxication, says, "What a delightful thing—drunkenness."[55]

Drunkenness represents the most extreme version of the festive rites, but, to a certain extent, it reopens the old debate about civilization at a time when America was in bondage to the Eighteenth Amendment. For is it not perhaps the case that the Americans who get drunk in Paris are thereby calling into question their way of life? Like the cannon shots that are also a part of festive celebrations, drunkenness seems to bring drowned bodies back to the surface, stirring up old issues and bringing pressure to bear in favor of a new hearing of the case of Europe vs. America, this time in the context of the 1920s.

CHAPTER 7

THE JUDGMENTS OF PARIS

In the novel by Gore Vidal from which this chapter takes its title, the hero arrives in the French capital after a long journey and prepares to set the seal on his destiny by choosing, out of three modern incarnations of the legendary goddesses, the one who represents Venus. This relatively recent work (1953) draws attention to the American protagonist who, ending his quest in Paris with a judgment and a choice, symbolizes successful expatriation. By no means all of the characters in novels of expatriation reach the same happy end and assign such importance to the capital, but this does not prevent them from passing their own judgments during their stay in the city. Paris is their forum, and the debates with which the city resounds are not simply the result of geographical hazard. Even when they have no direct bearing on the capital itself, they are a consequence of the protagonists' presence there and of their special status as expatriates, torn between their country of birth and their country of adoption. The preposition in the title has a twofold meaning: judgments passed on Paris and judgments provoked by Paris. The books of American authors are full of discussions, ranging from arguments between different stereotypical characters—Parisians, East Coast Americans, West Coast Americans, artists, tourists, and Babbitt figures—to interior monologues concerning the characters' quest for their true identity, like Dodsworth's soliloquy on the terrace of the Weber. In the midst of all these voices, that of the author may be heard discoursing on such divergent topics as the differences between Europe and America, bohemia, the nature of literary activity, and the significance of myths.

America vs. Europe

A convenient way of avoiding the seeming contradiction between America's prosperity and the expatriation of so many of its citizens is simply to ignore it, to focus instead on the disadvantages of life in Paris. Apart from the usual tourist complaints, which are far more numerous and specific than they had been heretofore, we gradually become aware of the appearance of a distinct sentiment that the New World is superior to the Old. Although this attitude is not new, and in any case is not common to all writers, the accumulated criticisms leave us with a picture of a postwar Paris that is not particularly attractive and reflects that of Europe in general. Some judgments are inspired by feelings of enthusiasm and enjoyment; others are the result of a sober lucidity in which the carefree gaiety of the Parisians is not sufficient to redeem their city's all too obvious shortcomings. The Americans are often amused by the lack of organization, the gratuitous complicatedness of the capital, but they do not find it so funny when they are forced to deal with Parisians who are dirty, stupid, narrow-minded, and dishonest—mean and petty creatures who seem to Thomas Wolfe to swarm through the city like rats. The capital, with its scandals, its corrupt press, its antiquated buildings, its soulless museums and war memorials, is the very embodiment of a spent and exhausted society. Such an image may appear unnecessarily gloomy and reductive. Yet it is one that recurs time after time in descriptions by Maurice Samuel, Thomas Wolfe, Donald Ogden Stewart, Homer Croy, and Lyon Mearson, and it foreshadows Henry Miller's image of a metropolis eaten away by cancer and syphilis. The Depression cannot be blamed for such moroseness and pessimism, since most of these works were written before it. The denigration of Paris quite simply underscores the general decline of Europe.

In *Mr. and Mrs. Haddock in Paris*, there is a sudden change in tone on page 240. Haddock, along with a character called Le Bottin, launches into a lengthy comparison between Paris and America. The author warns us that we must now be serious, for what is about to come is "too ghastly true to be funny."[1] In Haddock's opinion, Europe has well and truly lost her soul. As for America, she certainly has not found hers yet, but she will not do so by looking to Europe for inspiration. Underneath the surface jingoism of this passage, which comes at the end of an essentially comic book, lie fundamental preoccupations. Paris prompts Americans to ask themselves questions about their own civilization. Not all of them have the fine optimism of Haddock. In *The Web and the Rock* George Webber is horrified at the behavior of his fellow citizens at the American Express office, huge, rough individuals shoving and jostling in front of the windows, and is obliged to conclude that there is little to choose between these arrogant, self-righteous characters and the lowest type of Parisian. But what is to be learned from these differences, and how can America bring back to life on the other side of the Atlantic the grandeur of past centuries? It is questions like these that pass through Dodsworth's mind as he stands before Notre-Dame. "There was strength there; strength and endurance and wisdom. The flying buttresses soared like wings. The whole cathedral expanded before his eyes; the work of human hands seemed to tower larger than the sky. He felt, dimly and disconnectedly, that he too had done things with his hands; that the motor car was no contemptible creation; that he was nearer to the forgotten, the anonymous and merry and vulgar artisans who had created this somber epic of stone, than was any Endicott Everet Atkins . . . as he uttered pomposities about 'the transition in Gothic motifs.'"[2] At fifty-two, Dodsworth is part of an aging generation whose potential for achievement is drawing to an end. Even the name of his automobile company seems to portend a new order: the enthusiasm hinted at in the firm's former name, the Revelation Motor Company, has been replaced by the prosaic matter-of-factness of the giant that has taken it over, the Unit Automobile Company. Dodsworth's experience of the capital affects him profoundly, causing a rift to open between himself and his wife. He exemplifies the old pioneer virtue of America, while his wife is shown behaving with the frivolous irresponsibility of a spoiled child.

The Dodsworths' situation symbolizes the split between the representatives of Old America and the New Barbarians. Ranged alongside Dodsworth are Ross Ireland (the famous reporter who is Dodsworth's alter ego), Dev Evans, George Webber, and other characters with evocative names: Lilian Garfield in *The Left Bank,* Lincoln Peters in "Babylon Revisited," and Abe North in *Tender Is the Night.* It is no accident that both of the presidents recalled here were assassinated, for Old America is dying. Yet, the name of this last character seems to suggest that he is also one of the Barbarians, whose origin lies in the North. Dev Evans's sister Bess exudes "a kind of northern gloom,"[3] and Rosemary, Nicole, and Baby Warren, standing for the various destructive elements in *Tender Is the Night,* are all characterized by their coldness. Fran Dodsworth has "pale Swede hair" and chooses to appear as "the North Wind" for a masked ball. The German aristocrat von Obersdorf describes her as "a kind of Arctic beauty, shining like ice."[4] Dodsworth feels totally lost and cut off from this incomprehensible generation, and his perplexity increases when, on a brief visit to New York, he tries to speak to his son. Brent wants to become a bond broker in order to make money as fast as possible. Where the father wanted to create, the son wants to sell, consume, destroy. Paris focuses this antagonism, revealing these New Barbarians as the possible precursors of a growing totalitarianism. The references to the cold, the North, are reinforced by the fact that Fran Dodsworth and Nicole and Baby Warren are all of German stock. Also, Brent announces his life's plan in a German restaurant, where, in his father's eyes, he looks "real as a knife blade, and as shining."⁵ The opposition between these two groups of characters cannot be explained simply by reference to the antithesis implicit in puritan morality on the one hand and a desire for emancipation on the other. There is between them a difference of moral fiber, of character, and of basic human values resulting from their diverging reactions to the contemporary crisis affecting both Europe and America.

Bohemia on Trial

Two works that set out to judge bohemia produce, between them, a sort of debate: *On the Terrasse* and *The Left Bank*. In the first of these, Van Wyck acquits bohemia of all charges against it. Scott, the artist, rejects the materialistic arguments of Babbitt in the name of individual liberty, creativity, and love. In the second, Elmer Rice tries to temper criticism of Paris with criticism of America. Waldo Lynde, a character of reference for the spectator, is more like Babbitt than like Scott. At the end of the play, Waldo's wife stays in Paris with the writer John Shelby, while John's wife goes back to America with Waldo—an exchange in which the author's sympathies lie clearly with those who are leaving. Insofar as these two works deal exclusively with the subject of expatriation, they would appear to be critical to the topic under discussion here. On closer examination, however, their engagements with the problems of expatriation and bohemia seem like rearguard skirmishes fought in the aftermath of the real battle. *On the Terrasse* appeared in 1930, and the first performance of *The Left Bank* took place at the Little Theatre of New York on 5 October 1931. On the whole, both texts draw up a fairly banal inventory of the pros and cons of Montparnasse, with the poem tending toward apologia and the play toward condemnation. *On the Terrasse* was published by Edward Titus in an edition of one hundred copies and doubtless had little impact outside a small circle of friends. Rice's play, on the other hand, was one of the hits of the 1931–32 season, and reveals to what extent New Yorkers were aware of the latest happenings and general ambience of the Left Bank. To stage a New York production of a play set exclusively in Montparnasse presupposes a certain interest on the part of the audience. But the theater, even when dealing with contemporary subjects, is slow to get going. Its relative sluggishness is a function of public interest, which explains both the fact that the play did not appear until the end of the decade and the fact of its success. Its theme, a debate on expatriation, was not of central relevance to the majority of spectators, and is consequently specifically packaged for the home market. In neither work is the author's argument successful, and both the militant idealism of Scott and the sound common sense of Waldo are irritating rather than convincing.

In *The Gods Arrive* Edith Wharton takes the opportunity to settle a few old scores. In her account of Halo Tarrant's stay in Paris with her lover, Wharton launches a scathing attack on the group of characters who gravitate around the couple, in particular Halo's brother, Lorry, an avant-garde theater designer. Halo soon discovers that bohemia has its own laws, which are just as strict as those of more conventional society. Observing its members, she feels "a latent repulsion for them: for the capable free-spoken Jane, with her thriving trade in forbidden books and obscene drawings, for her friend and business partner Kate Brennan, whose conversation echoed and parodied Jane's, and for all the other women of the group, with their artistic and literary jargon, picked up from the brilliant young men whose lives they shared, and their noisy ostentation of emotions they seldom felt, and sins they probably did not always commit."[6] The most significant passage of the book occurs when Lorry, looking for a sponsor, finds himself hampered by the unorthodox situation of his sister and her lover. In consequence, the erstwhile champion of bohemia suddenly becomes an upholder of traditional bourgeois morality. Wharton's deliberate intent in the novel seems to be to disparage. Cut off from the younger generation, isolated at her home at Saint-Brice-sous-Forêt, the "grande romancière américaine" restates the case she put in her war novels: Paris, the real Paris, is hers; the only intellectual circles with any claim to authenticity are those she frequents.

There are various accounts of the way in which Sinclair Lewis was publicly snubbed by regulars at the Dôme. In spite of this, there is no special rancor in the depiction of bohemia found in *Dodsworth*. While not condemning artistic society outright, Lewis, like Glenway Wescott, Lyon Mearson, Harold Loeb, and Hemingway, was well aware of its failings and absurdities, its mimesis and its shibboleths. Lyon Mearson brilliantly parodies the literary gatherings at which each coterie has its cult expressions and its fashionable form of excess. In *The French They Are a Funny Race* the painter Stanton's studio is the epicenter of various tremors that shake the lives of real and imaginary characters. Seven pages are devoted to a "Dialogue between James Joyce and Gertrude Stein," devised by Aunt Minnie, a crazy old lady newly arrived from Chicago, who also invents a new method of painting, dispensing with the use of paint or indeed any sort of contact with the canvas, and christened the "Freedom from paint school of Art." Similarly, Hemingway, in *The Torrents of Spring*, parodies the obsessions, mannerisms, and well-worn anecdotes of Montparnasse, particularly in the conversation between Scripps O'Neil and Mandy, at Petoskey, Michigan.

A more serious and fundamental judgment criticizes the expatriates' ambiguous attitude toward money. While loudly decrying the baseness of commercial art, they are prepared to stoop pretty low in their efforts to lay their hands on ready cash, and the fact that most of their financial aid comes from America in no way deters them from disparaging their homeland. Glenway Wescott, in "The Whistling Swan," highlights the contradictions implicit in accepting patronage. Although the artists compete with one another for the favors of rich Americans, they have problems putting up with the constraints and restrictions that such financial patronage involves. The taste for money, once acquired, sometimes necessitates strange compromises, as is illustrated by the case of Hubert Redd, busy exploiting two patrons at the same time, while making sure that neither knows about the other.

But this double standard with regard to money has more far-reaching implications and calls into question the authenticity and integrity of the expatriates themselves. If not actual forgers—like Gus in *The Left Bank,* who makes a living painting "Renoirs"—many are fakes in the sense that their presence in the capital is the result of a process of autosuggestion in which they have succeeded in fooling themselves about the real reasons for their self-imposed exile. In *The Professors Like Vodka* John Mercado comments that Americans in Montparnasse are "failures, who found the tolerance of the older civilization more comfortable than the sharp edges of their own land, and sentimentalists, who enjoyed spouting the platitudes they had gleaned from third-rate sex and travel literature."[7] Some Americans seem to adapt quite naturally, whereas others give the impression of being displaced persons. For example, it is hard to imagine what keeps Robert Cohn there. The city makes him ill at ease; he dreams of setting off on a trip to South America or East Africa, and his restlessness prompts Jake Barnes to admonish him, "You can't get away from yourself by moving from one place to another."[8] This aphorism is central to the debate on expatriation, and the way it is expressed is characteristic of American attitudes and relationships. Each expatriate is anxious to justify his own presence in the city and finds fault with the reasons given by others in the same situation. The result is an avalanche of questions and self-doubt. The term "expatriate" itself, like the term "tourist," is often used pejoratively, implying a certain rootlessness, and each character can always think of someone who is more of an "expatriate" than himself. Perspectives vary from one work to the next, reflecting what is happening in reality, where people are constantly watching one another.

So there is a sort of guilt associated with the figure of the American expatriate of the twenties, which diminishes somewhat as Montparnasse gets rid of its less authentic elements. This seems to be the conclusion of *Tropic of Cancer:* Fillmore flees Paris because he has fallen too much under the influence of wine and women. Miller stays, despite the fact that he can now afford to leave, since the attitude of his friend provides him with the justification he needs. The expatriate's guilt also stems from the disorganization and waste of bohemian life, with its vain and frenzied activity, its frittering away of time and money, in short, its "dissipation." Fitzgerald, in "Babylon Revisited," explains the meaning of the verb "to dissipate." It is "to make nothing out of something."⁹ And does not art, on the other hand, consist precisely, in Racine's words, of "making something out of nothing"? The artist may have the feeling of being dissolved in the limbo of bohemia, yet bohemia redeems itself by permitting him to express himself and be creative.

Writers in the Witness Box

The greater number of writer-characters in the literature of Paris in the 1920s reflects the growing tendency toward autobiography and provides the reader with insights into how American authors went about the process of writing while in Paris. Such confidences are to be found particularly in *Of Time and the River,* where the twenty-five pages of Chapter 75 consist entirely of Eugene Gant's notebook, but also in *The Gods Arrive, A Voyage to Pagany,* and *A Moveable Feast.* The authors are highly susceptible to the influence of their new environment, where the presence of a sort of writers' fraternity is almost tangible and occasionally obsessive. The city contains the traces of Musset, Balzac, Nerval, Maupassant, Verlaine, and Apollinaire, as well as George du Maurier, George Moore, Oscar Wilde, and August Strindberg.¹⁰ Their memory, sometimes commemorated by plaques and statues, lives on almost palpably in hotels, streets, and cafés. The suffering and effort involved in the creative act takes place, therefore, in a particular context: that of a city that is simultaneously a pantheon and a sanctuary. In *A Moveable Feast* Hemingway, forced to skip a meal through lack of funds, reacts against his initial feeling of self-pity and pride by calling himself a "dirty phony saint and martyr."¹¹ The trace of past generations is also to be found in the vast number of books that can be seen everywhere in the city, but particularly on the stalls lining the river, and which draw the writer-characters like a magnet. Eugene Gant wants to read the lot, to absorb all this printed knowledge, but he is hampered by his poor French. Hemingway is able in part to appease the hunger he writes about by avidly reading the books lent to him by Sylvia Beach. He writes: "To have come on all this new world of writing, with time to read in a city like Paris where there was a way of living well and working, no matter how poor you were, was like having a great treasure given to you."[12]

Yet the presence of all these writers in time and space is a cause of anxiety for Eugene Gant, and he is particularly tormented by certain French authors whose names he repeats like a litany: Paul Reboux, Lavedan, Rosny, Gyp, Boylesve, Richepin, Bordeaux, Prévost, Margueritte, Duvernois, Feuillet, Capus, Donnay, Tinayre, Bazin, Theuriet, Courteline, Régnier, and Hermant. He is "haunted with the idea that the words of all this graceful, strange and fortunate company were written without effort, with the most superb casualness and ease." He is unable to banish the thought that "by the fortunate accident of race and birth each one had somehow been constituted an artist who could do all things gracefully and well."[13] Dev Evans has the same reaction and confesses to his sister his feelings of inadequacy when he contemplates the formal perfection of French poets. Although frustrated, he does not suffer from the sort of hallucination that Eugene Gant experiences, imagining a dialogue between two Parisian writers whom the reader may recognize as Maurice Donnay and Octave Feuillet. These two fantasy figures, with their badinage, their frivolous wit, their way of playing at writing, embody everything that Eugene hates most. The hero looks for ways of torturing himself through his imagination, and even his choice of location, the café de la Régence, stresses the cultural imperialism of eighteenth-century Paris. For him America is light years away, "with all the dumb hunger of its hundred million tongues, its unfound form, its unborn art."[14] Yet America is also vast and multifaceted. Dev Evans agrees with his sister when she contrasts the prolificness of American writers to the meager output of French poets, presumably with the examples of Whitman and Mallarmé in mind.

Moreover, the institutionalized nature of France's literary activity may be nefarious for a writer whose public lies across the Atlantic. In Gant's opinion, a French writer can make a career for himself so long as he complies with certain norms. He cites the case of Henri Bordeaux, whose mediocrity did not stand in the way of his success, as it certainly would have done for an American writer. Dev Evans reminds us that Jean Cocteau's literary reputation was helped by the fact that he was a darling of fashion, surrounded by influential friends. Also, the literary contacts of Americans in Paris are limited. There is, of course, the American colony, in which the aspiring writer may try to find a niche, as does, in *Dodsworth,* Endicott Everett

Atkins, who is well on the road to comfortable fossilization. In Montparnasse different dangers lie in wait, dangers inherent in the phenomenon Hemingway calls "literary life." For example, American magazines tempt writers with offers of handsome remuneration for articles of a commercial nature. Other risks include Natalie Barney's coterie, professional critics, and even, on occasion, the salon of Gertrude Stein.

Surrounded by so many perils, what can the American writer do except apply himself to discovering in Paris a way of life that is most favorable to the practice of his art? Uprooted from his native country, he is often beset by a restlessness, a desire to keep moving. Hemingway is a striking example of this sort of wandering writer. He is constantly packing up and moving from one place to another, from his hotel room to a café in the Place Saint-Michel, from the Place Saint-Michel to the Closerie des Lilas. In Paris, cafés have traditionally provided a privileged work place, and Hemingway, abandoning his typewriter, sits there writing for hours on end in his notebooks, using specially sharpened pencils. Similarly, Eugene Gant has a book that he fills with notes and sketches. Walks too are important. Dev Evans simply gets a feeling of well-being through these walks. Vance Weston, strolling along the banks of the Seine, finds himself carried away toward a kind of poetic meditation. The city's architecture and the beauty of its streets constitute a "great visual symphony" in which he can perceive the vibration of great minds. His walks help to develop his powers of receptiveness and awareness.[15] For Hemingway, walking is an essential part of the creative process. After several hours of writing, he sets off to tramp the streets, thus allowing his unconscious to get to work before the next spell of composition.[16] Gertrude Stein believed that the cadence of her footsteps had a direct influence on her style. In *The Autobiography of Alice B. Toklas* she says that the original style of *The Making of Americans* was a result of her research into automatic writing, combined with the rhythm of her long walks across the city to Montmartre to pose for Picasso.[17]

It would be possible to play down the importance of Paris by drawing a distinction between the physical act of walking and the place in which such activity occurs. Yet it is an undeniable fact that several texts talk about walking through the streets as being an essential part of the writer's life in Paris. But then another question arises: do these walks provide actual material used subsequently by authors in their texts, or do they serve some other function? In other words, to what extent does Paris itself constitute a veritable subject, as it did for André Breton and Aragon, for example? The answer is something of a paradox, for in these books about Paris, the writer-character totally ignores the city as soon as he begins to write. All the evidence supplied by the authors themselves points to the fact that the city acted as a creative catalyst rather than providing actual subject matter. Hemingway, writing a short story in a café, compares his struggles to get something on paper with the sexual act, a comparison arising out of the ambience of the place, the warmth of the glass of rum he is drinking, and the beautiful brunette waiting at a nearby table. The city's influence is diffuse, shaping the writing and affecting its form rather than its content. The writer absorbs the city in its entirety, without noticing the constituent parts. He is a medium who transcribes the message he receives. As Hemingway puts it, "All Paris belongs to me, and I belong to this notebook and this pencil"; but he makes the remark in the middle of writing something about America, not Paris, observing, "Maybe away from Paris I could write about Paris as in Paris I could write about Michigan."[18] For him, writing about Paris implied a knowledge that took time to acquire, which was different from simply being receptive to the city's influence.

This influence is hard to define without resorting to a suspect term like "inspiration." Yet inspiration is undoubtedly the word needed to describe what is felt by Vance Weston, abandoning himself to romantic revery, his sensibilities stripped bare by the city; or by Eugene Gant, in thrall to its magical atmosphere; or by Hemingway, whose creative mechanisms just seem to function better in Paris than anywhere else. It is as though the city were invested with mysterious attributes emanating directly from the supernatural powers watching over it. There is, for example, the incident that took place during Verlaine's funeral procession, recalled by Dev Evans: just as the cortege reached the Opéra, Apollo's lyre, which crowned the facade of the building, suddenly toppled and crashed on the pavement below.[19] Hemingway's belief in ritual can be seen against this background, and his struggles recall that of Jacob and the angel. When the author has the upper hand, he is able to make progress—the words seem to appear out of nowhere. When he is losing, he must abandon work entirely. Hemingway readily admitted to being superstitious, and he engaged in all sorts of propitiatory rites, touching wood, carrying a rabbit's foot in his pocket, and constantly entreating his luck to hold just long enough for him to get out one more sentence. All this confirms the idea of a city with transcendental powers, distributing or withholding favors to supplicant writers. These observations are in keeping with metaphors used by historians and critics. Paris is a factory for ideas, a laboratory of art, and—to sum it up in Hemingway's words—"the town best organized for a writer to write in that there is."[20]

But the city's influence can sometimes be counterproductive. Prostrate before a vision of Paris clad in all the unbearable radiance of its myth, the artist may react by renouncing life and taking refuge in aestheticism. This is the case of Starwick, in *Of Time and the River.* His idolatrous love for the city is accompanied by a complete disregard for its inhabitants. Paris is a purely intellectual and abstract concept standing outside time, and Starwick uses his cult of the city as a means of justifying and excusing his personal failure. The aesthete's Paris is the other side of the writer's Paris, and is dangerous, for its cult of formal beauty masks a skepticism damaging to other values. Starwick's attitude is diametrically opposed to that of Eugene Gant. He refuses the cultural nourishment that ordinary life can bring, loses all sense of ambition, and deliberately dissipates talent and will. Lycurgus Watts, the ridiculous and affected mandarin in *Dodsworth,* also belongs to this aesthetic fraternity. For Hemingway, aestheticism went hand in hand with the worldliness and elitism of artistic life, and in *A Moveable Feast,* as well as in *Of Time and the River* and *Dodsworth,* it is associated with homosexuality.

The Return to Myths

For both historical and cultural reasons, the decade of 1920–30 is particularly colored by a return to mythology. The huge wrinkle in time that occurred between 1914 and 1918 altered the normal flow of the present, and contemporary writers, reflecting the zeitgeist of the twenties and influenced by recent ethnographic and psychoanalytic discoveries, turned to the past for inspiration. Two great works of Anglo-Saxon literature, *Ulysses* and *The Waste Land,* typify this new perspective on the world. With the end of the war came an end to the image of a wartime Paris; and now, as the broken threads of the legend are taken up again, what remains of that mysterious capital whose climate of discreet eroticism was personified in the figure of Mme de Vionnet? The war's harsh searchlight has exposed the sordid reality of sex and death. Now the soldier has shed his uniform like an old skin, and the dazed tourist experiences something akin to a second birth trauma on arriving in the city. Like a child expelled from his mother's womb, he is literally ejected from the station into the newly created universe of 1920s Paris, whose elemental and primeval nature heralds the dawn of a new era.

Henry James, comparing the city to a jungle, underlined its inhuman, almost ferocious nature. In the twenties, new species emerge, odd variations spawned by the city's teeming slums, the "bas-fonds." Apaches, petty hoods, pushers, and addicts cluster on the outskirts of the plot in *The Outsider, The Professors Like Vodka,* and *Of Time and the River* or provide the central focus of stories such as those in *The Innocents of Paris.* There is an archaic, exotic feel to these works, which derives mainly from these grotesque characters, the new "innocents" whom C. E. Andrews compares to the Notre-Dame gargoyles to which he dedicates his book. But the title of Lyon Mearson's book goes further: the Parisians are a different *race.* They have strange customs, like eating horsemeat or treating on an equal footing black people, whose spontaneity, as *Dark Laughter* demonstrates, is an overt expression of the city's subconscious drives. Haddock is surprised to see a French woman sitting at the same table as "a large, black, well-dressed negro,"[21] and Edgar Bowman, at the Bal Nègre, experiences "a curious feeling of unreality"[22] upon hearing blacks speak French.

The Parisian universe simply cannot be bent to fit in with the fundamental concepts of the Christian world. Dev Evans's visit to Paris is a trip to "Pagany," and, when he stands before Notre-Dame, he sees a creation devoid of all Christian significance. For him, the great church is an incarnation of the abiding strength of paganism, and looking at the gargoyles, he thinks that "the pagan gods were turned into these stone images."[23] The harmonious linkage to Paris of characters like Bes Evans and Brett Ashley also harkens back to some ancient time. According to Robert Cohn, Brett, like Circe, has the power to change men into swine—and, indeed, in the heart of the city men and animals converge, sharing the same basic instincts. Aline Grey, in *Dark Laughter,* recalls "the stallions hitched to dustcarts and trumpeting to mares, lovers kissing each other openly in the streets in the late afternoons."[24] Characters are described by zoological metaphors,[25] and the disguises of the costume balls bring such metaphors to life. Curiously, the animals most frequently referred to are goats, and flocks of these animals can still be seen wandering through the streets of Paris in spite of municipal bans.[26] Edgar Bowman is highly disconcerted to find himself the object of the public advances of one of these creatures, called Suzanne. Lyon Mearson draws a further analogy between man and beast in his story about a joke-loving butcher who causes mayhem by engaging in a display of exhibitionism, in which his natural endowments are replaced by a cow's udder.[27] The city is complex and contradictory, and the forces of nature and culture are brought into play within its limits, linking the barbarous to the civilized. But the American character is not born of this urban chaos, with its echoes of myths of the creation, as is evident in the titles of various works: *The Outsider, Beggars Abroad,* "Babylon Revisited," *Paris Was Our Mistress.* Set against a background of genesis, he is an immigrant Adam, a postwar Henry Adams, a modern Christopher Newman pursuing his quest; but, unlike the latter, he is also a figure of flight, if not of revolt.

The works of Thomas Wolfe suggest various mythological avenues of pursuit. In *Of Time and the River* the author repeatedly draws parallels between the life of Eugene Gant and the adventures of Orestes, Telemachus, and Ulysses. Although the chapters relating to Paris are found in a section entitled "Jason's Voyage," the hero's adventures in the capital evoke more particularly the figure of the young Faust. Obsessed like Faust by the idea of complete knowledge, Eugene experiences in Paris a more intense version of the feeling of dizziness he had had in the Harvard University library. The novel is subtitled "A Legend of Man's Hunger in His Youth." Hemingway, too, has experienced such a hunger, but for Gant the phenomenon becomes a veritable torture. He wants to lock the entire city within his memory, to possess, to judge, to suck in the last drop of knowledge in which the city is steeped. But the scope of Paris, exceeding the young man's intellectual capacity, becomes an eternal temptation.

A different aspect of the city is revealed when Gant meets Starwick and plunges into the Parisian underworld. This view of the city foreshadows the infernal visions of Broadway in *You Can't Go Home Again.* Starwick becomes Eugene's Mephistopheles, as Alec will become Starwick's. In *Of Time and the River* the Parisian night swarms with fiendish figures expressing in concrete form the city's collective unconscious. In *Tender Is the Night* it is a vague limbo in which characters hang suspended. At other times it seems to be a vacuum standing outside of time, in which man is irrevocably swallowed up. In a strange scene in *The Outsider* Mortimer Long leans against the walls of the church of La Madeleine, gazing at the Obelisk of Luxor. He thinks he hears from within the church the sound of an entire congregation chanting his name. Soon only the first syllable can be heard, "Mort! Mort!," and the Egyptian monolith, glimpsed between the pillars of the neo-Greek temple, seems to beckon him to mythological kingdoms of the dead.[28]

The Parisian night, sometimes steaming with sulfurous fumes, sometimes dullingly analgesic, sometimes insidiously lethal, illustrates what Thomas Wolfe calls "death in life" and represents an objective version of hell, the corresponding subjective version consisting of an exploration of the dark abysses of the soul. There is no doubt that a thirst for knowledge and a desire for personal liberation have always been impelling motives for expatriation, but developments in the field of psychoanalysis, combined with exposure to Paris in the 1920s, provide particularly favorable conditions for introspection. The destruction of taboos, which is part of the bohemian ethic, can also trigger an iconoclastic landslide in which the profanation of moral or national values ends in a kind of Satanism. In *The Outsider,* for example, Mortimer and Carmen are united in a sacrilegious ceremony over which their friend Ezra Rich officiates, saying: "You shall further take to heart the responsibility of irresponsibility . . . you shall never know the meaning of that ordurous phrase, 'to be true to each other' . . . you shall love by a series of accidents . . . or not at all, and he or she that suspects that the other no longer loves, shall be the first to go. . . . With the authority vested in me by direct descent through the hereditary priesthood of the mighty Nobodaddy and calling the Great Spirit of Nothingness to witness, I hereby pronounce you man and—woman."[29] This union results, at the end of the book, in the suicide of the young French girl, while Ezra sinks into the icy solitudes of the opium addict.

Some of the characters wish to go beyond the temporary "high" induced by extreme forms of the festive rite like the use of alcohol and drugs. Their trip lies inward, toward more introspective territories. Bes Evans aims at reaching happiness by living in a sort of trance. Starwick, an admirer of Baudelaire, wants to pick the flowers of evil that lie on the dangerous slopes of his fractured ego. In a fit of hysteria, he cries, "You must show me all you know, all you have seen—you must teach me to smoke opium—take me where the opium smokers go—Alec! Alec! J'ai la nostalgie pour [*sic*] la boue."[30] Eugene Gant also yearns to embark on a voyage to the beyond, and Rose Frank and Aline Aldridge, in *Dark Laughter,* are obsessed by the urge "to go the limit," to plunge themselves in "up to the hilt,"[31] and to smash the last remaining barriers surrounding sexual taboos. This double descent into hell through the city's slums and the characters' psyches is a schema that can be stretched to include the experiences of many of the protagonists: Hubert Redd in "The Whistling Swan," John Mercado in *The Professors Like Vodka,* George Webber, Brett Ashley, and even Dodsworth. This introspective and urban odyssey is noteworthy in several regards. First, it sets up a chronological continuity by sanctioning, in peacetime, behavior and sensations previously dictated by wartime conditions. Second, it is related to contemporary preoccupations manifested in the work of the surrealists and the development of psychoanalysis. Finally, as regards its links with mythology, its main importance is not in its connections with the Faust legend but in those with fertility myths.

Adonis, representing the male principle of reproduction, spent half his time in the underworld, once Aphrodite had brought him back to life, drawing his virility from this period spent in the company of Persephone. It is conceivable that his alternating existence mirrors that of the expatriate. Perhaps, as Wolfe says, there is a "life in death," a hidden fertility that is contained in the infernal secrets of the city, and of the ego. Certainly, the writers' perception of Paris, which has traditionally swung between opposite extremes, shows this tendency more acutely after 1920. The city represents simultaneously life and death, abundance and famine, hope and disillusionment, human warmth and intellectual barrenness. It is perceived in terms of human temperament, with its changing moods, the movements of the day, and the cycle of the seasons, with the contrast between winter and spring constituting a leitmotif. In *The Gods Arrive* Paris is firmly associated with the idea of fertility and creative initiation, and the same is true in *Dark Laughter,* where the city is markedly Dionysian.

But Hemingway and Wolfe give us a different picture. In particular, *The Sun Also Rises,* which in many respects is the most representative work of the period, points to a clear interpretation of the city in the context of one specific myth. The novel contains explicit references to *The Waste Land,* and Eliot's influence on Hemingway is evoked here insofar as the two works have links with the legend of the Holy Grail. Eliot openly acknowledged his debt to Jessie L. Weston's book *From Ritual to Romance,* and Hemingway, in his turn, recollected Eliot's poem as he wrote *The Sun Also Rises.* Apart from specific echoes pointed out by Richard P. Adams,[32] parallels may be drawn between the settings and the characters, and their mythological counterparts. Like London in *The Waste Land,* Paris resembles the desolate kingdom of Amfortas, and the crisis of civilization already felt at the level of the tourist is here amplified through the image of these sterile metropolises. Other parallels exist for the characters. Jake Barnes, like Tiresias in *The Waste Land,* corresponds to the Fisher King, while Robert Cohn grotesquely images the hero engaged in his quest for the Holy Grail. We may compare him with Jay Gatsby and Dick Diver, whose knightly status is phonetically underlined in the "night" of the book's title.

Thomas Wolfe expresses the city's sterility by reference to the legend of Anteus. Eugene Gant, his vitality spent, can only regain his strength through renewed contact with the earth. Journeying to Orléans, he falls into conversation with a peasant and discovers once more "le soleil," "la pluie," and "la terre."[33] In Book VI, "Anteus: Earth Again," his visit to the Loire Valley helps him to get back in touch with the realities of life, after what now seems to him like his Parisian nightmare. Similarly, in *The Sun Also Rises,* Hemingway draws a fundamental opposition between city and country, France and Spain, Paris and the Pyrenees. At Burguete, Jake, like his tutelary hero, devotes his time to fishing in a sort of pre-Fall paradise that is the home of a virile brotherhood. In this he follows the advice of Bill Gorton, who accuses him of having "lost touch with the soil."[34]

The figure of the Fisher King, whose physical condition has direct consequences on the state of his kingdom, focuses our attention on Jake's relationship with the capital. The hero's castration, like Tiresias's blindness, confers on him a sort of superior wisdom. The couple formed by Jake, suffering from a war injury, and Brett Ashley, is symbolic. Brett belongs to the city as much as Jake does. She has dug herself in there, and it is she who says, "One's an ass to leave Paris."[35] Brett is portrayed as the kind of female who dominates in relationships with men, the winner in trials of strength, the irresistible corrupter of morals, and the psychological castrator of her victims. Jake, protected by his infirmity, is immune to this, as becomes his role as narrator. Neither Mike, however, nor Robert Cohn, significantly compared to an ox, is able to escape. Thus, Brett assumes the role of destroyer, spreading through the city the sterility embodied in Jake.

Brett is not the sole representative of this new breed of woman. Fran Dodsworth, Nicole Warren, Zelda Fitzgerald—as a character in *A Moveable Feast*—Elinor in *Of Time and the River,* Cleopatra in *The Professors Like Vodka,* all belong to the same race. They take their place in a gallery of female portraits differing noticeably from those that came before. Shorn of most of their national, cultural, and social characteristics, they are reduced to the sum of their sexuality. Indifferent partners or sex-crazed animals, they are classed more often than not with nature's predators, or, to borrow Leslie Fiedler's expression, belong to the category of "bitches." Zelda is compared to a hawk, in the chapter "Hawks Do Not Share." Cleopatra, a vertiginous and terrifying character of nighttime Paris, tells John Mercado how she used to operate in the Russian pogroms. "They would crucify some young man for me. I would put a dagger between my breasts, the point against his heart, and slowly embrace him."[36] There is in *The Torrents of Spring* an amusing parable of the dangers threatening virility in Paris. A beautiful woman entices Yogi Johnson to a secluded home and surrenders herself to him. A few days later, Johnson attends an erotic spectacle for rich voyeurs, and then realizes that he has been the unwitting male protagonist in this same spectacle. The discovery renders him impotent. Money, too, is a sterilizing factor and yet another arm in the female arsenal. Paris is a place where women are for sale, but it is also a sort of game reserve where rich heiresses come to hunt. It is in Paris that Harry in "The Snows of Kilimanjaro" and the narrator of *A Moveable Feast* find themselves outwitted and tamed.

The difficulties and confusion caused previously by local female types now extend to women of all nationalities. Formerly, it was the enigmatic Parisienne who caused all the trouble. Now, it is all women. Whatever their origin, they beleaguer the capital, clamoring for equal rights, like Brett Ashley, appropriating expressions, gestures, and clothing that are traditionally male. The special difficulties of "l'amour" in Paris are no longer the consequence of differences in language, culture, or material circumstances. They are basic differences of sex. A new climate of permissiveness, accelerated by the thoughtless flaunting of a recent and precarious emancipation, have brought Americans to an impasse: woman stands revealed as man's adversary. The fear of impotence and death, which is present in many texts written at the time, becomes obsessional for the aging author of *A Moveable Feast.* All Hemingway's phobias recur time after time in the pages devoted to Pascin and, above all, Fitzgerald. While Lawrence Durrell spoke of an "English death," there may be, beyond the ecstatic trances of the tourist, a similar disease in Paris, a "Mal Parisien," whose final stages are a sort of entropy, causing sterility and confusion of the sexes.

Hart Crane's poem, "For the Marriage of Faustus and Helen," written as a reply to *The Waste Land,* is a contemporary version of the union of Faust and Helen described by Goethe in Part II of *Faust.* In it, Helen stands for modern civilization—flashy and commercial, but capable of developing moral and aesthetic values. The texts studied in this chapter are less optimistic and tend toward the same conclusions as those drawn by Eliot. Even the names of some of the heroines, set against their personalities and their roles, stand in direct opposition to Crane's poem. Elinor in *Of Time and the River*—after Eleanor in *1919*—and Helen, the wife of Charlie Wales in "Babylon Revisited," may be seen as travesties of the legendary Helen. In "The Snows of Kilimanjaro" Harry's wife is simply referred to as "she" until the end of the story, at which point we find out that she is called Helen. Her name is mentioned only twice, but its presence is strongly felt in the magical and dreamlike passage where the dead novelist rises into space in an airplane, exactly like the hero at the end of Crane's poem. But Harry's wife, like the other women mentioned, represents failure rather than an ideal, and the novelist's ascent takes place at the expense of a petty Helen left behind on earth.

Yet, it would be misleading to end this chapter on a note of defeat, allowing ourselves to be unduly influenced by those myths that underline the negative elements of expatriation. To refer back to the wordplay of the title, it is clear that Paris, the Greek hero, has ended up making the wrong choice.

He has been hoodwinked by a dark, castrating Venus, who has rewarded him with an unworthy Helen, incapable of helping him to work out a new, modern relationship between the sexes. But the heroes never reach the end of their journey in Paris, which explains the cyclical and contradictory nature of their experiences there. One day, their adventure is interrupted, the circle is broken, and they return to the country whence they came. The experience of American writers in the capital may also be inconclusive, but, paradoxically, the "Mal Parisien" to which they are exposed nourishes the works in which its symptoms are described.

CHAPTER 8

CITIES OF THE INTERIOR

The period 1930–40 stands quite separate from the preceding decade. A smaller number of books is involved, and they have their own peculiar characteristics. The face of American Paris began to change in 1929 with the departure of large numbers of expatriates as a result of the Wall Street crash. But there were other non-economic factors at work. Fate, too, intervened to make the literature of this period distinct, by bringing about the chance encounter of two highly original writers, whose relationship with the city was to prove particularly harmonious. Henry Miller and Anaïs Nin discovered and depicted widely dispersed sectors of Paris. Their version of the city is strange, secret, and strongly autobiographical, and its essence is distilled for the reader by the medium of imperious and commanding personalities. The "cities of the interior" thus revealed are quite different from anything encountered in American writing about Paris up to this point. They occupy an important place in the works of both authors, who said on numerous occasions that their Parisian experiences were definitive for them. The body of work relevant to the topic under consideration here comprises almost half the novel sequence of Anaïs Nin, from which this chapter derives its title, as well as some of her short stories and at least two volumes of her *Diary*. In addition, it includes *Tropic of Cancer* and other texts by Miller and, finally, certain works by Djuna Barnes, most notably *Nightwood*.

It will come as no surprise that these three authors should be classed together. Each one's image of the capital has definite affinities with those of the other two, and their peculiar vision differs noticeably from that of the authors of the preceding chapter with whom, logically, Djuna Barnes ought to belong. Although the action of *Nightwood* takes place during the period between 1920 and 1928, it seems more appropriate to set the book alongside other avant-garde texts that blossomed partly through its inspiration. While *Nightwood* itself, published in 1936, was certainly not an influence on *Tropic of Cancer,* which appeared two years earlier, Djuna Barnes, in her role as writer, served as a model for both Miller and Nin. The latter's *Diary,* for example, bears ample witness to her continuing interest in Barnes, who is represented as a sort of heroic prototype of the emancipated woman. Furthermore, in her novel sequence Nin pays direct homage to Barnes by calling one of her main characters Djuna. A fairly widespread misconception should, however, be dispelled: the two women were not friends. Anaïs Nin made this perfectly clear in an interview with Priscilla English in 1971. Nin and Barnes apparently never met, and the only letter Nin wrote to Barnes remained unanswered.[1] Nin and Miller, on the other hand, were, of course, intimate acquaintances. The story of Nin and Miller's friendship can be found in their correspondence, in Volumes 1 and 2 of the *Diary,* and in various texts by Miller, particularly "Cet Etre étoilique" and "More about Anaïs Nin," dedicated to the woman who was for him half muse and half mother hen.

Although the lives of these three authors were not as closely linked as some critics would have us believe—at least as far as Djuna Barnes is concerned— the mistake is understandable. In the history of literature, this provocative trio stands hand-in-hand, though the popularity of Miller far surpasses that of the other two. Each of them was at one time or another a source of scandal or the object of derision, but Barnes was the forerunner, her notoriety established before that of Miller and Nin. The city depicted in *Nightwood,* in short stories like "The Passion" and "The Grande Malade," and in the anonymous *Ladies Almanack* has only tenuous links with reality. In contrast, the writings of Miller and Nin and, to a lesser extent, some of the short stories of James T. Farrell give a detailed chronicle of the 1930s, including a portrait of the Villa Seurat group in the work of the first two authors. Miller and Nin belong to a third wave of expatriates that Warren Irving Susman has called "the internationalists." Susman distinguishes two waves of immigrants during the 1920s: the Malcolm Cowley group and the Midwest group. In the thirties, a new generation appears, consisting of writers such as Michael Fraenkel, Samuel Putnam, Peter Neagoe and Kay Boyle, with Miller and Nin occupying a central position. As critics have often remarked, *Tropic of Cancer* stands diametrically opposed to *The Sun Also Rises,* and Edmund Wilson saw the former work as "the epitaph for a whole generation of American writers and artists that migrated to Paris after the war."[2]

In our memory the dead grow old much faster than the living, and it may come as a surprise to recall that Miller, born in 1891, and Barnes, born in 1892, were both older than Fitzgerald. Nin, who was born in Neuilly in 1903 and died in January 1977, was only three years younger than Thomas Wolfe. The longevity of Miller and Barnes, who died in June 1980 and June 1982 respectively, like that of Edith Wharton and, more recently, Natalie Barney and Romaine Brooks, underlines the relativity of literary generations. When *Tropic of Cancer* was published, Nin was thirty-one, Barnes forty-one, and Miller forty-three. This statistical digression is meant to emphasize the physical maturity of the authors at the time they were writing about the city. Older and less impressionable than others who are sometimes thought to be their elders, they used the city as a screen on which to project the fantasies of experienced adults, familiar with the old demons of literary creation. The image of the city we receive from them incorporates new and often shocking aspects, revealing the authors' interest in the avant-garde and, in particular, surrealism. With a few reservations in the case of Djuna Barnes, the works that emerge are essentially autobiographical and are strongly marked by the presence of the hypertrophied "I." They present a city shaped by the author's personality, and thus, in this special sense, a city of the interior.

The Staging of the Ego

The Contemporary Mood

It is hard to write only about oneself, and even the most intimate journal is to some extent a chronicle of the times. *The Diary of Anaïs Nin* and the series of short stories and novels to which it gives rise often mention happenings of the decade. We find, for example, references to artistic events, the Exposition Universelle, demonstrations and uprisings, and the 1937 air force maneuvers. Distant rumors from the outside world are even faintly heard in the great egocentric concert of *Tropic of Cancer,* and the authors' attitudes are affected by the particular tenor, the prevalent mood, of the period under study. Three short stories by James T. Farrell set the tone. "After the Sun Has Risen," "Scrambled Eggs and Toast," and "Paris Scene: 1931" are bathed in an atmosphere of melancholy that coincides with the arrival in Paris of a new kind of expatriate, a product of the world's political tensions. Since World War I, Paris had seen the arrival of increasing numbers of White Russians and Jewish-American intellectuals. In the opening pages of *Tropic of Cancer,* Miller humorously complains, "The Jews . . . are snowing me under."[3] But the Jew becomes the symbol of growing insecurity in the face of the rise of nazism. In "Fritz" James T. Farrell describes the problems encountered by a German Communist illegally resident in France, who is finally sent back across the border by the French authorities. The short story "Sorel" depicts the political background of the 1930s with great precision, relating the conversion of a young Parisian to fascism. *Tropic of Cancer* is not like that. Nonetheless, the Russian journeys of Tania and Sylvester clearly demonstrate the attraction of Stalinism for certain intellectuals of the period, and the figure of Gandhi is evoked through the raw disciple to whom the author reveals nighttime Paris.

In *The Four-Chambered Heart* the revolutionary ideal is embodied in the figure of Rango (called Gonzalo in the *Diary*), a Guatemalan revolutionary involved with various Parisian Marxist groups. Numerous pages of Volume 2 of the *Diary* and of *The Four-Chambered Heart* are devoted to the activities of this character, to his violent internal debates and to the secret meetings he attends, of which at least one is held on Djuna/Anaïs's barge. Paris thus appears as the center of intense political activity, which occasionally degenerates into violence and tragedy. At one point, Gonzalo finds himself in a situation where he is forced to execute a traitor to the cause. Another time, his own life is at stake after he is accused of being a fascist spy. Such concerns become even more pressing with the outbreak of the Spanish Civil War. La Pasionaria and André Malraux hold meetings; Republican refugees begin to arrive in the capital; food and shelter must be found for them in spite of government interdictions. At the same time that Anaïs Nin busies herself with these various matters, her mother is sending off funds to help Franco's Red Cross.

The Parisian atmosphere has grown considerably darker thanks to the imminent threat of totalitarianism, and the burning question facing artists and intellectuals is that of commitment. Miller may rage against racism, but nothing can drag him away from his typewriter. While Orwell gets ready to leave for Catalonia to join one of the Marxist militias, Miller contents himself, as Alfred Perlès relates, with making him a present of his jacket. Anaïs Nin, sensitive to the suffering of others, reproaches Miller with harsh words for his indifference and cynicism. She adopts a similar attitude, however, by insisting on the supreme importance of their vocation as writers, come what may. Djuna, her alter ego in *The Four-Chambered Heart,* is astonished to find Rango taking the path of revolution and war while she cleaves only to Rango, that is to say, to love: "Parties changed every day, philosophies and science changed, but for Djuna human love alone continued. . . . She smiled at man's great need to build cities when it was so much harder to build relationships, his need to conquer countries when it was so much harder to conquer one heart."[4] Miller himself loftily proclaims his neutrality: "I'm not an American any more, nor a New Yorker, or even less a European, or a Parisian. I haven't any allegiance, any responsibilities, any hatreds, any worries, any prejudices, any passion. I'm neither for nor against. I'm neutral."[5] This Olympian pose is in keeping with Miller's job as a proofreader at the Paris office of the *Chicago Tribune*. As he reads during the night about catastrophes extending across five continents, he feels a sovereign detachment: "A good proofreader is a little like God Almighty, he's in the world but not of it."[6] If Miller the writer identifies with this humble employee of the daily press, ultimately responsible for the formal perfection of the text, it is doubtless because he sees in him a sort of incarnation of the artist.

Ego and Company

Rarely have the life and works of an author been so closely bound up with one another as they were in the case of Miller and of Nin. The latter quite literally lived in order to be able to write her diary. Each minor daily occurrence was instantly perceived in terms of its potential for literary elaboration. Both Miller and Otto Rank protested strongly against this "sickness," this "drug" of Nin's and tried to get her away from her diary so that she could concentrate on her novels. One result of this is that Nin, amply fulfilling her need for analysis and introspection through her diary, does not write about herself directly in her other works. Instead she splits up and dilutes different elements of her personality among the four main female characters of the novel sequence and the short stories, Djuna, Sabina, Stella, and Lillian. She also gives them personality traits borrowed from other people. Thus Sabina occasionally recalls June Miller, as Stella recalls Luise Rainer. Basically, however, these four characters, who vary slightly from one work to the next, derive most of their characteristics from their creator. In particular, the way in which Djuna's character evolves in *The Four-Chambered Heart* corresponds exactly with what we know of Nin at the time she was living on the barge *La Belle Aurore,* even though the way she develops in this work does not entirely fit in with the way the same character is portrayed in the first part of *Ladders to Fire* (entitled "This Hunger") and *Children of the Albatross.*[7] But the *Diary* cannot be relied upon to provide parallels between the author's life and her work. It is not a biography, but an autonomous literary creation; and the fact that it was published in expurgated form for personal and legal reasons and that it employed a certain number of pseudonyms only complicates matters further.

Miller, who did not keep a diary, writes about himself directly in the first person. He also at times uses the real names of his family and friends. For example, the astrologer Conrad Moricand keeps his own name in *A Devil in Paradise*. Most of the time, Miller uses pseudonyms that remain constant from one work to the next, and nowhere in his work do we come across purely imaginary characters. They are all reworkings of people he has met in real life. Djuna Barnes's dense and symbolic writing is also autobiographical, but the emblematic nature of her descriptions makes it difficult to identify correctly the milieux she writes about. (Elisabeth Béranger, however, has attempted to do so, with useful results.)[8]

If we first set out to draw up a list of the people who form part of Miller's circle in *Tropic of Cancer,* "Max," and *Quiet Days in Clichy,* we find ourselves right in the middle of what might be called "the gospel of the Villa Seurat," of which there are several versions, according to Miller, Nin, Alfred Perlès, Michael Fraenkel, and others. The only close friend who does not appear in Miller's texts is Anaïs Nin, possibly because she was too involved with the development and publication of *Tropic of Cancer.* Most of the others have easily identifiable code names: Mona is June, Carl is Perlès, Boris corresponds to Michael Fraenkel, Van Norden to Wambly Bald, Fillmore to Richard Osborn, Marlowe to Samuel Putnam, Cronstad to Walter Lowenfels, and Sylvester and Tania to the Schranks. Quite clearly, Nin and Miller frequented the same circles for almost ten years. Thus, Moricand of *A Devil in Paradise* turns up again in a piece of writing by Nin, "The Mohican," and reappears later under the name of Manuel in "Bread and the Wafer" (the second part of *Ladders to Fire*) and *Delta of Venus.* Similarly, the painter Hans Reichel inspired both "The Cosmological Eye" by Miller and "The Eye's Journey" by Nin, as well as certain sections of the *Diary.* Although the presence of Miller is not immediately obvious in Nin's writing, it soon becomes clear that the character of the painter/pianist Jay is meant to embody the egotism, the smiling villainy, and the black humor of the author of *Tropic of Cancer.* In addition, the complex relationships that existed between Anaïs, Henry, and June are mirrored in those of Djuna, Jay, and Lillian in "This Hunger" and of Lillian, Jay, and Sabina in "Bread and the Wafer." Antonin Artaud appears as Pierre in "Je Suis le Plus Malade des Surréalistes" and figures prominently in the early volumes of the *Diary.* Jean Carteret appears as Jean in "The All-Seeing," and the reader of the *Diary* will easily recognize Louise de Vilmorin in the character of Jeanne in "Under a Glass Bell." Albertine, the young maid who often figures in Volume 2 of the *Diary,* also serves as model for the central character of "The Mouse." However, the homosexual couple, Donald and Michael, who appear in "The Sealed Room" (the first part of *Children of the Albatross*) and *Delta of Venus,* are not identifiable from the *Diary;* nor is Djuna's young lover Paul and his friend Lawrence. The wife of Gonzalo/Rango, known as Helba in the *Diary* and Zora in *The Four-Chambered Heart,* retains the same anonymity as her husband. Many secondary figures are also characters "à clef," and, for example, the famous man who attends Jay and Lillian's party in the Rue Montsouris can be recognized in the following passage:

> Manuel was displaced by a figure who moved with stately politeness, his long hair patined with brilliantine, his face set in large and noble features by the men who carved the marble faces in the hall of fame. He bowed graciously over women's hands with the ritualistic deliberateness of a Pope. His decrees, issued with handkissing, with soothing opening and closing of doors, extending of chairs, were nonetheless fatal: he held full power of decision over the delicate verdict: "Is it tomorrow's art," No one could advance without his visa. He gave the passports to the future. Advance . . . or else: "My dear man, you are a mere echo of the past."⁹

This untitled portrait of André Breton gives us ample reason to believe that Faustin, the Chess Player, the Chinese poet, the Irish writer, and other guests all correspond to real people.

Miller and Nin echo each other, but they also share a tendency to repeat things. The same anecdotes and the same encounters occur from one work to the next, particularly in the case of Nin. We may find an event recorded in the *Diary* at the time it actually happened and again when it becomes the germ of a short story; then it reappears when the story is published, when the story is incorporated into a novel, and when the novel is published. That would obviously be an extreme case but not entirely exceptional. In her bric-a-brac of erotic writing, Nin was not very particular about the novelty of her material. But the constant recurrence of characters like the prostitute with the wooden leg, the madwoman of the Place de la Concorde, and the exhibitionist artist, or of scenes like the embrace of a couple in a moving elevator, can, in the end, be wearyingly repetitive.

While Nin's works seem to spin material out endlessly, *Nightwood* strikes us as a particularly dense work. According to Elisabeth Béranger, Guido, the father of Felix Volkbein, recalls a number of famous personalities who were part of the author's circle—Rémy de Gourmont, whom Barnes may not have known personally; Henry Bernstein, who languished at the feet of Romaine Brooks; and finally Gabriele D'Annunzio, who also served as a source of inspiration for the characters of Felix and O'Connor. O'Connor, in his turn, sometimes evokes Freud and sometimes André Breton, whose ghostly presence in the book is indicated by numerous allusion to *Nadja.* Don Anticolo may remind the reader of Cocteau weeping over his chosen son, Radiguet.

Gertrude Stein appears as Mademoiselle Basquette, thinly disguised under the name of her poodle, Basket. Felix's son suffers from the same mental deficiency as the brother of Romaine Brooks. There are also similarities to be found between what happens in certain parts of the novel and the events of the summer Natalie Barney spent at Bar Harbor in the company of Renée Vivien, Olive Custance, and Lord Alfred Douglas. In addition, part of Romaine Brooks's diary contains an incident that is very similar to Jenny's kidnapping of Robin. It is clear that the book's primary source material comes from the salon in the Rue Jacob and from the numerous characters who form part of the circle of the Brooks-Barney ménage. Barney had in fact appeared as Evangeline Musset in *Ladies Almanack,* published anonymously in 1928 in Paris and immediately attributed to Djuna Barnes. Behind *Nightwood,* there doubtless lies some minor episode in the chronicle of lesbian Paris, which the book then enriches with multiple images of the surrounding milieu.

Barnes, Miller, and Nin were closely integrated with different intellectual and artistic groups of the capital: Barnes started out as an illustrator, Nin was a dancer, and Miller, although he had not actually begun to paint, was interested in the graphic arts. They were avant-garde artists, aware of their vocation, open to new ideas, and, in the case of Nin and Miller, theorists. But the Paris they describe can best be understood through purely literary criteria, and it seems that three words capture the essential quality of their city's life: romanticism, symbolism, and surrealism.

Romanticism and Symbolism

Although highly original writers, Miller and Nin sometimes fall into rather banal attitudes when they write about the city. In Nin's novel sequence we find vignettes of Montparnasse that strike the reader as dated and anecdotes about the Latin Quarter that seem even more outmoded. For example, the story of Peter, which Jay tells in *Ladders to Fire,* reminds us of Guy Wetmore Carryl's short stories.[10] Miller too, when the mood takes him, breaks into clichéd raptures at the spectacle of Paris. Contemplating the Seine and its quays, he claims to be "going mad with the beauty of it" and says he is "stabbed by the miracle of these waters that reflect a forgotten world." "I don't know what it is rushes up in me at the sight of this dark, swift-moving current," he writes, "but a great exultation lifts me up, affirms the deep wish that is within me never to leave this land." "When spring comes to Paris," he observes further, "the humblest mortal alive must feel that he dwells in paradise."[11] Such quotations, brought together somewhat unfairly perhaps, testify to a genuine if hackneyed enthusiasm that echoes the reactions of earlier writers like Booth Tarkington or even the juvenile ardors of Henry James's Bostonian aesthetes.

The romantic commonplace of absence and recollection is also a part of the way in which Miller and Nin view the city. Nearly all other writers perceive their expatriation as something immediate, and their recollection of the past concerns only America. Such nostalgia for his native country is entirely foreign to Miller, and, turning toward the past, he prefers instead to evoke memories of Paris, of the city he discovered in 1928 in the company of June, and to recollect still more recent moments. As for Nin, she spontaneously rediscovers childhood memories while passing through familiar neighborhoods. For Miller, in *Tropic of Cancer*, the Paris of 1928 is, first and foremost, Mona, who is now back in America but whose face rises up in the mind's eye of the narrator when he returns to the places that were part of their life together: "a little square, a few trees and a bench . . . some deserted spot, like the Place de l'Estrapade, for example, or those dingy, mournful streets off the Mosque or along that open tomb of an Avenue de Breteuil." Mona's presence provokes meditations on the nature of love, the fleetingness of time, and oblivion. "She wouldn't remember that at a certain corner I had stopped to pick up her hairpin, or that, when I bent down to tie her laces, I remarked the spot on which her foot had rested and that it would remain there forever, even after the cathedrals had been demolished and the whole Latin civilization wiped out forever and ever."[12] For all the difference in vocabulary, there are echoes of Lamartine in Miller's dialogues with the streets of the city. But Mona does not belong only to his memories of 1928, a year that plays a small part in *Tropic of Cancer*. Absent or present, she structures the entire past of the narrator. Remembering her, he remembers times when he heard from her, or places where some memory of her came back to him. He remembers, in short, the act of remembering, and thus Paris is the framework for the self-referential hall of mirrors where the overarching feature is the great egocentric "I" of the author. The city, "a Paris that has never existed except by virtue of [his] loneliness, [his] hunger for her," is a romantic city, gathering to it all "the tortured, the hallucinated, the great maniacs of love."[13]

Nin's approach is similar to that of Miller, but the memory that obsesses her is that of her father, for whom she began her *Diary*. Joachim Nin is not as integral to the vision of Paris in *The Cities of the Interior* as June is in *Tropic of Cancer*. Yet, as in many passages in the *Diary*, his personality dominates the memories evoked by the city to such an extent that Paris is divided up quite simply into two kinds of neighborhoods, those where the image of the father is present and those where it is absent. The crucial moment when the author finally manages to liberate herself from the past occurs in a passage from *Winter of Artifice* in which the city acts as a catalyst. Walking down the street where her father used to live she passes the window of his house and suddenly realizes that she has at last broken free of him. The place where this happens, recognizable as the area around the Conservatoire de Musique, assumes a symbolic value in the text. The name of the street is given as "Rue Saturne," suggesting both the passage of time and the figure of the father who devours his children. City and heroine share a joint metamorphosis, for the Rue Saturne is being renamed: "She saw that the name of the street was being changed. Already it said: 'Anciennement Rue Saturne . . . now changed to . . .' Now changed. As she was changed and beginning to move away from the past. She wanted to change with the city, that all the houses of the past may be finally torn down, that the whole city of the past may disappear."[14]

This example shows how Nin uses symbols in her writing. She explained this technique several times in various theoretical texts from *Realism and Reality* in 1946 to *The Novel of the Future* in 1968. Exterior reality must correspond to the interior world of her characters, and the author even goes so far as to say, "I never include the concrete object or fact unless it has a symbolic role to play."[15] The general title of the novel sequence, *The Cities of the Interior,* merits, therefore, an explanation. It recurs time after time in different works and stands for the psyche, for intimate thoughts, and for extreme withdrawal and introspection. The metaphor is accompanied by a multiplicity of architectural references to houses, windows, corridors, and labyrinths, as the titles of various works indicate: *The Four-Chambered Heart, A Spy in the House of Love, Seduction of the Minotaur.* Each time the expression recurs—twice in the first of these volumes, five times in the second, and once in the third—it is always with reference to the character of Djuna, who, introverted and inhibited in her relationships with others, flees reality through dream and memory. Of all Nin's heroines, Djuna is the one who has the most difficulty reconciling exterior and interior worlds. Djuna lives in Paris, and thus the city assumes the symbolic role of the "city of the exterior," a phrase that underlines its importance and defines its limits. Half of *Ladders to Fire,* the whole of *Children of the Albatross,* and almost all of *The Four-Chambered Heart,* as well as retrospective passages in the last two novels, *A Spy in the House of Love* and *Seduction of the Minotaur,* are set in the capital. Yet, in spite of this, the lack of concreteness resulting from Nin's symbolizing habit reduces Paris to a relatively minor presence.

The word "symbolic," in this context, may only be used loosely. Paris often appears in the text as a simple poetic amplification of the characters' feelings. For example, in the following passage the foggy, hostile environment suggests the crisis that Lillian and Djuna are going through: "Through the blurred city they walked hazily and half lost. . . . The buses came upon them out of the dark, violently with deafening clatter, and they had to leap out of their way, only to continue stumbling through dark streets, crossing bridges, passing under heavy arcades, their feet unsteady on the uneven cobblestones as if they had both lost their sense of gravity."[16] To cope with the city, Lillian needs Jay. When he is sitting with Lillian in a restaurant near the Gare Saint-Lazare, "the warmth of the day was like a man's hand on her breast, the smell of the street like a man's breath on her neck." But when she later returns alone, "the street is separated from the restaurant by little green bushes she has not noticed before. . . . Everything is distant and separate. It does not flow inside of her and carry her away."[17] The urban landscape takes on a masculine quality, and its harmony or discord for the heroine makes it a source of pleasure or anxiety.

Similarly, Djuna is caught in a network of descriptive symbols relating to the theme of prison. Djuna is the room where she waits for and clings to her seventeen-year-old lover. She is the house with the closed shutters, cozy interior, and bricked-up door. She is the barge in which she hopes for liberation, floating on the river, cut off from the world, yet moored in the very heart of the city. Djuna's destiny is like the traffic, revolving like a gramophone record around the Place de la Concorde. She also sees, in the local madwoman Mathilda, a pitiful image of herself. Every day for twenty years Mathilda has come to sit on the same bench to await the return of her faithless lover. In the same way, Djuna hopes for, and fears, the return of her father. Djuna is at times able to feel happy in her prison. She experiences a similar emotion to the one that Nin analyzes in her *Diary:* the fear of being rejected by a group linked with the fear of belonging to it.[18] For this reason, two Parisian rites—discussions at the café, and parties like the one in Rue Montsouris—force Djuna to take refuge in her cities of the interior.

In *Realism and Reality* Nin points out other symbols relating to this same character, and Evelyn J. Hinz explains, "The barge on which Rango and Djuna live is also a 'Noah's Ark,' the River Seine is both the river—the flow of the unconscious—and a French landmark; the policeman on the shore is also Djuna's conventional conscience." There are other examples: the Gare d'Orsay clock represents a domineering superego, as does the detective looking for Paul and the God to whom Djuna prays in a nearby church. For Hinz, "The locale of the Nin novels . . . is not the phenomenal, but the noumenal,"[19] and this explains the particular, stylized quality of the city. In fact, the Paris of Djuna and Rango's idyll resembles the scene of a French symbolist drama. There is the Seine, mysterious and occasionally sinister, on the bank of which the lovers exchange their first kiss. There is the barge, a former theater, with its private and exotic trappings, in which the frail heroine meets her magnificent, romantic lover; in such a setting the couple recalls the legend of Undine or of Beauty and the Beast. There is Zora, the wicked witch, lying in wait for them in her basement lair. There is Rango's chivalrous bearing during the flood. "He wanted to be the one to row his lady to the barge . . . to feel that he abducted her from the land, from the city of Paris, to shelter and conceal her in his own tower of love . . . and Djuna sat and watched him with admiration, as if this were a medieval tournament."[20] The threat of suicide hovers in the background too. There is the woman who tries to drown herself and is saved by the narrator of "Houseboat," or the tramp, driven to despair. Mystery cloaks the identity of "l'inconnue de la Seine," pulled out of the river, whose beauty is so extraordinary that a death mask is made from her face at the Morgue. One evening, Djuna too succumbs to this death wish. She makes a hole in the bottom of the barge and lies there, dreaming, waiting for the end. Then, on second thought, she plugs the hole and saves herself. There are also strong hints of a fin de siècle aesthetic: references to Ravel and Debussy, whose *Ile joyeuse* is mentioned—when we might have expected *Pelléas et Mélisande*—the story of Gaspar Hauser in "The Sealed Room," recalling a poem from *Sagesse;* and specific echoes of Baudelaire and Verlaine.[21]

The musical fluidity of the text combined with the hazy intemporality of the setting and of certain scenes link *The Four-Chambered Heart* and "Houseboat" to the tradition of French symbolism in its broadest sense. Occasionally the desire to integrate myth with daily life is accompanied by a certain heavy-handed insistence on the author's part. For example, the scene where Rango crosses the swollen river and lights a fire on the barge is followed by the comment, "Love and desire restored to small actions their large dimensions, and renewed in one winter night in Paris the full stature of the myth."[22] Elsewhere we see the influence not so much of Maeterlinck, but of Cocteau and Prévert. "The Sealed Room," in which we find characters such as Paul and Lawrence with their blue mouse and their phosphorescent birdcage, owes a debt to *Les Enfants Terribles*. The descriptions of the

Parisian quays, haunted by the music of the barrel-organ, and episodes such as the discovery of a drowned doll remind us of films by Marcel Carné or some of the poems of *Paroles*. There is a never-ending play of influences and echoes in the writing of an author who systematically draws on vast cultural and artistic resources. Nin's register extends from symbolism to surrealism, although the Paris she describes is more strongly marked by the former than the latter. Nonetheless, certain parts of her writing show clear links with surrealism, as do the works of Miller and Barnes.

A Surrealist Paris?

The areas of the city that, according to Marie-Claire Bancquart's study, make up surrealist Paris are mainly on the Right Bank. They include the grand boulevards and their many arcades, the neighborhood of the large newspapers, the area around the Square Saint-Jacques, the Buttes-Chaumont, and the Parc Monceau. And what stands out most clearly is the strangeness, the unexpectedness of their cityscape. The city described by Miller, Barnes, and Nin stands somewhere between the Paris of the expatriates and the Paris of the surrealists. It is often difficult to recognize parts of the Left Bank that have been transformed by an artist's particular vision. This is true of the Place Saint-Sulpice in *Nightwood;* the Rue de la Harpe and the whole Latin Quarter, which take on an exaggerated medieval air in "Max"; and Montparnasse, often described under the somewhat unusual light of early morning. Writing about the ninth arrondissement and the Rue Lamartine, which houses the office and press of the *Chicago Tribune,* Miller moves over to surrealist Paris. The Hindu Nanantatee lives in the Rue Lafayette, and there is frequent mention of the Rue Faubourg-Montmartre, the Rue Sucher, and the Rue Laffitte. The bistro run by M. Paul—referred to variously by Alfred Perlès and Elliot Paul as Chez Guillot or Chez Gillotte [*sic*], is the setting for a lengthy study of local life. Still more unusual is the grotesque and monstrous Cité Nortier, come upon by chance near the Place du Combat, known today as the Place du Colonel-Fabien, or the streets of the fifth, thirteenth, and nineteenth arrondissements through which Miller follows a photographer bent on an exclusively pornographic errand for a degenerate client from Munich. In the company of Gonzalo, Nin explores the outercity slums, where she visits a village of rag and bone men and the gypsy encampment where Django Reinhardt lives. Better known to the American reader is the Flea Market, dear to the heart of Breton and the surrealists, which Michael and Donald visit in *Children of the Albatross.*

Robin Vote's wanderings, in *Nightwood,* lead her from church to church, in particular to the Eglise de l'Adoration Perpétuelle in the Rue de Picpus, haunted by the memory of revolutionary executions, of Jean Valjean in *Les Misérables,* and of Lafayette, who is buried there.

Within these boundaries, sex is everywhere, and Miller and Nin push the sexual revolution preached by the surrealists to its furthest extremes. Both writers share the same total freedom of vocabulary, the same determination to scandalize the bourgeoisie, particularly in *Tropic of Cancer* and *Delta of Venus.* It is perhaps unfair to regard the erotic works of Anaïs Nin, for which she was paid at the rate of a dollar a page, as an authentic part of her literary output. Made up of bits and scraps, they are a rehash of her more serious writing. Yet such reworkings of old material contain striking observations. Sex abounds. We see it in the erotic literature of the booksellers; in the pornographic films of the penny machines; in the graffiti on lavatory walls; in the doors of these same lavatories, full of holes to look through; or quite simply through the mere fact of being in the city and succumbing to its atmosphere. "It was a soft rainy afternoon, with that gray Parisian melancholy that drove people indoors, that created an erotic atmosphere because it fell like a ceiling over the city, enclosing them all in a nerveless air, as in an alcove; and everywhere, some reminder of the erotic life—a shop, half-hidden, showing underwear and black garters and black boots; the Parisian woman's provocative walk; taxis carrying embracing lovers."[23] Nin devotes an entire page of Volume 2 of her *Diary* to a description of the voluptuousness of kisses stolen in taxis and promises herself she will write "a long *Promenade en Taxi*" where she will analyze "the reveries in anticipation of what is about to happen, the preparations, rehearsals to act, and then the retrospective analysis and reveries on what has happened."[24] Apparently she never wrote this piece, but on several occasions in *Delta of Venus* the taxi is chosen to play the role of private room.

The surrealists never reached a consensus about commercialized sex. Breton condemned it, and in the works of other writers prostitution appears far less often than it does in Miller's. Prostitutes abound in his books, as they do to a lesser extent in Nin's, as irrefutable evidence of the omnipresence of sex. Denizens of the common street or of select houses of pleasure, in Miller's writings they are given the names Claude, Germaine, Lucienne, and Adrienne. Sometimes they have code-names like Mara St-Louis or Mara-Marignan; sometimes, in spite of their importance to the plot, they remain anonymous, like the prostitutes the author meets at the Dôme, the Jungle, or the Wepler. In *Delta of Venus* they are called Linda or Bijou, the latter playing a central role in "Elena" and "The Basque and Bijou." The one who stands out most and who so impressed the authors that she appears in *Tropic of Cancer, Quiet Days in Clichy,* Volume 2 of the *Diary, Seduction of the Minotaur,* and *Delta of Venus,* has already been mentioned. Her peculiar feature is a wooden leg, and her beat is opposite the Gaumont Palace cinema.[25] "I have never seen a place like Paris for variety of sexual provender," writes Miller, shortly after spurning the advances of a pregnant woman, adding with humorous intent, "As soon as a woman loses a front tooth or an eye or a leg she goes on the loose."[26] But there is no humor involved when Conrad Moricand, in *A Devil in Paradise,* describes his complicated maneuvers to obtain the favors of a nine-year-old prostitute in the Passage Jouffroy. The ritual of the "maison close," idealized by Aragon, is explained on several occasions with a total lack of embarrassment and moral censure. In Volume 2 of the *Diary* Nin describes her visit with Henry Miller to 32 Rue Blondel and the ensuing spectacle provided by two of the ladies of the establishment. The comic scene in *Tropic of Cancer* in which the disciple of Gandhi mistakenly defecates in the bidet takes place at Miss Hamilton's, in the Rue Laferrière. On one occasion, Miller even acts as tout for a new establishment in the Rue Edgar-Quinet. In addition to this detailed panoply of commercial sex, the books deal with sexual obsession, from which most characters suffer. *Tropic of Cancer*'s success was initially a succès de scandale, due to the multiple scenes of copulation that form the background to Parisian life. In Miller's work we find an exaltation of virility, echoed in Nin's *Diary* and the novel sequence by an analysis of the female orgasm, but this vindication of physical love is accompanied by the revelation of many stranger forms of sex. In this respect the erotic texts of *Delta of Venus* constitute a veritable Pandora's box of the sexually bizarre: necrophilia, fetishism, exhibitionism, bestiality . . .

Miller does not bring up the subject of homosexuality very often, though he does recall sharing a bed with a homosexual and visiting Mme Delorme, a lesbian, like the protector of the Russian princess Macha. The homosexual couple, Michael and Donald, who appear in *Children of the Albatross,* resurface in "Elena." Manuel/Moricand, too, is homosexual. But the most remarkable example is found in *Nightwood,* in the transvestite Dr. O'Connor, discoursing interminably on "the Paris of the sodomites." Nin informs us in "Elena" that an English tearoom over a bookshop in the Rue de Rivoli is a meeting place for male and female homosexuals, and O'Connor gives a lengthy, detailed account of the similar role played by the pissoirs, elaborating on the opportunities provided by these public conveniences, in particular the one that adorns the place de la Bastille. Several of Nin's female characters have some sort of leaning toward sapphism. The author's liaison with June Miller is reported in Volume 1 of the *Diary* and taken up again on numerous occasions in the novel sequence, particularly in the relationship of Lillian and Sabina. *Nightwood*'s plot revolves around the suffering involved in Nora and Jenny's love for Robin Vote.

Such writing has affinities with surrealism in that the city revealed by these authors is a city of provocation in which traditional values are deliberately overturned. Behind the desacralization of bourgeois love stands the figure of Freud, whose influence can also be felt in these writers' preoccupation with other issues, notably madness and pathology. They directly engage the issue of excessive sexual tendencies and the relative degree of psychopathy that these imply. Nin writes, for example: "My neurosis is utterly different from Henry's, or Artaud's, or Helba's, or Gonzalo's. It is as if by a fluid quality, a facility for identification with others, I became like water and instead of separating from others, as Henry does, I lose myself in others."[27] Through the characters of her heroines and in her *Diary,* Nin sets up a sort of dialogue with herself in which she tries to throw light on her relationship with her father, her writing, and her life in general. Formerly the patient of René Allendy, and later the student and assistant of Otto Rank, Nin reveals remarkable powers of analysis in her work. Miller, Nin, and the characters they transform or invent are only too aware that neurosis and artistic talent are twigs from the same branch, as Rank explains in *Art and the Artist.* Both writers reflect on their own mental stability, but they also explore the madness of others. June Miller, mythomaniac and faker, is a case in point. Her behavior in Paris is totally aberrant. She represents an enigma that both Miller and Nin try to solve, a sphinx whom they question and who subjugates them. In March 1937 Nin writes: "I think now that June was like André Breton's Nadja, only Henry did not accept her."[28] On the subject of Nora Flood, Djuna Barnes writes in *Nightwood*, "Those who love a city, in its profoundest sense, become the shame of that city, the *détraqués,* the paupers," using a French slang expression that alludes to *Nadja.*[29] The link between love for the capital and madness is particularly apt in the case of Breton's heroine but also suits those tortured victims of love among whom Miller ranks himself in certain lyrical passages in *Tropic of Cancer.* But madness has other causes, and its outer manifestations often seem like an inability to adapt to the city. Misfits are both fascinating and disturbing. They appear in the work of these writers in the persons of the half-idiot Englishwoman who incongruously kisses Miller's hand; the hysterical surrealist girl writing poems in lipstick all over the bathroom of the Clichy apartment; Fillmore, whose debauchery provokes a brush with madness; Max, the pitiful victim of a vague and generalized persecution mania; Mathilda, ever-punctual for her appointment with eternity on the Place de la Concorde; and Zora, who is unaware of her progressive mental disintegration and tries to kill Djuna in a fit of rage.

These and other characters form a group around the city's most tragic instance of mental collapse: the artist who knows that he is going mad. Hans Reichel is one of these sad figures. His irrational behavior and drunken furies are described by Nin and Alfred Perlès. He is the Hans of "The Eye's Journey," setting off for the psychiatric hospital carrying his shoes so as not to be buried barefoot. But the most pitiful figure of all is Antonin Artaud, whose long friendship with Anaïs Nin enables us to follow the story of his suffering as it is reported in the first two volumes of the *Diary* and "Je Suis le Plus Malade des Surréalistes." In real life, his story ends behind the walls of the Hôpital Sainte-Anne. In Nin's account, it ends with a scene in which a doctor, after questioning the patient, treacherously gives him permission to leave the room. Pierre, forgetting that he is tied up, manages to take a couple of steps before collapsing on the floor. "He was permitted to fall."[30] The Asylum stands out in the Paris of insanity, representing for the artist a second, extreme, expatriation. Its blandly euphemistic labels—in *Tropic of Cancer* it is known as the "château"—mask a terrifying reality, like that of the Morgue in adventure novels. Anaïs Nin plucks up sufficient courage to step within its walls, in the company of Jean Carteret. Miller, on the other hand, prudently refrains from visiting Fillmore when he is an inmate. The Asylum is the double symbol of the atrocities of alienation and of the tyranny of the medical profession. Nin, in the *Diary,* joins in, albeit in more measured terms, the litany of abuse that André Breton heaped upon the heads of psychiatrists in *Nadja.*

What relationship exists between this city, haunted by sex and madness, and the lives and quest of the heroes? They are now interested in the ordinary street scene, which offers a new way to engage with the capital. In the course of their wanderings, the protagonists meet with surprises reserved for those who know where and how to look. In *The Four-Chambered Heart* a tramp walks the streets dressed in old theater costumes he has fished out of the trash cans of the Opéra Comique. In *Children of the Albatross* a children's merry-go-round breaks down, and Djuna, standing in the Place Clichy, watches the slow paralysis of the wooden horses grinding to a halt. Anaïs Nin is amused to read a headline in the financial pages of a newspaper announcing "Une timide reprise de la dynamite."[31] In the windows of the Galerie Zak, Miller sees a painting depicting "The Cosmos." Elsewhere he notices curious hotel names such as the Tombeau des Lapins—Rabbits' Grave—or the quaint-sounding Hôtel Pretty. The Place Violet appears mauve to him and the Impasse Satan frightens him. In *Seduction of the Minotaur* the Rue de la Fourche (Fork) evokes for Lillian the figures of the devil and Neptune, while the sonorities of the Rue d'Ulm remind her of a poem by Edgar Allan Poe, probably "Ulalume," though she does not name it.[32] The accumulation of such detail builds up an image of a strange townscape, surrealist in origin, creating a sudden bond of complicity between the stroller and the city.

Characters in earlier novels felt an urge to get out into the streets symptomatic of a state of crisis for which the rush outside is also the cure. Anaïs Nin, too, finds therapeutic virtues in her walks through the city, which soothe her inner turmoil and enable her to resist the temptation toward painful introspection. "I walk the streets. I tease Henry for filling my head with streets, names of streets. . . . One may have nothing when one has the name of a street, but one possesses a street in place of a thought. . . . Henry saved me. He took me down into the street. It is enough that a few hours ago I was obliged to think about my father in order to write about him. It is enough, enough. Come Square Montholon, Boulevard Jean-Jaurès, Rue Saint-Martin, like merry dice dancing in my empty head."[33] In *Tropic of Cancer* Miller, abandoning his meager belongings in Serge's filthy flat, escapes into the street and gets a lift downtown, where, alone and penniless, he gives vent to his delight in a long perambulation through the city. "When we get to the Place Péreire I jump out. No particular reason for getting off here. No particular reason for anything. *I'm free,* that's the main thing. Light as a bird I flit about from one quarter to another. It's as though I had been released from prison. I look at the world with new eyes. Everything interests me profoundly. Even trifles."[34]

The novelists find whatever it is they are looking for simply by stepping outside. Miller's natural inclination led him toward the ordinary and the commonplace, a predilection of which Nin heartily disapproved. Their long discussions on the city, reported in the *Diary,* revolve around the question of realism. Nin writes: "He loves the ordinary, the natural aspects of Paris. He is disillusioned when he travels because nothing is extraordinary as he expected it to be. I tell him his search for the natural, the ordinary, stands in the way of his finding the extraordinary. This he does not understand."[35] This was written in March 1937, but in an earlier text—May 1932—she acknowledges a debt to Miller for teaching her a new way of seeing the city:

I had never looked at a street as Henry does: every doorway, every lamp, every window, every courtyard, every shop, every object in the shop, every café, every hidden-away bookshop, hidden-away antique shop, every news vendor, every lottery-ticket vendor, every blind man, every beggar, every clock, every church, every whore house, every wineshop, every shop where they sell erotica and transparent underwear, the circus, the night-club singer, the strip tease, the girlie shows, the penny movies in the arcade, the bal [sic] musettes, the artists ball, the apache quarters, the flea market, the gypsy cart, the markets early in the morning.[36]

These diverse objects reflect Nin's own taste, but the atomizing, listing technique is almost a pastiche of Miller. Like Aragon in *Le Paysan de Paris*, Miller starts from a scrupulous realism in order to arrive at the visionary. Nin, on the other hand, tends to look for a symbolic fusion between herself and the object of her perceptions. Each builds a city of words where the real and the imaginary meet, a city composed of the authors' mental projections, especially their projection of the unconscious.

An example of this occurs in Nin's descriptions of empty streets, in particular of the Rue Dolent, which Jay declines like a Latin word as "dolorous, doliente, douleur," judging it to be the saddest street in Paris.[37] These streets impress her in the same way as certain paintings by de Chirico, especially his *Rue*, or Tanguy's *Jour de Lenteur* and *Rue de la Santé*. The author does not set up definite comparisons, but the townscape of the *Rue de la Santé* closely resembles that described in the novel. There is the same long perspective of the blank wall, the same atmosphere of desolation. In reality, the Rue Dolent and the Rue de la Santé converge, after running along different sides of the prison. The scene expresses an aesthetic impression of Nin's, which gave rise to a dream described in the *Diary* as "the edges, the dark spaces around them. Chirico. Vast deserts. Only a few objects in sight (Tanguy). Mutilations."[38] Similarly, in the character of Djuna, Nin describes herself going down the flight of steps leading to the quays of the Seine and being struck by the memory of Marcel Duchamp's most famous painting. The setting is similar, and the figure descending the stairs conveys not only a sense of physical movement but also an expression of the successive aspects of her multiple personality. In Nin's writing the inner world encroaches on the outer in a way that goes beyond symbolism, and Evelyn Hinz has observed that an opening up to the outer world is indicated by a shift from musical to pictorial references.[39]

Miller is, above all, visual, and his fantasies impose themselves as spontaneous metaphors on what he actually sees. The Avenue de Breteuil opens before him like a tomb; an anonymous, sordid little street calls up in his mind the image of "a big chancrous cock laid open longitudinally."[40] This reflex produces complex psychic mixtures of objects, times, and places. A simple example occurs in the author's description of a woman on a bus, just after a visit to the Zoo, where he has been admiring the peacocks: "I noticed a little French woman opposite me who sat stiff and erect as if she were getting ready to preen herself. She sat on the edge of the seat as if she feared to crush her gorgeous tail. Marvelous, I thought, if suddenly she shook herself and from her *derrière* there sprung open a huge studded fan with long silken plumes."[41] This vision of the peacock-woman, like the Eiffel tower as a bubbling champagne bottle "built entirely of numbers and shrouded in black lace,"[42] is closely linked to surrealist painting. A similar distortion of reality occurs in Jay's description of the pawnbroker's shop in *Ladders to Fire*, where he sees the clients "pawning their arms and legs, after seeing them pawn the stove that would keep them warm, the coat that would save them from pneumonia, the dress that would attract customers."[43]

But the most striking of such passages occurs halfway through *Tropic of Cancer*. In his proofreader's hutch Miller dreams about the prostitute Lucienne, who he imagines "sailing down the boulevard with her wings outstretched, a huge silver condor suspended over the sluggish tide of traffic, a strange bird from the tip of the Andes." Sometimes he follows her to Montparnasse, after work, as the night is drawing to a close, expressing his proliferating fantasies through long, cinematographic tracking shots in which the abstract and the concrete are mixed and through diffuse sensory impressions flooded with impulsions from the subconscious. The walker of Miller's writing is half asleep, exhausted by his work, and the visions that assail him, expressed in enigmatic phrases, belong to the hallucinatory state that precedes sleep. Following in the footsteps of the bird-woman, Miller wanders "through the court of the Louvre, over the Pont des Arts, through the arcade, through the fents and slits, the somnolence, the drugged whiteness, the grill of the Luxembourg, the tangled boughs, the snores and groans, the green slats, the strum and tinkle, the points of the stars, the spangles, the jetties, the blue and white striped awnings that she brushed with the tip of her wings." The journey ends in a landscape whose composition and color bring to mind the paintings of Yves Tanguy and Salvador Dali.

In the blue of an electric dawn the peanut shells look wan and crumpled; along the beach at Montparnasse the water lilies bend and break. When the tide is on the ebb and only a few syphilitic mermaids are left stranded in the muck, the Dôme looks like a shooting gallery that's been struck by a cyclone. Everything is slowly dribbling back to the sewer. For about an hour there is a deathlike calm during which the vomit is mopped up. It is like the signal that announces the close of the exchange. What hopes there were are swept up. The moment has come to void the last bagful of urine. The day is sneaking in like a leper.[44]

Here is a genuinely surrealistic description of Paris, based on an identifiable concrete reality that blends with the narration and the author's interior landscape, but this is not always the case with Miller. When his "dream-feeling" is triggered by some minor stimulus—the smell of rancid butter, the sight of a white worm, or a sordid room cluttered with odds and ends—the author abandons himself to a dream delirium that takes the form of unexpected description, aberrant collages, and lengthy scenarios in comic or tragic mood, sometimes lasting for several paragraphs. When this happens, Paris is just one of the many constituents of the magma flowing up from the unconscious and often seeming to have little to do with the city that provoked it.

The city itself, sometimes given as the alter ego of the characters, occasionally intervenes directly in their destinies, just as it does with the French surrealists, particularly André Breton. Anaïs Nin is sensitive to the play of chance, as is evident in certain passages from the *Diary*. "What a strange coincidence that I wrote on the title page of this diary: *Les Mots Flottants*. The Floating Words. A prophesy. *Les Mots Flottants* led me to the *Belle Aurore* on the Seine. I sit in it now, writing." A little further, she notes: "Coincidences. That I should pass the Café Zeyer and see standing there the proprietor of Louveciennes, and it was also at the Café Zeyer where I met Otto Rank, before Henry moved to the Villa Seurat. Gonzalo lives a few doors away from my first studio on the Rue Schoelcher."[45] In *Tropic of Cancer* an advertisement for cigarette paper suggests a particular way of behaving to Miller, the Zig-Zag, and a ticket found in the toilet of a bar more or less forces him to go to a concert in the Salle Gaveau. Later, the city, crushing Miller beneath its formidable weight, whispers to him in a dingy hotel room that he is a zero, a "nonentity"—a magic word that immediately conjures up the name of the Hindu Nanantatee, to whom the author flees.[46]

These examples do not reveal the existence of an occult city such as Breton's, and the comparisons made in this section show the necessity of putting a question mark after the heading: a surrealist Paris? Yes, in so far as the important themes of madness and sex tie in with the preoccupations of the contemporary avant-garde. Yes, because certain descriptive details correspond closely to the surrealist aesthetic. But it must be admitted that the rarefied Paris of *Nightwood* provides little to support this case and that the city described by Anaïs Nin, and chronologically situated in the first part of her works, shows some affinities with André Breton but owes far more to symbolism. Nin was not wholly untouched by the movement, but she never personally claimed to be a surrealist, although she applied the term freely to Miller. The only Paris truly meriting such an epithet is undoubtedly that of *Tropic of Cancer,* but even here its importance must not be exaggerated. Miller's writing reveals only the less important features of surrealism, and, when analyzed, proves to contain much that is gratuitous or irrelevant. The author, who did not agree with the underlying theoretical concepts of the movement, flattered himself when he said: "My surrealism is born of life. That is true surrealism."[47] The spontaneity, the vigor, and the truculence of the Parisian scenes he depicts are undeniable, but according to André Breton, Miller is merely a "distinguished erotomaniac."[48]

The Cosmic Theater

Although not everything in the approach of Miller, Nin, and Barnes is new, these authors' chief originality lies in the fact that they were the first to place the city in a context larger than that of a traditional opposition between Europe and America. In their writing, the city appears as a privileged observatory on the entire world. This lofty vantage point reflects their cosmopolitanism, but it is also particularly suited to their constant movement back and forth between the urban spectacle and the universal scheme of things, often accompanied by vertiginous and dreamlike distortions. The narrator of *Tropic of Cancer* and O'Connor in *Nightwood,* for example, embark on a series of acrobatic flights of rhetoric when describing minor aspects of the city. This does not mean that the usual comparisons between France and America do not appear in the writings of these authors, but they are rare. The *Diary* contains a certain number of such comparisons, made notably during Nin's curtailed visit to New York from November 1934 to June 1935, when she was thinking of establishing herself in the United States as a psychoanalyst. For Nin, New York seems artificial and synthetic in comparison with Paris, but it has a certain animal vitality and, dominated by its skyscrapers, it seems more surrealistic than the French capital. In *Children of the Albatross* she describes Paris as having "the languid beauty of a woman," while New York can only flaunt its "masculine and aggressive beauty."[49] Similar banalities can be found elsewhere, as when she takes up the old refrain "Paris was built for eternity, and New York only for the present."⁵⁰ Harping on the same theme, Miller contrasts the feeling of belonging, which the Parisian has in his hometown, with the feeling of indifference that weighs on the New Yorker, lost in a city that is "cold, glittering, malign."⁵¹ In *Quiet Days in Clichy* he opposes Broadway and Montmartre: "Broadway is fast, dizzying, dazzling, and no place to sit down. Montmartre is sluggish, lazy, indifferent, somewhat shabby and seedylooking, not glamorous so much as seductive, not scintillating but glowing with a smouldering flame. Broadway looks exciting, even magical at times, but there is no fire, no heat—it is a brilliantly illuminated asbestos display, the paradise of advertising agents. Montmartre is worn, faded, derelict, nakedly vicious, mercenary, vulgar. It is, if anything, repellent rather than attractive, but insidiously repellent, like vice itself."⁵² Miller's comparisons reflect for the most part the violent criticism of the United States that runs throughout his work. Like Nin and Barnes, he sees in the French a kind of superior wisdom that enables them to rise above the difficulties that constantly beset them. The ambience of Paris is set against the brittle optimism that glitters on the other side of the Atlantic. "It's just because the chances are all against you, just because there's so little hope, that life is so sweet over here. Day by day. No yesterdays and no tomorrows. The barometer never changes, the flag is always at half mast."⁵³ This attitude, drawn from the common fund of American opinion of France, is echoed by Barnes and Nin. The latter calls Parisians people who "are in love with life and even with their tragedies,"⁵⁴ while O'Connor declares in *Nightwood:* "The French are dishevelled, and wise, the American tries to approximate it with drink."⁵⁵

Such generalities should not be allowed to divert our attention from what is essentially new and subversive in these writers' attitudes. After Dos Passos, Miller reacts violently, for example, against his compatriots' passive acceptance of the cultural role of Paris. The museum masterpieces, the official glories of the Third Republic, leave Miller cold. To Molière, Racine, Corneille, and Voltaire, he prefers Villon, Rabelais, and Rimbaud. Paris is the mirror of a Europe sated with art, its soil stuffed with bones and its museums with stolen treasures. Yet it contains far more than it exposes to the public gaze. Letting himself be guided by his whims and his fancies, Miller, deliberately turning his back on "the gold standard of literature,"⁵⁶ creates his own imaginary Pantheon, housing a multitude of figures connected in one way or another with the capital. They people his imagination as he walks, figures from the present, figures from the past, Frenchmen and others, conjuring up imaginary worlds: Strindberg, Dante, Papini, Hamsun, Matisse, Proust, Balzac, and so on. Djuna Barnes denies the possibility of any exchange between the Old World and the New. The story of Robin Vote and Felix is a fairy tale gone sour. A young American woman in Paris marries an Austrian aristocrat, in reality a Jewish commoner from a poor family. Their marriage breaks up almost immediately, leaving in its wake a child who turns out to be abnormal. Robin, a lesbian and a debauchee, goes insane. Felix sinks into alcoholism, and his early dreams based on faith in the idea of the New World—he affirms naively, "With an American, anything can be done"[57]—fade and vanish one by one.

The city exists at the center of an imaginary cosmos. Around it lie other countries: Austria, to whose defunct imperialism Felix vows allegiance; Morocco and the city of Fez, greatly appreciated by Anaïs Nin; South American countries evoked by the figure of Rango in *The Four-Chambered Heart*. In Miller's works appear Luxembourg, racist and antiseptic; England, which he treats with scorn; the Germany of Elsa, sentimental and unpredictable; the Russia of Tania, whose artificial optimism recalls that of the New World. But there is also an unreal Dalmatia, belonging to certain watches of the night in the reveries of the proofreader; India, contaminated by cheap American idealism; and China, "a China rotting away, crumbling to dust like a huge dinosaur, yet preserving to the very end the glamor, the enchantment and the mystery and the cruelty of her hoary legends."[58] The city, proteiform and centrifugal, scintillates at the center of a target of images, crisscrossing, shading one into the other, permitting us to embark, motionless, on voyages of the mind. For Miller, the city may become "a crepuscular melange of all the cities of Europe and Central America."[59] Anaïs Nin, standing in the Rue de la Santé, the Rue Dolent, or the Rue des Saints-Pères, sees "Bombay, Ladona, Budapest, Lavinia."[60] In the titanic prophesying of *Tropic of Cancer*, Paris takes its place at the hub of a veritable cosmogony in space and time, defined by reference to the points of the compass, the poles, the tropics, the meridians and parallels, the era of quaternary glaciation, the age of volcanoes, and the evolution of the human skull. Miller, who seeks through literature to "erect a world on the basis of the *omphalos*, not on an abstract idea nailed to a cross,"[61] finds in the city the perfect point of departure. Paris is like some modern Delphi, and Miller, leaning over what he calls "the crack" and entering a kind of trance, reenacts the pythoness uttering her chthonic message.[62] Nowhere else in Miller's works, or in any of the works of the other two authors considered here, can we find metaphors that invest the city with such importance. Although, in *Tropic of Cancer*, the images of the omphalos and the crack cannot be taken only as the representation of Paris, they emphasize an essential aspect: the juxtaposition of the cosmos with basic biological fact. This juxtaposition can be seen in the works of all three authors—more in Barnes than in Nin, but above all in Miller, where, to some degree, scatology becomes eschatology. So Paris opens herself simultaneously to the movement of celestial bodies and the physiology of the human body, as the title of *Tropic of Cancer* indicates.

The city, externalizing man's unconscious, allows him at the same time to make an inventory of his body: vomit, excreta, fetuses, sperm, false teeth. Human tissue is shown eaten away by disease, whose presence permeates the texts of all three authors. It is felt in the multiple resonances of "cancer," in the title of "The Grande Malade," and in the fact that Barnes's supreme interpreter of Paris, O'Connor, is a doctor. Above all, it is shown by the fact that in *Tropic of Cancer* the sexual act carries with it a permanent threat of contamination. It is not necessary to insist on the genitourinary aspect of Miller's writing to realize to what extent physical love is bound up with disease and death. Sex here is not a source of fertility and enthusiasm, as it was for the surrealists; it is degraded and corrupt, the image of a rotting universe. *Tropic of Cancer* describes a plague-ridden place, full of cock-roaches, rats, and tombs, with abattoirs and morgues, a place in a slow process of disintegration. In *Nightwood* the prediction of the end of the world is more discreet. The executioner strolling down the Boulevard Saint-Michel, the proclamation by Dr. O'Connor of Altamonte's final erection, the prediction of a marquise who declared for Robin's benefit that one member of the group was nearly "at the end of her existence and would return no more"[63]— these are premonitory signs. Above all, at the heart of the work is the progressive decline of the human species, clearly brought out by Elisabeth Béranger, which finally reduces Robin to the level of an animal. The Paris of Djuna Barnes encloses, in its rarefied atmosphere, beings who are finished, spent, consumed, like the princess in "The Passion," who was "sèche," and was "living on her last suppuration."[64]

Death has always been a part of the city's landscape, but never so much as in the works of these three authors. "We're all dead, dying, or about to die," wrote Miller, a prisoner of streets in which he saw "no exit signs anywhere; no issue save death. A blind alley at the end of which is a scaffold."[65] From all sides, elements converge, heralding the final degeneration. "Birth" by Anaïs Nin, like James T. Farrell's short story "Honey We'll Be Brave," is the cruel account of the delivery of a stillborn child. O'Connor is an abortionist. In *Tropic of Cancer,* an anonymous midwife turns to prostitution, and the end of the human race is foreseen in homosexuality, perversions, and the practice of onanism that Van Norden sees as the final solution to sexual problems.

The myth of the hermaphrodite, used for pornographic ends by Anaïs Nin, is brought to nothing in the person of Robin. The aspirations of the surrealists point one way, but the city drifting slowly toward entropy is moving in entirely the opposite direction. If, for André Breton, the apocalypse represents the revelation of arcana, for Miller it is simply a violent ending. Although the narrator of *Tropic of Cancer* borrows an image from Henry Adams to invoke "a world of men and women with dynamos between their legs,"[66] he knows very well that from now on everything is finished: "I'll tell you, Max, what time it is—to the split second. *It is just five minutes before the end.*"[67]

Such pessimism corresponds to the history of the period, whose gloom affected Barnes and Nin as well as Miller. The despair in Djuna Barnes's writing seems, however, to stem largely from fundamental attitudes. Moreover, in Nin and Miller, there is a discrepancy between the romantic, symbolist, surrealist Paris, and this quite different city that has just been discussed. This is because, for both of them, individual salvation remained a permanent possibility. For Nin, it consisted of the search for a new definition of woman. For Miller, it involved faith in the individual and the refusal of despair. The persistence of such beliefs explains many of the contradictions in their different versions of Paris. Miller, in particular, often seems to give vent, with black humor, to a sense of tragedy that he does not completely feel. For him, the impending Second World War may be part of some general apocalypse, but it is revealing to find that this war predicted from *Tropic of Cancer* onward is an apocalypse from which he plans to escape, simply by leaving Paris.

How can we reconcile the different elements in the Paris of the 1930s? It is clear that the city was particularly suited to the mental universe of both Miller and Nin and that in these writers' mainly autobiographical works setting and plot complement each other perfectly. Furthermore, in a vision closely related to that of the surrealists, the urban landscape is seen as provoking and liberating the unconscious of the narrator and the characters. But this vision of a city that is simultaneously exterior and, psychologically and physiologically, interior, both dream and reality, poses a problem. Is it in fact Paris? No, says Joseph H. McMahon: as far as *Tropic of Cancer* is concerned, it could just as well be Brooklyn.[68] It is true that the descriptions of Miller, Nin, and Barnes would make a poor sort of guide for the tourist. Nonetheless, all the examples quoted in this chapter testify to the existence of a definite concrete base and a familiarity with certain milieux that seem to refute McMahon's objection. *Nightwood* is a parable about the fall of man in which the characters, with their lesbian tendencies, could hardly meet anywhere other than in Paris. The city of *Ladders to Fire, Children of the Albatross,* and *The Four-Chambered Heart,* even when reduced, as if we were looking at an X-ray, to a network of symbols, retains, particularly with the supporting evidence of the *Diary,* enough substance to be easily recognizable. In *Tropic of Cancer* Miller defines the role of the capital as follows: "It is no accident that propels people like us to Paris. Paris is simply an artificial stage, a revolving stage that permits the spectator to glimpse all the phases of the conflict. Of itself Paris initiates no dramas. They are begun elsewhere. Paris is simply an obstetrical instrument that tears the living embryo from the womb and puts it in the incubator. Paris is the cradle of artificial births."[69] In a passage quoted by Nin in the *Diary,* Miller writes,

> Things are rotting away on the outside and in this quick rot the ego buries itself like a seed and blooms. Here the body becomes a plant which gives off its own moisture, creates an aura, produces a flower. I see one big globule which swims in the blood of the great animal Man. This globule is Paris. I see it round, and full, always the whole globule at once. The globule will stretch and expand. It will permit him the most fantastic movement, but will not break. Suddenly I am inside the globule. I entered by osmosis. I seeped through between late afternoon and midnight. I am inside now. I know it.[70]

Metaphors abound to show that for Henry Miller, Anaïs Nin, and Djuna Barnes Paris was, above all, a theater, but a theater of cruelty like that of Antonin Artaud. The urban environment affects these authors like a play in which, to quote the hero of "Je Suis le Plus Malade des Surréalistes," the drama will take place "so near to them that they will feel it happening inside themselves."[71]

CHAPTER 9

THE DISINTEGRATING CITY

An examination of the literature written during the fifty or so years since the outbreak of the Second World War reveals few thematic patterns. The aim of this chapter is to draw together these patterns and to identify a shared image of postwar Paris. It is an image that, though somewhat anodyne, has characteristics that are peculiarly American. It is also an image that traces, during this long period, the gradual decline of Paris as a source of inspiration for American writers.

The Literature

When hostilities first broke out, the French authorities ordered all foreigners to leave the capital. Although this officially terminated the stay of all expatriates, Gertrude Stein remained, and she was apparently the only American writer who continued to live in Paris between 1940 and 1944. Her memoirs of the war and of the Nazi occupation, which partly involve the capital, were published in two volumes: *Paris, France* (1940), which describes the mobilization, and *Wars I Have Seen* (1945), published one year before her death. In 1954 Anaïs Nin returned to Paris, and part of Volume 5 of her *Diary* describes the surprises awaiting her after such a long absence. The portion relating to Paris was published separately under the title *Paris Revisited* in a limited edition signed by the author and containing various photographs. Postwar Paris also figures in stories by James T. Farrell and, briefly, in Upton Sinclair's *O Shepherd, Speak!*, the tenth volume of the adventures of Lanny Budd.

A more interesting case, as far as our story is concerned, is that of Elliot Paul. A volunteer in the Ambulance Corps during the First World War, he later worked as a journalist on the Parisian staff of the *Chicago Tribune* and was, with Eugene Jolas, the founder of *transition* in 1927. Though he spent some years in Ibiza, Paul lived for a long time in Paris, where part of his novel *The Amazon* (1930) is set. In 1939 he embarked on a series of detective novels about the capital, featuring millionaire-hero Homer Evans, whose penchant for amateur detective work involved him in close collaboration with the Parisian police. Evans's real-life counterpart was a 1930s expatriate named Homer Bevans, an opium addict and alcoholic, who started life as an engineer before turning to sculpture. A thumbnail sketch of this character is given by Samuel Putnam in *Paris Was Our Mistress*.[1] The Parisian exploits of Homer Evans begin in 1939 with *The Mysterious Mickey Finn; or, Murder at the Café du Dôme*, continue with *Hugger-Mugger in the Louvre* in 1940 and *Mayhem in B Flat* in 1951, and finish, again in 1951, with *Murder on the Left Bank*. The city forming the background of this detective series of more than a thousand pages has little to do with the Paris of mystery. It is a setting against which the craziest plots erupt and explode like fireworks, but in which Paul skillfully sketches the most stereotypical aspects of bohemia. The first three books are set predominantly in 1930s Montparnasse and the fourth in the Saint-Germain-des-Prés of the existentialists. This sort of writing enjoyed a commercial success because it appealed to a readership already familiar with the places and milieux described. In the first three novels, and to a certain extent the fourth, Paul makes capital out of the myth of the Lost Generation—a myth that was more American than French—and freely mixes popular detective archetypes with asides to the initiated,[2] thereby satisfying Peter Cheney fans on the one hand and Hemingway fans on the other. Paul takes neither his characters nor his plots very seriously, and he enters into a bond of complicity with the reader, accompanying the narration of the hunt for the criminal with a sort of underlying ironic commentary about the thousand and one surprises of Parisian life. A legendary "Left Bank" lends the novels an atmosphere that fits in nicely with the public's underlying image of Paris, but the final result is that Paul, in spite of his talent and genuine affection for the city, somewhat devalues the legend itself.

The same commercialization of the past occurs in the first part of Paul's diptych about the Rue de la Huchette. *The Last Time I Saw Paris,* the title of which is borrowed from the well-known ballet and song, is a remarkable example of what might be called "the literature of nostalgia." Published in 1942, at the darkest moments of the German occupation, this somewhat disconcerting book was a *succès de circonstances*. According to a review by Janet Flanner, it is, simultaneously, the biography of the author and that of the seventy-five people who live in the street, a work of local geography, a chapter in the history of France from the arrival of the Americans in 1923 up to the arrival of the Germans in 1940, and the epitaph of the Third Republic.³ It could also be described as the X-ray of a microcosm whose paradigmatic role as regards the city as a whole is questionable.

This unclassifiable book, whose subject matter, although filtered through the sentimental precipitate of the war, really puts it with the books in the three preceding chapters, is only the first volet of the diptych. The author, returning to Paris in 1949, followed it up with *Springtime in Paris,* in which he reuses the same technique, the same setting, and also some of the same characters, transposed to 1949. It is impossible to give a succinct and comprehensive account of the innumerable portraits, anecdotes, and intrigues of these two books. In *The Last Time I Saw Paris* the text is preceded by an engraving in which each house is clearly depicted, along with a list of the occupants. The work as a whole mixes various genres: reportage steeped in local color (cafés and brothels figure prominently), short stories, artistic and literary chronicle, and the odd bit of sociological analysis. Not surprisingly, such an amazing potpourri met with a certain amount of critical hostility, its polyvalence being seen as unsuitable in a work of this kind, whereas it had been well enough received in the detective novels. What remains, in 1989, of this same Rue de la Huchette, so lovingly described by the author? The Café Saint-Michel, the theater, and the Hôtel du Mont-Blanc (Hôtel Mont-Souris in the book) still exist, but boutiques and Greek restaurants have replaced the small shops and family businesses of yesterday. As for the cast of 150 characters, one wonders how many of their real-life counterparts were even aware of the existence of 795 pages glorifying their street.

Elliot Paul is not easily classifiable in the history of American Paris, for his writing spans the period from the First World War to the end of the Fourth Republic. Paris was quite evidently his favorite subject. He is the bard of the Rue de la Huchette and the attentive interpreter of French manners, which he tries to explain in a systematic fashion one last time in *Understanding the French,* resorting yet again to the tried and tested formula of piling up characters and anecdotes. Although something of a fringe author, given the nature of his writing, Paul represents an essential link between the Lost Generation and the contemporary period, and thus deserves mention in this study.

The other novelists discussed in this chapter differ considerably in their experience of the capital. Some, like Richard Wright, James Baldwin, Irwin Shaw, James Jones, and Mary McCarthy, spent several years there. Others, like Stefan Heym and Herbert Eliot French, drew on their brief experience as servicemen. Jack Kerouac, John Steinbeck, Gore Vidal, William Gardner

Smith, and Harold Flender had a few short stays in the capital. Art Buchwald first came to Paris after the war, left again, and finally returned after an
absence of several years. Reynolds Packard, the famous journalist, worked in
the city for some time. The authors in the first of these groups can be
considered as genuine expatriates. Richard Wright, accepting first an invita-
tion from the French Provisional Government in 1945, finally established
himself in the capital in 1946, living there until his death in 1960. James
Baldwin spent the years 1948–57 either in Paris or on the Riviera. He then
went back to the United States for thirteen years, returning to France in
1970, and finally leaving once more some years later. James Jones arrived in
Paris in 1958 and lived in an apartment on the Ile Saint-Louis until 1974.
Irwin Shaw arrived in 1951 and left in 1975.

Some of the books we shall look at are well known, if not famous: *The
Judgment of Paris* by Gore Vidal (published in 1952 and revised in 1965),
Giovanni's Room by James Baldwin (1956), *Satori in Paris* by Jack Kerouac
(1966), *Birds of America* by Mary McCarthy (1971), and *The Merry Month
of May* by James Jones (1971). Others, like *The Stone Face* by William
Gardner Smith (1963), *Paris Blues* by Harold Flender (1957), and *The Kansas
City Milkman* (1950) by Reynolds Packard, though less well known, nevertheless provide new perspectives on the city. We may add to this list a
dozen short stories by James T. Farrell and Irwin Shaw, Richard Wright's
unfinished novel *Island of Hallucination,* and several important fragments
from war novels like *The Crusaders* by Stefan Heym (1948) and *The Young
Lions* by Irwin Shaw (1948). There are also a number of lighter-weight
works: *My Yankee Paris* by Herbert Eliot French (1945); a collection of
articles published in French by John Steinbeck, *Un Américain à New York et
à Paris* (1956); Janet Flanner's *Paris Journal* (1972); Art Buchwald's *How
Much Is That in Dollars?* (1962); and a book called *Paris! Paris!* in which
Irwin Shaw recalls memories of his life in the capital that are not altogether
pleasant. These and other works not yet mentioned reveal a chronicle of the
city that varies in importance from one book to the next.

The Events

In the Second World War, Paris played a relatively minor role, and in 1944
American troops made a detour around the capital for strategic and political
reasons. In his study of American novels about World War II, Joseph Waldmeir, who served in France at the time, points out the rarity of Parisian
episodes, overshadowed by the dramatic events of the Normandy landings

and the battle of Alsace. When the capital does appear, it is shown as scarcely more than a halt for the protagonists, en route from the Normandy ports to Germany.[4] Although American troops did not take part directly in the liberation of Paris, three writers belonging to noncombatant units—Irwin Shaw, Stefan Heym, and Herbert Eliot French—were nonetheless witnesses to this event. Irwin Shaw, who belonged to a camera unit, was one of the first soldiers to enter the city on 25 August 1944. He witnessed the fighting on the Place de la Concorde and the storming of the Ministère de la Marine and the Chambre des Députés. All the great historical moments of the three extraordinary days of the Liberation, preserved in photographs, on film, and in popular works such as Collins and Lapierre's *Is Paris Burning?*, are to be found in Shaw's *Paris! Paris!* and *The Young Lions* and, in a different connection, in *The Crusaders* by Stefan Heym. Heym was in Propaganda Intelligence, and his novel is above all an exposé of the corrupt practices of the American army. His descriptions of Paris "en fête" are darkened by more sombre touches: the rape of Thérèse Laurent by Captain Loomis at the Hôtel Scribe; the black-marketeering of Loomis, Dondolo, and Millet; and the abuses of office perpetrated by Major Willoughby, who uses his job with Propaganda Intelligence to further business deals with a pro-Nazi Frenchman under cover of a civilian company.

Shaw's accounts of the German army's entry into Paris in 1940 and its headlong flight in the hours before the liberation are obviously fictional. Through the characters of Diestl and Brandt, Shaw tries, rather unsuccessfully at times, to present the way of thinking of the Germans. For instance, when the soldiers of the Reich arrive in the capital for the first time, their surprise and wonder at the city's venerable antiquity are more typical of Americans than Germans. "Retreat," a short story by the same author, also strikes a false note. A Wehrmacht officer, fleeing from the city, encounters a Parisian Jew and tries to justify his behavior. Understandably, he doesn't make a very good impression and ends up being roundly abused for his pains. Two other books relate to the period of the war. In *One Clear Call* the protean Lanny Budd, now an officer with the British Special Services, carries out several missions in the French capital. He is even admitted, thanks to the famous Colonel Rol-Tanguy, to the underground headquarters of the insurrection situated beneath the War Ministry, the existence of which went entirely undetected by the Germans. At the opposite extreme from the totally fictitious adventures of Upton Sinclair's hero, *My Yankee Paris* by Herbert Eliot French has all the freshness and immediacy of an eyewitness report. French, who was in a quartermaster unit, recounts his experiences in

Paris immediately after the Liberation. Although the book is of negligible literary worth, it is an interesting document of the period, showing the capital at a transitional moment in its history.

Moving to a more recent period, the events of May 1968 are the background of a novel of conjugal conflict, *The Merry Month of May,* by James Jones. The protagonists are an American couple, Harry and Louisa Gallagher, who live—like the author—on the Ile Saint-Louis. Their marriage founders with the arrival of a voluptuous young nymphomaniac, Samantha Everton, incidentally a lesbian and a drug addict totally lacking in any moral sense. She proceeds to seduce the husband, the wife, the son, and all the leading male characters with the exception of the narrator, Jack Hartley. The latter, an unsuccessful novelist but successful bon vivant, would appear to be the ironical self-portrait of James Jones. The novel begins in early May and ends on 17 June 1968. At this point, law and order have been restored to the streets, Samantha has left Harry, and Louisa, after a suicide attempt, lies totally paralyzed in the American Hospital. The novel's boost resides in the extraordinary sexual virulence of Samantha combined with the frenetic spasms shaking the capital. The emotional intrigue and the collective ups and downs of the city are interwoven with each other: Gallagher's son, Hill, becomes one of the leaders of the student movement, and Harry himself, a talented scriptwriter, is much in demand for public debates. The crisis in the streets punctuates the unfolding of the various human relationships, and analysis and introspection blend with reportage. Lengthy narrative passages describe a skirmish near the Place Maubert, the eternal discussions at the Odéon, the building of a barricade in the Rue Monge, and other events.[5] The reader's eye is drawn to strange and unexpected details: close-ups of graffiti scrawled across the walls, mountains of refuse piling up in the streets, or panoramic shots like the one describing the spectacle of the city on Sunday, 19 May: "In all that empty space the traffic lights blinked merrily from red to green to red again, serving only the Army trucks, and the police camions who totally ignored them. It was an eerie sight, like some shot from a science fiction horror film when for some reason or other the world has ended, and humanity no longer exists. But the traffic lights go on."[6]

Jones goes to great pains to explain the so-called freedoms of the universities, or the way studies were organized before 1968, but his explanations are either oversimplified or distorted. One gets the impression that the May uprising was triggered by the hot weather or by the machinations of a bunch of international conspirators, or that it was some sort of Parisian ritual similar to the running of the bulls in Pamplona. There is a lot of talk, mainly in relation to Samantha, about the atmosphere of sexual freedom, drug abuse, and the orgies in the Odéon and the Sorbonne. Many episodes have the air of being youthful pranks. McKenna, the Gallaghers' nine-year-old daughter, organizes action committees in her grade school and stands on her parents' balcony shouting "down with the government" at the policemen guarding Georges Pompidou's apartment. The book's central focus concerns the reactions of a group of expatriates caught up in events that are bewildering and unfamiliar, but it does not, unfortunately, present a very nuanced account of the student revolution and does little more than simply confirm, in the minds of American readers, already existing stereotypes.

Apart from events like the Liberation and the uprising of 1968, which affected the city directly, the repercussions of more distant events were felt in Paris and are reflected in the literature about the city. The Algerian War, for example, provides the context for the plot of *The Stone Face* and also that of the short story "The Man who Married a French Wife." And sometimes the shadow of American history falls across the city. The influx of blacks attests to America's growing racial problems, and the excesses of the McCarthy era are reflected in the increasing numbers of show business personalities who seek refuge in the capital. Other dramatic events are woven into the Parisian chronicle, like the assassination of John Kennedy and later that of his brother Robert, or the 1964 presidential campaign, in which, according to Mary McCarthy, many Americans participated under the auspices of the "American in Paris for Johnson" association.

Minor local events find their memorial in the literature. For example, Elliot Paul, opponent of the Marthe Richard law (which closed down all the brothels) laments its consequences on the ecology of his favorite street, and Jack Kerouac recalls the day in 1962 when a plane bound for Atlanta crashed as it was taking off from Orly. Also reported are various political duels, John Kennedy's visit to the Elysée Palace, the tragic police charge at the Charonne metro station, and the near arrest of the terrorist Carlos in the Rue Amélie.[7] This calendar of events, spanning more than forty years, is given a distinctive tone by the authors' selection of material, but it also concerns characters and milieux that have changed since the war.

The New Innocents

As real tourists become more numerous, their fictional counterparts are relegated to being background figures, and the descriptions of the capital that once accompanied their adventures are now of little interest to a reading public for whom Paris is no longer a novelty. Description of the city is now incidental: landmarks appear in the background of certain scenes or are pointed out by characters acting the role of temporary guide. Kerouac's adventures in *Satori in Paris* illustrate this new trend. He arrives in the capital with the specific intention of tracing his family origins, and his trip is divided between disappointing visits to libraries and less disappointing visits to bars, with very little time for sightseeing. His trip in June 1965 marks the turning point in the battle of the airplane versus the ocean liner. The fact that Kerouac was able to cross the ocean twice in order to spend a mere ten days in France, scarcely five of which were in Paris, radically changes our notions of travel and shows that the grand tour is a thing of the past. The plane plays a fundamental role in transporting the author to this satori. The adventure's magical quality, supposedly due to the virtues of a city that the author scarcely saw, owes much to the fact that his visit provided him with the opportunity to embark on a 124-hour bender and ego trip. The sudden illumination referred to in the book's title seems to have been caused by a series of internal short circuits due to a combination of alcohol, fatigue, and jet lag rather than the famous radiance of the City of Lights.

It is equally impossible to hang the label of "tourist" on Philip Warren, hero of *The Judgment of Paris*. This happy young man not only possesses a considerable fortune but also a network of personal contacts so influential that the doors of aristocratic circles everywhere swing open before him. Philip/Paris moves easily amid modern gods of politics and finance, ruled by Rex and Regina Durham. His approach to the countries he visits—Italy, Egypt, and France—is colored by his interest in their history and the eventual choice he must make concerning his own destiny, in which he will put love before power or intelligence. Philip discovers strange and unexpected aspects of the French capital, but his powers of philosophical analysis distinguish him from the common run of tourists.

The tourist, a disappearing species, is now glimpsed only in short, humorous pieces like those in Art Buchwald's *How Much Is That in Dollars?*, in particular the section entitled "Les Touristes Encore." Yet the innocence of Mark Twain's travelers, with its marvelous potential for development, is handed down to a new version of an old literary type: the student. While the middle-aged American hero, beholding the spectacle of Paris with innocence and naiveté has obviously lost some credibility after 1945, the situation is different when the hero is less than twenty years old.

The postwar American student in Paris appears as a conventional sort of person, uncontaminated by existential excess. Farrell's short story "I Want to

Meet a French Girl" is set in the Paris of the 1950s, and its hero, Lawrence, applies himself to following rules set down by Hemingway in order to become a writer. The students in Irwin Shaw's and Mary McCarthy's works belong to the more recent period of the 1960s, when it became fashionable for American universities to send students abroad for their junior year, a scheme that developed during John Kennedy's term at the White House and was part of the expansion of modern language teaching. Peter Levi, in *Birds of America,* embodies an idealism, an openness to the world, a lack of parochialism that has its roots in this political subsoil. The year in Paris allows these very young students—they are only juniors—to emerge in fact from adolescence, as Roberta James explains in "A Year to Learn the Language": "The Battle of Gettysburg was crystal clear compared to being nineteen years old. I want to get out of the fog of youth. I want to be *precise.* I don't want anything to be an accident. That's one of the reasons I came to Paris—everybody's always talking about how precise the French are. Maybe I can learn to be like that."[8] Peter Levi has not yet undergone his sexual education; nor has Roberta, who thinks she will get over this hurdle pretty soon, following the example of her roommate Louise. "Like all virgins who come to Paris, she was secretly convinced, or resigned, or delighted, by the idea that she would leave the city in a different condition from that in which she had arrived in it."[9] Professor Small, in *Birds of America,* calls the junior year abroad "a decision making device,"[10] and, on a much smaller scale and featuring far less experienced protagonists, this year is similar to the year that Philip Warren gives himself in order to reach his "judgment." Peter, Roberta, Louise, and their classmates, view the city in a way that corresponds not only to a particular phase in their development but also to a particular period in American consciousness as a whole. These students are basically serious. Roberta strives to get better at "precision," and Peter aims at judging everything on the basis of Kantian philosophy. They are intellectuals, who, when moved to express the common grievances of the tourists, do so with a certain amount of detachment, trying at the same time to understand and to explain. But the two works differ in one respect. "A Year to Learn the Language" takes place before Kennedy's assassination, whereas Peter Levi arrives in Paris in October 1964. Through him, the city is seen as the background of the disillusionment of an entire age group, the boys of which, as potential draft fodder, run the risk of ending up in Vietnam. Clearly marked out as a modern Candide, Peter rejects the argument of Pangloss/Small in favor of American political realism, but, with the first bombings of Hanoi, the ground shifts beneath his feet. Even his friends the birds betray him. After being attacked by a swan in the Zoo, he lies in the American Hospital and, in his delirium, sees the figure of Kant himself coming to announce that "nature is dead."

The infrastructure of the junior year abroad is laid bare, particularly in McCarthy's novel. The students are lodged with American families, or with French families vetted by the Embassy, or in maids' rooms, or in small hotels. The majority of them take courses at the Alliance Française, but—an important point—these courses do not count to defer military service. Other rallying points for the students include the American Student Center on the Boulevard Raspail, the American College, Reid Hall (where English classes are organized for the girls from Smith College), the cinémathèques of the Rue d'Ulm and the Palais de Chaillot, and Queenie's café.¹¹ But in the central position is the Sorbonne, where foreign students are dumped indiscriminately in childish civilization courses carefully scheduled for eight o'clock in the morning. This early hour discourages the weak while encouraging the bold to cram themselves into an amphitheater for 500 (there are more than 2,000 enrolled) so dark that it is impossible to take notes. Apparently, the Sorbonne relegates these students to the obscure limbo of a sham university filled with understudy teachers. Peter is only too aware of what is going on, but he also knows that the normal classes for first-year French students are too advanced for him. So, like his friends, he feels he is being exploited by a commercial and chauvinistic system whose syllabus seems to have been drawn up by the French Tourist Board. In her book, Mary McCarthy—with a wisdom born of hindsight, since it was written in 1971— outlines those grievances that were to form the basis of the student complaints in May 1968: boring, out-of-date courses with no audience participation, offering no scope for individual work, and final exams with no relation to the year's work.

The opposite side of the coin is the fact that the bad faith underlying the year abroad is more American than French. Set up on virtually commercial lines, the scheme is designed to enhance the prestige of the participating universities, and one of its spin-offs is the fat profit reaped by the teachers at the Paris end, of whom the mercenary Mr. Small is a typical example. Not surprisingly, McCarthy's description is presented in terms of a balance sheet, setting forth exact details of investment, profit, and loss, and exposing a sort of double talk that, on the one hand, heavily criticizes the Sorbonne, and on the other, makes a great case back home of the least of its diplomas. However, even if the teaching is admitted to be inadequate, there is still the possibility that some of the city's culture will rub off on the students and that their stay can be justified as being "a year to learn the language." This last argument is viewed with skepticism by Roberta James, whose French, after eight months in the capital, shows little progress due to the fact that everyone insists on talking to her in English. This is only one aspect of the general feeling of vague disillusionment. Transported en masse from America, enrolled in organizations that institutionalize what might perhaps have been "la vie de bohème," the students feel deprived of their personal adventure, lost in a cultural ghetto where Parisians are represented by landladies, concierges, post office clerks, teachers, and bums. Strangely, the latter hold a strong fascination for these young Americans, who use them as guinea pigs on whom to practice their French. Their existence poses serious moral problems, however, for Peter Levi, whose fundamental belief in humanity compels him to offer shelter for the night to a drunken woman he finds sleeping on the stairs. This episode, one of the last in the book, ends in a fiasco, and Peter/Candide, in behaving like a Peace Corps volunteer, receives yet another lesson in skepticism for his pains.

The New Colony

The most permanent American residents in Paris belong to the various worlds of business, journalism, diplomacy, and the armed forces. Some of them have vague connections with less respectable milieux and are the descendants of the racketeers denounced by Stefan Heym in *The Crusaders*. In *Murder on the Left Bank* Elliot Paul takes up the old theme of the postwar traffic in Nazi dollars, and some characters in Irwin Shaw's works are ex-soldiers involved in activities midway between the world of business and the world of adventure. In "Tip on a Dead Jockey" former pilot Lloyd Barber, working as an adviser for a war film, is asked to smuggle a large sum of money in a private plane from Egypt to France. He refuses, obeying a superstitious impulse after the jockey of a horse he has backed is killed during the race. Describing the lives of various groups adrift in the city, Shaw exposes the climate of moral decay, of profound despair, that attaches to their ritual pursuit of pleasure. His stories are stories of failure. In "Tip on a Dead Jockey" Lloyd Barber is brought face-to-face with his lack of courage. In "In the French Style" diplomat Walter Beddoes returns from a trip to find that his mistress, Christina, has left him to become the fiancée of a boring doctor from Seattle, who has come to Paris for a conference. In "God Was Here but He Left Early" Rosemary Maclain faces the problem of terminating a pregnancy resulting from a casual encounter. The nature and tone of the conversations underline the human emptiness in which the various characters struggle to survive: memories of the war in the Pacific, the Vietnam War, bits of sordid gossip relating to "the group." In opting for a marriage of reason, Christina, the understanding comrade who is always falling in love, decides to put an end to a life of pleasure that has finally become unbearable. "I'm tired of correspondents and pilots and promising junior statesmen . . . I'm tired of seeing people off . . . I'm tired of all the spoiled, hung-over international darlings . . . I'm tired of being handed around the group. I'm tired of being more in love with people than they are with me."[12] While she breaks the news of her engagement to Beddoes, a wreath-laying ceremony is taking place in the background, at the Arc de Triomphe. After refusing to act as courier, Barber says: "I better get out of here . . . this continent is not for me."[13] Rosemary tries to forget her worries in the arms of a reporter from the BBC, only to realize with bitter amusement that this time her bedmate is a harmless fetishist. Shaw paints a somber picture of these lost Americans, tied through their work to a capital in which the world's ills are felt with unusual intensity, especially the Vietnam War. The title of the third story, in fact, derives from a graffito on a wall in Vietnam, but it is also the epitaph for a city and milieu that seem, for Shaw, to have fallen from grace: "God Was Here but He Left Early."

The Kansas City Milkman, written by the legendary correspondent of the United Press and the *New York Daily News,* Reynolds Packard, constitutes a unique document on the lives of American journalists just after the war. The plot revolves around the relationship between the narrator, Clay Brewster, an old hand at the Paris office of the imaginary Interworld Press Association, and a young reporter, Don Shelby. Brewster narrates the day-to-day functioning of the agency, with its diverse intrigues and numerous incidents caused by errors of judgment or misinformation. He reveals the tortuous and often dishonest steps involved in the writing of articles aimed specifically at a reading public exemplified in the person of the "Kansas City milkman." The basic subject matter concerns the news items of a three-year period, 1946–49, and the city is an integral part of the plot. The news agency itself is in the Rue Auber. The journalists are regular customers at Prunier's, Rouzier's, and the Hôtel Scribe, and also the Montana Bar and Harry's Bar. One entire chapter is devoted to Parisian brothels, for the simple reason that potential clients from the United States arrive with the expectation that they will also be initiated into the pleasures of the city's nightlife. Brewster, who often finds himself in the difficult role of guide, has to be able to size up their degree of curiosity in relation to their imperviousness to shock. Such episodes reveal Packard's censure of a profession that he shows as entirely governed by financial considerations and, in sum, rather immoral. The excesses of the Parisian office, narrated with cynical humor, are shown as harmonizing perfectly with the venal aspects of the city.

Another distinctive social group is studied by James T. Farrell, Art Buchwald, and, above all, Mary McCarthy: the Americans who work for the North Atlantic Treaty Organization, and whose presence in Paris is a direct consequence of the 1949 treaty and the capital's role as NATO headquarters until 1966. During this period, these American civil servants and members of the armed forces enjoyed an original sort of lifestyle, given their enormous privileges combined with conditions in Paris at the time. These Americans could hardly have been unaware of the gulf that separated them from ordinary Parisians, since all the things that set them apart were officially spelled out in numerous rules and regulations. Over and above their generous salaries, they also enjoyed various perquisites that isolated them still more. Their cars, their gas, their food, the various domestic appliances they used all came directly from the United States and cost far less than they would have in France. A "PX economy" came into existence—and included not only regular use of the post exchange but also of the commissary and the Class VI store where spirits were sold. Peter Levi discovers the real significance of this supply system when he dines with General Lammers for the first time: "We had a big canned American ham, which the general carved with an electric slicer; it was baked with Dole's pineapple and brown sugar and with it were canned potato balls and frozen peas and lima beans, followed by American vanilla ice cream and Hershey's chocolate sauce and FFV cookies. . . . The wife kept announcing the brand names, like those butlers you see in the movies calling out the names of the guests.[14]

Is it possible to accept such inequalities without moral reservations? The question simply does not arise for the narrator of "French Girls Are Vicious," for whom it is enough, indeed her duty, to obey the rules: "I have a Chrysler. I paid for it out of my savings. I am not ashamed of driving my Chrysler around Paris. I was able to have it shipped over to me because I work for the Government; I believe in getting all the advantages I can from my position. But I don't cheat, because I never cheated in my life. But I use the PX as much as I can."[15] For Mrs. Lammers, buying from the PX constitutes a political act. The products on display in her apartment proclaim the excellence of the American way of life, arousing the envy of visiting French officers and their wives. Others, whose judgment is finer, find the extreme version of such economic sectarianism shabby and disgraceful and cannot accept that true patriotism consists of buying everything down to the last light bulb and stalk of celery at the PX. Through his connection with General Lammers, Peter has an opportunity to acquire a typewriter for a third off the normal American price. But, he argues with himself, can he do it, in all conscience? And if he did, would this not involve harming the French market in some way, though its exorbitant prices, in any case, would make such a purchase there impossible? The perplexity of Candide is total. His moral dilemma underscores the special situation of the NATO Americans. Trapped between the realities of their own country, generally referred to as "stateside," and the conditions of local life, they find themselves on a financial leash that leaves them little room for maneuver. This very dependence is an essential part of their existence, as illustrated by the case of the deserted wife who refuses to divorce her husband because this would mean giving up her PX card.[16] For many of these Americans, life in Paris is exactly the same as it would be anywhere else in the world. Mary McCarthy is unable to forgive their cultural amorphousness and their indifference to their surroundings. They are the prisoners of the physical and mental structures of their functions.

A particularly sharp focus for McCarthy's satire is found in her account of Thanksgiving Day celebrations. As far as Parisians are concerned, this is the least comprehensible of American traditions, and Art Buchwald, in a couple of humorous articles entitled "Thanksgiving Sounds Even Better in French" and "The Priscilla Pitch and Merci Donnant," shows that it is better not to look for a French equivalent. The spirit of this celebration, which, in a way, consists of thanking God for being American, harmonizes perfectly with the NATO philosophy. Listening to Mrs. Lammers trying to initiate her guests into the mysteries of the ritual, Peter Levi wonders if "maybe service wives abroad got directives from the Pentagon on what to tell the natives about Thanksgiving."[17] The French guests, a bunch of bemedalled reactionaries according to Peter, happily fraternize with the foreigners, as did the Indians of the first Thanksgiving, and the celebration becomes something of a public relations operation. But the earth's generous gifts, canned or frozen, come straight from the PX, and this parody of Thanksgiving is symbolic of the entire existence of the NATO Americans. In spite of being militant patriots, they are so cut off from their cultural heritage that as Art Buchwald claims in "Un-American Baseball in Paris," they have actually forgotten the basic rules of their national sport.

Homosexuals

It may seem strange to identify two new literary types, homosexuals and blacks, solely on the basis of their sexual preference and skin color. Yet these two factors enable us to identify a new and significant body of works in which the hero's process of self-discovery is radically influenced by his search for sexual or racial identity, a search that, apparently, is greatly facilitated by being in a city where the way of life is freer and more tolerant. Historically, this was true for blacks, and one immediately thinks of black writers drawn to Paris—of Richard Wright and of James Baldwin, who could write in *Nobody Knows My Name*, "And, in fact, in Paris, I began to see the sky for what seemed to be the first time."[18] In the case of homosexuals, matters are less clear; it is difficult to estimate the numbers involved and to pinpoint the precise reasons that caused them to come to Paris.

In the history of American literature, Paris is closely linked with the first fictional attempts to deal with the subject of homosexuality. In works like *The City and the Pillar* and *Other Voices, Other Rooms,* both published in 1948, Gore Vidal and Truman Capote, it is true, use material that is uniquely American. But in Vidal's *The Judgment of Paris* (1952) and "Pages from an Abandoned Journal" (1956) and in Baldwin's *Giovanni's Room* (1956), homosexual relationships evolve within the framework of the capital. In this last novel, James Baldwin chooses to make all his characters white, in order to remove any possible racial interference. The novel's fourth sentence shows the character of David looking in a mirror, which gives back to the reader the explicit image of blond hair. In "Pages from an Abandoned Journal" the Parisian experience is a decisive one for the anonymous narrator. He is shown in the first two parts of the story (21 May–4 June 1948) to be cautiously approaching the homosexual milieux of the capital. The reader then finds him five years later, in the third fragment of the journal (26–27 December 1953), working as an interior decorator in New York and involved in a series of homosexual love affairs. For Gore Vidal, the year 1948, marked by his second trip to Europe—which he had visited in 1939 on a St. Alban's School trip—seems to have been a turning point. The time he spent in Rome and, above all, Paris provides much of the material for *The Judgment of Paris* and "Pages from an Abandoned Journal."

In *Giovanni's Room* David's stay in Paris symbolizes the end of an evolution begun in childhood that necessitated the severing of all ties with his family and his society. His meeting with Giovanni rekindles memories of the adolescent affection of his friend Joey and reveals to him the existence of a

new sort of relationship based on virile passion. The failure of this relationship brings David to a moment of crisis. For him, Paris acts as eye-
opener, just as it does for the writer of the "abandoned journal." Some
parallels exist between these two works by different authors published in the
same year. Each of the protagonists has had a homosexual encounter in
adolescence (with Joey or Jimmy); each meets in Paris a person who is in
some way out of the ordinary (Giovanni or Elliot Magren); each leaves the
city for the seaside (the Riviera or Deauville), accompanied by a woman
(Hella or Hilda) whose physical presence soon becomes unbearable. But
while the hero of "Pages from an Abandoned Journal" makes a final choice
as to the path he will follow, it is not clear at the end of *Giovanni's Room*
whether David will in the future devote himself to an ideal of homosexual
love. We must wait until *Another Country* before the question is resolved.

Robert A. Bone, writing about *Giovanni's Room*, brings into his discussion the figure of André Gide, who appears to have influenced both Vidal
and Baldwin. Ray Lewis White refers to a meeting between Vidal and Gide
in Paris in 1948, and in *The Judgment of Paris* Vidal inserts an account of a
visit to the master by Philip Warren's friend Charles de Cluny. More significantly, Baldwin devotes an entire essay, "The Male Prison" in *Nobody Knows
My Name,* to Gide's *Madeleine.* Bone sees the relationship of Giovanni and
David as mirroring that of Gide and his wife. Like Gide's wife, David has the
chance to choose to play the role of redeemer and save his partner from the
threat of degradation but instead betrays him.[19] This interpretation highlights the fundamental duality of the homosexual caught between a sort of
platonic ideal and the sordidness of reality. Such idealism, expressed by the
character Jim in certain speeches in *The Judgment of Paris,* like the idealism
of Jacques and Giovanni in *Giovanni's Room,* is in strange contrast with
Jim's behavior and choice of friends. Jim, who previously appeared in *The
City and the Pillar,* at the end of which he kills his partner, launches into a
fervent explanation to Philip Warren of the beauty of reciprocal passion. Yet
in Paris, where he has fled to escape American justice, he turns to prostitution, first in order to survive, and later, to make money. Jacques, too, a
homosexual in his fifties who urges David to abandon himself to Giovanni,
has experienced nothing more fulfilling than furtive couplings in the dark.
Giovanni himself, transfigured by the purity of his love for David, nonetheless continues to act as bait for the clients in the special bar where he is a
waiter. The vision of the homosexual as fallen angel harmonizes well with
the city's more sinister aspects, particularly in Baldwin's novel.

Yet the capital appears as a haven of tolerance where homosexuality is an accepted part of literary and artistic life. It is no accident that Gide's name crops up frequently, and in "Pages from an Abandoned Journal" the narrator, who is writing his Ph.D. dissertation in Paris, is greatly impressed by the vast culture of Elliot Magren and his friends. The terraces of the Café de Flore, mentioned on several occasions in "Pages from an Abandoned Journal" and *The Judgment of Paris*,[20] show us the good-natured side of a city in which Stephen and Bill, in Vidal's novel, are able to enjoy a cozy idyll without having to make excuses and provide explanations. According to Charles de Cluny, Saint Germain, the great sixth-century liberator of slaves, lives on symbolically in the twentieth century as guarantor for other kinds of emancipation.[21] A Frenchman whom Philip Warren meets at Edmond Twill's explains to him that Paris belongs to a continent where "a gentleman can buy very nearly everything he wants, including the incorruptible,"[22] and in the same breath the distinguished fetishist makes an offer of 10,000 francs for the underpants Philip is wearing. The texts reveal the existence of a demimonde whose operations are greatly facilitated by the city's permissiveness; and Vidal and Baldwin, between them, provide the reader with a two-tiered description, featuring, on one level, an international aristocracy and, on the other, a Parisian subculture of dubious reputation.

The cosmopolitan circles of *The Judgment of Paris* provide excellent material for social comedy. Two Englishmen, Lord Glenellen and Clyde Norman, and an American, Edmond Twill, all relatively benign homosexuals and practiced transvestites, engage in long, worldly conversations, embroidered with delicate euphemisms and exquisite subtleties, which provide plenty of light-hearted entertainment. The tone changes, however, with the description of the Felliniesque gathering in the imaginary Hôtel de Lyon et Grénoble [*sic*]. It becomes even more disturbing when Elliot Magren and Jim are brought in to provide the indispensable spice to such pleasures. Magren, a long-time protégé of Lord Glenellen—who also appears in "Pages from an Abandoned Journal"—has become sufficiently successful as a prostitute to be able to choose his partners; but Jim, forced to rely on the protection of Twill, whom he finds unbearable, tries to find escape in drugs, and eventually dies from an overdose. In spite of these more somber aspects of the plot, the predominant tone of the book is high farce, particularly in the set piece, describing the cult of the hermaphrodite Augustus/Augusta. This cult is not mentioned in books on esotericism in Paris,[23] and probably the scene is pure invention. At the appointed hour, Augusta makes her appearance, choosing whichever form, male or female, happens to take her fancy, after which she is ritually clothed by her worshipers. Then all of his/

her ancestors are named, as far back as Julius Caesar, thus providing ample proof of direct descent from Venus. Because of their wealth, Twill, Norman, and especially Lord Glenellen soon rise to the highest ranks of the presiding dignitaries, whose role it is to spread the cult of the hermaphrodite through-out the world. Unfortunately, in the middle of one of these ceremonies of "revelation," just as Augusta is unveiling to her followers "primary and secondary sexual characteristics of unusual variety,"[24] the police rush in and arrest the participants. The episode ends in mock-heroic mode. Glenellen and Norman, after fleeing to the innermost sanctuary, struggle desperately to enable Augusta to escape, while engaging in a dialogue that parodies Act 4, Scene 3, of Shakespeare's *Julius Caesar.*

Such farce is totally foreign to *Giovanni's Room,* where the setting is permeated with the author's melancholy recollections of his first stay in France in 1948–57. The private gatherings of *The Judgment of Paris,* with their atmosphere of refined, discreet elegance give way to descriptions of humdrum, run-of-the-mill cafés and bars, made exceptional only by their homosexual clientele. In the working-class café on the Left Bank, or in Guillaume's bar where Giovanni works, or in Mme Clothilde's restaurant in Les Halles we discover a population both more pathetic and more frighten-ing than the collection of precious eccentrics who frequent Edmond Twill's salon and who are to some extent redeemed by the sparkling wit of their conversations. David, the narrator, casting an eye around Guillaume's bar, describes the customers as follows: "There were the usual paunchy bespec-tacled gentlemen with avid, sometimes despairing eyes, the usual, knife-blade lean, tight-trousered boys. . . . There were, of course, *les folles,* al-ways dressed in the most improbable combinations, screaming like parrots the details of their latest love affairs. . . . There was the boy who worked all day, it was said, in the post office, who came out at night wearing makeup and earrings and with his heavy blond hair piled high."[25] The regulars at Mme Clothilde's restaurant look equally strange and disturbing to David: "Giovanni was far from me, drinking *marc* between an old man, who looked like a receptacle of all the world's dirt and disease, and a young boy, a redhead, who would look like that man one day, if one could read in the dullness of his eye, anything so real as a future. Now, however, he had something of a horse's dreadful beauty; some suggestion, too, of the storm trooper; covertly, he was watching Guillaume; he knew that both Guillaume and Jacques were watching him."[26] Apart from the description of such characters, who may not, of course, be typically Parisian, the book's local color derives from Baldwin's attempts to reproduce the city's slang and from his evocative descriptions of Les Halles, whose atmosphere of semiclan-destinity suits the theme of homosexuality in the 1950s. Here we are on the fringes of the underworld, rubbing shoulders with pushers and drug addicts, weighed down by the feeling of decline and loss characteristic of the Fourth Republic and exemplified in the character of Guillaume, a disillusioned former member of the Gaullist resistance and the last of a long line of aristocrats. It is hard to say how much Baldwin based his settings and characters on real-life models, but there is a documentary aspect to his work that is striking.

Still, in spite of its wealth of concrete detail, *Giovanni's Room* leaves one with the impression, to borrow Robert Bone's phrase, that Paris incorpo-rates "the moral topography of Harlem."[27] Baldwin seems haunted by the spectacle of Giovanni's, and then David's, descent into the underworld, and we may ask ourselves whether such a sentiment of anguish is entirely valid in the Parisian context. In fact, the way the city is perceived changes as David's personality changes, and the initial stereotype, "no city is more beautiful than Paris,"[28] is replaced by more ambivalent feelings. As Giovanni's person-ality is more fully revealed to David, along with the true meaning of what it is to be a homosexual, the city becomes a symbol for the homosexual condi-tion. Paris is not seen as fundamentally evil, and Baldwin does not sink into profound despair; but if we take Giovanni's room as a representation of the city as a whole, it is a city that the author perceives as a labyrinth and a prison or even as the cave of Plato's parable. The room and the city that surrounds it form an encircling matrix squeezing Giovanni inside a body in which he feels ill at ease. For David, the discovery of his own homosexuality is also tied to this metaphor, hence his longing to escape toward the sun and the sea. Paris is a purgatory where David remains and suffers and from which Giovanni escapes at the price of his damnation through crime. In *Another Country* Rufus, who resembles Giovanni, ends up committing suicide in New York. Conversely, Eric, the literary descendant of David, achieves self-knowledge and fulfillment. Although the homosexual paradise described at the beginning of Book 2 is to be found on the shores of the Mediterranean, it is nevertheless in Paris that Eric first meets Yves. The latter is given the same name as the petty crook of Les Halles with whom Giovanni is last seen. The Yves of *Another Country* also has links with the world of crime but reforms under Eric's influence, and at the end of the book he is seen as the redeemer for whom Eric waits in New York. Thus, the Parisian experience, which remained ambiguous in the case of David in *Giovanni's Room,* leads to revelation in *Another Country.*

Although sexual ambivalence is a common theme in Gore Vidal's work (in particular *Myra Breckenridge*), it is surprising to find to what extent homosexuality figures in *The Judgment of Paris,* which supposedly sanctions the supremacy of Venus. Faithful to the guidelines implicit in the title, Anna/Venus, who is French—though the reader is apt to forget it—triumphs over her female rivals in Paris. She is also successful in routing her homosexual competitors: Jim dies, Stephen and Bill go back to America, and the cult of the hermaphrodite is brought to an end by the police. The book ends on this victorious note, but it is a victory that might be deemed more technical than real. By alluding indirectly to the first Kinsey Report of 1948, the author situates Philip's trip in the context of a great homosexual awakening in the United States, the repercussions of which are felt as far away as Paris:

> The city had been conquered by his homosexual countrymen, and he watched with wonder as the scandal grew, as mask after mask fell, from familiar and ordinary faces, to reveal the unexpected, the Grecian visage. Businessmen from Kansas City, good Rotarians all, embraced bored young soldiers on the streets at night or paid high prices for slim Algerian boys at those bordellos which catered to such pleasures. College boys, young veterans, the ones Philip had always known in school or in the Navy, athletes and æsthetes both, scoured the bars and urinals in search of one another, the nice girl back home forgotten, as they loved or tried to love one another in this airy summer city. . . . Those sturdy youths who had been ashamed of their secret practice now took much pleasure, at least in Paris, in openly doing what they pleased and, with the enthusiasm of zealots, they proselyted furiously.[29]

Clyde Norman expresses the hope that the various homosexual factions will now be united under the common banner of the "Third Way," a sort of homosexual fraternity whose origins lie in frontier society, with its scarcity of women, and that manifested itself more recently among American soldiers during the Second World War.

A close look at the book's hero makes the implied equivalence between the city of Paris and the triumph of Venus even more dubious. Philip is pictured as the fellow traveler of Norman, Glenellen, and Twill, the tolerant observer who, to the surprise of the participants, does not enter into the game. But as a modern Paris, does he not appear, through his acquaintance with homosexuality in all respects other than actual practice, as an admirer of Venus who is much too distant and abstract? There are striking similarities between Philip, who says to Sophia, "I've kept a journal off and on all my life,"[30] and that other keeper of journals who wrote "Pages from an Abandoned Journal." Both are young and cultured, and they frequent in the same year the same Parisian circles. They differ only in the particular orientation of their quest for love, and this difference, combined with what is complementary in their natures, makes the two into an ideal hermaphrodite figure. The hero of the short story, too, has links with the Greek legend, but of an antithetical nature, for he will finally reject the love of his fiancée, Helen. This second Paris may seem more convincing than the first and may raise doubts about the legitimacy of Philip's final verdict. Set side by side, novel and short story confirm the preeminence of homosexuality in Vidal's writing about the capital, despite the inevitable triumph of Venus. In fact, ten years after the novel's publication, Vidal admitted that he would hesitate to make the same choice a second time.[31]

Blacks

Blacks, as perceived by James Baldwin, William Gardner Smith, Richard Wright, and Harold Flender, may experience in Paris, in the Sartrean perspective of *Another Country,* a form of acute existential anxiety similar to that of homosexuals, but their search for identity through expatriation involves considerations that are largely political. Consequently, their presence in Paris is almost always accompanied by some sort of intellectual debate, if not an actual statement of revolt, and the literary version of their real migration is concerned, above all, with making its causes explicit.

In the literature written before 1940, white Americans are often surprised at the way in which blacks are a normal part of Parisian life and, under the aegis of Freudianism, are even shown as having a special relationship with the city whose unconscious drives are reflected in their natural spontaneity. After the Second World War, the feeling of surprise continues. For example, in 1945 the good-natured promiscuity of the Paris métro, where there are no notices obliging blacks and whites to sit separately, comes as a shock to the Southern narrator of *My Yankee Paris.* He becomes friendly with a rich Abyssinian, a great admirer of the United States, who promises to visit him there, and this promise causes the narrator a certain amount of embarrassment. Reflecting somewhat bitterly on conditions back home, he secretly hopes the visit will not materialize.[32]

Understandably, the reactions of black writers go far deeper than the occasional stabs of doubt or shame experienced by some of their white compatriots. In literature, several factors are at the origin of black expatriation: hatred of the climate of racism in America, fear and anxiety about the future, and, occasionally, firsthand experience of injustice or persecution. In *The Long Dream* Zeke, who is stationed in Orléans, writes to Fishbelly Tucker that he intends to stay in France after his military service: "Man, its good to live in this grayness where folks don't look mad at you just cause you are black." And later he adds, "France ain't no heaven, but folks don't kill you for crazy things. These white folks just more like human beings than them crackers back in Mississippi."[33] The plot of *The Long Dream* leads up to the departure of Fishbelly, who, after being unjustly persecuted by Cantley, the local police chief, flees from Clintonville, Mississippi, to Paris. Richard Wright presumably wished to justify his own actions and to stress the fact that even the so-called liberalism of the North did not inspire much confidence among black Americans in 1958. In Smith's novel *The Stone Face* the journalist Simeon Brown is tortured by a sadistic policeman and leaves Philadelphia so as not to succumb to his murderous desire for revenge. These characters are motivated by reasons similar to those expressed by James Baldwin in *Nobody Knows My Name:* "I left America because I doubted my ability to survive the fury of the color problem here . . . I wanted to prevent myself from becoming *merely* a Negro."[34]

The implicit protest of black expatriation is heightened by the explicit sacrifices it entails. But not everything is sacrificed: for blacks in Paris, jazz is an important part of life that attests to the existence of a black culture shared on both sides of the Atlantic. (Its role is particularly significant in *Paris Blues* by Harold Flender, the only white author discussed in this section.) For some of these expatriates there seems to be no possibility of a return to America or to its ways. In *Paris Blues* Marie, the owner of a nightclub, ends up marrying a French aristocrat, and Eddie Cook, the saxophonist, believes (wrongly as it turns out) that he has severed all ties with the United States. Simeon Brown, in *The Stone Face,* is also convinced that he will never go back home. On the other hand, bandleader Wild Man Moore plays down, in *Paris Blues,* the evils of segregation and puts his international career in the hands of a white impresario. Black visitors to the capital bring over the latest reports of significant changes across the ocean. One of these visitors is Connie Mitchell, who teaches school in Chicago and becomes Eddie Cook's friend. In Richard Wright's unfinished work, *Island of Hallucination,* a couple of despicable black characters serve as an indirect condemnation of the system that has made them what they are. Irene Stout gets rich by writing to her white compatriots for money, successfully exploiting their feeling of guilt, and Jimmy Whitfield blackmails the young white American women he has seduced in Paris, by threatening to tell their parents what they have done.

The spate of ideas, debates, and occasional fights that agitate this milieu constantly is reminiscent of the great debate about expatriation in the 1920s. Here, however, the fundamental preoccupation—the problem of blacks—is complicated by the presence of white characters. Based on the three variables of color, nationality, and political affiliation, the characters in these works offer as many solutions as is mathematically possible. The most vulgar kind of racists are found among Right Bank tourists. In diametric opposition to them, stand the Latin Quarter liberals, ex-soldiers, and artists: in *Paris Blues*, the Jewish musician Benny, and, in *The Stone Face*, white expatriates like Clyde and Jinx; Henri, an extreme left-wing French student; Maria, a Polish Jew who survived the concentration camps; and Lou, who stands for the ideal white American believing in his country's crucial role as the melting pot of races. In *Paris Blues* we meet Michel, a jazz guitarist, whose brother is a diplomat, and who comes from the Parisian upper classes. But with whom are we to class him, since he is also black?

The relationships between these characters embodying different ideologies take place in a context resting on one simple fact: in Paris, black Americans are able to enjoy the status of privileged whites. An example of this is provided by the episode in *Paris Blues* in which a white American, in the middle of a jam session, calls Eddie Cook a nigger and roughly orders him to play "Melancholy Baby," whereupon the surprised tourist is forced to make a hasty exit before the threatening reactions of the audience. A similar incident occurs in *The Stone Face*, where a group of tourists from Utah are thrown out of a nightclub by the owner after insulting Simeon Brown. The Parisians are a partial lot, and Eddie Cook begins to wonder if the applause that follows his number is due as much to the color of his skin as to his accomplishments as a musician. Gore Vidal, too, in *The Judgment of Paris*, tells the story of a New Yorker of Italian descent who has had a huge success in Paris by passing herself off as a black blues singer. But for a black American, finding oneself, as it were, in the skin of a white European is not a satisfactory answer to the search for an identity. This is all the more true insofar as the racist attitude of the French toward Arabs puts him in an extremely uncomfortable position as soon as he comes into contact with the North African minority. This special kind of segregation is occasionally condemned in *Birds of America*, *Nobody Knows My Name*, and Ursule Molinaro's novel *Green Lights Are Blue*. Similarly, in Chapter 10 of *Paris Blues*, Eddie Cook, finding himself stopped in a taxi during a demonstration by Algerians, is shocked by the hostile attitude of the taxi drivers. It is a problem that is central to the plot of *The Stone Face*, whose author sees in these Parisian aspects of the Algerian War additional proof of the universality of racism, which Simeon Brown attempts to exorcise by painting a picture that he calls *The Stone Face*.

Smith's belief in the ubiquity of racism is behind the numerous scenes involving the Algerian colony in Paris, which Simeon gets to know after he has accidentally caused the unwarranted arrest of customers in an Algerian café. Later, one of them explains to Simeon in English how he was sent on a mission to the United States while serving in the Free French army, and was therefore able to see for himself the way black Americans lived. This experience provokes a sarcastic tirade: "How does it feel to be the white man for a change? . . . We're the niggers here! Know what the French call us—*bicot, melon, raton, nor'af.* That means *nigger* in French. Ain't you scared we might rob you? Ain't you appaled by our unpressed clothes, our body odor? No, but seriously, I want to ask you a serious question—would you let your daughter marry one of us?"[35] This experience of color reversal is repeated when, in Chapter 5, Simeon vainly tries to get his new friends admitted to the Château Club, where he is a member.

Subsequently, guided by Ahmed, a medical student who is a member of the Algerian National Liberation Front, Simeon is taken on a tour of the Goutte d'Or Quarter.

> The further north the bus moved, the more drab became the buildings, the streets and the people. Cheap stores selling clothes, furniture, kitchen utensils: "Easy terms, ten months to pay"! Cafés became dimmer, the street narrower and noisier, more and more children filled the sidewalks. Men out of work, with nothing to do and no place to go, stood in sullen, furtive groups on street corners. Arab music blared from the dark cafés or from the open windows of the bleak hotels. Then suddenly, police were everywhere, stalking the streets, eyes moving insolently from face to face, submachine guns strung from their shoulders. It was like Harlem, Simeon thought, except that there were fewer cops in Harlem.

As the scene develops, further comparisons arise:

> The men he saw through the windows of the bus had whiter skins and less frizzly hair, but they were in other way like the Negroes in the United States. They adopted the same poses. . . . Street vendors shouted their wares in Arabic: fruit, clothes, vegetables. He remembered the pushcarts in his childhood on Tenth Street. . . . The odors of rotting food and of cooking mingled in the air, and he remembered how they had smelled to him—the fried chicken or the greens, the uncollected garbage in the

alleys and gutters. Arab music assailed them from all sides. The Blues. Where was the Blues Singer now? In the dismal cafés, men played pinball or football machines, or stood at counters staring at nothing, empty coffee cups in front of them. There were no women. The police paced the streets, their faces hard.[36]

The bitterness of these descriptions leaves no doubt as to what Smith thinks of French attitudes toward Arabs. He stresses the existence of shanty towns, internment camps, shakedowns, police raids, tortures, and summary executions. Three of Simeon's friends are tortured during interrogations. Ahmed, whose brother had died in the fighting in Algeria, is himself killed during an anticurfew demonstration on 1 October 1961, in which the death toll—according to Smith—was over 200. In *The Last of the Conquerors,* published fifteen years earlier in 1948, Smith had argued that American racism was the moral equivalent of the Nazi holocaust. In *The Stone Face* he makes a similar comparison, but this time with regard to French racism. Maria's recollections of her treatment by the Nazis in Poland, the equivocal use of the term "concentration camp," and the attribution to the French in general of the traditional excuse of the Germans—"Wir sind die kleiner Leuter [*sic*]"[37]—are all used to support this hypothesis. Such a condemnation is doubtless excessive. But Smith does give us an insight into the feelings of black expatriates brought up against the problem of belonging, by the experience of seeing other nonwhites desperately fighting to preserve an ideal and a country.

The presence of black Americans in Paris can be justified far more than that of whites, and as Simeon says, "When you have to get out from under the stick, life has a purpose."[38] But it is a purpose that soon turns out to be insufficient as blacks discover the artificiality of their situation. Violently opposed to many of their white compatriots, they finally realize that their life in Paris resembles a negative development, in the photographic sense. They are then faced with the idea of a possible return to the United States. After twelve years spent in Paris, Eddie Cook finally returns, persuaded by Connie Mitchell, who convinces him of their country's qualities of grandeur and vitality. His return takes place in an atmosphere of rosy optimism that could not fail to seduce Hollywood—a film version of the novel was made in 1962 starring Sidney Poitier. Simeon Brown also returns, more than ever convinced of the universality of racism. His experiences in Paris, during which he assaults a policeman in the demonstrations of 1 October 1961, influence his decision to go back to America and take up arms with his black brothers rather than follow the struggle from afar. His development is clearly charted in the book's different sections: "The Fugitive," "The White Man," and finally "The Brother." The moment of truth awaiting all black expatriates is thus described by James Baldwin:

> This crucial day may be the day on which an Algerian taxi-driver tells him how it feels to be an Algerian in Paris. . . . Or it may be the day on which someone asks him to explain Little Rock and he begins to feel that it would be simpler—and, corny as the words may sound, more honorable—to *go* to Little Rock than to sit in Europe, on an American passport, trying to explain it. This is a personal day, a terrible day, the day to which his entire sojourn has been tending. It is the day he realizes that there are no untroubled countries in this fearfully troubled world; that if he has been preparing himself for anything in Europe, he has been preparing himself—for America.[39]

The Decline of Paris

By insisting on the necessity of a return, James Baldwin underlines the transitory and limited nature of black expatriation, which today offers no further potential for renewal as a literary theme than the expatriation of homosexuals or NATO officials. In the context of the late 1980s, these three different Parisian milieux seem equally dated. It is inconceivable today that black Americans should en masse choose exile in Paris. As for the homosexuals who once saw the capital as a refuge, they are now probably better protected by the legislation of certain American states than they would be in France. NATO Americans were dispersed after 1966, when France ceased to be an active member of the organization, and they belong to a closed chapter of history. With regard to other groups, it is indeed likely that there are just as many businessmen, journalists, and diplomats living in Paris now as in the past and that the lure of the junior year abroad is as strong as it was previously. The main interest of the novels and short stories that have been examined in this chapter lies in their documentary nature. They illustrate the life of characteristic social groups. But the urban setting is, on the whole, one of extreme banality. This is true even of *Giovanni's Room,* where every description of the quays, with their bookstalls and their anglers, or of the American Express office with its waiting tourists seems to have come straight from the pages of Wolfe, Hemingway, or other 1920s writers. David's description of his meeting with Sue on the terrace of the Select and her instant seduction also recall works like *Tropic of Cancer.* Even Hella

Lincoln's last name is yet another instance of references to Old America. In *Paris Blues* the circuit of nocturnal Paris that Benny plans for the old school-mistress Lillian recalls half a dozen works written between the wars. Mary McCarthy, too, fails to reveal any new aspects of the Latin Quarter, describing hotels and markets as had Hemingway, Sinclair Lewis, or Lyon Mearson before her. Ten years or so after *Birds of America,* the same old clichés can still be found in Erica Jong's *Fear of Flying.* Among the most recent novels dealing with Paris are two best-sellers, *The French Passion* by Diane Du Pont and *Mistral's Daughter* by Judith Krantz. The former, set during the French Revolution, relates the adventures of a young aristocrat, Manon d'Epinay, who becomes the mistress of a poet and tribune called André—in reality an illegitimate son of Louis XV. André and Manon narrowly escape the guillotine and embark for America. The plot of the latter takes the reader from 1920s Paris to New York's modeling agencies in the years between 1950 and 1980 and revolves around three generations of red-haired beauties bound to the painter Julien Mistral, who in some respects reminds us of Picasso. The recent success of such books in which the theme of Paris is rather crudely treated seems to indicate that Paris may now be a subject of inspiration for popular literature and that its multivalence can be relied upon to yield material for historical, erotic, or fantastic plots, or even for "disaster" novels.

The works described in this chapter show that after 1945 it becomes increasingly difficult to be innovative in describing a city that a long literary tradition combined with technological advances in the media had rendered overfamiliar and, consequently, less exciting. The authors fall back on depictions of social groups like the ones we have just seen or of milieux that are somehow out of the ordinary—like the expatriate black basketball players in Peter Israel's *The Stiff Upper Lip.* The authors can only deal with the city in fragments rather than seeing it as a whole, and even such fragments rely heavily for inspiration on the great literature of the past. If it is true that Paris is associated with what John W. Aldridge considers the two most fruitful subjects for immediate postwar writing, homosexuality and racial conflict,[40] it is an association whose contribution to literary history remains modest. The authors often place themselves under the aegis of James, Hemingway, and Miller, in order to justify similarities in their works or give more authority to what they say. Explaining the black exodus, William Gardner Smith talks of a "New Lost Generation" and refers to *The Sun also Rises* and *Tropic of Cancer.*[41] Harold Flender remembers Henry James and, like him, compares Paris to a diamond.[42] In *The Merry Month of May* James Jones tries to come up with a name for the generation of McCarthyite victims and overloads his writing with references to Hemingway, Fitzgerald, Gertrude Stein, and Sylvia Beach.[43] Finally, Gore Vidal in *The Judgment of Paris* springs on the reader an unacknowledged but sufficiently explicit pastiche of the scene from *The American* where Christopher Newman meets the Duchess.[44] Such a technique, through its use of irony, superposition, and deliberate exaggeration, effectively forestalls the impression of "déjà vu" so common to many descriptions of contemporary Paris. But it also underscores the imprisonment of the subject in an archetype more suited to the adventures of Paris or Candide than of a modern Strether. The city is relegated to a position of inferiority compared with the place it occupied in novels written between the world wars. Like the modern imitation of "Shakespeare and Co.," in the Rue de la Bûcherie, attempting to bring back to life Sylvia Beach's famous bookshop, it is in some respects a hollow sham.

The decline of Paris can also be traced through the changing relationships between the city and Americans in general. The importance of politics has already been mentioned in references to racism, the Algerian War, and Vietnam. Simeon Brown, Eddie Cook, and Peter Levi all stand for clearly defined ideologies. America's rise as the first of the world's powers and its determining influence on the course of the Second World War deprive Americans of the neutral status they once enjoyed in the capital. The benevolent indifference with which they were treated by local Parisians changes after the Marshall Plan and the creation of NATO. A political polarity develops between the two countries of which the only previous example was the litigation over French debts after World War I. In 1950 Elliot Paul notes in *Springtime in Paris* that the local population can be divided into two groups, "Atlantiques" and "Continentaux," whose opinions on America differ widely.[45] These terms, which the author introduces rather misleadingly as being established expressions, underline for the first time an emotional confrontation between the two nations, which will be expressed later in more overt acts of reciprocal hostility. When Peter Levi arrives in Paris, anti-American sentiment is an established fact, which he examines in detail through his friendship with the Bonfante family, while Irwin Shaw remarks on the numerous graffiti inviting Americans to go home. Peter also becomes aware of the systematic criticism of France that is a constant feature of NATO conversations.[46]

There is a shifting of American attitudes from one of moral and individual superiority, occasionally justified by wealth or success, to a political and national superiority based on America's position in the forefront of the world powers. This feeling is behind the numerous criticisms directed at the various aspects of French life. While it is true that diatribes against the police and the press were not uncommon in earlier writers, they have now changed in tone, with the previous outbursts being replaced by a more cold and detached assessment of the indisputable imperfections of the French political system, particularly during the Fourth Republic. *The Stone Face* and Shaw's "The Man Who Married a French Wife" both stress the commonplace appearance of lawlessness during the Algerian War, while the narrators of *Giovanni's Room* and *The Merry Month of May* make much of the censorship of the media by the French government. The newspaper reports of Giovanni's crime and his subsequent arrest and trial are blatantly untrue. They reflect the nationalism and xenophobia (Giovanni is Italian) of a ruling class that feels threatened by Guillaume's murder. Similarly, in May 1968, Jack Hartley condemns the government's abuse of national radio and television networks. Peter Levi, who is slow to grasp the use of lead-lined capes by the police during a student demonstration, is later astonished to see what he considers to be the elementary rights of the citizens so openly flouted. Observing the forces of law and order in action in 1968, Jack Hartley echoes Peter's sentiments. Also, one of the reasons restraining Lloyd Barber from taking part in the smuggling operation in "Tip on a Dead Jockey" is fear of falling into the hands of the French police and being obliged to undergo one of their redoubtable interrogations. In *Birds of America* there is even a rumor among the students that the Deuxième Bureau will not balk at rigging the odd traffic accident in order to get rid of undesirable elements.[47]

While the last example is presented as being mere hearsay, it is clear that others represent the literal truth for authors, characters, and readers. Liberal and conservative Americans alike join forces to emerge as defenders of the democratic principles and basic human rights that they see as being trampled underfoot. In "The Man Who Married a French Wife" Beauchurch's attitude reflects Irwin Shaw's contempt for the state of affairs existing in the capital, even under normal conditions, and for the cynicism of the Parisians, who claim that the most reasonable thing to do is to go along with it. Simeon Brown, the only character who is a sincere admirer of the French Revolution and the Commune, has an identical reaction. For him, "the stone face" is also the Parisian policeman. Even in minor matters, these accounts of the manipulation of public opinion, of the lack of protection for the individual, and of various miscarriages of justice combine to affect the American's general view of Paris, and they are part of a more widespread feeling of disenchantment, the diverse causes of which are difficult to pin down. Ursule Molinaro makes an attempt to pin it down in *Green Lights Are Blue,* a novel of farewell in which Phil Lapparent compares France to a former mistress, now aging and overweight, whom he meets again on a journey and from whom he turns away without regret. In *Paris! Paris!* Irwin Shaw explains some of the reasons that made him finally decide to leave Paris in 1975, after living there for twenty-five years: "The number of Americans was rapidly falling in France anyway, for several reasons, chief among which was the disastrous rate of the dollar against the franc, plus the feeling that France was sliding into a political and economic crisis that would make living there considerably less agreeable than it had been in the halcyon days of the fifties. . . . I had no wish to be left stranded, a last, desolate, trans-Atlantic monument to a joyous invasion that had come and gone."[48] In works that span a period of more than thirty years, it is clear that Irwin Shaw became increasingly irritated by the petty annoyances of Parisian life that the atmosphere of the city could not make up for. Once he had treated with irony the breathless admiration of his compatriots on their visits to France, claiming that his own appreciation was fairer and more nuanced. But, little by little, his equanimity vanished, worn down by constant confrontations with flat owners or tenants, neighbors, and various bureaucracies. The title *Paris! Paris!* suggests a regretful shake of the head. Shaw, with his long period of expatriation and the circumstances under which he left France, is in many ways a symbolic figure in American writing after the war and in the decline of the Parisian theme. McLuhan's global village, with its permanent and planetary links, has put an end to Paris as a privileged meeting place of two continents and two civilizations. The city's famous charm has been damaged by the changing quality of urban life, by its growing material difficulties and increasing physical differentiation. Expatriation, finally, with its twin tenets of curiosity and exchange has also suffered in the battle of France's cultural colonization by the United States in which Paris stands in the direct firing line. Since 1945, the image of Paris presented by American writers is that of a slowly disintegrating city whose gradual decline seems irreversible.

CONCLUSION

When one attempts to draw conclusions about the particular significance of Paris for American writers, and the kind of work the capital inspired, perhaps the first thing one notices is the heterogeneity of the literature. Although the vast majority of works belong to two genres only, the novel and the short story, the Parisian theme imposes no particular form or distinctive continuity. The books range from simple travelogues written in the first person to complex novels where the authorial voice is practically inaudible. Sometimes the main focus is the city's local population, sometimes one or another of the expatriate groups who live there, sometimes the tourists who visit it. Falling somewhere between the broad general divisions of the novel and the short story, hybrid species exist that cannot be classified with any precision. *The Innocents of Paris* is one of these, in which the linking devices of a single narrator and recurring characters give a semblance of novelistic unity to a series of separate short stories. This is also true of *A Moveable Feast,* which may, at Hemingway's suggestion, be read as a work of fiction. *The Last Time I Saw Paris* and *Springtime in Paris* are even more difficult to label. They could perhaps be described as "synoptic studies," a term used by Blanche H. Gelfant in *The American City Novel* to characterize works in which there is no hero and the city is perceived immediately as a personality itself.[1] On the other hand, the fact that both these books about Paris focus on a specific neighborhood and group of people would seem to be best accounted for in Gelfant's second category, the "ecological study." Her third classification, the "portrait study," in which the city is revealed through the development of a single character, is more appropriate to the novels of Henry James, Edith Wharton, and Dorothy Canfield. But from another point of view, these categories are unsatisfactory, since, for the Americans, Paris is not simply one more metropolis among many. It is the crowning symbol, the concrete manifestation, of a foreign civilization. The Parisian novel cannot therefore be considered as one aspect of the urban novel in general. How, then, can we best describe these works?

Americans see the French capital in two different ways. The first brings into focus the exotic nature of the Parisian experience. The authors highlight everything that is new and original, often simplifying and exaggerating as they do so. The second views the city through the experience of expatriation. A central character provides the essential link between America and Paris, epitomizing through his dilemmas and his dramatic development the opposition between the Old World and the New. He is the cornerstone of the book's architecture, and his role to some degree is that of the protagonist in the "portrait novel." These approaches may coexist and are not a direct consequence of degree of fictionalization relative to degree of autobiography. Exoticism is an important element in *The French They Are a Funny Race* and parts of *Tropic of Cancer* but also in the portrait of the nobility given by James in *The American*. Between the two extremes represented by the search for local color and the analysis of expatriation, it would be possible to rank the books in order of ascending interest according to the relative importance of the two approaches. Obviously, the second has more potential for literary development, but "tourist Paris," which belongs to the first, is an essential part of the books' general harmony, and a variant of this theme that is of some consequence is to be found in the creation of "mysterious Paris." At the head of the list would stand the figure of the expatriate writer, whose particular significance for this study explains the interest of the Parisian episodes in *A Voyage to Pagany, Of Time and the River,* and part of *A Moveable Feast.*

Yet, even when we examine the literature in the light of these two approaches, no clear development can be seen. They exist as early as *The Innocents Abroad* and *Madame de Mauves,* and they continue up to the present day. There are slight changes and modifications: the long and detailed descriptions of well-known places and monuments gradually give way to little touches illustrating the city's strange and unexpected surprises, and the appearance of the writer-character in the literature between the wars entails a more penetrating analysis of the phenomenon of expatriation. But the almost total disappearance of the tourist after 1945, which might have heralded a new kind of maturity, is in fact accompanied by a second-degree exoticism involving uniquely American milieux and by the theme's decline.

From an imaginary and ideological point of view, other differences can be observed between the Parisian novel and the American city novel. The French capital, even in works on mysterious Paris, is never portrayed as a huge metropolis, the Leviathan city. Unlike their provincial counterparts in French literature, the American visitors, with their experience of New York and Chicago, are not struck by the city's vast dimensions. The image of the inhuman, gigantic city given in novels by Balzac, Hugo, and Zola, is totally foreign to their work. Indeed, as the capital continues to grow in reality, it appears to shrink in the eyes of Americans. In 1956, the narrator of *Giovanni's Room* is astonished that "in so small and policed a city"[2] as Paris, the hero can still manage to escape capture several days after his crime. The Paris métro, representing a condensation and accentuation of the problems of urban life, has never been the subject of any extended description in American literature.

This lack of gigantism is in harmony with the city's role as a cultural icon. The American artist easily adapts to an urban environment particularly favorable to reflection and creation. He does not feel crushed and oppressed by the encircling city. Usually, no ostentatious display of wealth or vulgarity jars his sensibilities. He is no longer assaulted by feelings of loneliness, frustration, or alienation. Here too there is a marked difference with his experience of the great American metropolises, at least until 1940. Yet the artist's harmonious integration with his environment is in one way misleading, for it masks a process of dissociation different from the one experienced by the heroes of American city novels. Henry James described Gaston Probert in *The Reverberator* as being "placed between two stools,"[3] and thus unsure of where to sit. The young man's dilemma is in many ways exemplary. The manner in which the characters of Parisian novels develop, the intellectual and moral judgments they make, the comic potential of both native and foreign social types, all have meaning only in relation to cultural references and values that are essentially American. In short, we are forced to the banal conclusion that the image of Paris found in these books is typically American. It is the sum of the shared experience of more than a hundred years. No matter how varied and diverse the literature, the same elements and evaluations constantly recur, as if shaped by an autonomous group dynamic that functions almost independently of real circumstances, creating a common fiction.

An illustration of the way this works is provided by what American authors say about Chablis. If we are to believe the novels, this is one of the great French wines, the one that is most widely known and appreciated by the Parisians and the Americans. Henry James, Ernest Hemingway, Henry Miller, Elliot Paul, and Maurice Samuel, for example, all contribute to this impression. The astonishing publicity bestowed uniquely upon this good, but not great, local wine epitomizes the genesis of American Paris. How did it acquire such an undeserved reputation? Did James, writing about Chablis in *The Ambassadors,* simply give Strether his own tastes? Was it known as the prince of wines in America thanks to Californian imitations? Was its final, undeniable supremacy the result of American advertising, or of the sheeplike behavior of the expatriates, or of the snowball effect of novel after novel contributing to its huge popularity? It is impossible to know who first started this oenological conspiracy. Like the exclusive veneration of Chablis, American Paris is the result of a combination of abstract and concrete factors radically affecting the writers' perception. Their version of Paris is sometimes at odds with historical reality. This is partly because their vision is refracted through an ocean of words and habits, partly because their experience of the city is restricted and partial. But, on the other hand, these American novels, with their scenes from domestic life matched by equally detailed street scenes, their long, imagistic sequences linked to the wanderings of various characters, their amusing anecdotes and arresting details, afford an interesting and potentially enriching perspective on what French observers tell us—even if it would be wrong to regard all of them as faithful mirrors of reality. The blithe insouciance of some of the authors when it comes to the rigors of spelling and grammar or the need for exactitude in giving locations, for example, is, alas, plainly evident from the frequency with which *sic* must be injected when quoting from their works.

Such observations make comparisons between French and American representations of Paris difficult. The Americans are in a situation of political, economic, and cultural separateness. They only partly apprehend the social implications of Parisian life. Their financial problems are apt to be easily resolved, and the events that interest them most are those that permit comparisons or parallels with their own history. The racism that becomes acute at the time of the Algerian War is invoked chiefly as a means of throwing light on America's own racial problem. The debates about expatriation serve principally to criticize or glorify the United States. While this attitude is perfectly understandable, it does reveal a certain powerlessness, of which the writers may or may not have been aware, to grasp a deeper reality kept at bay by a barricade of words. For a city is also characterized by the language of its inhabitants, and the way in which French is incorporated into these works underscores a crucial deficiency on the part of most writers: their inability to understand fully what is being said around them and their ignorance, in fact, of a mode of existence conveyed through the medium of language. It would be easy to draw up a long list of mistranslations, incorrect expressions, or misquotations bearing witness to this deficiency. One wonders, for instance, how the author of *The Left Bank,* in 1931, managed to pass off as authentic French the phrases he puts into the mouth of Claude, the bellhop, which were pronounced at least 242 times before a paying audience before being immortalized in print.[4] And there is not the slightest sign of progress. All the observations about the way in which French is used or abused in the literature, in Chapter 2, hold good for the later periods.[5] The most successful approach to the problem is found in writers like Fitzgerald, Dos Passos, Wolfe, and Miller, who all convey some sense of the mystery, form, and color of French words through literary or linguistic correspondences. But few characters express any impatience or frustration with the barrier that these unknown vocables raise between them and the city. Most tend to oversimplify the problems of communication, and this tendency is shared by the professionals of language themselves, the authors. Such an attitude partly affects their perception of the city of which they give a translated, transatlanticized version.

This representation of Paris, with its peculiar distortions, does, however, tell us things about America and the Americans. For the period up to 1914, the works highlight the difficulties that Americans experienced in coping with the Old World. The Parisian microcosm, the bright Babylon, dedicated to an art of living unconcerned with the dictates of a strict morality, brings out the puritanical reactions of the visitors. In addition, the importance of the French nobility in these works attests to wealthy Americans' desire for social refinement and to their repressed elitism. Then, again, the capital's rich and colorful history, its impressive monuments, offer a chronological perspective that is unfamiliar to these New World visitors. But above all Paris offers them a new version of woman and love. After 1917, a fresh wave of expatriates from widely differing social backgrounds gives a new image of America. The Parisian experience now becomes more acute, more fraught with personal implications. Arguments about America are echoed in crises of identity. The opposition between the two civilizations at whose junction the expatriates stand is accompanied by profound soul-searching and greater dissociation. Paris, with its elemental and primordial nature, is a magic place in which a disorienting play of mirrors provokes anamorphoses. Paris is the city of *la fête,* of drunkenness and debauchery, steeped in an atmosphere of transgression, sexual liberation, and Freudian release.

The poetry of Paris is best articulated by the writers of the Lost Generation. The metaphorical universe of *The Waste Land,* with its myths of fertility and sterility, stands at the beginning of a legendary epoch of American Paris, investing the city with a superior poetic dimension. If, as Joseph H. McMahon asserts, *The Ambassadors* is the American novel in which Paris is most completely and harmoniously integrated,[6] and if the writings of Henry Miller and Anaïs Nin show us, better than any others, the city's role as shaper of artistic talent, nevertheless it is in the 1920s that the Parisian theme in American literature is most richly orchestrated. The decline begins after 1940. Paris is no longer a haven, or a refuge, and its erotic appeal has suffered as a consequence of the disappearing of sexual taboos across the Atlantic. The American artist has adapted to life in his own country or has chosen other places of expatriation. The relentless shrinking of distances and the familiarizing effect of the media have lessened the salutary impact produced by the clash of two cultures, and even the rite of passage inherent in the six-day ocean crossing has been wiped out by the advent of the airplane. Paris has become a neutral territory where writers can no longer find very fertile soil. It has become a mere literary cliché. Will the capital ever inspire other major works of American literature? All signs point to the end of its role as a creative catalyst for successive generations of writers. It does not seem to offer a challenge any more, eliciting new and fresh responses from authors and shaping the destinies of their heroes.

NOTES

Introduction

1. There are several errors in the section on American Paris. The author describes Robert W. Chambers's novel *In the Quarter* as a collection of short stories. He mistakes the location of the Rue des Deux Amis in Frank Berkeley Smith's *The Street of the Two Friends,* and talking about *The Princess Aline* by Richard Harding Davis, he gets the name of the hero slightly wrong.

2. Citron, *La Poésie de Paris,* 1:7.

Chapter 1

1. Pollin, *Discoveries in Poe.*

2. Poe, *Tales of Mystery,* p. 415. "The rue des Drômes is a short and narrow but populous thoroughfare, not far from the banks of the river and at a distance of some two miles, in the most direct course possible, from the *pension* of Madame Rogêt."

3. The George Washington Bridge dates only from 1931. The absence of bridges over the Seine is mentioned several times in sentences such as: "It is no cause for wonder, surely, that a gang of blackguards should make *haste* to get home when a wide river is to be crossed in small boats . . ." (p. 449).

4. Twain, *Innocents Abroad,* p. 50.

5. Moffett, *Through the Wall,* pp. 201–2.

6. Smith, *The Street of the Two Friends,* pp. 317–18.

7. Vance, *Lone Wolf,* p. 86.

8. Ibid., p. 166.

9. Poe, *Tales of Mystery,* p. 442.

10. Belasco, *Stranglers of Paris,* pp. 85–88.

11. Vance, *Lone Wolf,* p. 166. Troyon's was an imaginary hostelry in the Latin Quarter, resembling Foyot's.

12. Gunter, *That Frenchman,* p. 90.

13. Moffett, "The Mysterious Card Unveiled," p. 10. This tale of fantasy appeared in two parts in *The Black Cat.* The first part was called "The Mysterious Card" and the second "The Mysterious Card Unveiled." The second part provided the solution to the mystery.

14. Vance, *Lone Wolf,* p. 159.

15. Poe, *Tales of Mystery,* p. 393. The location of the street is correct despite its fictitious name. When Poe wrote this, the Saint-Roch district was indeed a

slum area, but it was later cleared by Haussmann for the construction of the Avenue de l'Opéra.

16. Poe, *Tales of Mystery*, p. 382.

17. Moffett, *Through the Wall*, p. 20.

18. Vance, *Lone Wolf*, p. 2.

19. One house in *That Frenchman*, p. 90, has two entries, like most of the Lone Wolf's hideouts: Troyon's, the café on p. 168, and the mansion on p. 181. Michael Lanyard escapes once through an underground passage (p. 159).

20. Moffett, *Through the Wall*, p. 291.

21. Ibid., p. 283.

22. Ibid., pp. 389–90.

23. Mitchell, *A Madeira Party*, pp. 163–65, and *Adventures of François*, pp. 287–307.

24. Vance, *Lone Wolf*, p. 233.

25. King, *Inner Shrine*, p. 6. Basil King was born in Canada and became a minister in the Episcopal church, later giving up his post at Christ Church, Cambridge, Mass., due to ill health. He devoted the rest of his life to writing, producing twenty or so sentimental, didactic, and moralizing novels. As he got older, he became particularly interested in spiritualism and wrote eight books on the subject. He enjoyed considerable success as a writer. His biography can be found in *Who's Who in America*, 1928–29.

26. Poe, *Tales of Mystery*, p. 458.

27. Gunter, *That Frenchman*, p. 75.

28. Gunter, *Baron Montez*, p. 266.

29. Poe, *Tales of Mystery*, p. 470.

30. Gunter, *Baron Montez*, p. 250.

31. In *Lone Wolf*, for example, Louis Vance alludes to Balzac and Dumas. Michael Lanyard, on the point of being blindfolded in order to be taken to a secret rendezvous, exclaims, "Blindfold? I should say not! This is not—need I remind you again?—the Paris of Balzac and that wonderful Dumas of yours" (p. 76).

32. Sherlock Holmes made his first appearance in literature in 1880, Maurice in 1889, Arsène Lupin and Rouletabille in 1907, and the Lone Wolf in 1914.

33. Lucy, Michael's companion during his adventures, says to him, "You're very like the other lone wolf, the fictitious one—Lupin—you know—a bit of a blagueur" (p. 289).

34. Poe, *Tales of Mystery*, p. 381.

35. In *A Princess of Paris*, an adventure story set during the period of the French Regency, Gunter gives his opinion in the following aside: "For the *gendarmes* of France of that day had very much the same idea of justice as the police of the present time. They must have a guilty man, and when they could not find the guilty, generally took the innocent, if he were worth the plucking" (p. 231).

36. Gunter, *That Frenchman*, p. 121.

37. Moffett, *Through the Wall*, p. 167.

38. Ibid., pp. 299–340.

39. Caillois, "Paris, Mythe Moderne," p. 685.

40. Sue, *Les Mystères de Paris*, p. 247.

41. Citron, *La Poésie de Paris*, 2:133–34, 209.

42. Moffett, *Through the Wall,* p. 169.

43. Guides Noirs, *Guide de Paris Mystérieux,* pp. 370–75.

44. This is what C. E. Andrews claims. He often mentions Apaches in *The Innocents of Paris,* pp. 157–93, and even writes, "And now fiction is so full of the *apache* that some day he will be the subject of a doctor's thesis" (p. 157).

45. Stone, *The Passionate Journey,* pp. 92–93.

46. Twain, *Innocents Abroad,* p. 57.

47. Holmes, "La Grisette," p. 326.

48. The author explains in the preface that Peter Whiffle, who died on 15 December 1919, specifically requested in his will that Van Vechten write a book about him. Peter does not appear until p. 34, and in the first four chapters Van Vechten speaks principally about his own experiences in Paris, where he arrived on 10 May 1907, and about his relationships with Arthur Machen and Cunninghame Grahame.

49. Mitchell, *A Madeira Party,* pp. 64–65.

50. Chambers, *The King in Yellow,* p. 229.

51. Chambers, *The Haunts of Men,* p. 293.

52. Gethryn's studio is described at length in *In the Quarter,* pp. 13–15. The Pension Marotte is in "The Street of Our Lady of the Fields," pp. 230–32, with the Crémerie Murphy, pp. 278–79, and the Restaurant Mignon and Restaurant Boulant, p. 255. The trip to La Roche is described in the same short story, pp. 267–72. The ball held at the Opéra takes up twenty-two pages (pp. 144–66) of *In the Quarter.* The Café Vachette is in "Another Good Man," p. 287, and in "Rue Barrée," p. 288. The Café du Cercle appears also in "Rue Barrée," p. 288.

53. Chambers does this, for example, in "The Street of the First Shell," p. 187, and *In the Quarter,* p. 46.

54. Carryl, *Zut,* p. 28.

55. Smith, *The Street of the Two Friends,* p. 1.

56. Ibid., p. 340.

57. The most complete account of La Ruche is given in Chapiro, *La Ruche.*

58. Smith, *The Street of the Two Friends,* p. 128.

59. Murger, *Vie de Bohème,* p. cix.

60. His sermons are often delivered through the character of Braith. The author follows the title of "Another Good Man" with a quote from Lamartine: "Une conscience sans Dieu est un tribunal sans juge."

61. Chambers, *The Red Republic,* p. 27.

62. Chambers also wrote an operetta, *Iole,* in which the chief protagonist resembles the chansonnier Aristide Bruant.

63. Chambers, *In the Quarter,* pp. 55–56.

64. The names "Julian" and "Bouguereau" are frequently misspelled as "Julien" and "Bougereau," not only by Chambers but also by other American writers, and even in serious reference works.

65. Stone, *The Passionate Journey,* pp. 138–39.

66. Chambers, *In the Quarter,* pp. 23–24.

67. Details can be found in "Another Good Man," p. 270, "Rue Barrée," p. 301, and *In the Quarter,* p. 96.

68. Chambers, *In the Quarter,* pp. 102–3. This same taste for comic exaggeration can be found in the character of Kate Shipley in Bronson Howard's play *One of Our Girls.*

69. Chambers, *The Haunts of Men,* p. 289, and Stone, *The Passionate Journey,* p. 104.

70. Chambers, *In the Quarter,* pp. 12–13.

71. Ibid., pp. 108–14.

72. Ibid., p. 17.

73. Wilson, *Ruggles of Red Gap,* p. 84.

74. James, *The Ambassadors,* p. 58.

75. James, *The Madonna of the Future,* pp. 254–81. The cousin invents a story about a marriage to a Provençal countess and pressing debts to be paid off.

76. Tarkington, *The Guest of Quesnay,* p. 13.

77. Ibid., p. 16.

78. James, *The Ambassadors,* pp. 120–22. Gloriani lives in an *hôtel particulier* in the faubourg. Not only aristocrats but also students like Chad and Little Bilham are invited to his receptions.

79. James, *The American,* p. 207.

80. Wharton, *The Reef,* pp. 38–39.

81. James, *The Ambassadors,* p. 59.

82. Ibid., p. 80.

83. James, *Madame de Mauves,* p. 62.

84. Ibid., p. 67.

85. Ibid., pp. 62–67. The couple of the painter and Claudine prefigures that of Chad and Mme de Vionnet. The innkeeper, for example, tells Longmore what she thinks of Claudine: "It is my belief that she's better than he. I've even gone so far as to believe she's a lady,—a true lady—and that she has given up a great many things for him" (p. 67).

86. James, *The Ambassadors,* p. 337. The narrator describes the change in atmosphere as "a marked drop into innocent, friendly Bohemia."

87. Chambers, *The Red Republic,* p. 28.

88. Murger, *Vie de Bohème,* pp. 293–94.

89. Holmes, *Our Hundred Days,* p. 266.

90. Jules Janin uses the same technique in *The American in Paris.* The book can be found in English at the Bibliothèque Nationale. It is presented as the retranslation of a work originally written in English and then translated into French, after which the original English version was lost. Jules Janin claims to be the second translator, from French back into English.

91. Twain, *Innocents Abroad,* p. 49.

92. Ibid., p. 50.

93. Ibid., p. 59.

94. Ibid., p. 51.

95. Ibid., p. 48.

96. James, *The American,* p. 58.

97. James, "A Bundle of Letters," in *The Complete Tales,* 4:430–31.

98. James, *The Ambassadors,* p. 127.

99. *Madame de Treymes* by Edith Wharton relates the story of Mme de Malrive, née Fanny Frisbee, an American separated from her French husband. John Durham wants her to get a divorce so that he can marry her. But her husband's family, represented by Fanny's sister-in-law, Mme de Treymes, makes

sure this is impossible, while at the same time taking advantage of John Durham's hopes.

100. The Nouveau Luxe appears principally in *The Custom of the Country,* pp. 199 and 243. It also appears in "Les Metteurs en Scène," p. 1, and *A Son at the Front,* pp. 116 and 229. In *The Glimpses of the Moon* hotels of the same name exist in Rome and London, emphasizing the international character of this imaginary chain.

101. James, *The Ambassadors,* pp. 183–86.

102. Tarkington, *The Beautiful Lady,* pp. 26–29.

103. The Café Anglais is often mentioned, in particular in *The American,* p. 6, and in *The Siege of London,* p. 258. The Café Riche is in *The Ambassadors,* p. 49. The Café de Madrid is in *The Beautiful Lady,* p. 41. In *That Frenchman,* p. 119, Vance writes of the Café Le Peletier that it is "so much patronized by transatlantic visitors that the waiters nickname it the café Américain." The Grand Café is mentioned in *The Siege of London,* p. 258.

104. Laurent appears in Richard Harding Davis's *Princess Aline,* p. 58, and Durand appears in *The Reverberator,* p. 47. Paillard appears in *The Custom of the Country,* p. 135. The Bignon is mentioned in *The Ambassadors,* p. 257, and *The Siege of London,* p. 258. The Brébant is in *The Ambassadors,* p. 258, and *Madame de Mauves,* p. 8. The Pavillon d'Armenonville is in *The Beautiful Lady,* p. 40. The Pavillon Henri IV is in *The Reverberator,* p. 55.

105. James, *The Ambassadors,* pp. 49, 230, and 257.

106. Davis, *The Princess Aline,* p. 59.

107. James, *The American,* pp. 201–13.

108. James, *The Ambassadors,* pp. 81–85.

109. *The Siege of London,* in *The Great Short Novels,* p. 236.

110. James, "A Bundle of Letters," p. 432.

111. Gunter, *Baron Montez,* p. 252, and Tarkington, *The Guest of Quesnay,* p. 5.

112. James, *The American,* p. 26.

113. Tarkington, *The Beautiful Lady,* p. 66.

114. James, *The Ambassadors,* p. 57.

115. James, "A Bundle of Letters," p. 428.

116. Wharton, *Madame de Treymes,* p. 1.

117. James, "A Bundle of Letters," p. 428.

118. Canfield, *The Bent Twig,* pp. 406 and 409.

119. Tarkington, *The Beautiful Lady,* pp. 26–27.

120. James, *The Ambassadors,* p. 73.

121. Ibid., p. 260.

122. Wilson, *Ruggles of Red Gap,* pp. 53–65.

123. James uses the term ironically in *The Ambassadors:* "in the well, the great temple, as one hears of it, of pleasure" (p. 259).

124. Tarkington, *The Guest of Quesnay,* pp. 30–31.

125. Davis, *The Princess Aline,* p. 55.

126. Tarkington, *The Guest of Quesnay,* p. 5.

Chapter 2

1. James, *The American*, p. 75.
2. Wharton, *Madame de Treymes*, p. 121.
3. Mrs. Marshall-Smith in *The Bent Twig* owes her fortune to her late husband, as does Mrs. Temperly, in "Mrs. Temperly." Mrs. Headway in *The Siege of London* became rich through a series of divorces.
4. James, *The Reverberator*, pp. 38–39.
5. For example, at one point she tells Newman, "Thank God I am not a Frenchwoman" (p. 157).
6. James, *The American*, p. 314.
7. Ibid., p. 128.
8. Wharton, *The Custom of the Country*, p. 201.
9. Ibid., p. 368. Wharton is on the whole more critical of the English than is James. Her attitude is part and parcel of her Francophile sentiments, which grew more pronounced with the advent of the First World War.
10. James, *The American*, p. 75.
11. Smith, *The Street of the Two Friends*, p. 22.
12. Wilson, *Ruggles of Red Gap*, p. 53.
13. Tarkington, *The Guest of Quesnay*, p. 4.
14. James, *The American*, p. 43.
15. Ibid., p. 104. In addition, Young Mme de Bellegarde says, "You owe me a famous taper" (p. 143), and M. Nioche says, "She makes me walk as she will" (p. 180).
16. Ibid., p. 37. Similarly, the narrator writes, "Newman was, according to the French phrase, only abounding in [Mrs. Tristram's] own sense" (p. 114). On p. 148, Valentin tells Newman, "Mademoiselle Noémie has thrown her cap over the mill, as we say." On p. 34, Mrs. Tristram asks Newman, "Should you like me, as they say here, to marry you?" and later adds: "As the French proverb says, the most beautiful girl in the world can give but what she has."
17. Smith, *The Street of the Two Friends*, p. 26.
18. Carryl, *Zut*, pp. 13, 16, and 23. Other stories in the same collection afford similar examples. In "Caffiard," p. 37, "Art thou jealous, species of thinness of a hundred nails?" and p. 45, an oath like "name of a pipe." In "In the Absence of Monsieur," p. 266, there are phrases such as "type of cow," and, in reference to a frame with nails in it, "pig of a frame" and "sacred nails."
19. Poli, *Le Roman Américain*, p. 190.
20. James, *The American*, p. 30.
21. Ibid., p. 27.
22. The Farlows are Sophy Viner's friends in Wharton's novel *The Reef*. Mrs. Lister is a character in *The Transgression of Andrew Vane*; she is nicknamed "the jail breaker" because she never finishes a sentence (p. 153). In *The Custom of the Country* Mrs. Shallum, "though in command of but a few verbs, all of which, on her lips, became irregular, managed to express a polyglot personality as vivid as her husband was effaced" (p. 123).
23. James, *The Ambassadors*, p. 101. From what Chad tells Strether, the latter assumes that "the moral of it seemed to be that he went about little in the 'colony.'"

24. James, *The Reverberator*, p. 42.
25. Carryl, *The Transgression of Andrew Vane*, pp. 46–47.
26. Wharton, *Madame de Treymes*, pp. 44–45.
27. James, *The American*, p. 30.
28. Ibid., p. 196.
29. Wharton, *Madame de Treymes*, p. 46.
30. Canfield, *The Bent Twig*, p. 380.
31. Carryl, *Zut*, p. 45.
32. Carryl, *The Transgression of Andrew Vane*, p. 46.
33. Davis, *About Paris*, pp. 189–90.
34. There is a duchess at the Bellegardes' in *The American*, p. 193, and also at Gloriani's reception in *The Ambassadors*, p. 133, and the Malrives' reception in *Madame de Treymes*, p. 56. In "Mrs. Temperly" a duchess presides over a debutantes' ball that Effie attends.
35. James, *The American*, p. 35.
36. Ibid., p. 72.
37. Wharton, *Madame de Treymes*, p. 18.
38. Ibid., p. 59.
39. James, *The American*, p. 217.
40. King, *Inner Shrine*, p. 347.
41. Ibid., p. 6.
42. Howells, *A Hazard of New Fortunes*, p. 551.
43. King, *Inner Shrine*, pp. 342–43.
44. Fiedler, *Love and Death*, p. 53.
45. James, *Madame de Mauves*, p. 49.
46. James, *The Ambassadors*, p. 141.
47. Wharton, *Madame de Treymes*, p. 144.
48. Wharton, *The Custom of the Country*, p. 282.
49. Ibid., p. 249.
50. James, *The American*, p. 94.
51. Ibid., p. 132.
52. Rahv, *The Great Short Novels of Henry James*, p. 225.
53. James, *The Siege of London*, p. 241.
54. James, *The American*, p. 30.

Chapter 3

1. James, *Madame de Mauves*, p. 49.
2. Carryl, *The Transgression of Andrew Vane*, pp. 137–38.
3. Wharton, *Madame de Treymes*, p. 23.
4. Chambers, *In the Quarter*, pp. 148–49.
5. Brownell, *French Traits*, p. 64.
6. Michael Millgate, ed., Introduction to *The Custom of the Country*, p. 15.
7. James, *The American*, p. 187.
8. Wharton, "The Last Asset," in *The Best Short Stories*, p. 149.
9. James, "Mrs. Temperly," in *The Complete Tales*, 6:231.
10. Ibid., p. 232.
11. King, *Inner Shrine*, pp. 24–25.

12. Ibid., p. 3.
13. Wharton, *The Custom of the Country*, p. 341.
14. Howells, *A Hazard of New Fortunes*, p. 551.
15. James, *The Siege of London*, p. 268.
16. James, "The Point of View," in *The Complete Tales*, 4:500.
17. Ibid., p. 510.
18. Canfield, *The Bent Twig*, p. 401.
19. Wharton, *Madame de Treymes*, p. 11.
20. Garnier, *Henry James et la France*, p. 75.
21. Wegelin, *The Image of Europe in Henry James*, p. 84.
22. Wharton, *Madame de Treymes*, pp. 35–36.
23. James, *The Ambassadors*, pp. 93–94.
24. Wharton, *Madame de Treymes*, pp. 36–37.
25. James, *The Ambassadors*, p. 259.
26. James, *The Reverberator*, p. 18.
27. Wharton, *The Custom of the Country*, p. 205.
28. James, *The Ambassadors*, p. 191.
29. Ibid., p. 342.
30. Canfield, *The Bent Twig*, p. 423. The statue is now in the Rodin Museum, at 77 Rue de Varenne.
31. Ibid., p. 401.
32. James, *The Ambassadors*, p. 179.
33. Carryl, *The Transgression of Andrew Vane*, p. 199.
34. Brownell, *French Traits*, p. 204.
35. Wharton, *Madame de Treymes*, pp. 39–40.
36. Fiedler, *Love and Death*, p. 287.
37. James, *The Ambassadors*, p. 163.
38. Knoepflmacher, "O Rare for Strether!," p. 108.
39. Fiedler, *Love and Death*, p. 287.
40. For example, "tropical swamp" is in *The Transgression of Andrew Vane*, p. 138; "jungle" is in *The Ambassadors*, p. 135, as is "Babylon," p. 57; and "Eastern Bazaar" is in *Madame de Treymes*, p. 62.
41. James, *The Ambassadors*, pp. 100 and 105.
42. Carryl, *The Transgression of Andrew Vane*, p. 137.
43. Carryl, *Zut*, p. 236.

Chapter 4

1. Martin S. Day, *History of American Literature* (Garden City: Doubleday, 1970), 1:vi.
2. Mitchell, *Adventures of François*, p. 21.
3. Day, *History of American Literature*, 1:232.
4. Probably Commandant Léonce Rousset, author of *Les Combattants de 1870–1871* (Paris: Librairie Illustrée, 1891).
5. Although Mitchell calls him Jean-Pierre Amar (p. 112), his real name was Jean-Baptiste André Amar, and he was known for his hostile attitude toward the Girondists. Grégoire is Abbé Grégoire, a priest who became a senator during the

Empire. Flourens is Gustave Flourens, killed by a sabre thrust from a gendarme in 1871.

6. Chambers, *The Red Republic,* p. 8.

7. Mitchell, *Adventures of François,* p. 100.

8. Chambers, *Ashes of Empire,* p. 280.

9. Ibid., p. 280.

10. Chambers, *The Red Republic,* pp. 428–29.

11. Chambers, *Ashes of Empire,* p. 95.

12. Chambers, *The Red Republic,* pp. 94–95.

13. James, *The Ambassadors,* p. 344.

14. Chambers, *The Red Republic,* p. 117.

15. Citron, *La Poésie de Paris,* 2:8–10.

16. Faulkner, *A Fable,* p. 248.

17. Wharton, *The Marne,* p. 81.

18. Ibid., p. 87.

19. Ibid., pp. 88–89.

20. Ibid., p. 91.

21. Ibid., p. 22.

22. Stein, *Autobiography of Alice B. Toklas,* p. 185.

23. Wharton, *A Son at the Front,* p. 70.

24. Stein, *Autobiography of Alice B. Toklas,* p. 176.

25. Wharton, *The Marne,* pp. 20–21.

26. Wharton, *A Son at the Front,* pp. 22–23.

27. Ibid., p. 67.

28. Stein, *Autobiography of Alice B. Toklas,* p. 89.

29. Canfield, *The Day of Glory,* pp. 147–48.

30. Dos Passos, *1919,* p. 293.

31. Ibid., p. 233.

32. Wharton, *The Marne,* p. 23.

33. Canfield, *The Deepening Stream,* p. 287.

34. Dos Passos, *1919,* p. 247.

35. Canfield, *The Deepening Stream,* p. 330.

36. Stein, *Autobiography of Alice B. Toklas,* pp. 235–36.

37. Canfield, *Home Fires in France,* p. 159.

38. Ibid., p. 149.

39. Wharton, *A Son at the Front,* p. 133.

40. Dos Passos, *1919,* p. 357.

41. Ibid., p. 383.

42. Dos Passos, *Three Soldiers,* p. 342.

43. Ibid., pp. 299–300.

44. The Café de la Paix appears in *1919,* pp. 226 and 302, and *Chosen Country,* pp. 200 and 259; the Ritz in *1919,* p. 357; Chez Maxim's in *One Man's Initiation,* p. 53, *The Deepening Stream,* p. 299, and *1919,* pp. 226 and 415; and the Opéra in *1919,* p. 300.

45. The Tour d'Argent appears in *1919,* p. 218; Larue in *1919,* p. 357; Voisin in *Chosen Country,* p. 205 and *1919,* p. 357; Noel Peters in *1919,* p. 329. In *1919* the Poccardi is mentioned on p. 300, the Weber on pp. 357 and 387, and the

Médicis on p. 297. In *A Son at the Front* the Madrid is mentioned on p. 27. The Rat Qui Danse is the little restaurant in Montmartre where John Andrews meets Jeanne in *Three Soldiers,* pp. 313–18. The Taverne Nicolas Flamel is mentioned in *1919,* p. 218 (Dos Passos spells it "Nicholas"), as is Rumpelmeyer, p. 383.

46. John Andrews and Jeanne see *Louise* at the Opéra Comique in *Three Soldiers,* p. 333. Later, John meets Geneviève Rod there, at a performance of *Pelléas et Mélisande,* p. 363. In *1919* Freddy Seargeant and Eveline Hutchins also go to the Opéra Comique to see this same opera, p. 319. The Odéon and the Olympia are in *Three Soldiers,* pp. 304 and 306. The Théâtre Caumartin is in *1919,* p. 385.

47. Dos Passos, *One Man's Initiation,* p. 94, and *Three Soldiers,* p. 307.

48. Dos Passos, *1919,* pp. 296–97.

49. Dos Passos, *Three Soldiers,* p. 251.

50. Dos Passos, *1919,* p. 97.

51. Dos Passos, *One Man's Initiation,* p. 88.

52. Dos Passos, *Chosen Country,* p. 208.

53. Dos Passos, *1919,* p. 99.

54. Ibid.

55. Ibid., p. 361.

56. Dos Passos, *Chosen Country,* p. 201. The picture cannot be the famous painting by Watteau, which is not of Venice and in which there are no quays.

57. Dos Passos, *1919,* pp. 361–62.

Chapter 5

1. Wharton, *A Son at the Front,* p. 203.

2. Ibid., p. 313.

3. Stein, *Autobiography of Alice B. Toklas,* p. 234.

4. Canfield, *Home Fires in France,* p. 166.

5. Wharton, *A Son at the Front,* p. 44.

6. Ibid., p. 17.

7. Ibid., p. 163.

8. Wharton, *The Marne,* p. 64.

9. Wharton, *A Son at the Front,* p. 123.

10. Ibid., pp. 173–74.

11. Wharton, *The Marne,* pp. 26–27.

12. Dos Passos, *1919,* p. 136.

13. Dos Passos, *Chosen Country,* p. 211.

14. Dos Passos, *One Man's Initiation,* p. 53.

15. Dos Passos, *1919,* p. 215.

16. Canfield, *The Deepening Stream,* p. 299.

17. Wharton, *A Son at the Front,* p. 5.

18. Dos Passos, *1919,* p. 219.

19. Wharton, *A Son at the Front,* p. 32.

20. Canfield, *Home Fires in France,* p. 243.

21. Canfield, *The Deepening Stream,* p. 333.

22. Stein, *Autobiography of Alice B. Toklas,* p. 207.

23. Wharton, *A Son at the Front,* p. 278.

24. Ibid., p. 279.
25. Ibid., p. 173.
26. Ibid., p. 198.
27. Ibid., p. 187.
28. Ibid., p. 285.
29. Canfield, *The Deepening Stream*, p. 291.
30. Ibid., pp. 292–93.
31. Dos Passos, *1919*, p. 217.
32. Wharton, *A Son at the Front*, p. 285.
33. Dos Passos, *1919*, p. 218.
34. Ibid., p. 359.
35. Canfield, *The Deepening Stream*, p. 330.
36. Ibid., p. 335.
37. Coolidge, *Edith Wharton*, p. 164.
38. Canfield, *Home Fires in France*, p. 161.
39. Wharton, *The Marne*, p. 12.
40. Ibid., p. 114.
41. Wharton, *A Son at the Front*, p. 314.
42. Canfield, *The Deepening Stream*, p. 327.
43. Lyde, *Edith Wharton*, pp. 166–68.
44. Ibid., p. 168.
45. Dos Passos, *1919*, p. 12.
46. Cowley, *Exile's Return*, p. 43.
47. Dos Passos, *1919*, p. 359.
48. Ibid., p. 466.
49. Ibid., p. 328.
50. Cowley, *Exile's Return*, p. 38.
51. Dos Passos, *Three Soldiers*, p. 309.
52. Ibid., p. 358.
53. Dos Passos, *Chosen Country*, p. 208.
54. Dos Passos, *1919*, p. 461.
55. Dos Passos, *Three Soldiers*, p. 322.
56. Ibid., p. 320.

Chapter 6

1. McMahon, "City for Expatriates," p. 144.
2. In *We Were Interrupted*, for example, Rascoe speaks of Guy (Georges) de la Fouchardière and Jean Juarès (Jaurès) on p. 182, of Jules Bréton (André Breton) on p. 183, and of the Ballet Suédois (Ballet Russe) of Diaghilev on p. 189.
3. Hemingway, *A Moveable Feast*, unnumbered preface.
4. Kohner, *Kiki*, p. 16.
5. Paul, *The Amazon*, p. 333.
6. Samuel, *The Outsider*, pp. 5 and 7.
7. Cather, *One of Ours*, p. 173.
8. Earnest, *Expatriates and Patriots*, p. 259.
9. Lewis, *Dodsworth*, p. 113.
10. Ibid., pp. 114–15.

11. Rice, *The Left Bank*, p. 11.

12. Ibid., p. 57.

13. cummings, "Conflicting Aspects of Paris," pp. 154–58.

14. Hemingway, *The Sun Also Rises*, p. 76.

15. Lewis, *Dodsworth*, p. 113.

16. Van Wyck, *On the Terrasse*, p. 11.

17. Stewart, *Mr. and Mrs. Haddock in Paris*, p. 194.

18. Garnier, *Henry James et la France*, p. 200, n. 3.

19. Several texts underline this experience: in *Dodsworth*, "An incessant, nerve-cracking, irritating, exhilarating blat-blat-blat of nervous little motor horns" (p. 110); in *Mr. and Mrs. Haddock in Paris*, "Off they drove in the custody of that sinister-looking driver with a dirty linen duster and a mustache. . . . There seemed to be millions of other taxicabs all going just as fast and honking just as loudly" (pp. 43–44); and in *A Voyage to Pagany*, "In the crowd at the Gare St. Lazare the porter was drunk and started to put up a scene. . . . The dilapidated taxi started out madly into the rain in the disordered whirl about the station front" (p. 26). The same impression of Paris's bustling traffic can be found in *They Had to See Paris*, p. 54.

20. Williams, *A Voyage to Pagany*, p. 24.

21. Stewart, *Mr. and Mrs. Haddock in Paris*, p. 237.

22. Wolfe, *The Web and the Rock*, p. 638.

23. Stewart, *Mr. and Mrs. Haddock in Paris*, p. 193.

24. Ibid., p. 26.

25. Croy, *They Had to See Paris*, p. 76.

26. cummings, *Him*, p. 80.

27. Fitzgerald, *Tender Is the Night*, pp. 54–55.

28. Ibid., p. 97.

29. The Dôme appears in *A Voyage to Pagany*, pp. 58–60; *Dodsworth*, p. 295; *The Sun Also Rises*, p. 46; "Mr. and Mrs. Elliot," in *The Snows of Kilimanjaro*, p. 98; and *Of Time and the River*, p. 688.

30. Hemingway, *A Moveable Feast*, p. 101.

31. Wolfe, *Of Time and the River*, p. 688, and Hemingway, *The Snows of Kilimanjaro*, p. 98.

32. Hemingway, *The Sun Also Rises*, p. 42.

33. See *A Moveable Feast*, pp. 56, 57, 72–73, 81, 82, 91–96, 99, 101, 147, 152; *The Sun Also Rises*, pp. 6, 74–75, 78, 81, 83; *A Voyage to Pagany*, pp. 43, 49, 60–62, 64; *Kiki of Montparnasse*, p. 100; *Of Time and the River*, p. 688.

34. Ibid., p. 44.

35. Ibid., p. 3.

36. Hemingway, *The Snows of Kilimanjaro*, p. 25.

37. Williams, *A Voyage to Pagany*, pp. 33–36 and 58–60.

38. Hemingway, *The Snows of Kilimanjaro*, p. 21.

39. Lewis, *Dodsworth*, p. 299.

40. Ibid.

41. Anderson, *Dark Laughter*, p. 156.

42. Van Wyck, *On the Terrasse*, p. 19.

43. Hemingway, *A Moveable Feast*, pp. 93–94.

44. Lewis, *Dodsworth*, pp. 300–301.

45. Hemingway, *A Moveable Feast*, p. 37.
46. Ibid., p. 72.
47. In *Tender Is the Night* Dick and Rosemary go to a reception in the Rue Monsieur, pp. 71–76. Dodsworth is invited to Jerry Watts's reception, pp. 125–28. In *The Gods Arrive* Lorry Spear gives a party for the millionaire Mrs. Glaisher, p. 124. In *Dark Laughter* Rose Frank gives a reception in her apartment on the Quai Voltaire, pp. 171–86.
48. Fitzgerald, *Tender Is the Night*, p. 76
49. Wolfe, *Of Time and the River*, p. 781.
50. Lewis, *Dodsworth*, p. 266.
51. Hemingway, *The Sun Also Rises*, p. 226.
52. Croy, *They Had to See Paris*, p. 71.
53. Stewart, *Mr. and Mrs. Haddock in Paris*, p. 224.
54. cummings, *Him*, pp. 77–78.
55. Williams, *A Voyage to Pagany*, p. 63.

Chapter 7

1. Stewart, *Mr. and Mrs. Haddock in Paris*, p. 240.
2. Lewis, *Dodsworth*, p. 113.
3. Williams, *A Voyage to Pagany*, pp. 51–52.
4. Lewis, *Dodsworth*, pp. 192–220.
5. Ibid., p. 164.
6. Wharton, *The Gods Arrive*, p. 91.
7. Loeb, *The Professors Like Vodka*, p. 17.
8. Hemingway, *The Sun Also Rises*, p. 11.
9. Fitzgerald, *The Crack-Up*, p. 115.
10. For example, there are allusions to Nerval in "The Whistling Swan," p. 355; to Verlaine in *A Voyage to Pagany*, p. 29, *The Snows of Kilimanjaro*, p. 25, and *A Moveable Feast*, p. 4; and to Oscar Wilde in *Of Time and the River*, p. 685.
11. Hemingway, *A Moveable Feast*, p. 72.
12. Ibid., p. 132.
13. Wolfe, *Of Time and the River*, p. 657.
14. Ibid., p. 660.
15. Wharton, *The Gods Arrive*, p. 76.
16. Hemingway, *A Moveable Feast*, p. 13.
17. Stein, *Autobiography of Alice B. Toklas*, p. 27.
18. Hemingway, *A Moveable Feast*, pp. 5–6.
19. Williams, *A Voyage to Pagany*, p. 29.
20. Hemingway, *A Moveable Feast*, p. 180.
21. Stewart, *Mr. and Mrs. Haddock in Paris*, p. 237.
22. Mearson, *The French They Are a Funny Race*, p. 184.
23. Williams, *A Voyage to Pagany*, p. 51.
24. Anderson, *Dark Laughter*, p. 167. Hemingway makes fun of this passage in *Torrents of Spring:* "In Paris there are no geldings. All the horses are stallions" (p. 21).

25. Wolfe often uses the expression "rat-like." In *Of Time and the River* there are phrases such as "bestial grimace" (p. 708), "the feature of a rodent" (p. 712), and "a serpent's eye" (p. 724), and in *The Web and the Rock*, "reptile's eyes" (p. 641), "vulpine face" (p. 641), and "rattler's fangs" (p. 647).

26. The policeman called Emile explains in *The French They Are a Funny Race*, p. 135, that these flocks are allowed to cross through Paris on condition that they are on their way to the slaughterhouse but that the goatherd has only to pretend he is on his way to the slaughterhouse in order to be able to take his goats into the streets and sell their milk.

27. Mearson, *The French They Are a Funny Race*, pp. 215–16.

28. Samuel, *The Outsider*, pp. 114–15.

29. Ibid., p. 48.

30. Wolfe, *Of Time and the River*, p. 727.

31. Anderson, *Dark Laughter*, pp. 181, 193–94, and 203.

32. Adams, "Sunrise out of the Waste Land."

33. Wolfe, *Of Time and the River*, pp. 800–801.

34. Hemingway, *The Sun Also Rises*, p. 115.

35. Ibid., p. 75.

36. Loeb, *The Professors Like Vodka*, p. 176.

Chapter 8

1. Priscilla English published her interview with Anaïs Nin in Zaller, *A Casebook on Anaïs Nin*, pp. 185–97.

2. Quoted in Susman, "Pilgrimage to Paris," p. 343.

3. Miller, *Tropic of Cancer*, p. 11.

4. Nin, *The Four-Chambered Heart*, pp. 72–73.

5. Miller, *Tropic of Cancer*, p. 157.

6. Ibid., p. 152.

7. Djuna's childhood and youth, as they are described in *Ladders to Fire*, pp. 31–36, and *Children of the Albatross*, pp. 8 and 17–22, do not correspond to what the author tells us in *The Four-Chambered Heart*, pp. 12–13 and 36–37.

8. Béranger, "Une Epoque de Transe."

9. Nin, *Ladders to Fire*, pp. 141–42.

10. To avoid paying his concierge, Peter pretends that he stands a good chance of winning first prize in a painting competition. When his deception is discovered, he hangs a dummy in his studio to make it look as if he has committed suicide, reappearing only when everyone is ready to forgive him.

11. Miller, *Tropic of Cancer*, pp. 14, 23, 73–74.

12. Ibid., pp. 182–83.

13. Ibid., pp. 183 and 186.

14. Nin, *Winter of Artifice*, p. 102.

15. Nin, *Realism and Reality* (New York: Gemor Press, 1946), p. 14.

16. Nin, *Ladders to Fire*, pp. 131–32.

17. Ibid., p. 89.

18. Nin, *Diary*, 2:240–41.

19. Hinz, *The Mirror and the Garden*, pp. 53–55.

20. Nin, *The Four-Chambered Heart*, pp. 30–31.

21. For example, a phrase from *Children of the Albatross,* "A soft rain covered the city with a muted lid" (p. 114), recalls both Verlaine and Baudelaire.

22. Nin, *The Four-Chambered Heart,* p. 31.

23. Nin, *Delta of Venus,* p. 137.

24. Nin, *Diary,* 2:215.

25. Claude is the heroine of "Mademoiselle Claude," but she reappears in *Tropic of Cancer,* pp. 49–54, where she is compared with Germaine. Lucienne is a regular of "Chez Paul" in *Tropic of Cancer,* pp. 161–65. Adrienne and Mara-St-Louis are mentioned in *Quiet Days in Clichy,* pp. 67 and 81. The second part of *Quiet Days in Clichy* is about Mara-Marignan. The prostitute from the Dôme appears in *Tropic of Cancer,* pp. 145–49, like her counterpart from the Jungle, pp. 214–20. The one from the Wepler appears in *Quiet Days in Clichy,* p. 9. The prostitute with a wooden leg is mentioned in *Tropic of Cancer,* p. 79, in *Quiet Days in Clichy,* p. 54, in Nin's *Diary,* 1:77–78, in *Seduction of the Minotaur,* p. 134, and in *Delta of Venus,* p. 245.

26. Miller, *Tropic of Cancer,* p. 166.

27. Nin, *Diary,* 2:285.

28. Ibid., p. 186.

29. *Les Détraquées* is the title of the play Breton sees at the Théâtre des Deux-Masques in *Nadja.*

30. Nin, *Under a Glass Bell,* p. 59.

31. Nin, *Diary,* 2:273.

32. Nin, *Seduction of the Minotaur,* p. 141.

33. Nin, *Diary,* 1:322–23.

34. Miller, *Tropic of Cancer,* p. 79.

35. Nin, *Diary,* 2:185.

36. Ibid., 1:113.

37. Nin, *Ladders to Fire,* p. 106.

38. Nin, *Diary,* 2:289.

39. Hinz, *The Mirror and the Garden,* p. 60.

40. Miller, *Tropic of Cancer,* p.47.

41. Ibid., p. 166.

42. Ibid., p. 70.

43. Nin, *Ladders to Fire,* p. 107.

44. Miller, *Tropic of Cancer,* p. 165.

45. Nin, *Diary,* 2:125 and 229.

46. Miller, *Tropic of Cancer,* p. 85.

47. Quoted in Nin, *Diary,* 2:115.

48. Quoted in Alexandrian, *Les Libérateurs de l'Amour,* p. 231.

49. Nin, *Children of the Albatross,* p. 138.

50. Nin, *Diary,* 2:46.

51. Miller, *Tropic of Cancer,* p. 74.

52. Miller, *Quiet Days in Clichy,* pp. 6–7.

53. Miller, *Tropic of Cancer,* p. 155.

54. Nin, *Diary,* 2:35.

55. Barnes, *Nightwood,* p. 131.

56. Miller, *Tropic of Cancer,* pp. 241, 244, and 279.

57. Barnes, *Nightwood,* p. 61.

58. Miller, *Tropic of Cancer*, p. 201.
59. Ibid., pp. 11–12.
60. Nin, *Children of the Albatross*, p. 147.
61. Miller, *Tropic of Cancer*, p. 244.
62. Ibid., pp. 247–50.
63. Barnes, *Nightwood*, pp. 41–42, 44, and 105.
64. Barnes, "The Passion," p. 493.
65. Miller, *Tropic of Cancer*, pp. 46 and 186.
66. Ibid., p. 258.
67. Miller, *Max*, p. 132.
68. McMahon, "City for Expatriates," p. 148.
69. Miller, *Tropic of Cancer*, p. 35.
70. Quoted in Nin, *Diary*, 2:44–45.
71. Nin, *Under a Glass Bell*, p. 50.

Chapter 9

1. Putnam, *Paris Was Our Mistress*, pp. 84–85.
2. For example, in *Mayhem in B Flat*, p. 206, Homer Evans, unsure of where to keep some particularly dangerous tarantulas (they have been carefully fed with crickets, which in turn have been fed on death cups!) finally wraps them in a sheet of *L'Action Française*.
3. *Book Review Digest*, 1942, p. 592.
4. Waldmeir, *American Novels of the Second World War,* and correspondence with the author, August–September 1977.
5. Jones, *The Merry Month of May*, pp. 100–103 and 213–15.
6. Ibid., p. 195.
7. Local events can be found in *Birds of America*, pp. 168, 218, and 292–94; *Springtime in Paris*, pp. 219–21 and 230–32; *The Kansas City Milkman*, p. 86; *Satori in Paris*, p. 11; and *Paris! Paris!*, p. 117.
8. Shaw, *Love on a Dark Street*, p. 78.
9. Ibid., p. 80.
10. McCarthy, *Birds of America*, p. 208.
11. The American College and the American Student Center are mentioned in *Paris! Paris!*, pp. 130 and 191; Reid Hall and the cinémathèques are in *Birds of America*, pp. 125 and 210; and Queenie's is mentioned in "A Year to Learn the Language," p. 73.
12. Shaw, *Short Stories*, p. 557.
13. Ibid., p. 526.
14. McCarthy, *Birds of America*, p. 128.
15. Farrell, *French Girls Are Vicious*, p. 17.
16. McCarthy, *Birds of America*, p. 176.
17. Ibid., p. 173.
18. Baldwin, *Nobody Knows My Name*, p. 20.
19. Bone, *The Negro Novel*, p. 227.
20. The Flore is mentioned in "Pages from an Abandoned Journal," p. 124, and in *The Judgment of Paris*, pp. 231–33.
21. Vidal, *The Judgment of Paris*, p. 257.

22. Ibid., p. 251.

23. The following books have been consulted: Geyraud, *L'Occultisme à Paris* and *Sectes et Rites;* Ziegler, *Histoire Secrète de Paris;* and Guides Noirs, *Guide de Paris Mystérieux.*

24. Vidal, *The Judgment of Paris,* p. 274.

25. Baldwin, *Giovanni's Room,* p. 38.

26. Ibid., p. 73.

27. Bone, *The Negro Novel,* p. 226.

28. Baldwin, *Giovanni's Room,* p. 46.

29. Vidal, *The Judgment of Paris,* p. 228-29.

30. Ibid., p. 299.

31. Quoted in White, *Gore Vidal,* p. 89.

32. French, *My Yankee Paris,* p. 180. "I don't want to see the look on his face when we try to go into a restaurant together, or when he tries to book a room at a hotel, or when he asks for so many of those things that he's been so used to having without any difficulties in Paris."

33. Wright, *The Long Dream,* pp. 360 and 370.

34. Baldwin, *Nobody Knows My Name,* p. 17.

35. Smith, *The Stone Face,* p. 57.

36. Ibid., pp. 86-87.

37. Ibid., p. 174.

38. Ibid., p. 139.

39. Baldwin, *Nobody Knows My Name,* pp. 21-22.

40. Aldridge, *After the Lost Generation,* p. 90.

41. Smith, *The Stone Face,* pp. 10 and 139.

42. Flender, *Paris Blues,* p. 86.

43. Jones calls his generation the "cunt-struck Generation" (p. 52) and the "Drunk Generation" (p. 115). There are five mentions of Hemingway (pp. 115, 121, 145, 213, and 274) as well as two of *The Sun Also Rises* (pp. 87 and 213), two of Fitzgerald (pp. 115 and 145), and one of Gertrude Stein and Sylvia Beach (p. 307).

44. Vidal, *The Judgment of Paris,* pp. 266-68. The scene in *The American* is on pp. 192-94.

45. Paul, *Springtime in Paris,* pp. 209-10.

46. Details on anti-Americanism can be found in *Birds of America,* pp. 97, 183, and 204-5, and *Paris! Paris!,* p. 9.

47. McCarthy, *Birds of America,* p. 166.

48. Shaw, *Paris! Paris!,* p. 6.

Conclusion

1. Gelfant, *The American City Novel,* p. 11.

2. Baldwin, *Giovanni's Room,* p. 201.

3. James, *The Reverberator,* p. 39.

4. According to Burns Mantle, ed., *The Best Plays of 1931-32* (New York: Dodd, Mead, 1932), p. 208. The spectators must have heard phrases like "Si vous veuillez attendre" (p. 50); "C'est vite faite, ne c'est pas" (p. 52); and "Pas de tout, monsieur. Ne dérangez vous pas" (p. 66).

5. For example, in *Giovanni's Room,* Baldwin's French is rather inexact. In addition to many misspellings, there are phrases like "il fait beau bien" (p. 87). In *The Judgment of Paris,* pp. 284–85, why does Gore Vidal have the president of the "Académie Française des auteurs de romans policiers"—who is a Frenchman—deliver a ten-line speech in highly dubious French that a high school student could easily have corrected? In *Mistral's Daughter* most of the French words and phrases used by Judith Krantz are erroneous—for example: "une enfante naturelle" (pp. 226 and 314), "une enfante adultérine" (pp. 314 and 404), "certaine âge" (p. 319), "Union Sportif" (p. 388), "Fichier Centrale" (p. 513); and "Code Civile" (p. 516).

6. McMahon, "City for Expatriates."

BIBLIOGRAPHY

PRIMARY SOURCES

American Primary Sources

Novels

Anderson, Sherwood. *Dark Laughter.* New York: Liveright, 1960.
Baldwin, James. *Another Country.* New York: Dell, 1963.
———. *Giovanni's Room.* New York: Dell, 1969.
Barnes, Djuna. *Nightwood.* London: Faber, 1974.
Boyle, Kay. *Monday Night.* London: Faber, 1938.
Bromfield, Louis. *The Green Bay Tree.* Paris: Phoenix, 1949.
Canfield, Dorothy. *The Bent Twig.* New York: Holt, 1915.
———. *The Deepening Stream.* New York: Harcourt, Brace, 1930.
Carryl, Guy Wetmore. *The Transgression of Andrew Vane.* New York: Holt, 1904.
Cather, Willa. *One of Ours.* New York: Knopf, 1940.
Chambers, Robert W. *Ashes of Empire.* New York: Stokes, [1898].
———. *In the Quarter.* Chicago and New York: Neely, 1894.
———. *The Red Republic.* New York: Putnam, 1895.
Coates, Robert M. *The Eater of Darkness.* Paris: Contact Editions, [1926].
Croy, Homer. *They Had to See Paris.* London: Readers Library Publishing Company, 1926.
Davis, Richard Harding. *The Princess Aline.* New York: Harper, 1895.
Dos Passos, John. *Chosen Country.* Boston: Houghton Mifflin, 1951.
———. *The 42nd Parallel.* New York: Random House, 1930.
———. *1919.* New York: Random House, 1932.
———. *One Man's Initiation: 1917.* Ithaca: Cornell University Press, 1970.
———. *Three Soldiers.* New York: Random House, 1932.
Du Pont, Diane. *The French Passion.* Greenwich: Fawcett, 1977.
Faulkner, William. *A Fable.* New York: Random House, 1954.
Fitzgerald, F. Scott. *Tender Is the Night.* New York: Scribner, 1962.
Flender, Harold. *Paris Blues.* New York: Ballantine, 1957.
Graham, Dorothy. *The French Wife.* New York: Stokes, 1928.
Green, Anne. *The Selbys.* New York: Dutton, 1930.
Gunter, Archibald Clavering. *Baron Montez of Panama and Paris.* New York: Home, 1893.

————. *Mr. Barnes of New York.* New York: Home, 1888.

————. *A Princess of Paris.* New York: Home, 1894.

————. *That Frenchman.* New York: Home, 1889.

Hemingway, Ernest. *Islands in the Stream.* New York: Scribner, 1970.

————. *The Sun Also Rises.* New York: Scribner, 1954.

————. *The Torrents of Spring.* London: Penguin Books, 1976.

Henry, O. [William Sydney Porter]. *Roads of Destiny.* New York: Doubleday, Page, 1909.

Heym, Stefan. *The Crusaders.* Boston: Little, Brown, 1948.

Howells, William Dean. *A Hazard of New Fortunes.* New York: Dutton, 1952.

Israel, Peter. *The Stiff Upper Lip.* New York: Crowell, 1978.

James, Henry. *The Ambassadors.* New York: New American Library, 1960.

————. *The American.* New York: New American Library, 1963.

————. *Madame de Mauves.* In *The Great Short Novels of Henry James,* edited by Philip Rahv. New York: Dial, 1944.

————. *The Reverberator.* New York: Grove, 1957.

————. *The Siege of London.* In *The Great Short Novels of Henry James,* edited by Philip Rahv. New York: Dial, 1944.

Johnson, Owen. *In the Name of Liberty.* New York: Century, 1905.

————. *The Wasted Generation.* Boston: Little, Brown, 1921.

Jones, James. *The Merry Month of May.* New York: Fontana Books, 1971.

Jong, Erica. *Fear of Flying.* London: Granada, 1978.

Kerouac, Jack. *Satori in Paris.* New York: Grove, 1967.

King, Basil. *The Inner Shrine.* New York: Harper, 1909.

Koningsberger, Hans. *A Walk with Love and Death.* London: Macmillan, 1961.

Krantz, Judith. *Mistral's Daughter.* New York: Bantam, 1983.

Lewis, Sinclair. *Dodsworth.* New York: New American Library, 1967.

Loeb, Harold. *The Professors Like Vodka.* New York: Boni and Liveright, 1927.

McCarthy, Mary. *Birds of America.* London: Penguin Books, 1973.

Mearson, Lyon. *The French They Are a Funny Race.* New York: Mohawk Press, [1931].

Meeker, Arthur. *American Beauty.* New York: Covici, Friede, 1929.

Merwin, Samuel. *The Honey Bee.* New York: Bobbs, 1915.

Miller, Henry. *Black Spring.* Paris: Obelisk Press, 1936.

————. *A Devil in Paradise.* London: Four Square, 1963.

————. *Quiet Days in Clichy.* London: New English Library, 1969.

————. *Tropic of Cancer.* London: Panther Books, 1965.

Mitchell, S. Weir. *The Adventures of François, Foundling, Thief, Juggler and Fencing Master during the French Revolution.* New York: Century, 1898.

Moffett, Cleveland. *The Seine Mystery.* New York: Dodd, 1925.

————. *Through the Wall.* New York: Grosset and Dunlap, 1909.

Molinaro, Ursule. *Green Lights Are Blue*. New York: New American Library, 1967.

Nin, Anaïs. *Children of the Albatross*. Chicago: Swallow, 1959.

———. *The Four-Chambered Heart*. Chicago: Swallow, 1959.

———. *Ladders to Fire*. Chicago: Swallow, 1959.

———. *Seduction of the Minotaur*. London: Owen, 1961.

———. *A Spy in the House of Love*. New York: Bantam, 1974.

———. *Winter of Artifice*. Chicago: Swallow, 1945.

Packard, Reynolds. *The Kansas City Milkman*. New York: Dutton, 1950.

Paul, Elliot. *The Amazon*. New York: Liveright, 1930.

———. *Hugger-Mugger in the Louvre*. New York: Random House, 1950.

———. *Mayhem in B Flat*. London: Corgi, 1951.

———. *Murder on the Left Bank*. New York: Random House, 1951.

———. *The Mysterious Mickey Finn; or, Murder at the Café du Dôme*. New York: Avon, 1942.

Prokosch, Frederic. *The Skies of Europe*. New York: Harper, 1941.

Samuel, Maurice. *The Outsider*. Boston: Stratford, 1929.

Shaw, Irwin. *The Young Lions*. New York: Random House, 1948.

Sinclair, Upton. *Between Two Worlds*. New York: Viking, 1945.

———. *One Clear Call*. New York: Viking, 1948.

———. *O Shepherd, Speak!* New York: Viking, 1949.

———. *Wide Is the Gate*. New York: Viking, 1944.

———. *World's End*. New York: Viking, 1945.

Smith, William Gardner. *The Stone Face*. New York: Farrar, Straus, 1963.

Sontag, Susan. *The Benefactor*. New York: New American Library, 1963.

Stewart, Donald Ogden. *Mr. and Mrs. Haddock Abroad*. New York: Doran, 1924.

———. *Mr. and Mrs. Haddock in Paris, France*. New York: Harper, 1926.

Stone, Irving. *The Passionate Journey*. New York: Doubleday, 1949.

Strunsky, Simeon. *Little Journeys towards Paris, 1914–1918*. New York: Holt, 1918.

Tarkington, Booth. *The Beautiful Lady*. New York: McClure, Phillips, 1905.

———. *The Guest of Quesnay*. Toronto: Musson, 1908.

Vance, Louis. *The Lone Wolf*. New York: Burt, 1914.

Van Vechten, Carl. *Peter Whiffle, His Life and Works*. New York: Knopf, 1929.

———. *The Tattooed Countess*. New York: Knopf, 1924.

Vidal, Gore. *The Judgment of Paris*. London: Panther Books, 1976.

Wharton, Edith. *The Custom of the Country*. With an introduction by Michael Millgate. London: Constable, 1965.

———. *The Glimpses of the Moon*. London: Appleton, 1922.

———. *The Gods Arrive*. London: Appleton, 1932.

———. *Madame de Treymes*. New York: Scribner, 1907.

———. *The Marne*. London: Macmillan, 1918.

———. *The Reef.* London: Macmillan, 1913.

———. *A Son at the Front.* London: Macmillan, 1923.

Williams, William Carlos. *A Voyage to Pagany.* New York: Macaulay, 1928.

Wilson, Harry Leon. *Ruggles of Red Gap.* New York: Hillary, 1957.

Wolfe, Thomas. *Of Time and the River.* New York: Scribner, 1952.

———. *The Web and the Rock.* New York: Scribner, 1939.

Wright, Richard. [*Island of Hallucination*] "Five Episodes from an Unfinished Novel." In *Soon, One Morning: New Writing by American Negroes, 1940–1962,* edited by Herbert Hill. New York: Knopf, 1963.

———. *The Long Dream.* Chatham: Chatham Bookseller, 1969.

Short Stories

Barnes, Djuna. "The Passion." *Transatlantic Review* 2 (Nov. 1924): 490–96.

———. *Spillway.* London: Faber, 1962. (This collection includes "The Grande Malade.")

Canfield, Dorothy. *The Day of Glory.* New York: Holt, 1919. (This collection includes "The Day of Glory.")

———. *Home Fires in France.* New York: Holt, 1918. (This collection includes "A Honeymoon . . . Vive l'Amérique" and "A Little Kansas Leaven.")

Carryl, Guy Wetmore. *Zut and Other Parisians.* Boston and New York: Houghton Mifflin, 1903. (This collection includes "Caffiard," "In the Absence of Monsieur," "A Latter-Day Lucifer," "Little Tapin," "The Next Corner," "The Only Son of His Mother," "Papa Labesse," "Le Pochard," "Poire," "The Tuition of Dodo Chapuis," and "Zut.")

Chambers, Robert W. *The Haunts of Men.* New York: Stokes, [1895]. (This collection includes "Ambassador Extraordinary," "Another Good Man," and "Enter the Queen.")

———. *The King in Yellow.* Chicago and New York: Neely, 1895. (This collection includes "In the Court of the Dragon," "The Mask," "Rue Barrée," "The Street of Our Lady of the Fields," "The Street of the First Shell," and "The Street of the Four Winds.")

Davis, Richard Harding. *From "Gallegher" to "The Deserter".* New York: Scribner, 1927. (This collection includes "Somewhere in France.")

Farrell, James T. *French Girls Are Vicious.* New York: Vanguard, 1955. (This collection includes "A Dream of Love," "French Girls Are Vicious," and "I Want to Meet a French Girl.")

———. *An Omnibus of Short Stories.* New York: Vanguard, 1957. (This collection includes "After the Sun Has Risen," "Scrambled Eggs and Toast," and "Sorel.")

———. *When Boyhood Dreams Come True.* New York: Vanguard, 1946. (This collection includes "Fritz" and "Paris Scene: 1931.")

Fitzgerald, F. Scott. *The Crack-Up.* London: Penguin Books, 1965. (This collection includes "Babylon Revisited.")

Hemingway, Ernest. *The Snows of Kilimanjaro.* London: Penguin Books,

1968. (This collection includes "Mr. and Mrs. Elliott," "My Old Man," and "The Snows of Kilimanjaro.")

Irving, Washington. "The Adventure of the German Student." In *Fantastic Tales,* edited by Roger Asselineau. Paris: Aubier, 1979.

James, Henry. *The Complete Tales of Henry James.* Edited by Leon Edel. 12 vols. Philadelphia and New York: Lippincott, 1962–63. (This collection includes "A Bundle of Letters" [vol. 4], "Collaboration" [vol. 8], "Gabrielle de Bergerac," [vol. 2], "Mrs. Temperly" [vol. 6], and "The Point of View" [vol. 4].)

————. *The Madonna of the Future.* New York: New American Library, 1962. (This collection includes "Four Meetings.")

Lovecraft, Howard Phillips. *The Haunter in the Dark.* London: Panther Books, 1963. (This collection includes "The Music of Erich Zann.")

Miller. Henry. *Max and the White Phagocytes.* Paris: Obelisk Press, 1938. (This collection includes "Max.")

————. *Selected Prose.* London: Macgibbon and Kee, 1965. (This collection includes "Mademoiselle Claude.")

Mitchell, S. Weir. *A Madeira Party.* New York: Century, 1895. (This collection includes "A Little More Burgundy.")

Moffett, Cleveland. "The Mysterious Card." *The Black Cat* 5 (Feb. 1896): 1–10.

————. "The Mysterious Card Unveiled." *The Black Cat* 11 (Aug. 1896): 1–17.

Nin, Anaïs. *Delta of Venus.* New York: Harcourt Brace, 1977. (This collection includes "Artists and Models," "The Basque and Bijou," "Elena," "Linda," "Manuel," "Marcel," "Marianne," "Mathilde," and "Pierre.")

————. *Under a Glass Bell.* London: Penguin Books, 1978. (This collection includes "The All-Seeing," "The Eye's Journey," "Houseboat," "Je Suis le Plus Malade des Surréalistes," "The Mohican," "The Mouse," and "Under a Glass Bell.")

Poe, Edgar Allan. *Tales of Mystery and Imagination.* London: Dent, 1968. (This collection includes "The Murders in the Rue Morgue," "The Mystery of Marie Rogêt," and "The Purloined Letter.")

Shaw, Irwin. *Love on a Dark Street.* New York: Dell, 1975. (This collection includes "Love on a Dark Street," "The Man Who Married a French Wife," and "A Year to Learn the Language.")

————. *Short Stories: Five Decades.* New York: Delacorte, 1978. (This collection includes "God Was Here but He Left Early," "In the French Style," "Retreat," and "Tip on a Dead Jockey.")

Smith, Frank Berkeley. *The Street of the Two Friends.* New York: Doubleday, Page, 1912. (This collection includes "The Arrangement of Monsieur de Courcelles," "By the Grace of Allah," "The Enthusiast," "Natka," "The Refugees," "Straight-Rye Jones," and "Thérèse.")

Vidal, Gore. *A Thirsty Devil.* New York: Zero Press, 1956. (This collection includes "Pages from an Abandoned Journal.")

Wescott, Glenway. *Good-bye Wisconsin*. New York: Harper, 1928. (This collection includes "The Whistling Swan.")

Wharton, Edith. *The Best Short Stories of Edith Wharton*. Edited by Wayne Andrews. New York: Scribner, 1958. (This collection includes "The Last Asset.")

————. *Les Metteurs en Scène*. Paris: Plon, 1909. (This collection includes "Les Metteurs en Scène," a short story written in French by Edith Wharton.)

Texts of an Autobiographical Nature

Aldrich, Mildred. *A Hilltop on the Marne*. London: Constable, 1918.

Andrews, C. E. *The Innocents of Paris*. New York and London: Appleton, 1928.

Baldwin, James. *Nobody Knows My Name*. New York: Dell, 1975.

[Barnes, Djuna]. *Ladies Almanack*. Paris: Titus, 1928.

Buchwald, Art. *How Much Is That in Dollars?* Greenwich: Fawcett, 1961.

————. "The Priscilla Pitch and Merci Donnant." *International Herald Tribune*, 22 Nov. 1979, p. 16.

————. "Thanksgiving Sounds Even Better in French." *Chicago Sun-Times*, 22 Nov. 1979, p. 104.

Callaghan, Morley. *That Summer in Paris*. Toronto: Macmillan, 1963.

Cooper, James Fenimore. *A Residence in France*. Paris: Baudry, 1836.

Crosby, Harry. *Shadows of the Sun*. Paris: Black Sun Press, 1928-29.

cummings, e. e. "Conflicting Aspects of Paris." In *e. e. cummings: A Miscellany*, edited by George Firmage. London: Peter Owen, 1966.

Davis, Richard Harding. *With the Allies*. Toronto: Copp Clark, 1915.

Flanner, Janet. *An American in Paris*. New York: Simon and Shuster, 1940.

————. *Paris Journal, 1944-1965*. New York: Atheneum, 1965.

————. *Paris Journal, 1965-1971*. New York: Atheneum, 1972.

————. *Paris Was Yesterday 1925-1939*. Edited by Irving Drutman. New York: Viking, 1972.

French, Herbert Eliot. *My Yankee Paris*. New York: Vanguard, 1945.

Hemingway, Ernest. *A Moveable Feast*. New York: Bantam, 1965.

Holmes, Oliver Wendell. *Our Hundred Days in Europe*. New York: Arno, 1971.

Irving, Washington. *Journals and Notebooks*. Vol. 1, *1803-1806*. Edited by Nathalia Wright. *The Complete Works of Washington Irving*. Madison: University of Wisconsin Press, 1969.

James, Henry. *Within the Rim and Other Essays (1914-1915)*. London: Collins, 1918.

Kohner, Frederick. *Kiki of Montparnasse*. New York: Stein and Day, 1967.

Loeb, Harold. *The Way It Was*. New York: Criterion, 1959.

————. "The Young Writer in Paris and Pamplona." *Saturday Review* 49 (29 July 1961): 25-26.

McKay, Claude. *A Long Voyage from Home*. New York: Lee Furman, 1937.

Mowrer, Paul Scott. *The House of Europe.* Boston: Houghton Mifflin, 1945.

Nin, Anaïs. *The Diary of Anaïs Nin.* Edited by Gunter Stuhlmann. Vols. 1–3. New York: Swallow and Harcourt, Brace and World, 1966, 1967, and 1969.

———. *The Journals of Anaïs Nin.* Edited by Gunter Stuhlmann. Vols. 4 and 5. London: Quarter Books, 1974 and 1976.

———. *Paris Revisited.* Santa Barbara: Capra Press, 1972.

Paul, Elliot. *The Last Time I Saw Paris.* New York: Random House, 1951.

———. *Springtime in Paris.* New York: Random House, 1950.

———. *Understanding the French.* London: Muller, 1954.

Putnam, Samuel. *Paris Was Our Mistress: Memoirs of a Lost and Found Generation.* New York: Viking, 1947.

Rascoe, Burton. *We Were Interrupted.* Garden City: Doubleday, 1947.

Shaw, Irwin. *Paris! Paris!* London: Weidenfeld and Nicolson, 1977.

[Stein, Gertrude]. *The Autobiography of Alice B. Toklas.* New York: Harcourt, Brace, 1933.

Stein, Gertrude. *Paris France.* London: Batsford, [1940].

———. *War I Have Seen.* New York: Random House, 1945.

Steinbeck, John. *Un Américain à New York et à Paris.* Translated by Jean-François Rozan. Paris: Julliard, 1956. (The English text of this work apparently has never been published in book form.)

Tully, Jim. *Beggars Abroad.* Garden City: Doubleday, Doran, 1930.

Twain, Mark. *The Innocents Abroad.* London: Routledge, 1872.

Vidal, Gore. *Matters of Fact and of Fiction: Essays, 1973–1976.* New York: Random House, 1977.

Wharton, Edith. *Fighting France from Dunkerque to Belfort.* London: Macmillan, 1915.

Plays

Belasco, David. *The Stranglers of Paris.* In *America's Lost Plays,* edited by Glenn Hughes and George Savage, vol. 18. Bloomington, Indiana University Press, n.d.

cummings, e. e. *Him.* In *Three Plays and a Ballet.* New York: October House, 1967.

Howard, Bronson. *The Banker's Daughter.* In *America's Lost Plays,* edited by Glenn Hughes and George Savage, vol. 10. Bloomington: Indiana University Press, n.d.

———. *One of Our Girls.* In *America's Lost Plays,* edited by Glenn Hughes and George Savage, vol. 10. Bloomington: Indiana University Press, n.d.

Rice, Elmer. *The Left Bank.* New York and Los Angeles: French, 1931.

Poems

Crosby, Caresse. *Crosses of Gold.* Paris: Messein, 1925. (This collection includes "Daybreak: Ile Saint-Louis" and "Le Cimetière de l'Abbaye de Longchamp.")

Crosby, Harry. *Red Skeletons*. Paris: Narcisse, 1927. (This collection includes "Gargoyle.")

———. *Sonnets for Caresse*. Paris: Narcisse, 1927. (This collection includes "Nocturne de Paris.")

cummings, e.e. *And*. New York: Liveright, 1925. (This collection includes "little ladies / more than dead," and "Paris; this April sunset completely utters.")

———. *Is 5*. New York: Liveright, 1926. (This collection includes "16 heures / l'Etoile / the communists have fine Eyes.")

Holmes, Oliver Wendell. "La Grisette." In *The Complete Works of Oliver Wendell Holmes*. Boston and New York: Houghton Mifflin, 1895.

Van Wyck, William. *On the Terrasse*. Paris: Titus, 1930.

Non-American Primary Sources

Aragon, [Louis]. *Le Paysan de Paris*. Paris: Gallimard, 1926.

Augier, Emile. *L'Aventurière*. Paris: Hetzel, 1848.

Bourdet, Edouard. *Le Sexe Faible*. Paris, 1929.

Breton, André. *Nadja*. Paris: Gallimard, 1964.

Dickens, Charles. *A Tale of Two Cities*. London: Nelson, n.d.

Dumas, Alexandre, fils. *Le Demi-monde*. Paris: Lévy, 1855.

Du Maurier, George. *Peter Ibbetson*. London: Osgood, McIlvaine, 1892.

———. *Trilby*. London: Osgood, McIlvaine, 1895.

Hall, Radclyffe. *The Well of Loneliness*. Paris: Pegasus, 1928.

Janin, Jules. *The American in Paris*. London: Longman, 1843.

Marshall, Bruce. *Yellow Tapers for Paris*. Boston: Houghton Mifflin, 1946.

Merrick, Leonard. *A Chair on the Boulevard*. London: Stoughton, n.d.

Murger, Henri. *Scènes de la Vie de Bohème*. Paris: Garnier, 1929.

Orwell, George. *Down and Out in Paris and London*. London: Penguin Books, 1975.

Rhys, Jean. *After Leaving Mr. Mackenzie*. London: Penguin Books, 1975.

———. *Good Morning, Midnight*. London: Penguin Books, 1975.

———. *Tigers Are Better Looking*. London: Penguin Books, 1972.

Sue, Eugène. *Les Mystères de Paris*. Paris: Agence Parisienne de Distribution, 1950.

Valentino, Henri. *Les Américains à Paris, Au Temps Joyeux de la Prospérité*. Paris: Perrin, 1936.

SECONDARY SOURCES

Literary Criticism

General Studies

Aldridge, John W. *After the Lost Generation*. New York: McGraw-Hill, 1951.

Alexandrian, [Sarane]. *Les Libérateurs de l'Amour.* Paris: Seuil, 1977.

Bone, Robert A. *The Negro Novel in America.* New Haven and London: Yale University Press, 1965.

Brodin, Pierre. *Vingt-Cinq Américains: Littérature et Littérateurs Américains des Années 1960.* Paris: Debresse, 1969.

Fiedler, Leslie. *Love and Death in the American Novel.* London: Paladin, 1970.

Gelfant, Blanche Housman. *The American City Novel.* Norman: University of Oklahoma Press, 1970.

Hoffman, Frederick. *The Twenties.* New York: Viking, 1955.

Poli, Bernard. *Le Roman Américain 1865–1917: Mythes de la Frontière et de la Ville.* Paris: Colin, 1972.

Tibert, Michel. *La Ville.* Paris: Hachette, 1973.

Waldmeir, Joseph J. *American Novels of the Second World War.* The Hague and Paris: Mouton, 1969.

Weston, Jessie L. *From Ritual to Romance.* Garden City: Doubleday, 1957.

Zeraffa, Michel. *Roman et Société.* Paris: Presses Universitaires, 1971.

Studies on Specific Authors

Adams, Richard P. "Sunrise out of the Waste Land." *Tulane Studies in English* 9 (1959): 119–31.

Astre, Georges-Albert. *John Dos Passos.* Paris: Minard, 1974.

Baker, Carlos. *Ernest Hemingway.* New York: Scribner, 1962.

———. *Hemingway: The Writer as Artist.* Princeton: Princeton University Press: 1956.

Béranger, Elisabeth. "Une Epoque de Transe: L'Exemple de Djuna Barnes." Doctoral thesis, Université de Paris III, 1977.

Bory, Jean-Louis. *Eugène Sue: Le Roi du Roman Populaire.* Paris: Hachette, 1962.

Brignano, Russell Carl. *Richard Wright: An Introduction to the Man and His Works.* Pittsburgh: University of Pittsburgh Press, 1970.

Brown, E. K. *Edith Wharton.* Paris: Droz, 1935.

Cestre, Charles. "La France dans l'Oeuvre de Henry James." *Revue Anglo-Américaine* 10 (1932): 1–13, 112–22.

Chalon, Jean. *Portrait d'une Séductrice.* Paris: Stock, 1976. (This is a study of Natalie Barney.)

Coolidge, Olivia. *Edith Wharton, 1862–1937.* New York: Scribner, 1964.

Evans, Oliver. *Anaïs Nin.* Carbondale: Southern Illinois University Press, 1968.

Field, Andrew. *The Formidable Miss Barnes.* London: Secker and Warburg, 1983.

Garnier, Marie-Reine. *Henry James et la France.* Paris: Champion, 1927.

Hinz, Evelyn J. *The Mirror and the Garden.* New York: Harcourt Brace, 1973. (This is a study of Anaïs Nin.)

Knoepflmacher, U. C. "'O Rare for Strether!': *Antony and Cleopatra* and

The Ambassadors." In *Twentieth Century Interpretations of the Ambassadors,* edited by Albert Stone. Englewood Cliffs: Prentice Hall, 1969.

Le Vot, André. *Scott Fitzgerald.* Paris: Julliard, 1972.

Lewis, R. W. B. *Edith Wharton: A Biography.* New York: Harper and Row, 1976.

Lyde, Marilyn Jones. *Edith Wharton: Convention and Morality in the Work of a Novelist.* Norman: University of Oklahoma Press, 1959.

Norman, Charles. *e. e. cummings, The Magic Maker.* Boston: Little, Brown, 1972.

Perlès, Alfred. *My Friend Henry Miller.* New York: Day, 1956.

Pollin, Burton R. *Discoveries in Poe.* Notre Dame: University of Notre Dame Press, 1970.

Wegelin, Christof. *The Image of Europe in Henry James.* Dallas: Southern Methodist University Press, 1958.

White, Ray Lewis. *Gore Vidal.* New York: Twayne, 1968.

Wrenn, John H. *John Dos Passos.* New Haven: College and University Press, 1961.

Zaller, Robert. *A Casebook on Anaïs Nin.* New York: New American Library, 1974.

Studies on Paris and Expatriation

Bancquart, Marie-Claire. *Paris des Surréalistes.* Paris: Seghers, 1972.

Benstock, Shari. *Women of the Left Bank: Paris, 1900–1940.* London: Virago, 1987.

Brownell, William Crary. *French Traits.* New York: Scribner, 1889.

Caillois, Roger. "Paris, Mythe Moderne." *Nouvelle Revue Française* 284 (May 1937): 682–99.

Carpenter, Humphrey. *Geniuses Together: American Writers in Paris in the 1920s.* London: Unwin Hyman, 1987.

Citron, Pierre. *La Poésie de Paris dans la Littérature Française de Rousseau à Baudelaire.* 2 vols. Paris: Minuit, 1961.

Cowley, Malcolm. *Exile's Return.* New York: Viking, 1956.

Earnest, Ernest. *Expatriates and Patriots.* Durham: Duke University Press, 1968.

Fabre, Michel. *La Rive Noire: De Harlem à la Seine.* Paris: Lieu Commun, 1985.

Ford, Hugh. *Published in Paris: American and British Writers, Printers, and Publishers in Paris, 1920–1930.* New York: Macmillan, 1975.

Lewin, David. "The Literary Expatriate as Social Critic of America." Ph.D. dissertation, New York University, 1952.

McMahon, Joseph H. "City for Expatriates." *Yale French Studies* 32 (Oct. 1964): 144–58.

Maurice, Arthur Bartlett. *The Paris of the Novelists.* London: Chapman and Hall, 1919.

Munson, Gorham. "The Fledgling Years, 1916–1924." *Sewanee Review* 40, no. 1 (1932): 24–54.

Susman, Warren Irving. "Pilgrimage to Paris: The Background of American Expatriation, 1920–1934." Ph.D. dissertation, University of Wisconsin, 1958.

Wickes, George. *Americans in Paris, 1903–1939.* New York: Doubleday, 1969.

Reference Works on Paris

Bourgin, Georges. *La Commune.* Paris: Presses Universitaires, 1971.

Chapiro, Jacques. *La Ruche.* Paris: Flammarion, 1960.

Child, Theodore. *The Praise of Paris.* New York: Harper, 1893.

Davis, Richard Harding. *About Paris.* New York: Harper, 1895.

Ferro, Marc. *La Grande Guerre, 1914–1918.* Paris: Gallimard, 1969.

Geyraud, Pierre. *L'Occultisme à Paris.* Paris: Emile-Paul-Frères, 1953.

———. *Sectes et Rites.* Paris: Emile-Paul-Frères, 1954.

Guides Bleus. *Paris.* Paris: Hachette, 1968.

Guides Noirs. *Guide de Paris Mystérieux.* Paris: Tchou, 1976.

Rémy, Tristan. *La Commune à Montmartre.* Paris: Editions Sociales, 1970.

Sédillot, René. *Paris.* Paris: Fayard, 1962.

Smith, Frank Berkeley. *How Paris Amuses Itself.* New York: Funk and Wagnalls, 1903.

———. *Parisians Out of Doors.* New York: Funk and Wagnalls, 1905.

———. *The Real Latin Quarter.* New York: Funk and Wagnalls, 1901.

Ziegler, Gilette. *Histoire Secrète de Paris.* Paris: Stock, 1967.

INDEX OF PERSONS

INDEX OF PLACES